Also by Charles M. Robinson III

Bad Hand: A Biography of General Ranald S. Mackenzie
The Buffalo Hunters
Satanta: The Life and Death of a War Chief
A Good Year to Die: The Story of the Great Sioux War

THE MEN WHO WEAR THE STAR

Random House New York

THE MEN WHO WEAR THE STAR

The Story of the Texas Rangers

Charles M. Robinson III

Library of Congress Cataloging-in-Publication Data

Robinson, Charles M.
The men who wear the star: the story of the Texas Rangers /
    Charles M. Robinson III.
        p.   cm.
    Includes bibliographical references and index.
    ISBN 0-679-45649-X
    1. Texas Rangers—History.   2. Texas Rangers—Biography.   3. Texas—
History—1846–1950.   4. Texas—History—To 1846.   5. Frontier and
pioneer life—Texas.   6. Law enforcement—Texas—History.
I. Title.
F391.R647   2000   976.4—dc21   99-27160

Random House website address: www.atrandom.com
Printed in the United States of America on acid-free paper
9 8 7 6 5 4 3 2

Book design by Mercedes Everett
Maps by Anita Karl and Jim Kemp

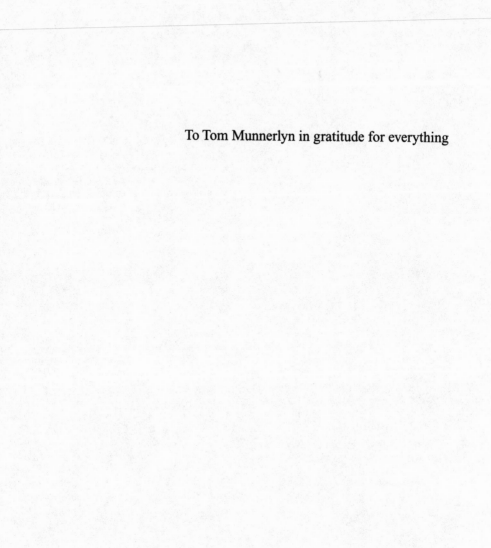

To Tom Munnerlyn in gratitude for everything

Los diablos tejanos! (The Texan devils!)

—Mexican expression for Texans in
general and Rangers in particular

No man in the wrong can stand up against a fellow
that's in the right and keeps on a-comin'.

—Ranger saying attributed variously
to Capt. Leander H. McNelly
and Capt. William J. McDonald

Acknowledgments

The idea for this book came almost simultaneously from three people: Douglas Plaisted of Houston, a lifelong friend; Tom Burks, then curator of the Texas Ranger Hall of Fame and Museum in Waco; and Thomas A. Munnerlyn of State House Press, in Austin. Tom Munnerlyn, whose press reprints many rare and hard-to-find books by and about Rangers, as well as original material, has encouraged the project from its inception, offering continued support in the form of books, papers, leads, comments, and advice. I am particularly grateful to him and his partner, Deborah Brothers, who provided virtually every book in the bibliography attributed to State House Press.

Special thanks also goes to my editor, Robert D. Loomis, of Random House, Inc., for his faith and patience with this project.

Others who deserve special mention are:

The Hon. George W. Bush, governor of Texas, and the Hon. Antonio O. Garza, former Texas secretary of state, for their comments and encouragement.

Leon C. Metz of El Paso, Chuck Parsons of Luling, Texas, and Robert M. Utley of Georgetown, Texas, for their advice, help, and encouragement.

The late Dr. C. L. Sonnichsen for his advice and criticisms concerning some aspects of Texas feuds, and whose books have been an inspiration since junior high school.

Robert A. Clark of the Arthur H. Clark Co., Spokane, Washington, through whose patience and tireless efforts I was able to secure many of the references needed.

At the risk of leaving some out, individuals and institutions deserving mention are:

Joan Farmer, former director of the Old Jail Art Center and Archive, Albany, Texas; Donaly E. Brice and John Anderson, Archives Division, Texas State Library and Archives, Austin; Mike Cox, chief of media relations, Department of Public Safety Public Information Office, Austin; Thomas Carroll and Aaron Mahr-Yanez, Palo Alto Battlefield National Historic Site, Brownsville; George Gause, Rio Grande Valley Regional Collection, University of Texas–Pan American, Edinburg, and the Interlibrary Loan Department at UTPA; James M. Day of El Paso; the library of the University of Texas at El Paso; Harold Weiss, Jr., of Leander, Texas; and the Texas Ranger Hall of Fame and Museum in Waco.

Grateful acknowledgment is extended to the following individuals, publishers, and holding institutions for permission to quote from various sources:

Courtesy of the Center for American History, the University of Texas at Austin

Caperton, John. "Sketch of Colonel John C. Hays, The Texan Rangers, Incidents in Texas and Mexico, Etc." John Coffee Hays Collection 2R35.

DeShields, James T. "Indian Raid, Pursuit and Fight." John Coffee Hays Collection 3F176.

DeShields, James T. "Jack Hays Fight on the Gaudaloupe [*sic*]." John Coffee Hays Collection 3F176.

Elm Creek Raid Statements (various). Earl Vandale Collection 2H481.

Gholson, Benjamin Franklin. "The Death of Nocona." Earl Vandale Collection 2H464.

Hamby, Thornton K. "An Indian Raid in Young County, Texas, Oct. 13th 1864." Elm Creek Raid Statements. Earl Vandale Collection 2H481.

Kuykendall, J. H. "Col. Samuel H. Walker." Samuel Hamilton Walker Vertical File. Texas Collection Library.

Lockhart, John W. "Jack Hays' Visit to Washington, Texas." John Coffee Hays Collection 3F176.

Courtesy of Eakin Press, a division of Sunbelt Media, Inc.

Roemer, Ferdinand. *Roemer's Texas, 1845 to 1847.* Special heritage ed. Austin: Eakin Press, 1995.

Courtesy of Gerald Barry Hurst, Jacksonville, N.C.

Barry, James Buckner. *Buck Barry, Texas Ranger and Frontiersman.* Bison Books ed. Lincoln: University of Nebraska Press, 1984.

Courtesy of State House Press, Austin, Texas

Jenkins, John Holmes III, and H. Gordon Frost. *"I'm Frank Hamer":* *The Life of a Texas Peace Officer.* Austin: State House Press, 1993.

Martin, Jack. *Border Boss: Captain John R. Hughes—Texas Ranger.* Austin: State House Press, 1990.

Wilkins, Frederick. *The Legend Begins: The Texas Rangers, 1823–1845.* Austin: State House Press, 1996.

Courtesy of Texas State Historical Association

Chamberlain, Samuel. *My Confession: Recollections of a Rogue.* Unexpurgated and Annotated Edition. Austin: Texas State Historical Association, 1996.

Erath, Lucy A. "Memoirs of Major George Bernard Erath." *Southwestern Historical Quarterly,* Vol. 26, no. 3 (January 1923); Vol. 26, no. 4 (April 1923); Vol. 27, no. 1 (July 1923); Vol. 27, no. 2 (October 1923).

Holland, James K. "Diary of a Texan Volunteer in the Mexican War." *Southwestern Historical Quarterly,* Vol. 30, no. 1 (July 1926).

Thompson, Jerry Don, ed. *Fifty Miles and a Fight: Major Samuel Peter Heintzelman's Journal of Texas and the Cortina War.* Austin: Texas State Historical Association, 1998.

Courtesy of Texas Western Press

Clayton, Lawrence R., and Joseph E. Chance, eds. *The March to Monterrey: The Diary of Lieutenant Rankin Dilworth, U.S. Army.* El Paso: Texas Western Press, 1996.

Justice, Glenn. *Revolution on the Rio Grande: Mexican Raids and Army Pursuits, 1916–1919.* El Paso: Texas Western Press, 1992.

Courtesy of University of North Texas Press

Roberts, Madge Thornall, ed. *The Personal Correspondence of Sam Houston.* Vol. 1: 1839–1845. Denton: University of North Texas Press, 1996.

Courtesy of University of Oklahoma Press

Haley, J. Evetts. *Charles Goodnight, Cowman and Plainsman.* New ed. Norman: University of Oklahoma Press, 1949.

Nye, Wilbur Sturtevant. *Carbine and Lance: The Story of Old Fort Sill.* Third ed. Revised. Norman: University of Oklahoma Press, 1969.

Sterling, William Warren. *Trails and Trials of a Texas Ranger.* Norman: University of Oklahoma Press, 1959, 1968.

Courtesy of University of Texas Press

Durham, George, as told to Clyde Wantland. *Taming the Nueces Strip: The Story of McNelly's Rangers.* Austin: University of Texas Press, 1962; reprinted 1990.

Ford, John Salmon, edited by Stephen B. Oates. *Rip Ford's Texas.* Austin: University of Texas Press, 1963; reprinted 1995.

Jenkins, John Holmes III, ed. *Recollections of Early Texas: The Memoirs of John Holland Jenkins.* Austin: University of Texas Press, 1958; reprinted 1986.

Peterson, John Allen, ed. *"Facts as I Remember Them": The Autobiography of Rufe LeFors.* Austin: University of Texas Press, 1986.

Webb, Walter Prescott. *The Texas Rangers: A Century of Frontier Defense.* Austin: University of Texas Press, 1965.

Courtesy of Yale University Press

Gillett, James B., edited with an introduction by M. M. Quaife. *Six Years with the Texas Rangers, 1875 to 1881.* New Haven: Yale University Press, 1925. Reprint. Lincoln: University of Nebraska Press, 1976.

Contents

Introduction:

Are They Still There?

When Richard McLaren, self-styled "ambassador of the Republic of Texas," holed up in the dry, rugged mountains of west Texas during a weeklong standoff in the spring of 1997, many Texans feared a bloodbath. Federal law enforcement has not been universally admired or trusted in Texas since the Branch Davidian debacle near Waco, and McLaren had threatened destruction. Later it was discovered that his refuge was booby-trapped and rigged for defense against assault. Yet he released his hostages the second day and, six days later, surrendered peacefully with most of his followers.

Several things separated the relatively quiet McLaren standoff from the fiery end of the Branch Davidians. First, the state maintained jurisdiction; federal authorities functioned in a strictly "advisory" capacity, which is to say virtually no capacity at all. Second, the man in charge was a Texas Ranger; McLaren trusted the Rangers because they predated American rule. Finally, the Ranger in charge was a soft-spoken company commander from Midland named Barry Caver, who, at thirty-nine, was the youngest captain in the service.

In classic Ranger tradition, Caver made his own rules based on the immediate situation, educated guesses, and simple instinct. Where conventional hostage wisdom calls for procrastination in hopes of wearing down the suspects, he made decisions. First, he accommodated McLaren by swapping a jailed Texas separatist for the hostages. With the hostages safe, Caver had more freedom of action, and he dealt with McLaren with one hand while tightening the cordon around him with the other. McLaren finally saw the hopelessness of his situation and surrendered. Two of his followers escaped into the mountains, where one was later killed, but he and the majority of his group surrendered without a fight.[1]

The McLaren case reaffirmed the prestige and skill of the Texas Rangers at a time when a small but vocal minority had begun to question whether they were even relevant to the modern age. Despite all the advances in criminology, they retain the nerve and sense of duty that have made them legendary throughout the world. In 1968, when I spent a weekend with a family in Glasgow, Scotland, I was introduced to their friends as a "Texas Ranger" for no other reason than that I am from Texas, and the Glaswegians viewed the words "Texas" and "Ranger" as inseparable. When the Washington Senators baseball team relocated to Dallas, they became the Rangers.

The name and the legend go far toward making the Rangers effective. Former adjutant general William W. Sterling, who commanded the Ranger Service in the 1920s and 1930s, once wrote:

> There is no question but that a definite potency exists in the name "Texas Ranger." Take two men of equal size and arm them with identical weapons. Call one of them a deputy sheriff and the other a Ranger. Send each of these officers out to stop a mob or quell a riot. The crowd will resist the deputy, but will submit to the authority of the Ranger.[2]

Seventy years later, it still holds true.

Texas historian Harold Weiss, Jr., recently divided Ranger history into three distinct periods: 1823–74, the era of the citizen-ranger who defended the frontier; 1874–1935, the era of the professional Western lawman who ultimately developed into a career peace officer; and 1935 onward, when the Rangers became a modern police force.[3] Today's Rangers assist local law enforcement agencies in criminal investigations, investigate public corruption, provide security for the governor when he or she travels in the state, and oversee elections when the potential for fraud exists. As such, the modern Texas Rangers are beyond the scope of this book. This is the story of the "classic" Rangers from the formation of the first frontier defense company in 1823 through the era of Mexican rule and the Republic of Texas, the Mexican War and Civil War, Indian fights, hunts for outlaws, and suppressions of blood feuds. The story of these classic Rangers ends with the overhaul of the service in the mid-1930s, after which the service entered the world of modern criminology.

Ranger history often is controversial. Part of this is because much of the material comes from sources in the nineteenth and early twentieth centuries, when the lines between good and evil were much more clearly and arbitrarily established than they are today. Good was white. Evil was black. The possibility that there might be large areas of gray was not considered. Evil itself being foul, any means to combat it—fair or foul—were justified. This often colored the actions of the Rangers, as well as their recollections of events.

Aside from the difficulty in obtaining a balanced and complete picture of the Ranger character, there is also a paucity of accurate information on their performance, a situation encountered more than eighty years ago by pioneer historians Andrew J. Sowell (himself a former Ranger) and James T. DeShields. DeShields described the problem in 1910, as he and Sowell tried to sift through the many fights of Capt. Jack Hays's Rangers some sixty years earlier.

> One of the difficulties encountered . . . has been in securing reliable material—sifting the facts from the fiction; and in fixing exact dates and even locations to the incidents known to have transpired, and in the manner presented. This arises from the fact that most of the reports of engagements and records of the Adjutant[']s office of the Republic were lost when the Capitol burned in 1881. The narratives of fights as supplied by survivors of that time, and even participants, while they bear the stamp of truth and in the main are no doubt reliable and sufficiently full are often lacking of dates and bearings.[4]

Hays's Rangers are a good example of the blurred line between myth and reality. By his twenty-fifth birthday, Hays was already a legend in Texas, and he later became prominent in California as a businessman and public official and one of the founders of Oakland. During his ranging days, his men were in the field almost continuously, and the tales of their many fights are often confused. Many times there is only an oral account transcribed many years after the events purportedly occurred. Some stories have been disputed because the names of the witnesses do not appear on muster rolls for the unit in question at that particular time. But the muster rolls contain large gaps, and the fact that a person's name is missing from the list doesn't necessarily mean he was not part of the unit at the time.

The Capitol fire cited by DeShields was the second destruction of Ranger records; the Adjutant General's Office previously burned in 1855. Fires, deterioration, thoughtless disposal, and ordinary theft have taken their toll. Files that were known to exist sixty years ago can no longer be found. Ledger books refer to letters and reports that have long since disappeared. Others exist only as transcript copies in the University of Texas's Center for American History. As Donaly E. Brice, reference specialist at the State Library and Archive in Austin, observed in 1996, "After 150 years, it's a miracle we have anything."[5] Yet much does remain, and a fairly comprehensive history can be assembled—at least from the Ranger point of view.

Like any organization closing out its second century, the Rangers have skeletons in their closets. Ranger officers were not always careful about the men they enlisted, and some were troublemakers or worse. During the border disturbances of the early 1900s, some Ranger units were little more than officially sanctioned lynch mobs, earning contempt even from other Rangers. In the Starr County farm labor disturbances in the late 1960s, the Rangers were justly accused of being strikebreakers, and their methods ultimately were condemned by the United States Supreme Court. In the early 1970s, there were even calls in Texas for their abolition. More recently, they have been involved in controversy over female and minority members, in part because they rushed too quickly into female and minority hiring, sometimes enlisting by quota or political pressure rather than talent. Until the McLaren standoff, many believed the Rangers were an anachronism, and there was widespread feeling that they needed to reexamine their mission as they approached the twenty-first century.

Yet the McLaren incident confirmed the belief of most Texans that the Rangers should continue as the senior state law enforcement agency. More than other peace officers, the Ranger continues the frontier tradition of a self-reliant person, capable of making decisions on his own, without consulting some centralized authority. And as Capt. Barry Caver demonstrated with McLaren, a modern Ranger acting on his own can handle a situation responsibly and with dignity for himself and the state.

In telling the story of the Texas Rangers, I have concentrated on the "forgotten" Rangers—the citizen-militiamen who answered the call to defend their homes during the period of Mexican rule, those who served honestly and ably during the Civil War and Reconstruction, and those who served less nobly during the border disturbances from about 1915 to 1918. Despite the hatred and prejudices of the past, and the occasional rogue Ranger, each Ranger performed his duty as he saw it. Each was molded by the time and place in which he lived.

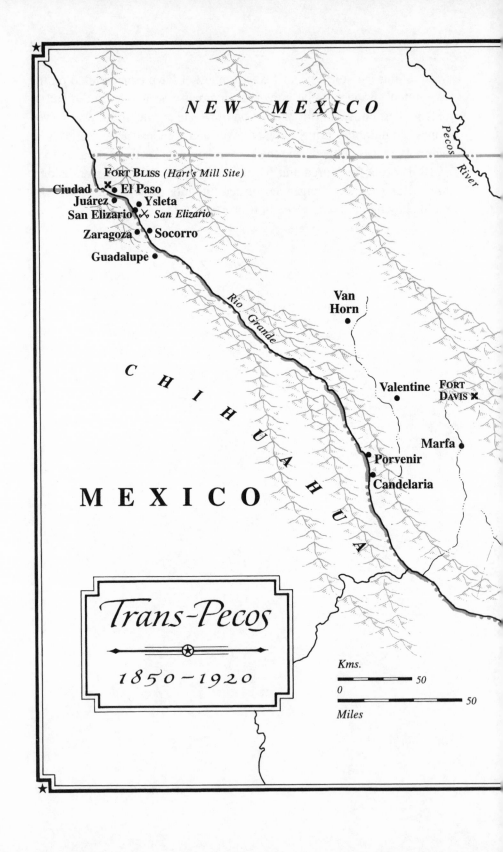

NEW MEXICO

Pecos River

FORT BLISS (Hart's Mill Site)
Ciudad • El Paso
Juárez •   • Ysleta
San Elizario • San Elizario
Zaragoza • • Socorro
Guadalupe •

Rio Grande

CHIHUAHUA

MEXICO

Van
Horn •

Valentine   FORT
•   DAVIS ✗

Marfa •

Porvenir •
Candelaria •

Trans-Pecos

1850–1920

Kms.
0 ———— 50
———————— 50
Miles

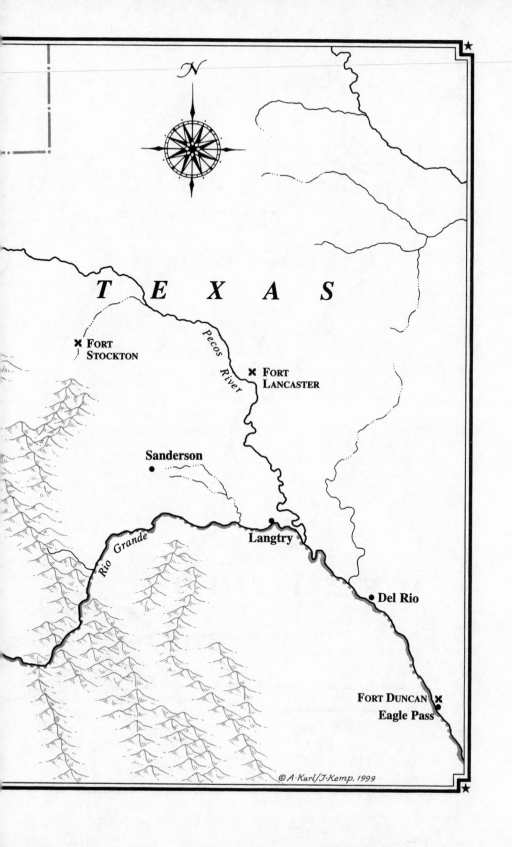

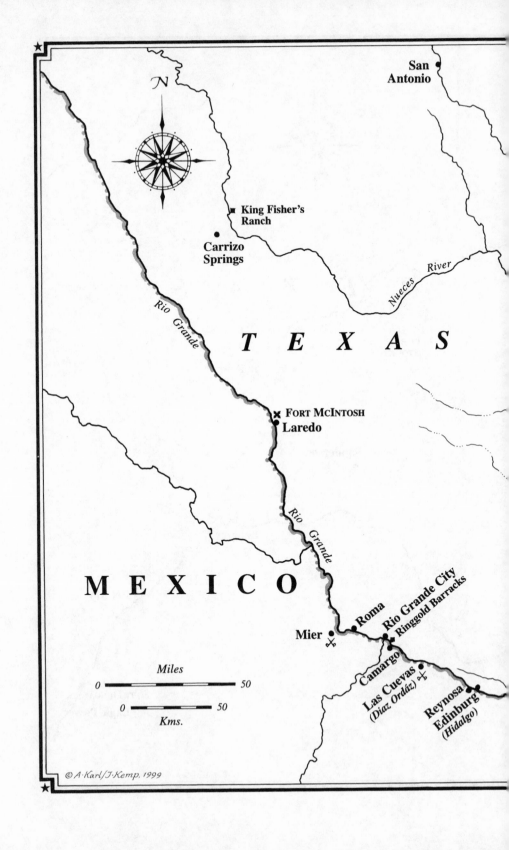

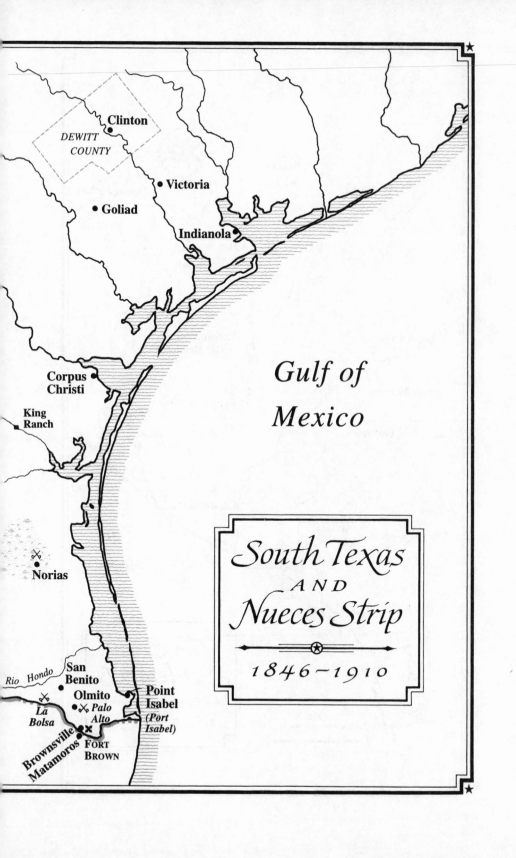

Clinton

DEWITT COUNTY

• Victoria

• Goliad

Indianola •

Gulf of

Mexico

Corpus
Christi •

King
Ranch

⚔ Norias

Rio Hondo

San
Benito •
⚔ • Olmito
La ⚔ *Palo*
Bolsa *Alto*
Brownsville ✕
Matamoros FORT
BROWN

Point
Isabel
*(Port
Isabel)*

South Texas
A N D
Nueces Strip
✪
1846–1910

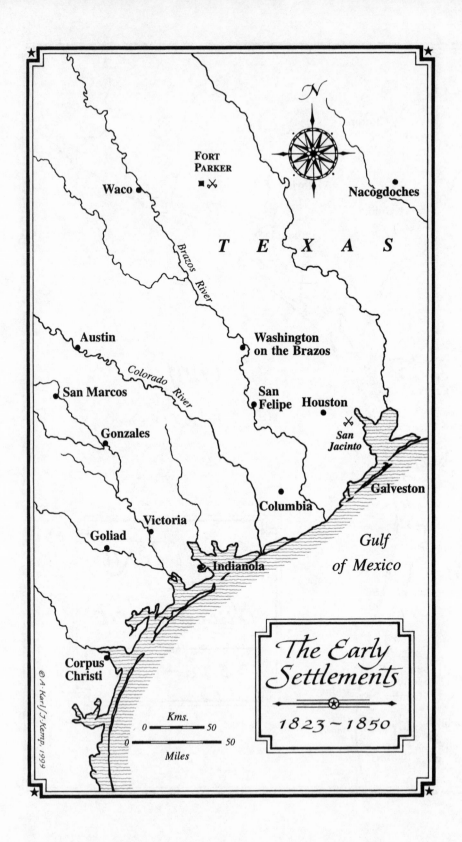

Waco

FORT
PARKER

Nacogdoches

N

T E X A S

Brazos River

Austin

Washington
on the Brazos

Colorado River

San Marcos

San
Felipe

Houston

Gonzales

*San
Jacinto*

Galveston

Columbia

Victoria

Goliad

Indianola

*Gulf
of Mexico*

Corpus
Christi

© A. Karl/J.Kemp, 1999

Kms.
0 —————— 50
0 —————— 50
Miles

*The Early
Settlements*

⊛

1823 ~ 1850

[OKLAHOMA]

Kiowa-Comanche Agency
FORT SILL

Red River

N

The Northwest Frontier
1848~1880

Salt Fork of the Brazos

FORT BELKNAP
Loving's Ranch
Camp Cooper
Jacksboro
FORT RICHARDSON
Lost Valley Fight

Dallas

Clear Fork of the Brazos
FORT GRIFFIN
Albany
FORT PHANTOM HILL

Fort Worth
(Military post until 1852)

T E X A S

Comanche
Brownwood
Colorado River
Waco

Brazos River

San Saba River
Menard
Camp San Saba
Lampasas
MASON CO.
Mason
FORT MASON
Burnet
FORT McKAVETT
Enchanted Rock
Round Rock
Fredericksburg
Austin

Guadalupe River
San Marcos
Plum Creek

Kms.
0 — 50
0 — 50
Miles

San Antonio

© A. Karl/J. Kemp, 1999

PART 1
THE FIRST RANGERS

Chapter 1

Life and Death in a Harsh Land

"Texas Ranger" is a blanket term that has meant different things at different times. Since 1874, it generally has described a full-time, professional state peace officer, originally charged with protecting the citizens from Indians and desperadoes, and later with investigating crime in the modern sense. Prior to 1874, however, the term was, in the words of one nineteenth-century writer, "somewhat vague when sought to be historically applied to the various volunteer and irregular organizations that have figured in the frontier service of Texas."[1]

The earliest ranger-style forces in Texas often were minutemen—much like those of colonial America—who agreed to hold themselves ready and come together under the authority of the Texas government when necessary, after which they would return home and resume their normal lives until needed again. Other times they might be volunteers who served for a specific length of time, electing their own officers, much the same as the ninety-day volunteers of the Union Army. Occasionally, they were ad hoc companies formed with the sanction of the local community to handle a specific emergency—and on the frontier at that time, the sanction of the local community was all the authority they needed.

During the period of the Republic through the Civil War, which is to say from 1836 to 1865, Rangers often served as auxiliaries for the military, and sometimes they were even incorporated into the army—at least theoretically. Yet the Texas Ranger always retained his separate identity and was never a soldier in the classic sense. He belonged to a unique group of men—neither military nor civil—banded together in an official or semiofficial capacity to defend the frontier. As Sgt. James B. Gillett, one of the outstanding Rangers of the nineteenth century, explained:

> Scant attention is paid to military law and precedent. The state furnishes food for the men, forage for their horses, ammunition, and medical attendance. The ranger himself must furnish his horse, his accoutrements, and his arms. There is, then, no uniformity in the matter of dress, for each ranger is free to dress as he pleases and in the garb experience has taught him most convenient for utility and comfort. A ranger, as any other frontiersman or cowboy, usually wears heavy woolen clothes of any color that strikes his fancy. . . . A felt hat of any make and color completes his outfit. While riding, a ranger always wears spurs and very high-heeled boots to prevent his foot from slipping through the stirrup, for both the ranger and the cowboy ride with the stirrup in the middle of the foot.[2]

The Ranger was a unique frontiersman on a unique frontier, for in all the annals of the American West there was nothing quite like Texas. One single state held every hope and hardship that pioneers faced in the nation's westward expansion. Texas's natural barriers included rivers, mountains, deserts, and extremes of weather. Some of the most tenacious Indians on the North American continent contested white pretensions of ownership. Nevertheless, the Texans settled their vast frontier within a single lifetime. Beginning as outsiders in a neglected province of Mexico, they turned that province into a sovereign republic, and made the republic into a prosperous state.

In building Texas, people on the frontier depended on the citizen-ranger far more than on any soldier or sheriff, because he was one of them and he knew the dangers they faced. He also understood the people he had to fight and adjusted his thinking accordingly. He risked his life because he had family and friends to protect, and sometimes he lost his life. For death was a constant companion to the Rangers during the first hundred years of their existence in a state that assumed more or less its present boundaries in 1850.

At 268,601 square miles, twentieth-century Texas is almost 56,000 square miles larger than France. The original area was even greater, but as part of the Compromise of 1850, the northwestern portion of the state was ceded to the United States and partitioned, eventually to become sections of New Mexico, Kansas, Colorado, Oklahoma, and Wyoming. Despite its size, its 1992 population was estimated at only 17,655,650, which is roughly as many people as Texas can conveniently support.[3] Like everything else about the state, this small population in relation to its immensity is dictated by two great immutable facts—climate and geography. The eastern half of the state is arable, has a reasonably secure water supply, and can support moderate development; the area to the west is arid and cannot. Most population centers are in east and central Texas; as one proceeds westward, cities become smaller and more isolated.

Most of the state is a plain shelving into three distinct tiers rising one above the other almost like stairs. The lowest is a relatively fertile coastal prairie anywhere from fifty to two hundred miles wide, where American settlement began and where the Texas Rangers were created. The coastal region ends at an escarpment of rugged hills that lead up to a second tier consisting of rolling plains that gradually slope to the northwest. These plains abruptly halt at the caprock, a line of sheer cliffs hundreds of miles long and seamed with deep, rugged canyons. Above these cliffs is the final tier, the Staked Plains, or *Llano Estacado,* to use their local names—flat and featureless tableland that reaches beyond the horizon to Canada, and gives credence to a local saying that there is nothing between Amarillo, Texas, and the North Pole but barbed wire. In the far western part of Texas, beyond the Pecos River, the terrain assumes yet another character totally different from the other three. Here one struggles among the highest mountains in the state, descending from the passes onto the flat, dry, sand-swept floor of true desert.

Even within one particular type of terrain, no two areas have the same environment. In the southernmost tip of Texas, the Rio Grande marks the transition from tropical jungle to temperate forest. Here the whitetail deer and bobcat of the north coexist with the coatimundi and ocelot of the south, and until it was hunted out midway through the twentieth century, the jaguar was considered a native.

The temperate forest hugs the river. A few miles above the mouth of the Rio Grande, the beaches of the coast give way to a region that is less a prairie than a desert. In modern times it is kept green and lush by irrigation from the Rio Grande and underground aquifers, but left to itself it soon would revert back to dust, scrub grass, and cactus. In the immediate coastal area, the easterly breezes from the Gulf of Mexico meet the southwest wind from the Chihuahuan desert, forming a pocket of hot, damp air and making the area around Brownsville a Turkish bath in summer. Farther north, the coast blends into true prairie with tall grass and groves of live oak until, in east Texas, one reaches the vast pine forests of the American South.

Along the escarpment, in the Hill Country, and beyond, spring rains carpet the land with wildflowers—blue, yellow, red, and white—wrapping around hills and buttes and extending as far as the eye can see. But with summer the flowers wither, the color fades to a dull beige, and dust coats everything.

ONLY SINCE THE 1950s, with construction of superhighways and expansion of commercial aviation, has travel been convenient in Texas. The Rangers gained their fame before the age of the automobile and airplane, traversing the country by horseback. In those days, the six-hundred-mile trip from San Antonio to El Paso took weeks through broken mountains and across searing desert. Here, Texans say, every form of plant or animal life bites, slashes, stabs, or stings. One shakes one's blanket for rattlesnakes and checks boots for scorpions and venomous spiders. The native cacti include a low-growing species that botanists know as *Echinocactus texensis,* but that locals call "horse crippler," with good reason.

Rangers scouting the country accepted temperatures in excess of a hundred degrees Fahrenheit as a normal condition of summer, when the sun beats down like a glowing ball. In the winter, they faced subzero temperatures in the north, and even in the southernmost sections of the state, sustained temperatures in the twenties and thirties are not uncommon. Often the cold arrives suddenly, with temperatures dropping as much as forty or fifty degrees within a few hours. Even in the driest months, rain is more of a curse than a blessing, for it is not the gentle showers of the East Coast or northern California, but sudden, torrential downpours bringing deadly flash floods.

And no matter where the Rangers went, they had to guard against attack by Comanches, Kiowas, Apaches, and various other Indian bands, for the Anglo-Saxon colonists who established the first Texas Rangers inherited a war of extermination between white and Indian that was already almost a century old when the first English-speaking settlers arrived in the country.

RANGERS DID NOT originate in Texas, but were a concept carried over from the British colonies in the East, where local militia forces called rangers protected the frontiers of Virginia, the Carolinas, Georgia, and the Old Northwest. In 1759, during the French and Indian War, a battalion commanded by Maj. Robert Rogers served with distinction on the northwest frontier as Rogers's Rangers. The English-speaking people who settled in Texas in the 1820s were predominantly Southern frontiersmen with a ranging tradition, and they brought with them a strong sense of community and of personal honor, together with a martial spirit that became infectious even among non-Southerners and pacifists. These traditions were the most basic foundations of what ultimately became the Texas Rangers.[4]

The original Texas Rangers were organized under Mexican law, because the state belonged to Mexico at the time. One of the Mexican motives for permitting these English-speaking pioneers to settle the area was frontier defense against Indian raids, which had been chronic since Spanish colonial times.

Although Europeans ventured into Texas as early as the 1520s, permanent settlement—and by extension Indian conflict—did not begin until the second decade of the eighteenth century. In 1716, in response to French incursions from the Mississippi Valley, the Spanish government placed Texas under the jurisdiction of the adjacent province of Coahuila, a situation that would continue off and on for the next 120 years. Two years later, the Spaniards initiated a formal and permanent entry into Texas, establishing the settlement that ultimately became San Antonio.[5]

The Spanish entry more or less coincided with the arrival in Texas of the vanguard of another group of invaders, the Kiowas and Comanches, nomadic wanderers who originated in what is now the northwestern United States. At some point in their history, they began separate migrations out onto the Plains to the southeast, and by the middle of the eighteenth century, the Spaniards were encountering them in Texas and New Mexico. Although the two tribes initially fought each other for domination of their new territory on the Southern Plains, by about 1790 they had confederated, forming an alliance that was to last until their defeat by the United States in the Red River War of 1874–75.[6]

One of the most pronounced aspects of Kiowa and Comanche society was its unending warfare. They were a raiding people, and a man's prestige was determined by his ability as a warrior. Depredations against other peoples—Indian and white—became such a pronounced part of their culture that an annual raiding season was established, beginning in the spring when grass was high enough for their ponies to feed and warm, moonlit nights allowed them maximum mobility. Each year they burst out from their strongholds on the Plains of the American Midwest, rapidly covering thousands of miles and marauding with impunity to within five hundred miles of Mexico City.[7]

Although the Kiowas viewed Texas less as a potential homeland than as raiding grounds, some Comanche bands were determined to make it their own. As they moved into Texas, they began displacing numerically weaker native tribes. The Tonkawas and the Lipan Apaches, to name only two, were driven from their traditional lands by the Comanche wedge from the north. It was only a matter of time before this wave of newcomers would clash with the Spaniards, who then were entering the territory from the south.[8]

The pivotal confrontation between these two alien races occurred at a mission on the San Saba River, near what is now Menard, some 150 miles northwest of San Antonio. In the early-morning hours of March 16, 1758, the Comanches and allied tribes attacked the mission and massacred its people.[9] This massacre opened a war between the whites and the Kiowa-Comanche confederation that would rage across Texas for more than a century.[10] The hostilities would be passed down among the Indians from generation to generation. When the Spaniards ultimately abandoned Texas, their Mexican successors inherited the war, and they would in turn pass it on to the Anglo-Saxons. The area between the Red River and the Rio Grande became a battleground with no quarter given and none expected.

After the San Saba massacre, Spain made no further effort to colonize or settle the frontier. The Spaniards acquired Louisiana from the French at the end of the Seven Years War, removing the military necessity for settlement. No private colonizer wanted to leave the relative safety of the interior provinces and risk destruction in a wild unknown. In what is now

Texas, the Spaniards were content to huddle around the only settlements strong enough to provide some semblance of security: Laredo, San Fernando de Béxar (San Antonio), and La Bahía (Goliad).[11]

OVER THE NEXT seventy years, little changed in Texas, and by 1820 the Spanish empire was in its death throes, exhausted by the Napoleonic Wars and with most of its American possessions in armed rebellion. This only accelerated the neglect of its northernmost province. There had been a brief flurry of interest in Texas at the beginning of the century when Madrid ceded Louisiana back to France, resurrecting old border disputes. Then, to Spain's outrage, the French sold the territory to the Americans, who soon convinced themselves that they had purchased Texas as well. In response, the Spaniards moved to strengthen their position in Texas. Anglo-Americans, who previously had been allowed to settle in the Spanish-controlled portions of the Mississippi Valley, were prohibited from obtaining land grants in Spanish territory, and the government planned accelerated colonization of Texas to serve as a barrier against the acquisitive, expansionist Americans. But like so many previous efforts, this one played out simply because Spain was overextended. The empire had become a liability.[12]

The American threat was removed in 1819, when the Adams-Onís Treaty established the Sabine and Red rivers as the border between Spanish Texas and American Louisiana. Thus, after more than a century, most boundaries were finally established, but others remained vague. In the far south the Nueces River was generally considered the division between Texas and Nuevo Santander (now the Mexican state of Tamaulipas), and in the southwest the Rio Grande marked the line with Coahuila. In the west, however, no one was sure where Texas ended and New Mexico began, and no one really cared. Here the Comanches and Apaches reigned supreme, and there was little the government in San Antonio could do about it.

Yet as the Spanish empire drew to a close, an opportunity to settle Texas suddenly presented itself in the person of Moses Austin, a speculating chameleon who had been born a British subject in colonial Connecticut and at various times had held either Spanish or U.S. nationality, according to what best served his interests. His arrival in San Antonio on December 23, 1820, was opportune, because Spain was searching for a solution to the settlement problem, and Austin wanted land.

MOSES AUSTIN WAS fifty-nine when he came to Texas. He had followed the frontier until he arrived in Ste. Genevieve, Missouri, then part of Spanish Louisiana, where he became a Spanish subject, and developed lead mines in the vicinity. Louisiana's transfer, first to France and then to the United States, did not affect Austin, who prospered until the War of 1812 paralyzed trade along the Mississippi. A postwar depression aggravated the situation, and when the Bank of St. Louis, in which Austin was a major stockholder, failed in 1818, he was ruined. His attention now turned to Texas. Once before, he had succeeded in Spanish territory, and he believed he could do it again.[13]

Upon his arrival in San Antonio, Austin presented himself to Governor Antonio Martínez in the Spanish residency that still stands on the city's Military Plaza. The immediate timing was bad. Spain had only recently put down the latest in a procession of uprisings led by adventurers from the United States who had made trouble in Texas over the past seventeen years. Despite the overall relaxation of restrictions under the Adams-Onís Treaty, the civil and military officials responsible for security in Texas and the other northeastern provinces took a dim view of Americans. Austin was an American. Governor Martínez listened perfunctorily, and then ordered him to leave the country.

Dejected, Austin was walking across the plaza from the residency to his lodgings when he encountered the Baron de Bastrop, an old acquaintance from Missouri days. Although he now lived in genteel poverty in San Antonio, Bastrop had influence with the governor and offered to intervene.[14]

BASTROP WAS ONE of the most important people in the development of Texas, yet he seems almost deliberately elusive. Indeed, little was known about him until the latter part of the twentieth century, when records were located in the Netherlands, his country of origin. It is now reasonably certain that his name was Philip Hendrik Nering Boegel (Hispanicized as Felipe Enrique Neri), and he was born in Paramaribo, Suriname, in 1759. His will, prepared shortly before his death in 1827, stated that Bastrop was a hereditary title that came from his father.[15] To some pioneers, however, he claimed that he had entered the Prussian service as a youth and had been ennobled by Frederick the Great.

The truth, however, is more prosaic. "Baron de Bastrop" was a title he bestowed on himself, for Philip Hendrik Nering Boegel was hiding from the law. After growing up in the Netherlands, he was appointed collector-general of taxes for the province of Frisia. Accused of embezzlement, he fled the country about 1793, arriving in Louisiana, where he became a Spanish subject. He was granted thirty square miles, but after several years abandoned his grant and moved to Texas. Some said he had lost his Louisiana holdings in title disputes once the United States took over the territory, and was bitter against the United States because of it. Others maintained that he crossed into Texas when Louisiana reverted briefly back to France, possibly finding that his adopted Spanish nationality was politically safer than coming under French jurisdiction with its Napoleonic ties to Holland.[16]

Whatever Bastrop's past, his chance meeting with Moses Austin in the Military Plaza bound his future firmly to Texas. He intervened with the governor using several arguments. First, he said the Comanches were becoming increasingly brazen in harassing the settlements, and Americans had a proven record as Indian fighters. Second, Spanish subjects simply were not immigrating to Texas; after more than a century the province was still almost empty. Third, American colonization had been successful during the Spanish regime in Louisiana. Finally, and no doubt the clincher, Austin had been a Spanish subject in good standing once before; he would not do anything to undermine the status quo.[17]

The next day, Austin was back at the residency, showing the Spanish passport he originally had used to obtain his Ste. Genevieve grant, declaring he was a Roman Catholic and a former Spanish subject, and requesting a grant on which to settle some three hundred families who would emigrate from the United States and become Spanish subjects. Governor Martínez convened his council and eventually agreed to forward Austin's application to the military headquarters for the northeastern provinces in Monterrey, where the authorities eventually approved it.

Austin, meanwhile, had returned to the United States, where he began preparations for a massive movement of people and equipment to the new country. By now, however, he was suffering from a severe cold, which, aggravated by his age and the exhaustion and exposure of the trip to Texas, developed into pneumonia. On June 10, 1821, he died, leaving instructions that his son, Stephen, take over the Texas project.[18]

STEPHEN F. AUSTIN is a shadowy, one-dimensional figure, despite the fact that his entire life is thoroughly documented. Texans speak of him respectfully, generally calling him by his full name, including the middle initial, but he is more a symbol than a man. Upon his death at the age of forty-three, Sam Houston called him "the Father of Texas." The capital is named for him. And it is generally agreed that without Austin the development of Texas would have been substantially delayed, and neither Houston nor any other of the early leaders and heroes would have been important to the process. Yet he remains elusive, never completely studied or understood. Part of that was the character of the man himself. Blacksmith and sometime Ranger Noah Smithwick remembered, "Dark hair and eyes, sparely built, and unassuming in manner, there was little in Austin's outward appearance to indicate the tremendous energy of which he was possessed."[19]

Austin was one of the most complex and sophisticated men ever to influence the course of Texas. When his fortunes were at their height, he was devious and cynical. He dispensed land titles as though they were the largesse of a feudal lord, which, in effect, they were. As the sole administrator of the colonization laws and the only person authorized to deal with the government, he was suspected by many settlers of manipulating the laws to his own benefit and at their expense. But when fortune left him and others usurped his leadership, he became magnificent, giving the colonies what Smithwick called "his protecting care," which, in the end, was Austin's greatest gift.[20]

A native of Virginia, where his father had business interests, Stephen Fuller Austin was five years old when the family immigrated to Missouri, and the cosmopolitan mixture of French-speaking Canadians, Spaniards, and newly arriving Americans grounded him early in the social and diplomatic niceties that would serve him in good stead as an adult. He was twenty-seven when his father's death gave him responsibility for the Texas colonies. Arriving in San Antonio on August 12, Austin met with Governor Martínez, who pointed out that the region that Austin planned to colonize was a wilderness, and that the government was not yet in a position to extend civil administration that far beyond San Antonio and the other principal settlements. Once Austin brought the colonists, Martínez said, "You will cause them all to understand that until the government organizes the authority which is to govern them and administer justice, they must be governed by and subordinate to you."[21]

Perhaps the most important asset Austin inherited from his father was the friendship with Bastrop. The worldly old schemer took the younger man under wing and soon made himself indispensable by securing an appointment from the governor to serve as Austin's land commissioner. As such, he ordered surveys, handed out titles, and, as the situation required, bullied or bluffed both the settlers on their tracts and officials in San Antonio.

Austin, meanwhile, had inspected the area of the Brazos and Colorado rivers and determined the boundaries of his grant, which he dispatched back to Governor Martínez. By late fall, the first of some three hundred families carefully screened by Austin—known in Texas history as the "Old Three Hundred"—were beginning to move in.

Now a new complication arose. After eleven years of sporadic rebellion and civil war, the three-hundred-year-old Spanish regime collapsed, and Mexico became independent. This raised the question of whether Austin's Spanish grant was even valid. Of more immediate concern to the colonists, however, were Indian depredations that commenced almost from the outset of their arrival.

IN THE EARLY days of Austin's grant, the trouble came not so much from Kiowas or Comanches, who ranged to the west of the colonies, but from native tribes. Austin's cousin Mary Austin Holley wrote:

> The Carancuhua [i.e., Karankawa] Indians were very hostile on the coast. The Wacos and Tawakanies were equally so in the interior, and committed constant depredations. Parties of Tankaways [Tonkawas], Lepans [Lipans], and other tribes, were intermingled with the settlers. These Indians were beggarly and insolent, and were restrained from violence the first two years, only by presents, forbearance, and policy. There was not force enough in the colony to awe them. One imprudent step with these Indians, would have destroyed the settlement. . . .[22]

The Lipans and Tonkawas were more of a nuisance than a threat, but the Karankawas did not hesitate to attack small groups of settlers when the opportunity presented itself. A coastal people, they lived among the estuaries and barrier islands running south from Galveston to Corpus Christi, traveling in canoes and waylaying colonists who went downriver to get supplies from ships anchored in the bays. The warriors averaged six feet tall. They painted their faces half red and half white, and smeared themselves with alligator grease as protection against mosqui-toes. Each carried a bow equal to his height, and could shoot a three-foot arrow one to two hundred yards with accuracy.[23]

Most colonists insisted, and many authorities agree, that they prac-ticed at least a ritual form of cannibalism, as did many of the Texas tribes.[24] Nevertheless, of all the Indians of that period, the Karankawas appear to have been the most hated. Pioneer settler and historian J. W. Wilbarger called them "the Ishmaelites of Texas, for their hands were against every man, and every man's hand was against them."[25]

Although the scrapes between Indians and settlers did not have the character of the later systemized Kiowa and Comanche raids, encounters were frequent enough to demonstrate the need for some sort of organized frontier defense force.

LIKE MANY TEXAS institutions, the militia force that developed into the Rangers was a hybrid of Anglo-Saxon and Hispano-Mexican traditions. The ranger concept itself came to Texas with Austin, who, given the re-sponsibility of protecting a colony beyond the pale of white civilization, recognized the need for a ranger-style defense force. Yet it was not Austin but the new Mexican governor, Col. José Félix Trespalacios, who or-dered the American colonists to establish a frontier police using a Span-ish militia system that had been carried over into Mexico. This called on citizens to organize armed companies to preserve local order. The struc-ture was such that there was no need for a large force, just one that could come together as needed. It was ideal for the colonists.[26]

Austin himself was in Mexico City when the first ranger-style militia company was created. He spent most of 1822 and the early part of 1823 in the capital in an effort to resolve legal disputes concerning the valid-ity of his Spanish colonial land grant under an independent Mexican government. In Texas, meanwhile, Indian depredations and cloudy land titles had so discouraged the settlers along the Colorado that by the fall of 1822 many were preparing to repatriate to the United States. The problem of titles could not be immediately resolved, but Governor Tres-palacios could take measures toward defense and at least give the colonists some feeling of permanence. Accordingly, he directed Bastrop to convene the Americans in the two main settlements to elect an *alcalde*, or political chief, and ranger commanders. On November 20, Bastrop called a convention in the Colorado settlement, which elected John Tumlinson *alcalde,* Robert Kuykendall captain, a man named Jackson as first lieutenant, and Moses Morrisson as second lieutenant.[27] At his direction a convention of the Brazos settlement elected Josiah H. Bell *alcalde,* Samuel Gates captain, and Gibson Kuykendall, Robert Kuykendall's nephew, lieutenant. Despite these efforts, the colonists were slow to organize. They were still new to the country, and in the absence of Austin with clear instructions, they feared taking any action that might bring them into conflict with the Mexican government.[28]

By January 1823, however, the Indian situation reached a point where the *alcalde* Tumlinson and Robert Kuykendall wrote Trespalacios asking permission to enlist expert riflemen from among the Colorado settlers. They would build blockhouses along the coast and boats for cruising the bays to protect vessels landing cargo for the settlements. Trespalacios ordered the enlistment of fourteen men, who mustered on May 5 and were posted near the mouth of the Colorado.[29]

The record of this unit is sketchy, and it appears that only ten men were actually recruited and their length of service is not certain. The commanding officer, Lt. Moses Morrisson, was listed on an 1823 census of American settlers as thirty years old and a farmer who also raised horses and hogs. He had served in the United States Army on the upper Mississippi, where he gained experience in fortifications and boat construction. Another thirty-year-old farmer, John McCroskey, was named corporal. The other eight were privates. All were armed with rifles except Pvt. John Frazer, who carried a musket. Morrisson's pay was set at $40 a month, McCroskey's at $26, and the privates at $24 each. From this beginning came the Texas Rangers.[30]

The new unit immediately encountered problems, the most critical of which seemed to be a shortage of ammunition. By July, after two months in the field, the company's total supply was reduced to only 111 charges of powder and a like number of ball. Explaining the shortage, Morrisson advised the governor that

> as we are altogether Depending upon hunting for our Subsistence at present it will be but a short time in all probability that what we have will be Expended. I therefore Dispatch two men to St. Antonio[31] to endeavour to procure a supply from the Government Charging the Company with the amount to be deducted from their pay as there is ma[n]y of my men who is destitute of

money at present [and] therefore would be unable to procure any [ammunition] from an individual at St. Antonio.

Likewise, he said, powder was completely unavailable in the vicinity, and the need to keep his men hunting for food had made it impossible to begin work on blockhouses.[32]

The following day, the *alcalde* John Tumlinson and a companion, Joseph Newman, started for San Antonio with Morrisson's letter, hoping to obtain the ammunition. They had reached the Guadalupe River within forty miles of the city when they encountered three Indians. Newman was suspicious, but Tumlinson advised friendliness, and extended his hand to one of the Indians. The warrior jerked him off his horse and lanced him. Newman spurred his pony and escaped, although the Indians chased him six miles before giving up.[33]

SHORTLY AFTER TUMLINSON'S death, Luciano García succeeded Trespalacios as governor. Far from adversely affecting the situation, the change strengthened Bastrop's hand, for on July 16, García advised him that Austin's grant had been confirmed, as was the administrative apparatus that Bastrop had already set into motion under Trespalacios. Austin's authority included the responsibility

> to administer justice in that District and to form a Regiment of National Militia of which, for now, he may serve as first chief with the grade of Lt. Colonel; to which end You [Bastrop] will serve notice to all the inhabitants of the aforementioned District to recognize Austin's authority and when ordained relative to good order, to serve the Fatherland and in the defense of the Nation to which they are dependent [i.e., Mexico].[34]

Morrisson's company of volunteers now had full legal sanction of the government and military authorities.

Official sanction did not alleviate the shortages Morrisson had listed in his report, and these imposed limitations on the ability of his company to effectively pacify the area under its jurisdiction. Late that summer, five colonists took a boat down to the mouth of the Colorado, where they bought corn for the settlers upriver. A short distance above the mouth of the river, they were waylaid by a band of Karankawas near the confluence with Skull Creek. Four were killed, and the fifth, J. C. Clark, received a gunshot wound that broke his thigh. Bleeding profusely, he managed to slip into the water and swim to a canebrake, where he hid while he tried to stanch the flow of blood. The Indians apparently lost interest and moved on, leaving Clark to hope he would be found.

The same night about fifteen miles upriver, settler Robert Brotherton encountered a band of Indians on the road, probably the ones who had attacked Clark's party earlier in the day. Believing they were friendly, he continued toward them until one opened fire, severely wounding him. Dismounting, Brotherton managed to hide in the brush, leaving his horse and gun to the Indians.[35]

When Brotherton reported the attack, Capt. Robert Kuykendall, ranger/militia chief of the Colorado, organized about a dozen settlers to go after the Karankawas. A band of Tonkawa Indians was camped near the settlement, and to assure these Indians' good behavior while the men were away, they invited the Tonkawa chief Carita to accompany the expedition as guest and hostage.

The settlers halted about nightfall near the mouth of Skull Creek, where Kuykendall, John H. Moore, and a man named Strickland left the main group and scouted ahead for the Indians. In the darkness, Moore heard an unusual sound and stopped the others. Strickland said it was the thumping of wild turkeys, but Moore believed the Indians were pounding brier root into a starchy pulp for food. Then they heard a baby crying, confirming they had found the Indian camp. Returning to the others, Kuykendall left the horses in charge of Judge William Rabb and Chief Carita, while he took the remaining settlers back to the Karankawa camp. The Indians, in the meantime, had finished their work and gone to sleep. About dawn, the settlers slipped down between the camp and the creek and began moving up among the sleeping Karankawas. They were almost inside the camp when one warrior awoke and grabbed his bow. Kuykendall killed him and the other settlers came in shooting, driving the Indians out of the thicket and onto the prairie. Several were killed and the others escaped. The scalp of one warrior was taken, together with his six-foot bow, which Kuykendall later gave to his nephew Gib.[36]

The badly wounded J. C. Clark, still hiding in the canebrake after his encounter with the Indians on the river, heard the shooting and managed to make his way to the camp, where he was rescued by the other whites. He recovered and lived for many years afterward.[37]

"The fight was an entire surprise [to the Indians]," Moore later recalled. "We all felt it was an act of justice and of self-preservation. We were too weak to furnish goods for Carankawaes [Karankawas], and had to be let alone to get bread for ourselves. . . .

"This was the first fight with the Indians in Austin's colony."[38]

DESPITE SUCH PUNITIVE actions, the Karankawas still moved openly near the mouth of the Colorado and Matagorda Bay, and Morrisson, whose company was charged with keeping them under control, could do little about it. On August 3, he wrote Kuykendall that his men had discovered a party of Karankawas by the bay, but because the powder was now completely depleted he felt it was not "altogether safe to attack them in our present fix, if you would come down and join us with a party of your men immediately I think we would be able to give them a good drubbing and clear them from our Coast."[39]

Austin arrived at the Colorado settlements the following day. Returning from Mexico City, he had paused in Monterrey to clarify his authority with military officials of the independent Mexican government.[40] This conference gave him essentially full dictatorial powers to maintain order, with the exception of capital cases, in which the record of trial would be referred to the authorities in San Antonio.[41]

Determined to use his new power to assist the beleaguered Morrisson (and to remind the colonists of their dependence on himself), he issued a proclamation on August 5, pledging his own resources to pay ten additional men for Morrisson's company "to act as rangers for the common defence." Not having cash, he offered each man $15 a month payable in land from his holdings.[42] This proclamation is significant because it appears to be the first time the word "rangers" was applied to a Texas defense force.

It is uncertain whether the ten rangers were ever enlisted. No record has ever been found indicating that this detachment was ever formed.[43] In a letter to military authorities in Monterrey in November, Austin indicated he had had second thoughts about organizing them on his own and wanted formal government sanction before recruiting them. So far, he said, the only full-time defense force was Morrisson's original unit mustered the previous May by order of then governor Trespalacios, and who "as of now have not received nothing in pay." Besides failing to pay the men, the government had provided only eighteen pounds of powder for ammunition, and that powder was of too coarse a grain to be serviceable for their rifles.[44]

Far from being able to maintain order, Austin told the military authorities:

> The roads are full of errant thieves united with the Indians, and without a small force of mounted troops to clean-up and guard them, I cannot respond to the security of travelers. . . . If it is possible to permit me to continue in service the 14 men and augment them with 10 more and a Sergeant, I can respond to the security of the roads.[45]

In other words, he needed rangers.

Chapter 2

Indian Raids and Revolution

It is estimated that nine tenths of the fatal encounters between colonists and Indians between 1821 and 1824 involved Karankawas. By late June 1824, depredations had reached such an extent that Austin organized a formal campaign against them. Capt. Amos Rawls was detailed to take a detachment of rangers and chase a band that had been stealing cattle. The rangers found the Indians, and in the ensuing fight one warrior was killed and a settler was permanently crippled by an arrow through the elbow. The Karankawas fled into the canebrakes, and Rawls sent for reinforcements. Austin dispatched more volunteers, who moved against the main Indian camp on the coast. This unit got into a fight near the mouth of the Colorado River, and five warriors were killed.[1]

In August, Indian movements indicated about fifty Karankawas planned a retaliatory raid against both the lower and upper settlements of the Colorado. Austin himself organized a company of sixty-two men, which he divided to reconnoiter both banks of the river. Finding nothing, the company reunited and scouted southwest toward the Lavaca River.

"Most of our route was through a prairie country without road or path," Gib Kuykendall recalled. "Bordering many of the creeks which we crossed were very dense thickets. Austin detailed pioneers to open roads through such places."[2]

By September 7, Austin concluded that the Indians had left the area and moved toward the San Antonio River, which runs through the *tejano* town of Goliad, where a mission had been established in the eighteenth century to evangelize the Karankawas. By now, however, Austin's provisions were almost exhausted, and he ordered his company back to San Felipe to resupply and gather reinforcements. Once that was done, he planned a direct march 110 miles southwest to Goliad.

The company, when it left San Felipe for Goliad in mid-September, was augmented by thirty armed and mounted slaves under the leadership of their owner, Col. Jared C. Groce. September is one of the hottest months in Texas, and the sun beat down and baked the prairies along the route. A short distance above the present city of Victoria, "one of our men fainted and fell from his horse," Gib Kuykendall remembered. "He was bled and soon revived."[3]

Camp that night was on the banks of the Guadalupe River, a little over thirty miles short of their goal. The men were in a good mood. William Pettus, known to the others as Uncle Buck, and Gustavus Edwards ran a foot race. Both were middle-aged, overweight, and hopelessly out of shape, and their comrades thought it was hilarious.

The following morning, the company was intercepted some twelve or fifteen miles outside of Goliad by a courier from the local authorities, who requested that the men stay away from the town. They went into camp on a creek about four miles out, and soon they were visited by the *alcalde* and mission priests. The Karankawas had taken refuge in the mission and had asked the priests and civil authorities to propose a truce whereby they would never again go east of the San Antonio River. Austin accompanied the Mexicans back to town to finalize the agreement. In the meantime, the Karankawas had reconsidered, realizing the San Antonio River would severely restrict their hunting and fishing grounds, and asked that instead the line be extended eastward to the Lavaca River. Since the priests and *alcalde* stood surety for the Indians, Austin agreed, but warned them to keep west of the Lavaca. The following day, the troops broke camp and returned home, having completed the first successful expedition of its kind in Texas.[4]

THE AGREEMENT WITH the Karankawas was never completely workable, and raids and counter-raids continued. Yet for the time being, at least, it bought some breathing space with that tribe. The Karankawas, however, were not the only Indians in conflict with the settlers, and as the colonists moved west and out onto the prairies, the Wacos and Tawakonis proved equally dangerous. The Americans' hold was still tenuous at best. For all their progress on their river bottoms in eastern Texas, the colonists were still strangers in a hostile and unknown country. Austin's Karankawa campaign demonstrated the need for an organized, extensive defense system. The necessity became even greater when Mexican military authorities in San Antonio began pressing the colonists to uphold their responsibilities as citizens and initiate a campaign against the Wacos, Tawakonis, and Tawaheshes.

After a fight between Colorado settlers and Tawakoni horse thieves in April 1826, Austin sent an order to the ranger-militiamen calling on them

> to protect your own homes, your own property, to shield your wives and children from the arrows of a savage and merciless enemy—your adopted country now also called [*sic*] upon you to rally around the national flag and fight its enemies the Wacos and Tahuacanies—every honorable and ardent impulse Therefore that can animate the bosoms of free men burns in yours and urges you forward to meet the enemy—the defence of your firesides—of your wives and children, your friends—yourselves— your property and your country. . . .
>
> The depredations of your enemies the W[acos] and T[awakonis] indians and there [*sic*] hostile preparations, has driven us to the necessity of taking up arms in self defence. The frontier is menaced—The whole colony is threatened—under these circumstances it became my duty to call the militia to the frontier to repel the threatened attacks and to teach our enemies to fear and respect us. . . .[5]

The plan was to form an alliance with the Cherokees, Shawnees, and Delawares and simultaneously attack the main villages of Wacos and Tawakonis along the Brazos and at the headwaters of the Navasota River. But the military authorities in San Antonio vetoed the alliance because they did not want the Cherokees, Shawnees, and Delawares to feel the whites depended on them. Austin therefore was forced to postpone a major campaign, but kept the rangers in the field for frontier defense.[6]

BESIDES INDIANS, THE settlers had to contend with "border ruffians," Mexicans, Frenchmen from Louisiana, and the occasional desperado fleeing the law in the United States. Most of their activities involved horse theft, a serious offense because the horse was the only reliable means of transportation. Although the American colonists had the legal right to handle all but capital cases, the colonies had extended to the point that they were more conveniently located to the formal legal system in San Antonio than in the beginning. Nevertheless, the settlers preferred to mete out punishment on their own. There was a growing distrust between the Anglo-Saxons and the Mexicans, and the Anglo-Saxons were not convinced the Mexicans would issue punishment, particularly when their own people were involved. In one early instance, a Frenchman and a Mexican were detained for stealing horses, and Josiah Bell, *alcalde* of the Brazos settlement, instructed Gib Kuykendall to take them to San Antonio. En route, he ran into Moses Morrisson "and one or two other Americans" who were returning from the city. They advised him to take the prisoners back to the Brazos because "the Mexican authorities would set the prisoners at liberty without punishment." He returned them to the settlement, where they were flogged and expelled without the benefit of Mexican authority.[7]

Despite their dim view of Mexico's system of justice, the colonists of Austin's original Old Three Hundred generally were law-abiding and attempted to coexist with the people of their adopted country. There was enough distance between the American settlers along the Brazos and Colorado and the Mexicans in San Antonio and Goliad that most contact was official and cordial. Austin himself noted:

> The settlers have done their duty, and have been much clearer from internal dissensions, than could be expected, under all the circumstances. They have uniformly been unshaken in their fidelity, and ready and willing to discharge their obligations as Mexican citizens; they have borne, with the most inflexible fortitude, all the privations to which their situation exposed them, and have contributed largely in laying a foundation for the future prosperity of Texas, by commencing the settlement of its wilderness.[8]

Nevertheless, the basic cultural differences, combined with what they often saw as abandonment and indifference on the part of the authorities, created tensions between the American colonists and their Mexican counterparts. The problem was aggravated by the newer *empresarios,* as the American land-grant colonizers were called, who were far less discriminating than Austin as to whom they allowed to enter their colonies. These new arrivals never abandoned cultural prejudices inherited from their ancestors as far back as Elizabethan conflicts with Spain. The Mexicans, having been under Spanish rule at that time, viewed the same history from the opposite direction and upheld a legacy of Castilian intolerance against the English-speaking world. The American felt it a solemn duty to bring a Protestant-based "Christian order" to a world of Spanish chaos.[9] Conversely, the Spanish language often used—and still uses—the word *católico* (Catholic) as a synonym for "Christian" and the word *cristiano* (Christian) as a synonym for the Spanish language itself.[10]

The friction was not entirely one-sided, for the Mexicans contributed their share to the growing atmosphere of suspicion and contempt. Despite the guarantees of political liberty contained in a federal constitution adopted in 1824 and the good intentions of those who framed it, three centuries of autocratic Spanish rule had left Mexico better prepared for despotism than popular sovereignty. A liberal faction advocated a republic of semiautonomous states modeled on the United States that offered personal liberty and limited the influence of the great landholders and the church. The powerful conservatives, made up of the great landholders, urban elite, monarchists, and clergy, wanted a strong central government that maintained their ancient privileges. As the conservatives gained control, the federal government became increasingly authoritarian, and state governments existed primarily to ratify federal degrees. State officials in Saltillo, now capital of the combined state of Coahuila-Texas, were quick to support whatever faction held power in Mexico City, and representatives to the state assembly were chosen by electors rather than by direct vote. The system went directly against the traditions of personal freedom the American immigrants had brought from their native country.[11]

For their part, the American immigrants—particularly those who came after Austin's Old Three Hundred—never totally accepted the fact that they were now in a foreign country with different laws and traditions; that their own rights and privileges as United States citizens were no longer applicable; that, indeed, they were no longer U.S. citizens but citizens of Mexico. Even in the United States, the Southern states were beginning to dispute the growing power of the American federal government, and a large percentage of colonists in Texas came from the South. The rigid Mexican system and the routine involvement of the military in many aspects of civil life seemed all the more alien and unacceptable. The possibility that the Americans themselves were the aliens was never seriously considered by the rank-and-file colonists.[12]

Historical and cultural differences were complicated by race. The Mexican, of varying shades from light olive to dark brown, was regarded as a backward, indolent, and irresponsible person, and the sooner Mexican territory was put into the hands of the pale, industrious Anglo-Saxons, the better for all.[13] The attitude of the United States during this period did nothing to allay the fears of the Mexicans. Although Texas never, at any time in its history, belonged to France and was not part of Thomas Jefferson's Louisiana Purchase, the scope of the purchase grew in Jefferson's mind. Ultimately he came to believe that it did include Texas, and this profoundly influenced U.S. foreign policy for the next half century. The United States government became increasingly dissatisfied with the 1819 treaty with Spain that fixed the boundary at the Sabine River, and officials in Washington adopted the stance that the Mexican presence in Texas was an illegal occupation of American territory.

In 1825, as Austin was struggling with Indians and with the general administrative problems of his colony, the United States proposed relocating the boundary by offering Mexico $1 million for a border on the Rio Grande, or $500,000 for the Colorado. This was, in effect, a bid to buy Texas, which Mexico had never offered to sell. It was the first of several unwanted attempts to purchase the region, and Mexican officials became suspicious of Washington's intentions regarding their country. These suspicions were carried over to the American colonists, whom the Mexicans began to see as part of a sinister conspiracy of territorial aggrandizement by the United States.[14]

Mexican suspicions deepened in the fall of 1826, when the colonists of the *empresario* Haden Edwards of Nacogdoches, near the Louisiana border, began defying the federal government. Soon the defiance broke into open revolt. On December 16, Edwards's followers unfurled their own flag and proclaimed the Republic of Fredonia.

Shaken from its lethargy, Mexico reacted by dispatching troops to east Texas to put down the rebellion. Seeing his own situation threatened, Austin issued a proclamation condemning the "Nacogdoches madmen," and the majority of the American colonists joined him in supporting the government.[15] In fact, so many men went with militia units aiding federal forces against Edwards that Austin feared the settlements would be unprotected from depredations by the prairie Indians. To counter that threat, he ordered Abner Kuykendall to take eight rangers and patrol the country "between the Colorado and Brazos along the San Antonio road to detect any inroad of the Wacoes or other northern tribes[.]"[16]

The rebellion was suppressed, and Edwards was expelled. Nevertheless, the Mexicans began to see an American plot at every turn.[17]

MEXICO NOW TOOK steps to strengthen its hold on Texas. Although the rights of the states and people were being suppressed throughout the country, specific actions were taken dealing with the American colonists. Tariffs were imposed on the imports on which the Texans depended for even the most basic goods. Further emigration from the United States was banned, and the settlements were garrisoned by federal soldiers, often convict troops who opted for the army instead of prison. These acts are considered among the first links in the chain of events that led to the rupture with Mexico.[18]

Even as relations deteriorated between the colonists and the government in Mexico City, Indian depredations continued on the frontier. In 1828 and 1829 there were numerous murders and thefts by prairie tribes. Indian war parties prowled the countryside, disrupting trade between the colonists and the Mexican interior. The settlers believed the time had come for some sort of decisive action.

The first organized war against these Indians broke out in July 1829, after a group of whites killed four Indians during a fight on the Colorado about twenty-five miles east of the present city of Austin. Retaliation was certain, and Austin called up two companies of fifty volunteers each. A third company was organized in Gonzales, seventy miles east of San Antonio, in response to murders and depredations in that area, and together the three companies moved up the Colorado looking for hostile bands. Near the confluence of the Colorado and the San Saba rivers, scouts reported a camp of Wacos and Tawakonis. The Indians, however, had spotted the colonists and fled, leaving much of their equipment behind. Capt. Bartlett Simms took fifteen men and chased the fleeing Indians several miles before overtaking their pony herd and capturing many of the animals. The volunteers returned home, hoping the loss of camp, equipment, and animals would discourage the Indians from raiding in the future.

This expedition seems to have ranged farther than any previously, and it was a learning experience. They spent thirty-two days on the march, reaching a point about 150 miles northwest of San Antonio, well beyond the pale of any settlement, Mexican or American. Poorly prepared, they ran out of provisions, and at one point lived for three days on acorns and wild persimmons.[19]

THE COLONISTS ALSO faced danger closer to home. Despite the truce with Austin, the Karankawas continued sporadic raiding. In 1831 about seventy warriors attacked the home of Charles Cavina, one of the earliest of Austin's Old Three Hundred.[20] Cavina himself was absent, and the house was undefended. The Karankawas killed Cavina's wife and three of his four daughters. A visiting neighbor named Mrs. Flowers was killed as she tried to escape. The fourth Cavina daughter, a girl of about five or six, was shot through with one of the Indians' three-foot arrows and left for dead. Mrs. Flowers's daughter was also wounded. Both eventually recovered.

The Indians were sacking the house when Cavina arrived home with his black retainers. Being unarmed, they had to retreat and wait until the Indians left. Cavina then raised a company of about sixty men under the command of Capt. Aylett C. Buckner, a veteran Indian fighter, who tracked the Karankawas to a spot on the Colorado River. Nearing their camp, he sent Moses Morrisson ahead to reconnoiter.

In the eight years since he had been placed in command of the very first ranger company, Morrisson had become an experienced Indian fighter. Slipping quietly up to a bluff overlooking the Indian position on the riverbank, he leaned over to get a better view. But the bluff crumbled under his weight, and he slid some forty feet into the middle of the startled Indians. He managed to keep hold of his rifle, and before the Karankawas recovered from their surprise, he dove into a hole in the riverbank and opened fire.

Buckner's men heard the shots and hurried to the rescue, charging into the Karankawas, firing indiscriminately and killing men, women, and children. One man killed a mother and her baby with a single shot that passed through both their bodies. Some of the Indians swam across the river, but were shot down as they tried to crawl up the opposite bank. Altogether between forty and fifty were killed, and one eyewitness later claimed the river was tinted red from their blood. This was the last real engagement between the colonists and the Karankawas. Never a large tribe, they appear to have been devastated by their losses in this fight, and they gradually faded from history; within a generation they were extinct.[21]

With the coastal tribes subdued, the colonists began turning their attention toward the western prairies, and beyond to the Great Plains. They were now undergoing a metamorphosis. Despite their brief tenure, they were being transformed by this land, becoming a new people. They no longer identified with the United States, but neither were they truly Mexican. The Mexicans still might consider them Americans, but they were rapidly becoming a different people. They began calling themselves "Texians," the first stage of a process that would create the classic Texan.

THE INDIAN THREAT aside, the Texans were optimistic, particularly now that it appeared relations might be improving with the government. A liberal general, Antonio López de Santa Anna, vocal in his support for constitutional rule, rose up in revolt against the current regime in Mexico City. Although Austin questioned Santa Anna's sincerity, he nevertheless violated his usual rule of staying aloof from Mexican politics and urged the colonists to declare for the general as the alternative to continued anarchy.[22]

By now, Austin no longer wielded the power he originally had held. Bastrop was dead. The colonists were electing their own officials, and quarrels had broken out with some of the newer American colonizers. Land fees, from which much of his income was derived, had been nullified by the government, and he had sold off much of his holdings to pay debts. His old sense of grandeeism was gone. Whether or not he benefited, the great Texas enterprise was a success, and for him that had become enough. The colonists no longer turned to him for governing authority, but for wisdom and experience, and he was determined to use that wisdom and experience in their best interests. Meanwhile, in Mexico City, the government was undergoing yet another reorganization— Santa Anna had won.[23]

If this period has left any common historic bond between Texans and Mexicans, it is their joint loathing for Santa Anna, the man who more than any other influenced events for the next two decades. In Texas, he is remembered as the butcher of the Alamo, Goliad, and Mier. In Mexico, he is viewed as an opportunist at best, and at worst as a traitor who sold out his country for his own wealth and comfort.[24] All of these images are true. It is doubtful whether he ever had any cause other than himself, and his entire life seems to have been centered around his own aggrandizement. Even toward the end, when he had outlived his enemies and existed in poverty and exile, he continued to feed his own vanity, portraying himself as a misunderstood patriot whose only motive was love of country.

Yet for all his well-known faults, Mexico continued to turn to him for leadership during national crises. The reason is not as complicated as it might seem. During three centuries of Spanish rule, the army was the only means by which colonial subjects could advance; every important civil position was filled by administrators sent from Europe. Independence meant the departure of virtually the entire governmental machinery, and the army filled part of the void.[25] Against such a background, in which the military habitually intervened in civil affairs, Santa Anna was simply the best Mexico could do.

At the time he seized the government, he was thirty-eight years old, dissipated, and obsessed with money and fame. But he was also shrewd, and could be patient when he wanted to be. Now he was patient as he represented himself as the liberal who only reluctantly had seized power to save the nation.[26] Soon, however, he realized there was strong opposition to reform, and he quietly began working with the conservatives and the clergy. Assuming executive power, he dissolved the national congress and the state legislatures and strengthened the privileges of the church. A new, handpicked *Congreso Nacional* ratified his actions, repudiating the 1824 constitution. Santa Anna was absolute master of Mexico.[27]

Mexicans did not quietly accept Santa Anna's dictatorship. Opposition in Puebla, a state southeast of Mexico City, had to be suppressed by military force. Then Zacatecas, a mineral-rich northern state, rebelled and called up five thousand troops against the new central government. Santa Anna put down this rebellion with particular ferocity, allowing his troops to sack the wealthy city of Zacatecas. Then came Coahuila's turn. The army arrived before the state could organize a rebellion and arrested Governor Agustín Viesca and his staff as they tried to transfer the government to San Antonio in Texas. The Texas members of the state legislature managed to escape and make their way home.[28]

Now Santa Anna turned his attention to Texas. Already he had received Stephen F. Austin, who was in Mexico City to present the Texans' views on their future. After an initially cordial relationship, Austin was jailed for eleven months, and under house arrest for another six months before being allowed to return home. In 1835, soldiers sent to Anahuac in east Texas to collect customs duties clashed with local citizens. The colonies organized committees of public safety, and by autumn, when Austin arrived back in Texas, many believed armed resistance to Santa Anna was the only option. As Mirabeau B. Lamar, later president of the Republic of Texas, wrote, "The Gov[erno]r of the State was a prisoner, the Constitution was broken down, and all Coahuila overrun by the military."

When they learned that Santa Anna's brother-in-law, Maj. Gen. Martín Perfecto de Cos, was en route to San Antonio with additional troops, the Texans organized a convention to prepare the state for defense. Before it could assemble, however, the citizens of Gonzales clashed with federal troops. News of the fight created so much excitement that few were aware when General Cos arrived in San Antonio with substantial reinforcements. As far as Santa Anna was concerned, Texas was in rebellion.[29]

With the state now at war, the convention that opened in San Felipe on October 11 established itself as the Permanent Council to organize a government and give some legitimacy to the citizens who were gathering to form an army. There was also the matter of frontier defense while the army faced Mexico, and on October 17, Daniel Parker of Nacogdoches moved that his brother Silas, Garrison Greenwood, and D. B. Fryer be authorized to form companies of "rangers whose business shall be to range and guard the frontiers. . . ."

The motion, as approved, designated Silas Parker, Greenwood, and Fryer as superintendents. The companies would elect the officers who would hold immediate command. The duties of the superintendents included enlisting and organizing the companies, overseeing their operations, and arranging their provisions, obligating public funds for the purpose. They were specifically enjoined "not to interfere with friendly tribes of Indians on our borders." The companies would elect their own officers. Each Ranger—from this point the term can reasonably be capitalized—was to provide his own horse, arms, ammunition, and equipment, and would receive $1.25 a day. The government would indemnify any losses of personal gear. Greenwood's company would muster at Houston, while Parker and Fryer would assemble "at the Ouaco [Waco] village on the Brazos" where the city of Waco now stands.[30]

The parsimonious pay initially may have been an expediency for a provisional government that was barely organized and had no treasury or means of revenue. However, it would become standard practice. Not until the oil boom of the early twentieth century did the government of Texas have financial resources appropriate to its responsibilities. Throughout the nineteenth century, the government had to carefully nurse its limited monies, and chronic underfunding would become the bane of the Ranger Service.[31]

Over the next few weeks, the concept was refined. A military ordinance was approved, creating a regular army of 1,120 men enlisted for two years under command of a major general. As part of the overall defense establishment, the ordinance stated:

> There shall be a corps of rangers under the command of a major,
> to consist of one hundred and fifty men, to be divided into three
> or more detachments, and which shall compose a battalion under
> the commander-in-chief, when in the field.[32]

Rangers were enlisted for one year rather than the two required of soldiers, and if discharged prior to the end of their enlistments, they were to hold themselves available in case they were needed. A separate article created a state militia, so that the line between Rangers and militia was now clearly defined, although both served under the jurisdiction of the military.

More refinements were made until finally, on November 28, the council elected officers. Robert McAlpin Williamson, a tough, self-reliant jurist known as "Three-Legged Willie" because he reinforced a polio-wasted right leg with a wooden peg, was named major of the proposed corps of Rangers. Company captains were Isaac W. Burton, William H. Arrington, and John J. Tumlinson. Various lieutenants were also elected. Despite Williamson's title as corps major, the real authority rested with the company captains; the corps itself was considered in service only when all three companies were assembled as a single unit.[33]

MOST HISTORIES OF the War of Independence center around the conflict with Mexico. In reality, it was a two-front war, not only against the Mexicans in the south and east, but against the Plains Indian tribes in the north and west. The fighting on the frontier was especially serious because it now involved the Comanches. Although initially indifferent to the Americans, they had begun growing restless when white expansion pushed other tribes into their hunting grounds. Then the whites themselves moved onto the edge of the Plains. Between these two groups, the buffalo herds on which the Comanches depended began to dwindle, and they retaliated.[34]

Trouble erupted in the spring of 1835, when a band of warriors raided one of the Colorado settlements, killed a wagoner, and stole some horses. A company hastily formed by pioneer Indian fighter Edward Burleson started in pursuit. On the trail, they encountered the friendly Caddo chief Canoma, who, traveling under a safe conduct, had managed to find the raiders and recover the horses and was en route back to the settlement. Without bothering to inquire, Burleson's men killed Canoma and his son, alienating the Caddos. Soon after, Indian depredations prompted some Brazos settlers to raid a Keechi village on the Trinity River, killing several people, destroying the village, and capturing horses, disrupting the fragile truce between the Indians and the Brazos whites.[35]

Then, in July 1835, a company of men under Capt. Robert M. Coleman attacked a Tawakoni village in what is now Limestone County, east of Waco. Though surprised, the Indians outnumbered the whites, forcing them to retreat to Parker's Fort, seat of the Parker clan, some forty miles east of Waco. Coleman sent for help and was reinforced by three companies under Col. John H. Moore. The Indians retreated. Moore's Rangers combed the countryside as far as the present site of Dallas before returning home.[36] These various skirmishes, insignificant on their own, would have far-reaching repercussions, not only with the local tribes but with the powerful Comanches of the Plains.

For all its efforts to bring this fighting to an end, the Permanent Council itself aggravated the situation by giving command of one of the new official Ranger companies to Capt. John Tumlinson. Like Burleson with his ad hoc rangers, Tumlinson was unlikely to inquire about an Indian's intentions before killing him. Neither he nor his brothers ever forgot the murder of their father, and "the Fighting Tumlinsons," as the clan would be known, nursed a lifelong hatred of Indians.[37]

Because they were moving into Comanche country, Tumlinson's Rangers could expect all the justification they needed for starting a fight.

The sixty-man company probably organized in late 1835, because by early January 1836 it was ready for duty. The Rangers were assigned to rendezvous at Hornsby's Station on the Colorado, collect equipment, and ride to the headwaters of Brushy Creek, about thirty miles northwest of the site of modern Austin. There they were to build and garrison a block-house.

One of the privates in the company, Noah Smithwick, left a memoir that has become a classic account of Texas's early years. Smithwick came to Texas in 1827, when he was about twenty, "with all my worldly possessions, consisting of a few dollars in money, a change of clothes, and a gun, of course, to seek my fortune."[38] He lived for a while in De-Witt's Colony before settling in San Felipe, where he established himself as a blacksmith. He was part of the force that captured San Antonio and, erroneously believing the fighting with Mexico was over, joined Tumlin-son's company to see more action. This probably saved his life, because it kept him away from the Alamo.[39]

A FORMER MISSION secularized and converted to a military post by the Spaniards, the Alamo was garrisoned by regular troops and volunteers commanded by Lt. Col. William Barrett Travis.[40] On February 23, 1836, a vanguard of Mexican dragoons under Gen. Joaquín Ramírez y Sesma arrived in San Antonio. Later that day, Santa Anna himself rode into the city with the main Mexican force and invested the fort. Faced with the prospect of a long siege, Travis penned a hasty note to the nearest help, seventy miles away in Gonzales.

> The enemy in large force is in sight. We want men and provi-sions. Send them to us. We have 150 men and are determined to defend the Alamo to the last. Give us assistance.
>
> W. B. Travis, Lieut.-Col. Commanding
>
> P.S. Send an express to San Felipe with the news night and day.
>
> Travis[41]

The note was given to Dr. John Sutherland and Capt. John W. Smith, who arrived in Gonzales the following day. Among those who saw it was Major Williamson of the recently authorized Ranger Corps, who wrote a letter advising the provisional government:

By express from San Antonio under date of 23rd inst. I have received information that 2,000 Mexicans under command of [Ramírez y] Sesma have arrived in Bexar [San Antonio] and have taken possession of the Public Square, compelling the American troops (150 in number) to confine themselves to the Alamo. The American troops are determined to defend the place to the last and have called upon their fellow-citizens for help.

> Yr. obt. servt.,
> R. M. Williamson,
> Comd'g the Rangers.[42]

Williamson's title was impressive but empty. The three companies were scattered, and until they assembled as a unit, he had no authority.

The same was not true, however, of the Gonzales Ranging Company of Mounted Volunteers, recently organized by the citizens under command of Lt. George Kimball. Because they were a strictly voluntary force with no sanction other than the support of the local community, they did not fall under Williamson's jurisdiction. In common with so many other ad hoc Ranger companies of the period, "they were voluntary combinations of freemen held together by the cohesive power [of] patriotism," according to nineteenth-century Ranger and historian John Henry Brown. The company was composed of only twenty-two men, and initially no one had expected a fight anytime soon. Nevertheless, Travis's call spurred them to action and they prepared to ride to San Antonio.[43]

Travis, meanwhile, had written a second letter, which, until recent years, could be recited by virtually every schoolchild in Texas.

Comandancy of the Alamo—.
Bexar, Feby. 24th 1836—
> To the People of Texas & all Americans *in the* world—
> Fellow citizens & compatriots—
> I am besieged, by a thousand or more of the Mexicans under Santa Anna—I have sustained a continual Bombardment & cannonade for 24 hours & have not lost a man—The enemy has demanded a surrender at discretion, otherwise, the garrison are to be put to the sword, if the fort is taken—I have answered the demand with a cannon shot, & our flag still waves proudly from the

walls—*I shall never surrender or retreat. Then,* I call on you in the name of Liberty, of patriotism & everything dear to the American character, to come to our aid, with all dispatch—The enemy is receiving reinforcements daily & will no doubt increase to three or four thousand in four or five days. If this call is neglected, I am determined to sustain myself as long as possible & die like a soldier who never forgets what is due to his own honor & that of his country.

> *Victory or death*
> William Barret Travis
> Lt. Col. comdt.

P.S. The Lord is on our side—When the enemy appeared in sight we had not three bushels of corn—We have since found in deserted houses 80 or 90 bushels & got into the walls 20 or 30 head of beeves—

> Travis[44]

The letter was given to Capt. Albert Martin of Gonzales, who reached his hometown late in the afternoon of the next day. Travis's new plea added a sense of urgency, and several more volunteered for the Gonzales Rangers, including Martin himself, who intended to go back and rejoin the garrison. At 2 P.M. on February 27, the company assembled and, led by Kimball and Martin, rode out toward San Antonio. Because Mexicans blocking the road ahead might force them to cut across open country, Captain Smith served as their guide. An experienced frontiersman and old San Antonio hand, he knew the country better than anyone. Picking up more men on the way, the company had risen to thirty-two men by sunset February 29 as it neared the Alamo.

In the distance, they saw the shadowy form of a horseman, who politely inquired if they wanted him to guide them through the Mexican lines into the fort. They accepted, but as they fell in behind the man, Smith was uneasy. The rider kept too far ahead, and his English was simply too precise. It was a trap. Someone suggested killing the man, but before they could shoot, the rider spurred off into the darkness.

Listening now for the sound of men and equipment on either side of their column, the Gonzales Rangers edged through the Mexican army toward the Alamo. As they neared, a rifle sounded from the walls, and the bullet grazed the foot of a Gonzales man, who responded with a loud string of Anglo-Saxon epithets. The shooting stopped, the gate swung open, and at 3 A.M. on March 1, the Gonzales Rangers entered the Alamo.[45]

The appearance of these reinforcements caught the attention of the Mexicans. Gen. Vicente Filisola, Santa Anna's second-in-command, who preferred to think of the rebels as newly arrived American adventurers rather than "colonists or inhabitants of Texas," grudgingly acknowledged that the Gonzales contingent was local. Santa Anna preferred to ignore them.[46]

The Gonzales Ranging Company raised the garrison to approximately 186, but it was not enough to resist Santa Anna's divisions. At dawn on March 6, Mexican troops overwhelmed the Alamo, killing all the defenders, including the Ranger volunteers.

IN THE WILDERNESS more than a hundred miles to the northwest, Tumlinson's Rangers were unaware of events in San Antonio. Leaving the city well before the arrival of the Mexicans, they had arrived at their rendezvous at Hornsby's Station and were just settling down to supper when "a young white woman, an entire stranger, her clothes hanging in shreds about her torn and bleeding body, dragged herself into camp and sank exhausted on the ground," according to young Noah Smithwick.[47] It took time to get a coherent statement from her, but at length the Rangers learned she was Sarah Hibbons. She had been traveling with her husband, brother, and two small children when they were attacked by Comanches. The two men were killed and the wagon was plundered. She was tied to one of the wagon mules and her three-year-old son to another. The younger child, however, irritated the Indians with its crying, and they silenced it by smashing its head against a tree.

As the Indians reached the Colorado, a norther blew in, and they sought shelter in a cedar brake. Confident Mrs. Hibbons would not escape and leave her three-year-old behind, they didn't bother to tie her up or post a guard. Realizing her only hope for herself or her son was escape, she waited until they were asleep and slipped away. The following night, she found the camp.

The Rangers finished their supper and prepared to ride. Their host, Reuben Hornsby, knew the country and acted as guide. They rode through the night until they judged they were near the Indian trail, then halted and waited until daylight, so they wouldn't miss it in the dark. Scouts went out at first light and soon found the trail. Smithwick remembered it was "fresh and well defined as if the marauders were exercising neither haste nor caution . . . having no doubt spent a good portion of the previous day in a fruitless search for their escaped prisoner."

They tracked the Indians to Walnut Creek, about ten miles northwest of Austin, and found them preparing to break camp. The surprised Comanches dashed for shelter in one of the numerous cedar brakes, leaving everything except weapons. Smithwick's horse took him right in among them, and one warrior barely missed him with a musket shot. Knowing the Comanche's gun was empty, Smithwick jumped off his horse and fired at him. The Indian dropped, and, presuming he was dead, Smithwick reloaded and ran after the others.

The warrior, however, was only wounded, and managed to reload his musket while lying on the ground. He fired at Tumlinson, killing his horse. Another Ranger grabbed the musket away and smashed the Comanche's head with it. The other Comanches managed to get into the brakes, where, according to Smithwick, "it was worse than useless to follow them."

A tragedy almost occurred when a Ranger prepared to fire on what appeared to be a bundled Indian fleeing on a mule. As he pulled the trigger, another Ranger knocked the barrel up, and the ball went over the rider's head. The mule was recovered and the rider proved to be the Hibbons boy, who had been bundled Indian-fashion and tied to the mule. When the Rangers attacked, the frightened mule had bolted, giving the impression of fleeing.

The dead Comanche's scalp was awarded to Smithwick, because the Rangers determined the wound from his shot would have been mortal. He wasn't necessarily pleased with the honor, but kept the scalp, "thinking it might afford the poor woman, whose family its owner had helped to murder, some satisfaction to see that gory evidence that one of the wretches had paid the penalty of his crime."[48]

Eventually, Tumlinson's company reached Brushy Creek and built the blockhouse. Their stay was uneventful. Two months later, they were recalled to the settlements to cover the rear of the army as it retreated eastward after the fall of the Alamo. Nevertheless, their fight on Walnut Creek was a turning point in Texas history, because it opened almost forty years of war with the Comanche nation.[49]

IT IS SOMETIMES said that the only battle that really matters is the last one. Such was the case of Texas. Despite losses at the Alamo, Goliad, and Refugio, the Texans won their independence on the bloody afternoon of April 21, 1836, when a ragtag army under Maj. Gen. Sam Houston overwhelmed Santa Anna's forces at San Jacinto. Although several Mexican armies were still undefeated and in the field, Santa Anna himself was a prisoner, and initially this did much to discourage the generals from any further campaigning. Santa Anna's influence was declining, however, and the detention of Texas peace commissioners in Matamoros on the Rio Grande raised suspicions that Mexico was planning another invasion. Gen. Thomas J. Rusk, who assumed command of the army after Houston was wounded at San Jacinto, ordered Capt. Isaac Burton's Ranger company to scout the area from the Guadalupe River to Refugio near the coastal bend.

On June 2, Burton learned that a suspicious vessel had put in at Copano Bay. Burton had his twenty-man force in position on the beach by dawn the next day. At 8 A.M., they signaled the ship to send a boat ashore. The ship's unsuspecting captain sent five men, who were taken prisoner on landing. Sixteen Rangers rowed out and captured the ship, which proved to be the *Watchman,* loaded with provisions for the Mexican army.

Burton wanted to send the ship up the coast to Velasco, but she was held in Copano Bay by contrary winds. During the wait, the *Camanche* [*sic*] and *Fanny Butler,* also loaded with freight consigned for the Mexicans, anchored off the bar. On Burton's orders, the captain of the *Watchman* decoyed their commanders, and their ships were captured as well. All three ships eventually were taken to Velasco, where they were condemned. Value of the prizes came to $25,000, a substantial amount to support the beleaguered Texas Army. Burton and his Rangers became known as the "Horse Marines."[50]

If one views the War of Independence purely in terms of the Mexican front, the Rangers might seem peripheral; the only ranging company involved in that campaign was the one from Gonzales, whose members died at the Alamo. The purpose of the Rangers, however, was not to fight Mexico but to defend the frontier. And while a serious Indian threat never really materialized, they remained ready to perform their duty, allowing the army to concentrate on Santa Anna.

PART 2
BIRTH OF A LEGEND

May 1836 was deceptively quiet. The immediate Mexican threat was over, and despite sporadic Indian raids in the vicinity of the Brazos settlements, the tribes were relatively peaceful. Yet, the sporadic raids were the early signs of a general uprising brought on in part by the Ranger attacks of the previous year. The death of Chief Canoma at the hands of Burleson's men had alienated the Caddos. The raid by the Brazos settlers against the Keechi village and Coleman and Moore's campaigns had brought sporadic retaliatory attacks in the vicinity. One Indian told settler Daniel Parker that about five hundred tribesmen had gathered on the Trinity River and were sporting two captive white women and several children, but the Parkers did not try to ascertain whether this was true.[1]

Daniel and his brother Silas Parker were among those who had been authorized by the Permanent Council to form Ranger companies to defend the frontier during the Mexican crisis. In private life, they and their other brothers headed a fortified settlement that had many characteristics of a religious commune; most of the settlers were either Parker kin or followers of a Predestinarian Baptist movement headed by Daniel. Originally from Virginia, the clan and its congregation had migrated to Texas from Illinois in the early 1830s. By the spring of 1834, they had chosen their land, staked their claims, completed their fort, and cleared and planted their fields. Surviving floods and Indian scares, they prospered, and in the fall of 1835 the War of Independence brought Silas and Daniel to prominence with the convention.[2]

Because the Rangers of this era were citizen volunteers, they used periods of relative peace to return home and tend their crops and handle other chores. With the frontier reasonably quiet and the immediate Mexican emergency over, May 1836 found Silas Parker back at the family seat of Parker's Fort near the headwaters of the Navasota River. The fort was not a military post but a fortified settlement of several families such as were built on the Indian frontier up through the 1860s. The modern reconstruction, erected on the original site based on archaeology and contemporary accounts, is a stockade of upright cedar logs enclosing a communal square and stock pens. The families lived in cabins built against the interior of the stockade. Between each cabin and the next was a rifle stage and loopholes for defense. Blockhouses were built over the northeast and southwest corners. The northeast blockhouse covered the main gate, and the southeast blockhouse overlooked the "spring gate," a waist-high portal that led to the springs where the families drew their water.

On May 19, 1836, most of the men were working in their fields some distance away, leaving only a handful of men in the fort with the women and children. The day was hot, and the main gate, which closed would have made the stockade virtually impregnable, was open to catch the breeze. About mid-morning, a large band of Indians appeared outside the gate, and before a defense could be prepared, they overran the fort. By the time the men arrived from the fields, the fort had been sacked. Five were dead, including Silas Parker; one was badly wounded, and five were taken captive.[3]

Eventually, every captive of the raid was ransomed except Silas's daughter, Cynthia Ann. For the next quarter of a century, whenever the Texas Rangers recovered a female white captive of the appropriate age, the question in everyone's mind was: Is this Cynthia Ann Parker?

NEWS OF THE attack on Parker's Fort created a sensation on the frontier. Many settlers in the outlying farms and ranches moved in closer to the settlements for protection. Indian depredations spread, and Bastrop County, about sixty miles northeast of San Antonio, suffered especially badly. Even as the financially battered Republic cut back on its army, it had to raise new Ranger units from those scattered after the War of Independence. On August 12, 1836, Acting Secretary of War F. A. Sawyer ordered Robert Coleman "to raise for the term of one year three companies of mounted men for the Special purpose of protecting frontier inhabitants. . . ." Many of these were Rangers from Tumlinson's company, called back into service because their previous enlistments had not expired. Among them was the twenty-eight-year-old Noah Smithwick, who appeared at a dance during this period "resplendent in a brand new buckskin suit, consisting of hunting shirt, pantaloons and moccasins, all elaborately fringed."[4]

Buckskin, which was common attire in those days, made good, durable clothing in dry weather. But when saturated in a heavy rain, the leather stretched and trouser legs might lengthen as much as a foot, then would shrink on drying. Wet buckskins also had a slimy, clammy feel that made their wearers uncomfortable. In an effort to clothe the Rangers, the Texas government made one of history's few attempts to provide them uniforms, buying them surplus from the United States. When they arrived, the uniforms were all too small. Smithwick recalled:

> Isaac Casner, who tipped the beam at 200 [pounds], got a suit that would have been a snug fit for a man of 140. . . . Wolfenberger, who would have measured six feet barefooted, got a suit of which the bottoms of the pantaloons struck him about half way to his knees, the jacket failing to connect with them by full six inches, and his arms protruding a foot beyond the end of the sleeves.[5]

The Rangers were promised $25 a month as well as 1,280 acres of public land for every year of service. Men were expected to provide their own horses and arms. Horses and equipment were major expenditures.

Austrian-born Ranger George Bernard Erath remembered more than one man who had to promise his land rights and pay in advance to procure a horse, bridle, and saddle. Noah Smithwick traded one of his 1,280-acre land certificates "for a horse which the Indians relieved me of in less than a week."[6]

The government theoretically furnished ammunition and rations, but in fact government support was largely limited to ammunition. According to Erath, the only rations were "some beef now and then." The rest of the time they fed themselves by hunting.[7] The food shortage was chronic in the early years. John C. Duval, a soldier in the War of Independence who became one of Texas's first men of letters, remembered encountering a company of Rangers who had been in service six months, subsisting solely on beef and game without any bread the entire time. Duval and his party shared their supply of moldy, worm-eaten hardtack, which the Rangers "devoured . . . with as keen a relish as if it had been the greatest delicacy."[8]

COLEMAN'S RANGERS BROKE up into two detachments. Coleman took the main body to build a fort at the junction of Walnut Creek and the Colorado about six miles below the present site of Austin, while Erath was detailed with two sergeants and twenty men to build a fort on the Leon River. Similar to Parker's Fort, these posts consisted of stockades enclosing some log cabins with blockhouses on opposite corners.[9]

Much of the duty appears to have been routine. Recalling the construction of his fort on the Leon River, Erath remarked:

> My memory for details on almost all subjects is good, but I am at a loss how to account for the amount of work done that winter [1836–37] by men who had to guard, hunt, cook, dress deerskin, and make clothes of it, particularly moccasins, and in all ways provide everything, and yet in six weeks time, by Christmas, I had up seven or eight houses with wooden chimneys, well covered, and with buffalo hide carpets down.[10]

There were some farms abandoned by settlers fleeing the Indian outbreak, and foraging parties managed to procure autumn corn growing untended in the fields. Erath issued the men one ear apiece per day for cornbread, and they ground it in a steel mill. Cooking utensils and other household wares were gathered from deserted cabins. "Our meat was wild game which was plentiful," he said. "Honey had to be kept in rawhide or deerskin sacks with the hair outside, and at Christmas we had several hundred pounds of it about the Fort." Coffee was scarce and brewed sparingly.[11]

Colemen's men had more trouble supplying themselves. The area surrounding his fort was more settled, perhaps because, as Smithwick commented, "the Indians were not depredating in our beat." Whereas Erath's foragers could supply themselves without complaint from abandoned farms, Coleman had to requisition food and supplies from the settlers, and his high-handed methods made him unpopular.

Matters came to a head when a Lieutenant Robel, a martinet who some said was a deserter from the U.S. Army, ordered a drunken Ranger tied to a post overnight. The man passed out, slumped away from the post, and was strangled to death by the cord around his neck. The death created a furor that frightened Robel into deserting the Rangers, leaving Coleman to bear the responsibility. Coleman was relieved of command and ordered to report to the War Department in the provisional capital at Columbia, where he drowned in a boating accident while awaiting investigation.[12]

Local and internal disputes aside, service at Coleman's Fort appears largely to have been tranquil, although occasionally the Indians provided some distraction. One evening in the spring of 1837, the men were relaxing on the parade ground, smoking, swapping stories, and dancing to Smithwick's fiddle, when a flame suddenly burst from a high knoll across the river, and shadows were seen dancing around it. "Our scouts had seen no sign of Indians," Smithwick wrote, "still, we knew no white men would so recklessly expose themselves in an Indian country, and at once decided they were Indians."

Lt. Nicholas Wren took fifteen mounted men across the river. By the time they assembled on the opposite side, the fire had gone out, and Wren, Smithwick, and Ranger Jo Weeks scouted in the direction from which it had been seen. Locating the vicinity, they returned for the others and moved ahead, and in the darkness blundered into the Indian pony herd. They calmed the nervous ponies, hoping the animals' pawing and snorting had not given them away, then moved into a cedar grove.

The Rangers were completely lost in the darkness until one Indian coughed in his sleep, revealing the location of the camp. The whites crept forward and saw the sleeping forms, but hesitated because they still could not identify them. Finally, one of the sleepers turned over, revealing them to be warriors. Suddenly, one jumped to his feet and appeared to be listening.

"Plug him, Weeks!" Ranger Tom McKarnan whispered. Weeks fired, and the Indian fell. The others stampeded into a dense thicket as the Rangers ran into the camp. One turned and fired, hitting Ranger Philip Martin in the mouth and killing him instantly. The others escaped, including Weeks's victim, who apparently was only wounded. The Rangers were left in possession of the camp, its equipment, and the pony herd. They returned with their prizes to the fort, where they buried Martin next to the man who had strangled on the post.[13]

Soon afterward, the Indians made a retaliatory raid on the pasture where the Rangers' horses were grazing, stampeding the herd and making off with many of the animals. The Rangers chased them for three days before finally giving up. Lieutenant Wren was suspended, unjustly in the minds of his men, and they successfully petitioned for his reinstatement. The Rangers continued to occupy Coleman's Fort, sporadically skirmishing with Indians, until the post was abandoned in November 1838. After that, the settlers organized scouting parties, patrolling the district in turns much like a twentieth-century neighborhood watch.[14]

ONE REASON FOR the vehement hatred whites held for Indians was the cruelty with which the Indians waged war. It is remarkable that the whites, with their own heritage of atrocity in the Thirty Years War and the religious upheavals of Europe, should have been so sensitive. Nevertheless, by the nineteenth century, battle was viewed as a set-piece, almost drill-field affair, and the Indian customs of mutilation, torture, rape, and wanton murder were seen as total depravity. Marauding Indians generally killed their victims outright or tortured them to death soon after capture. They rarely kept prisoners, because they did not have the means to confine them and very often did not even have the means to feed them. Those who were kept alive were spared because of the disposition of their individual captors or because they might be useful around camp. Boys and girls beyond the age of infancy were spared because they were useful—the boys to be groomed as warriors and the girls as wives. Infants, however, often were killed as liabilities.[15] Captive women and even young girls could expect to be gang-raped, although sometimes a warrior with prestige might claim a captive as exclusively his own. Girls placed under the supervision of Indian women might be subject to routine acts of sadism, such as burning with firebrands or hot irons, or laceration.

Nelson Lee, who occasionally served as a Texas Ranger, spent three years as a Comanche captive and described the fate of three Englishwomen brought into his camp. The women told Lee the men in their train had been massacred, the children separated and carried away, and crying babies killed by cutting a hole under their chins and hanging them "on the point of a broken limb." Already, the women had been repeatedly raped. Once in camp, Lee wrote:

> The mother, whose health had broken down under the hardships and sufferings she had endured, was made a common drudge in the camp, while the daughters were appropriated by two burly warriors, and compelled to serve them, both in the capacity of slaves and wives.[16]

Lee was the rare case of an adult male captive who managed to avoid a slow, excruciating death. Herman Lehmann, a German captured as a boy and reared as a warrior, recalled one joint Apache-Comanche raid near the headwaters of the Llano River. "We burned a house and killed a man, his wife and four or five children. We tortured them before we killed them," he commented matter-of-factly.[17]

THE EFFORT TO organize an effective frontier defense force was difficult because the government itself was barely organized. During the first months of the Republic, a provisional government functioned under the Permanent Council, with David G. Burnet as interim president and Lorenzo de Zavala as vice president. Then, on the first Monday in September 1836, Texans went to the polls, approving a constitution and electing Sam Houston to a two-year term as president, and Mirabeau B. Lamar, whom Houston detested, as vice president. The legislature consisted of a bicameral congress modeled on that of the United States. Voters also approved a resolution to seek annexation to the United States, which the American government, concerned about relations with Mexico as well as the admission of another slave state, politely ignored. As time passed and the American attitude remained tepid, the mood of many Texans changed to favor continued independence from any power.[18]

Houston and Lamar were inaugurated October 22 in Columbia, which served as capital until April 1, 1837, when the government was moved to the newly established city of Houston. One of the last official functions in Columbia was the state funeral of Stephen F. Austin, who died of pneumonia on December 27. The body lay in state for two days, then was carried aboard the steamer *Yellowstone* for the trip down the Brazos to the Austin family seat at Peach Point for burial.[19]

AMONG THE MYRIAD problems facing the new republic was frontier defense. On December 10, 1836, the Texas Congress passed a bill giving official sanction and establishing pay for all Rangers who had been in service since July of the previous year, as well as those who might enter the service in the future. Captains were to receive $75 a month; first lieutenants, $60; second lieutenants, $50; orderly sergeants, $40; and riflemen (i.e., privates), $25. Besides pay, Rangers and their officers were entitled to bonuses in the form of "bounties of land."[20]

Legislation aside, information on the Rangers for the remainder of the 1830s is at best sketchy, in part because of the confused conditions in the Republic in general and on the frontier in particular, and in part because so many records of the era have been lost. Although a national Ranger Corps existed in theory, the government often was not able to continually maintain it. When the terms of service specified in Ranger legislation expired, companies were mustered out and the cost-conscious Texas Congress did not always attempt to replace them or organize new Ranger companies until some crisis on the frontier required it. Often it appears to have been more expedient for the government to give official sanction and assume financial responsibility for locally organized companies. The activities of some of these local Ranger companies are recorded in official reports, diaries, letters, and newspaper accounts. Others are known only through muster rolls and pay sheets on file in the State Library and Archive in Austin. Nevertheless, such records as do remain indicate the Rangers were active throughout the decade.

WHETHER ORGANIZED BY the general government or by their own communities, Rangers revised their attitudes and tactics to fit changes in the nature and scope of Indian fighting. Houston obtained a permanent treaty with the Lipans and the Tonkawas, securing their aid as scouts against the Comanches and other Plains tribes. Although they had occasionally conflicted with the early settlers, the two tribes had been more of a nuisance than a threat. Overall, they remained friendly, and their goodwill increased in direct proportion to the growing hostility between the whites and the Plains tribes.[21] Describing the Lipans of the 1830s and 1840s, Ranger Robert Hall said:

> They were great friends to the Texans, and were a great help to us. They were always after the wild [Plains] Indians, and when-

ever they caught them they killed them. They were brave warriors in battle.[22]

The Tonkawas especially were interested in assisting the whites; gen-
erations earlier, the Comanches had driven them from their ancient
homeland along the fringes of the Hill Country west of Austin, and now
they looked to even the score. For the next forty years, until the end of
the Indian Wars in Texas, the Tonkawas remained steadfast allies.[23]

Although the whites were grateful for the support from these Indians,
they found some Lipan and Tonkawa customs unsettling, particularly the
practice of eating the corpses of slain enemies. Hall was invited to a cannibal feast after one Lipan skirmish with the Comanches. "They offered
me a choice slice of Comanche," he remarked, "but I politely informed
them that I had just eaten a rattlesnake and was too full to eat any
more."[24]

It was all the more horrifying when the whites themselves, by necessity of war, became unwilling contributors to the feast. Noah Smithwick
recalled one incident when a band of Tonkawas joined settlers chasing
Comanche horse thieves. Spotting the Comanche rear guard, three of the
Tonkawas galloped ahead and killed a warrior. With the body as a trophy,
they rode to one of the neighboring farms.

> Having fleeced off the flesh of the dead Comanche, they bor-
> rowed a big wash kettle . . . into which they put the Comanche
> meat, together with a lot of corn and potatoes—the most revolt-
> ing mess my eyes ever rested on. When the stew was sufficiently
> cooked and cooled to allow of its being ladled out with the hands
> the whole tribe gathered round, dipping it up with their hands and
> eating it as greedily as hogs. Having gorged themselves on this
> delectable feast they lay down and slept till night, when the en-
> tertainment was concluded with the scalp dance.[25]

HOUSTON'S TERM EXPIRED in the fall of 1838, and he was constitutionally
prohibited from succeeding himself. Subsequent presidents, though still
bound to the nonsuccession clause, would serve three years. Even before
the election, it was obvious Vice President Lamar would become the next
head of state. He had widespread support in the Texas Senate and with
the public, and Houston's anti-Lamar faction was unable to find a viable

candidate.[26] Modern historians often view Lamar as the buffoon of the Republic. He was, however, no worse suited for the presidency than Sam Houston, and in many ways he was well qualified to lead Texas into the 1840s. Lamar was shrewd, and his selection of cabinet ministers not only pleased the various political factions but assembled a broad array of education and talent. More cultured than the average frontiersman, Lamar became the father of public education in Texas, and his policies toward Indians, Mexico, and the United States reflected the public attitude.[27]

Affronted by the indifferent American attitude toward Texas, Lamar hoped to negotiate a peace with Mexico and obtain recognition of its independence. War, he believed, not only placed an excessive economic burden on both countries, but also threatened to disrupt a potentially profitable trade along the border. Because Santa Anna was back in power, however, peace was highly unlikely. If the differences could not be resolved, Lamar felt, Texas should aid revolutionary groups in Mexico.

Mexican relations took a disturbing twist when Burleson's Rangers killed a Mexican agent and recovered papers showing an apparent agreement with the east Texas Cherokees whereby the Mexican government would aid them in an uprising against Texas. Although there was little evidence that the Cherokees did more than simply listen to the Mexican proposals, the incident led to the eventual expulsion of the east Texas Cherokees. On the western frontier, meanwhile, the government was preparing to deal with the Plains Indian tribes.[28]

AS HORSEMEN AND guerrilla fighters, the Texans and Indians were about evenly matched, and Indian fights often were inconclusive. Plains warriors themselves rarely attacked unless they had overwhelming numerical superiority, and would scatter when attacked. The rationale was simple: consisting of small, nomadic bands, they could not sustain heavy losses. When a warrior died, he could not be replaced until a youth had reached fighting age; but they were vaguely aware that the loss of even a large group of whites would not materially affect the white ability to make war.[29]

The disadvantage was that Indians were always in position to fight, whereas economics often tempted the Texas Congress to delay funding for replacement Ranger companies until the next series of raids forced the issue. Even then, the Rangers might prove inadequate for the job at hand. Such was the case in 1839, when Indian depredations on the upper Brazos, Colorado, and Trinity rivers prompted the Texas Congress to pass a series of laws to activate several companies of volunteer Rangers for three months' service. Each company was to consist of three officers in charge of fifty-six sergeants and privates.[30]

One of the companies was mustered into service on April 21 under Capt. John Bird and marched from Fort Bend, just south of Houston, to Fort Milam, about twenty miles southeast of the present site of Waco. The detail was ill-starred from the beginning. Provisions soon gave out and the men had to hunt game. Some became so insubordinate that Bird decided to court-martial them. As there were not enough officers for a board, he formed a detail to take the prisoners south to Bastrop, and decided to accompany them.

On the afternoon of May 26, the party of thirty-five men reached a point near the present city of Temple, where they saw a small band of Indians. After checking his men's weapons, Bird ordered them to give chase. The Indians fled into a thicket, the whites in close pursuit. In an open prairie on the other side, they found themselves confronted by about three hundred Kickapoos, Caddos, and Comanches. The Rangers had been led into a trap by a decoy party, and the main party quickly surrounded them.

One of the men spotted a ravine a short distance away. Bird ordered his men to dismount, and, using their horses for cover, they moved to the ravine. "My heart rose to my throat," one of the Rangers remembered, "and I felt like I could outrun a race-horse and I thought all the rest felt just as I did."[31]

The Indians charged around the ravine several times, and each time Rangers fell, either killed outright or mortally wounded. But Indian losses also were mounting, and about sunset they "raised a hideous yell" and broke off the fight. Five Texans, including Bird and all the officers, were dead or mortally wounded.[32] Even so, the Houston *Telegraph* called the fight a victory that

> will undoubtedly be of immense benefit to the citizens of the frontier settlements in that section, as these hordes of savages have infested that region for many months, and have hitherto held complete possession of the country. They will now be compelled to retire further northward, and leave those settlers in the undisputed possession of their improvements.

There was no mention of casualties.[33]

The *Telegraph* was overly optimistic. Far from discouraging the Indians, the beating they had inflicted on the Rangers only made them bolder, and they stepped up their depredations.[34]

WHILE THE GOVERNMENT worried about Indians on the one hand, it had to deal with Mexico on the other. One of the great disputes was the exact border of Texas. In the Treaty of Velasco, which ended the War of Independence, Santa Anna recognized the Rio Grande as the boundary. Such it always had been, at least in the southwest where Coahuila was concerned. But from its earliest organization as a Spanish province, the southernmost boundary of Texas was the Nueces River, running westward from Corpus Christi Bay, some 150 miles north of the Rio Grande. The area between the Nueces and the Rio Grande was part of the Spanish province of Nuevo Santander, which, after independence from Spain, became the Mexican state of Tamaulipas.

As far as Mexico was concerned, however, any boundary discussion was a moot point, because immediately after the War of Independence the Mexican Congress had repudiated the Treaty of Velasco and temporarily deposed and exiled Santa Anna. Officially, at least, Texas continued to be a state in rebellion, although few in the Mexican government realistically believed it would be recovered. Both sides therefore settled into an armed truce, with the mostly uninhabited area between Nueces and the Rio Grande more or less a no-man's-land except for Laredo, which remained under Mexican jurisdiction.

Realities notwithstanding, in December 1836, the First Congress of the Republic of Texas had passed the Boundary Act, attempting to establish a permanent border. The Sabine and Red rivers were fixed as the demarcation between Texas and the United States, with the entire Rio Grande as the southern and western border. This encompassed the so-called Nueces Strip to the south, along with fully half of the Spanish-Mexican province of New Mexico, where the centuries-old towns of Santa Fe and Taos still considered themselves under Mexican jurisdiction.

There was an odd rationale behind Texas's extravagant claim. Expansionism aside, Lamar realized occupation of the western Rio Grande would give Texas control of the lucrative Santa Fe trade. The country would become the middleman between the United States and Cuba on the one hand and the interior of Mexico on the other. New Orleans merchants, who stood to gain substantially from their end of the trade, encouraged Texas to establish jurisdiction. Many believed the people of Santa Fe would welcome it; even the Mexican governor, Manuel Armijo, doubted their loyalty to Mexico.[35]

In June 1841, an ill-conceived expedition was organized at Brushy Creek outside of Austin, which, almost two years earlier, had been established specifically as the permanent seat of government. Composed largely of traders and adventurers, the expedition nevertheless had official sanction, carrying a proclamation from Lamar "To the Inhabitants of Santa Fe and other portions of New Mexico, to the East of the Rio Grande," whom he addressed as "Fellow Citizens."[36]

The thirteen-hundred-mile trail between Austin and Santa Fe crossed a region virtually uninhabited except by nomadic Indian tribes, and the Texans knew little of the country. By the time they reached New Mexico, they were starving, short on water, and ready to surrender. Governor Armijo, who had known about the expedition even before it left Austin, burned Lamar's proclamation in the plaza of Las Vegas, New Mexico. Brutally marched to prison in the Mexican interior, the survivors were repatriated during the spring of 1842, giving the Texans another grievance against Mexico, and historians another grievance against Lamar.[37]

DESPITE FORMAL HOSTILITIES between Texas and Mexico, trade between the two countries continued, encouraged by Lamar because import duties were virtually the only source of revenue for the Republic. The southern part of Texas around Victoria particularly depended on the Mexican trade, and when bandits began attacking trading expeditions, a group of Victoria citizens petitioned the president for protection.

They pointed out that two "Americans of Credibility" gave depositions that four weeks earlier, in February 1840, a gang of bandits (or "cow-boys" as they were known) had attacked a company of Mexican traders near San Patricio on the north side of the Nueces, severely wounding one of them.[38] These cow-boys had hardly gone when "another company of Americans" overhauled them and took their horses. Although the matter was being investigated by the courts, the Victoria citizens doubted any action would be taken, because the bandits "are able at all times to exculpate themselves by means of pliant witnesses."

"We could mention to your Excellency a number of these outrages which had been committed in defiance of Law and common decency and their motto being *'Dead men tell no tales'* it is probable many [raids] are never known but to the perpetrators thereof," the Victoria men told Lamar.

As a result, they said, trade with Mexico had come to an almost complete standstill, not only hurting the local economy but robbing the Republic of import duties on the Mexican goods.[39]

In response, the Texas War Department authorized formation of local ranger-type militia companies in Victoria. These, however, proved little better than the bandits themselves, because they took their commissions to mean a license to operate against Mexicans on the pretense that they were enemies of the Republic. Not only did it further disrupt trade, it alienated the Mexicans of the borderlands who otherwise wanted friendly commerce with Texas. One ad hoc company even went so far as to confiscate horses from the Corpus Christi trading firm of Aubrey & Kinney on the grounds that they were "Mexican property" (Henry Lawrence Kinney was suspected of being a Mexican sympathizer).[40]

On August 18, 1841, Corpus Christi settler S. L. Jones wrote Lamar, detailing the problems caused by the local companies and suggesting "that a force should be stationed somewhere in this Vicinity under the command of a disinterested and responsible officer such a Gentleman as Capt Hayes [*sic*] or any other equally respectable."[41]

Little appears to have been done, and the depredations continued. One of the most notorious bandits, who one day would earn an equally odious reputation as a Ranger, was Mabry B. Gray, better known as Mustang Gray, described by one contemporary as "a cold-blooded assassin."[42] In 1842, Gray belonged to a band of cow-boys who accepted the hospitality of a small group of Mexican traders camped outside Goliad. After joining the Mexicans for supper, Gray calmly announced the Texans intended to kill them. The victims were roped together, given a few minutes to pray, and then gunned down. The Mexican train was plundered and the bodies of the victims were stripped. One Mexican survived and, badly wounded, managed to reach Victoria. No one was ever brought to trial for the crime, no doubt because of the "pliant witnesses" cited by the Victoria men in their original petition.[43]

The "Capt Hayes" mentioned in Jones's letter was John Coffee "Jack" Hays, who, more than any other leader, came to symbolize the Rangers of the Republic.

Chapter 4

A Great Captain and a New Weapon

Jack Hays was only one of several outstanding Ranger captains during the Republic, but he is the most famous because he was the type of frontiersman who inspires legends. Barely an adult when he rose to command, he nevertheless won the admiration of Sam Houston himself, who observed, "The frontier of our country would have been defenceless but for his gallantry and vigilance united With fine capacity."[1] Indeed, he was so widely known by reputation that people were surprised when they saw him for the first time. Pioneer John W. Lockhart, who met Hays in a hotel lobby in Washington-on-the-Brazos, said:

> I thought that my eyes had deceived me. Could that *Small, Boyish Looking Youngster,* not a particle of beard on his face, homely palefaced young man, be the veritable Jack Hays, the celebrated Indian fighter, the man whose name was sung with praise by all Texians? It could not be, I thought, but I soon found out that it was the veritable "Captain Jack."[2]

John Coffee Hays had the right credentials to achieve greatness in Texas. Like Sam Houston, he was a Tennessean, born on his family's plantation near Nashville on January 28, 1817. His father, Harmon

Hays, was related to Andrew Jackson's wife, Rachel, and named his son for longtime family friend and Jackson protégé Col. John Coffee. The area's social life centered around the Hermitage, which the Jacksons had built on land purchased from Harmon Hays. Here Jack and his brothers met the great men of the frontier and nation, including the up-and-coming Houston, who numbered Harmon among his friends.

Harmon Hays died when Jack was fifteen years old, and he was placed with a well-meaning uncle who urged him to try for West Point. Not liking the prospect of military regimentation, he left his uncle's home and worked his way westward over the next four years. He arrived in Texas shortly after the Battle of San Jacinto and, finding the new republic's rough-and-tumble army suited him better than the spit and polish of the American military, promptly enlisted as a scout and surveyor. After a stint in the army, he joined a Ranger company commanded by Henry Karnes, distinguishing himself in fights against Indians and Mexicans and developing a reputation for cool, daring leadership.[3]

Besides being an outstanding leader, Hays more than any other individual is responsible for arming the Rangers with another great Texas legend—the Colt's revolver.

HAYS ACHIEVED HIS reputation as a leader in the 1840s, a decade unusually rife with bloodshed, for the Texans were beset by both Comanches and Mexicans. Despite several peace treaties, Comanche raids had stepped up during the second half of the 1830s, and the number of captive women and children had grown.[4]

Hostilities opened with a seemingly innocuous event. On January 9, 1840, three Comanches brought a Mexican captive to San Antonio, saying they had been delegated to negotiate a peace. Their message was passed on to Secretary of War Albert Sidney Johnston (later a noted Confederate general), who instructed Lt. Col. William S. Fisher of the First Infantry to meet with the Indians in San Antonio. If the Comanches brought their white captives, it would be considered a pledge of good faith, and they could depart unmolested after the treaty conference. If, however, they did not bring the captives, the chiefs would be detained as hostages.[5]

The Comanches returned on March 19. The party consisted of sixty-five men, women, and children, but only one captive, fifteen-year-old Matilda Lockhart, who had been taken two years earlier. She obviously had been tortured during much of her captivity; her nose was almost completely burned off, her hair had been singed to the scalp, and she was covered with fresh bruises and sores.[6]

Twelve of the main chiefs were escorted into the "Council House," as the old Spanish government house was sometimes known, while the other Indians passed the time in the courtyard. A quick conversation with Matilda Lockhart determined the other white prisoners were held at the main Comanche camp and would be brought in one or two at a time in hopes of large and continuous ransom payments.

Assembling his troops around the building, Colonel Fisher told the chiefs they would remain as hostages while the Comanche women, children, and warriors returned to their camp for the captives. Troops were brought into the room, and the chiefs drew knives and strung their bows. Fisher told the soldiers to fire if the Indians did not surrender calmly. At that moment, one chief stabbed a sentry and was shot. The others attacked the troops, who opened fire. Within moments all twelve chiefs were dead.

Hearing the commotion, the warriors and soldiers outside began fighting. Some Comanches headed toward the nearby San Antonio River, while others barricaded themselves into outbuildings around the Council House. When the shooting stopped, thirty chiefs and warriors, three women, and two children were dead, and twenty-seven women and children and two old men were prisoners. Among the Texans, seven soldiers and bystanders were killed and eight wounded.[7]

During the weeks following the Council House Fight, an uneasy truce prevailed while the two sides negotiated and exchanged prisoners. The death of the twelve chiefs left the Comanches temporarily demoralized, and it took them time to recover. By early summer, however, they had retreated into the hills west of Austin and San Antonio and begun planning a revenge raid. They were encouraged by Gen. Valentín Canalizo, the Mexican commandant in Matamoros, near the mouth of the Rio Grande. As word of the Mexican involvement filtered north into Texas, Dr. Branch Archer, who succeeded Johnston as secretary of war, called up volunteer units against a potential raid. But when the weeks passed and nothing happened, the volunteers were mustered out and allowed to return home.[8]

THE GREAT COMANCHE Raid of August 1840 took the Texans completely by surprise. Mexican agents in Texas had kept in touch with the Indians and apparently convinced them to delay until the volunteers disbanded. On August 4, a war party consisting of about six hundred Comanches and

Kiowas moved out of the hills and descended onto a relatively uninhabited area of the coastal plains. By the afternoon of August 6, they were spotted on the outskirts of Victoria, where the citizens prepared a defense. Avoiding the town itself, the Indians spent that day and the next in the immediate vicinity, stealing horses, burning and killing, and taking some women and children prisoner.

From Victoria, the raiders rode on to the small coastal settlement of Linnville. They struck that town on the morning of August 8, taking the citizens completely by surprise. Most fled in boats to the steamer *Mustang,* anchored in the bay. Those who didn't make it were captured or killed. The refugees on the steamer spent the rest of the day watching as the Indians burned and plundered the town. When they finally retreated, they carried several hundred horses and mules loaded with plunder taken from warehouses at the port.[9]

Even before the sack of Linnville, the Texans were gathering their forces. Early reports of Indian movement had prompted two ad hoc Ranger units, under Capts. Adam Zumwalt and Ben McCulloch, to head out in pursuit. The two units came together on the morning of August 7. By noon they were joined by the old Indian-fighting Ranger John Tumlinson with sixty-five men from Victoria and Cuero, who, unaware of the raiding around Victoria, were returning from a scouting expedition.[10]

As word of the attack on the towns spread, more soldiers, Rangers, and militia assembled, and Maj. Gen. Felix Huston assumed command. Guided by Tonkawa scouts under their veteran Chief Placido, the Texans moved inland and on August 12 intercepted the returning Comanches at Plum Creek, about twenty-seven miles southeast of Austin. Huston sent Ranger Robert Hall ahead with five men to reconnoiter. The Indians were strung out along the prairie, and to Hall the column "looked to be seven miles long." Skirting the column to the Comanche rear, the Texans could see warriors decked out in the plunder of Linnville.

> Many of them put on cloth coats and buttoned them behind. Most of them had on stolen shoes and hats. They spread the calico over their horses, and tied hundreds of yards of ribbon in their horses' manes and to their tails.

By the condition of their fighting equipment and tribal regalia, Hall surmised they had been preparing for the raid for a long time.[11]

At that moment, an officer and a private inexplicably blundered into the Indian line and were surrounded. The officer managed to break free and escape, but the private was killed in sight of the Rangers. Hall told his men to keep back a safe distance and fire whenever they had a target. The men obeyed, and they skirmished for about two miles until they got back to the main body of Texans, and the battle opened in earnest.

The cautious General Huston ordered the Texans to dismount, form into line, and open fire, but the bullets glanced off the tough rawhide of the Comanche shields. Seeing this, veteran fighters waited until the Indians wheeled about on their ponies, then shot them as they turned. As their losses mounted, the Comanches began pulling back out of range. Pressed by Ben McCulloch and Edward Burleson, Huston ordered a charge.

The sudden Texas assault startled the Comanches, but some fought back. A load of buckshot hit Ranger Nelson Lee near his elbow. He dropped his reins and his uncontrolled horse carried him straight into the Indians. Other members of his company rode after him and rescued him.

Hall took a bullet in his thigh. "It made a terrible wound and the blood ran until it sloshed out of my boots." He fell off his horse, but managed to stagger to his feet just as an Indian rode up. Hall raised his rifle, but the Indian threw up his hands and shouted, "Tonkaway!"—identifying himself as one of old Placido's scouts.

The Comanches were routed, and the Texans chased them until their horses gave out. In the confusion, the Comanches left behind their plunder and captives. Some of the captives were recovered alive, but several had been killed when the Comanches realized they were defeated. One woman was seriously wounded but saved from death because her steel corset had deflected her captor's arrow. A considerable amount of Mexican equipment was found, indicating the Comanches had been supplied from that quarter.[12]

Two months later, on October 14, an ad hoc Ranger company under Capt. John Moore with Lipan scouts attacked a large Comanche camp on the upper Colorado River. The Indians were completely routed, bringing public demand for more campaigns. These were the last major expeditions for the time being, however. The Republic was completely penniless.[13]

JACK HAYS WAS in the Battle of Plum Creek, although not a key participant; the day really belonged to veteran Rangers Ben McCulloch and Ed Burleson. Nevertheless, Hays had already earned a solid reputation with a military expedition against Laredo under Col. Eurastus "Deaf" Smith in 1837, returned on two separate occasions in 1839 with Ranger expeditions of his own, and was in several Indian fights with Henry Karnes's Rangers.[14] His prestige was such that when the Texas Congress reorganized the frontier defense forces in January 1841, the twenty-three-year-old Hays was appointed to command one of three new Ranger companies. Records of these units are sketchy, but apparently Hays and the other two captains, John Price and Antonio Pérez, were responsible for enlisting the men.[15]

Nelson Lee, who had recovered sufficiently from his buckshot wound to join Hays's company, recalled:

> He was a slim, slight, smooth-faced boy . . . and looking younger than he was in fact. In his manners he was unassuming in the extreme, a stripling of few words, whose quiet demeanor stretched quite to the verge of modesty. Nevertheless, it was this youngster whom the tall, huge-framed brawny-armed campaigners hailed unanimously as their chief and leader when they assembled together in their uncouth garb in the grand plaza of Bexar [San Antonio] . . . for young as he was, he had already exhibited abundant evidence that, though a lamb in peace, he was a lion in war. . . .[16]

Hays's calculated aggressiveness inspired frontiersmen to say an enemy fled "as if Jack Hays, himself, were after them."[17]

Yet to say he was a daring youth amid grizzled pioneers does injustice to his men. The frontier drew people from all walks of life, and Hays's Rangers were no exception. One of the company, Benjamin Highsmith, remembered many of them as "men of education and refinement. Around the campfire at night it was not uncommon to hear men quoting from the most popular poets and authors, and talking learnedly on ancient and modern history."[18]

In addition to Highsmith, who had carried messages out of the Alamo for Travis, Hays's Rangers at various times included such men as Samuel Walker, who, while not an intellectual, would help design the first purely military Colt's revolver; Ben McCulloch; P. H. Bell, a future governor of Texas; and Creed Taylor, around whom would one day center the most vicious blood feud in Texas history. As Rangers, however, they were young men looking for excitement.[19]

"Discipline is almost wholly lacking," a visiting German naturalist observed, "but this lack is made up for by the unconditional devotion to the leader, who by example leads all in the privations and hardships they usually endure. No one is punished. The coward or incompetent must face the disgrace of dismissal. A uniform is not prescribed and everyone dresses to suit his taste and needs."[20]

Creed Taylor remembered that before one fight, "[w]e dismounted and tightened up our saddle girths belts and etc, and while doing this I was struck with the spirit of dare-devil levity that seemed to have siezed every man."[21]

When the new company organized, Hays's salary was set at $75 a month, later raised to $150. The men were listed at $30 a month, although at first no one was paid because the Republic was in the process of stabilizing its badly inflated currency. It was not a terribly critical problem, however, because the militia acts that governed the Rangers initially allowed only fifteen men. They furnished their own arms, horses, and equipment. The government supplied ammunition and, officially at least, provisions. In reality, the Rangers in the field were cut off from supply and so lived by hunting or on provisions seized from Mexican trains. As a long arm, most carried single-shot muzzle-loading Jaeger rifles across the pommels of their saddles. Hays and a handful of others carried Col. Samuel Colt's revolver.[22]

COLT WAS NOT the first to invent a multishot revolving firearm, and he undoubtedly was inspired after seeing British attempts. Nevertheless, the Colt handgun, patented on February 25, 1836, was the first practical revolver, and by the end of that year, Colt was producing revolving pistols and rifles in his newly established factory in Paterson, New Jersey.[23] The handguns included a pocket model in .28 caliber, and two .31-caliber belt models. The No. 5 (actually the fourth model produced) was a holster pistol in .36 caliber. Colt's Patent No. 5 had a total production of a thousand, many of which went to Texas, and for that reason it is known as the Texas Paterson.[24]

By almost any later standard, the Texas Paterson was a crude, clumsy weapon. It was a cap-and-ball arm, with the five chambers in the cylinder charged from the front, the powder and ball being loaded separately. Each chamber had a nipple in the rear for a percussion cap that, when struck by the hammer, flashed directly into the chamber and ignited the powder charge. Once the chambers were loaded, they were sealed with grease, so that the powder blast from one would not ignite the others and cause the cylinder to explode in the hand of the user. The trigger normally folded into the frame and popped out when the gun was cocked; there was no trigger guard. The single-action mechanism required the hammer to be pulled back manually in order to turn the cylinder and cock the gun.

Yet for all its faults, the Texas Paterson was revolutionary. It fired five times before it was empty, compared to other contemporary handguns that had to be reloaded after each shot. And it was wonderfully uncomplicated, with only three basic components—frame, cylinder, and barrel. When it was empty, one simply removed the barrel, charged the chambers in the cylinder simultaneously from a five-spout powder flask, inserted the bullets, sealed the chambers, capped each nipple, replaced the barrel, and resumed firing. Paterson boxed sets often included an extra cylinder, doubling the amount of firepower before reloading. For its time, it was a brutally efficient weapon, and on the frontier, it could be used with devastating effect. J. W. Wilbarger, who was familiar with the arm, later wrote, "With these improved fire arms in their hands, then unknown to the Indians and Mexicans . . . one ranger was a fair match for five or six Mexicans or Indians."[25]

Oddly enough, the advantages of the Colt's Patent Revolver were not immediately evident in Texas. The War of Independence had left the country penniless and enormously in debt. Given Houston's peace policy and his aversion to a standing army, such weapons as remained after the war were deemed sufficient for the Republic's needs. But President Lamar's decision to take the offensive against the Indians and maintain a state of preparedness against Mexico required new arms purchases from abroad.[26]

In the spring of 1839, Lamar received a visit from an old friend, John Fuller, owner of a successful Washington, D.C., hotel. Before embarking on his trip, Fuller had obtained several samples of the company's products, including the No. 5 pistol.[27] Upon arriving in Texas, Fuller demonstrated the arms to Col. George W. Hockley of Texas's Bureau of Ordnance. A conservative officer who preferred the old-fashioned single-shot flintlock pistols and muskets, Hockley was unimpressed.[28] The expanding Texas Navy, however, was delighted with the Colt's revolver, and on April 29, 1839, Navy captain Edward Moore, on a procuring mission to the United States, was instructed to negotiate purchase of 180 of these handguns for use by naval boarding and landing parties. According to Moore, "The Colt's pistols used by the Texas Rangers before annexation were all supplied from the Navy, after they had been in constant use by that arm of the service for upwards of four years. . . ."[29]

Thus Colt's Texas Paterson revolver, ancestor of the gun that became synonymous with the American West, originally went west as navy surplus!

Jack Hays apparently obtained his first Colt's revolver in 1839, not long after it appeared in Texas. He may have purchased it through David K. Torrey, a prominent Waco trader, who wrote him from New York about Colt's "beautiful pattern of belt pistol." At the time, Colt's revolvers were almost unknown outside government circles, scarce, and very expensive for private citizens on the frontier, so several years would pass before they became commonplace among either citizens or Rangers.[30]

WITH OR WITHOUT Colt's revolvers, the Rangers still had to contend with Indians. The Comanches had begun to recover from the shock of Plum Creek and were moving back down toward the settlements. By the summer of 1841, they once again were raiding ranches and driving off cattle in the vicinity of San Antonio. On June 24, Hays led an expedition that struck a trail that led northwest to Uvalde Canyon. The command consisted of Hays's own company, now made up of sixteen Texans, and a company of twenty *tejano* Rangers under a captain identified as "Flores" but who probably was Antonio Pérez.

About two miles from the entrance to the canyon, they encountered a raiding party of ten Indians bound for San Antonio. The Rangers charged, pushing the Indians into a thicket. The Comanches gave ground grudgingly, forcing the Rangers to fight the distance. The thicket was too dense for a charge, so Hays had it surrounded while he and two others slipped in. Fighting broke out, and a fourth Ranger joined. Eight of the Indians were killed, and a wounded warrior and woman were captured. A Ranger named Miller was slightly wounded.

Hays reckoned that the main Comanche camp was within striking range, but when he followed the trail he realized it was farther than he had thought. His horses were becoming jaded, so he returned to San Antonio.[31]

Still determined to find the main camp, Hays took a company of fifty Rangers and ten Lipan scouts under the war chief Flacco and headed back toward Uvalde Canyon. The Comanches, meanwhile, had retreated westward, deep into the Hill Country, "where the white men had never before made a track."

As the Rangers and Lipans neared the camp, they ran into a Comanche hunting party, which turned about and rushed back to alert the others. Taking twenty-five of his best riders on fast horses, Hays chased them eight miles, catching the main band as the women were packing to flee. About a hundred warriors rode out to block the Rangers and lead them away from the camp, and a running fight ensued for about ninety minutes. Hays's exhausted horses finally forced him to abandon the chase. Several Rangers were wounded. Hays could not determine Indian losses, because they recovered their dead and wounded.

The search for the Comanche camp had taken the Rangers so far west of the line of settlement that they were completely out of provisions. On their return trip, they slaughtered and ate their worn-out horses. Nevertheless, the expedition had carried the Texans into an area the Comanches had previously believed secure, and they abandoned their depredations around San Antonio.[32]

Part of Hays's success in these early expeditions was attributable to his skill as a tracker who could find an enemy trail that was almost invisible. John W. Lockhart observed:

> In the dry and rocky portions of West Texas a squad of fifteen or twenty Indians could go through the country without leaving much sign, consequently a trailer was considered a very effective man. This faculty Captain Hays had to a very marked degree, it almost amounted to instinct with him; he could ride along at a good pace and see the signs where other men could see nothing, hence his great tact in overhauling and finishing Indians. It is said that often he would dismount and observe the small pebbles, and by noticing the slightest displacement made by the horses, could, in a moment, tell in what direction they had gone.[33]

In the field, Hays would halt his men a couple of hours before sunset, preferably near fresh water. Some were sent to hunt game for supper, while others tended the horses and built fires. After dark, when they had finished eating, they mounted up and rode until they found a secluded spot for camp. The object was to get far away from their cooking fire, whose telltale curl of smoke could be seen for miles. Two hours before dawn, they were in the saddle again. "Thus we passed day after day, and night after night, scouring in all directions the wide plains of Texas," Nelson Lee wrote.[34]

GIVEN THE HISTORICAL record of Hays's daring and audacity, it is not surprising that he inspired legend as well. The most famous story concerns a single-handed stand against a band of Comanches atop Enchanted Rock near Fredericksburg, some seventy miles west of Austin. The story first appeared in Samuel C. Reid's *The Scouting Expeditions of McCulloch's Texas Rangers,* published in Philadelphia in 1847. It was among the Hays exploits that Reid picked up around Ranger camps during the Mexican War.

According to Reid, the incident occurred about 1841 or 1842, when Hays and his men were attacked by Indians near the base of the "hill." Separated from his men, Hays retreated "to the top of the hill. Reaching the 'Enchanted Rock,' he there intrenched himself, and determined to sell his life dearly, for he had scarcely a gleam of hope left to escape."

For almost an hour, he held them off by bluff, the mere act of raising his rifle enough to keep the Indians under cover. Finally, they grew bolder, and started to rush his position. Hays discharged his rifle, "and then seizing his five-shooter, he felled them on all sides." After three more hours, his men finally made their way through the horde of warriors and rescued their leader.[35]

> "This," said the Texian, who told us the story, "was one of *'Jack's'* most narrow escapes, and he considers it one of the *tightest little places* that he ever was in. The Indians who had believed for a long time that he bore a charmed life, were then more than ever convinced of the fact."[36]

Reid himself obviously never saw Enchanted Rock, because he described it as "forming the apex of a high, round hill, very rugged and difficult of ascent. In the center there is a hollow, in the shape of a bowel, and sufficiently large to allow a small party of men to lie in it, thus forming a small fort, the projecting and elevated sides serving as a protection."[37] In fact, Enchanted Rock is the hill itself, a giant granite dome, formed by a volcanic upheaval about a billion years ago, and one of the oldest geological features of North America. Eons of rain and wear have pitted the top with shallow depressions ranging from a few inches to hundreds of feet across, but scarcely deep enough to protect a man against attackers. But the slopes of the rock are broken by rifts and caves that could shelter a man in a fight. Thus, like many legends, the Enchanted Rock Fight probably was based on an actual event that was embroidered in Ranger camps over the passage of time. Whatever the case, it illustrates the nerve and imagination that made Hays the great captain of the 1840s.

WHILE HAYS AND his men dealt with Indians, the government struggled to keep afloat. Lamar's term expired, and on December 13, 1841, Sam Houston resumed the presidency with the finances in shambles. Nine days later, Dr. Anson Jones, the brilliant, Machiavellian secretary of state, bluntly told the cabinet, "The country is *absolutely* without present means of any kind: her resources are large, though *prospective,* but her credit is utterly prostrate." The government's entire annual revenue, he continued, would not be sufficient to pay even the interest on the national debt.

To reduce the pressure on the administration, Jones proposed a virtual shutdown of the country's military, and a corresponding overhaul of priorities.

> Our policy, as regards Mexico, should be to act strictly on the *defensive.* So soon as she finds we are willing to let her alone, *she will let us alone.*
>
> The navy should be put in ordinary; and no troops kept in commission, except a few Rangers on the frontiers.
>
> The Indians should be conciliated by every means in our power. It is much cheaper and more humane to *purchase* their friendship than to *fight* them. A small sum will be sufficient for the former; the latter would require millions.
>
> By a steady, uniform, firm, undeviating adherence to this policy for two or three years, Texas may and will recover from her present utter prostration. It is the stern law of necessity which requires it, and she must yield to it, or perish!

Jones concluded with a direct attack against the national preoccupation with adventure, stating bluntly that Texas "cannot afford to raise another crop of 'Heroes.' "[38]

Houston proposed drastic cuts in the national budget. The navy, cruising the Bay of Campeche to support insurgents in Yucatán, was to be brought home and laid up. New peace emissaries would be sent to the Indians. Government departments would be consolidated, and many positions established under Lamar would be eliminated. Inflated paper money would be recalled, and replaced with a strictly controlled currency.[39]

The president believed if the Texas Congress adopted his recommendations he might "yet save the country." Nevertheless he was uneasy about troubles on the Indian frontier, and the Mexican attitude plainly worried him. The Santa Fe Expedition had infuriated Mexico, as did the Texas Navy's presence in the Bay of Campeche. More than anything else, however, the Mexicans were enraged because some of the "cowboy" gangs of the Nueces Strip had joined an ill-fated effort by rebel leader Antonio Canales to establish an independent republic of Mexican states along the Rio Grande. Despite Jones's wait-and-see position, on December 29 Houston wrote his wife, "Our chance . . . for invasion by Mexico is greater than it has been since 1836."[40]

HOUSTON'S FEARS WERE realized. In March 1842, the Mexican general Rafael Vásquez invaded Texas and occupied San Antonio. The city was largely deserted, because Rangers had shadowed the invading force and the citizens were more or less prepared for evacuation. After two days of plundering, Vásquez freed three of Hays's Rangers whom he had captured and started back for Mexico.[41]

Throughout the spring and summer, fear mounted over the prospect that Vásquez's incursion was only a prelude. By August, the Texans in San Antonio were unable to obtain ammunition locally, because it had all been sold to Mexicans. Ranger William A. A. Wallace, called "Big Foot" because his feet were outsized even for his six-foot-two-inch, 240-pound frame, told Hays he had seen "at least a dozen strange Mexicans in town . . . who did not live there." Because Wallace knew virtually every *tejano,* this was ominous.[42]

Hays sent Wallace and another Ranger to Austin to obtain ammunition. Upon arriving, they found the capital in an uproar over an Indian raid and were pressed into service to hunt down the marauders. When they finally headed back to San Antonio, they encountered a couple of Hays's men, who told them the city was occupied by a large Mexican expeditionary force under Gen. Adrian Woll.[43]

Woll's invasion caught San Antonio completely off-guard. Hays and most of the Rangers were on a scouting expedition, and those who had remained in town barely escaped the Mexican cavalry. The Mexicans found the district court in session, and judge and attorneys were among the prisoners marched in chains back to Mexico. Besides the immediate blow to the legal system in San Antonio, the threat of a repeated invasion canceled courts in at least four other western counties over the next several months. Austin was only sixty miles to the north, and Houston, who despised Lamar's artificial capital almost as much as he despised Lamar himself, used the invasion as an excuse to relocate the government to Washington-on-the-Brazos. It remained there for over two years until returning permanently to Austin.[44]

Woll held San Antonio until September 20, when he started back toward Mexico. In November a force of 750 Rangers and militia under Gen. Alexander Somervell marched toward Laredo on a retaliatory raid. They occupied the town on December 8, then continued down the Rio Grande, and on December 19, the force was ordered to return to Gonzales. A retaliatory blow—however minor—had been struck in Laredo, and as Jones had warned, Texas could not afford more heroes.

Hays and many of the other ranking Rangers joined Somervell in obeying the order. But some three hundred men, including prominent Rangers Big Foot Wallace and Samuel Walker, refused. Organizing themselves into a separate command under Col. William Fisher, they started toward Mier, southwest of the Rio Grande, about ten miles from the present city of Roma, Texas. The ensuing debacle, known to history as the Mier Expedition, was an act of sheer mutiny not involving Rangers in any sort of legitimate capacity. However, the roster included former and future Rangers, and the fate of the expedition had a far-reaching impact on Texan-Mexican relations. For those reasons, some discussion is in order.

The three hundred Texans seized Mier, but soon found themselves surrounded and vastly outnumbered by Mexican regular troops. After a desperate battle on the town square, the survivors surrendered and were marched south into the Mexican interior. At Hacienda Salado, south of Saltillo, they overpowered their guards and escaped. Some died in the wastes of northern Mexico, and others simply disappeared. A scant handful, including Ranger Nelson Lee, managed to reach Texas and safety. The remainder, unfamiliar with the country, were rounded up and returned to Salado, where Santa Anna ordered them decimated by firing squad. There being 176 prisoners, a jar was filled with 159 white beans and seventeen black beans. A white bean meant life; a black one death.[45]

The drawing was in alphabetical order, and when it reached *W,* Big Foot Wallace found only a few beans left on the bottom of the jar. His hand, which was as outsized as his feet, barely fit in the neck, and he had to feel around for a bean with two fingers. It was white. When he gave it to the Mexican officer supervising the drawing, the latter grasped his hand and called the other officers to come look at its size. Wallace would remember the man because of that incident.[46]

The men who had drawn the black beans were shot immediately after the lottery, and an eighteenth man, Capt. Ewen Cameron, was later shot near Mexico City on special orders of Santa Anna because Cameron had led the initial break at Hacienda Salado. The remainder, including Wallace and Sam Walker, joined Woll's prisoners from San Antonio in the grim fortress of Perote on the road between Mexico City and Veracruz.

WHILE THE SAN Antonio and Mier prisoners sat in Perote, waiting repatriation and nursing their hatred toward Mexico and all things Mexican, life at home returned to normal. Texans are a resilient people, and Houston, eager to reestablish some semblance of peace, confined his efforts against Mexico to diplomacy. As early as September 14, 1842, with Woll in San Antonio, the president had written Jack Hays:

> The situation of our frontier is very unhappy in its influence upon the prosperity of individuals, as well as upon the general interests, settlement and growth of our country. To remedy existing evils is a matter of primary importance to our situation. You are so situated [in San Antonio] that you can determine what course will be proper and safe to pursue. I have thought that advantage might result to us if trade were opened to San Antonio and to such other points as would be safe. In 1838 we had friendly relations and commerce with Mexico, so far as the frontiers were concerned, and had it not been for the cow boys and Canales and his gang, we would never have had any further troubles. . . .[47]

Hays himself appears to have been willing enough to comply. He realized that his Rangers were primarily scouts and mounted riflemen, more adept at fighting Indians and keeping an eye on Mexican movements than provoking an open conflict with Mexico. Most of his efforts continued around his Indian expeditions.

Between these expeditions the Rangers passed their time amusing themselves with the social and sporting life of San Antonio. Their profession was dangerous, and about half of all Rangers were killed every year. The life expectancy of the average Ranger upon joining the service was two years, and they intended to make the most of their leisure time. Cockfighting was a major event in San Antonio on Sundays. After church everyone, including the priest, joined in the sport. Most nights, the *tejanos* held dances and the Rangers attended. Hays himself "was sometimes seen whirling around with some fair señorita."[48]

Economics still plagued Texas, and eventually the Ranger companies authorized under the 1841 defense acts were disbanded. Houston, however, was certain the Texas Congress would authorize a new peacekeeping force, and when Hays called on him in January 1844, the president suggested he arm his men from the Texas Navy's supply of Colt's revolvers. From his own experience, Hays knew the value of the weapon. After getting an order from the secretary of war, he went to the naval depot at Galveston, where he drew the revolvers, extra cylinders and bullet molds, and other accessories. The Colt's revolver's time had come.[49]

AS ANTICIPATED, THE Texas Congress approved a new defense act, designating Hays by name to command a Ranger company of forty privates and one lieutenant. They were to be enlisted for four months, although this could be extended by presidential order in an emergency.[50] And, thanks to Houston's foresight, they were armed with revolvers. As a frontier weapon, the Colt's had its baptism of fire on June 8, 1844, after reports arrived in San Antonio of Indian depredations along the Guadalupe River northwest of the city. Hays, who was now a major, took fifteen of his new Rangers, including Sam Walker, who had returned to Texas following his release from Perote. They hunted for the Indians as far as the Pedernales River west of Austin and, finding nothing, were returning home when they discovered the Comanches had crossed their trail and were following them.

A small group of warriors taunted the Rangers, retreating when the Texans started toward them. Surmising this was a decoy party trying to lead him into a trap, Hays ordered his men to take cover in a stand of timber. As the Rangers neared the woods, however, the main band of Comanches emerged from the trees. Hays estimated "some sixty-five or seventy warriors . . . led by two especially brave and daring chiefs."

The Rangers charged, and after a vicious hand-to-hand fight, the Indians slowly began falling back. One of the chiefs, however, started exhorting the warriors, raising himself up in his saddle and gesturing to hit the Rangers one more time.

"Any man who has a load, kill that chief," Hays ordered.

"I'll do it," Richard Addison (Ad) Gillespie answered, and, taking careful aim with his long rifle, he shot the chief out of his saddle.

The Indians charged a second time. The Rangers used their revolvers, "two cylinders and both loaded," one survivor recalled.

"The repeating pistols, the 'five shooters' made great havoc among [the Indians]," Indian Superintendent Thomas Western reported to Houston, "some 30 or more were the killed and wounded, finally they fell back carrying off their dead and wounded and encamped in sight, where they remained, the belligerent camps in sight of each other. . . ."[51]

Sam Walker was badly wounded—at first the Rangers feared mortally—and Gillespie was severely injured. Hays was afraid to move them, so he sent one of his men into San Antonio for help. The Indians were too badly battered to travel far, and the two camps glared at each other across the prairie until Ben McCulloch arrived with twelve more men. The Indians departed, and the Rangers remained in place until Walker and Gillespie were well enough to be moved.[52]

Walker recovered from his wounds and drew a sketch of the fight showing a small band of pistol-packing Rangers chasing a horde of Indians. He sent the sketch to Sam Colt, who had artist W. L. Ormsby engrave it on the cylinders of the heavy .44-caliber six-shooters introduced in 1847. Ormsby's imaginative interpretation erroneously depicts the Rangers as uniformed soldiers, but this does not detract from the cold, functional beauty of the weapon.[53]

Chapter 5

Bound for the Rio Grande

As frontier defenders of an independent nation, Hays, Walker, and other Rangers were fighting for a lost cause. But in 1844, most Texans never would have admitted their days as a sovereign people were drawing to a close. In that year's presidential election, when annexation to the United States was a key issue, they supported Dr. Anson Jones, an opponent of annexation, over frontiersman Ed Burleson, who advocated it.

Jones probably was the most capable of Texas's three constitutional presidents. Despite his election stand, his service as Houston's secretary of state made him cold-bloodedly realistic. He knew that if the Republic could not stabilize its finances and conclude a formal peace with Mexico, its position in the international community would be increasingly precarious.

During his second term, Sam Houston had bowed to public sentiment by strengthening commercial relations with Great Britain and France. This, combined with the dispute between the United States and Great Britain over possession of Oregon, awakened American fears of European encirclement. American emotions also were stirred by the treatment of the Santa Fe and Mier prisoners. Thus, even as Texas was electing an anti-annexation president in Jones, the United States elected a pro-annexation president, James K. Polk.

Whether Jones actually believed his own campaign rhetoric or simply was playing the United States against the European powers to secure the best bargaining position remains debatable. Whatever his own thoughts, when the United States finally offered favorable annexation terms, Jones started the machinery in motion for a convention and public referendum on the issue.[1]

In June 1845, as the question was being decided, the United States ordered Bvt. Brig. Gen. Zachary Taylor to assemble two thousand troops at Fort Jessup, Louisiana. The Texas government had demanded a strong American military presence for protection in case the country opted for annexation. American expansionism had alarmed Mexico, and the Mexican government was now prepared to formally recognize the independence of Texas as a buffer state against the United States. But Mexico was equally clear that annexation could lead to armed conflict.[2]

THE CONVENTION ASSEMBLED July 4 in Austin and opted to join the United States. Now the American troops were needed along the disputed area between the Nueces and Rio Grande to block any move Mexico might make during Texas's last months as a sovereign nation. The first of Taylor's troops embarked for Corpus Christi Bay on July 22.[3]

On August 6, the U.S. adjutant general, Roger Jones, ordered Taylor to contact the Texas government about raising local troops. Because the United States had no provision for paying Texans (they were still foreign citizens), they would be called into service only in the event of a Mexican invasion. In that case, however, Jones was certain the U.S. Congress would authorize pay.[4]

Taylor also got a letter from Jack Hays, offering to form "a Volunteer Company of Mounted Men" in San Antonio. The general was already aware of Hays's "reputation as a partisan," and on September 12, Taylor's adjutant and son-in-law, Capt. W. W. Bliss, wrote to advise him the company would be mustered into service in conformity with U.S. Militia regulations. Hays would serve as major, and the company would function as Rangers.

> This company will be particularly charged with the duty of procuring intelligence of the movements of the Mexicans and protecting the Frontier against Indian Depredations, and the General desires me to say that he places great confidence in your

known activity and experience in Frontier service. [Taylor's] own instructions from the U.S. War Department enjoin him not to disturb any Mexican Establishment on this side [of] the Rio Grande unless it be rendered necessary by an attack or demonstration . . . and he therefore wishes it particularly understood that you are not to push your scouts into the Mexican settlements or commit any overt act calculated to provoke hostilities.[5]

Taylor and Bliss saw no problem with these instructions. They were professionals, prepared to carry out the military policy of their government without any personal animosity toward the Mexican people. But in Texas and Mexico, it was an entirely different matter. As U. S. Grant, then a young second lieutenant in the United States Army, noticed upon arrival at Corpus Christi, "The hostilities between Texans and Mexicans was so great that neither was safe in the neighborhood of the other. . . ."[6]

A. J. Sowell, whose cousin was shot after drawing a black bean at Hacienda Salado, remarked that many Rangers "had old scores to settle with the Mexicans. Only three years before, some in the regiment had drawn [beans] for their lives and worked on the streets in chains, footsore and nearly starved." They were not interested in policy. They wanted revenge.[7]

No doubt Taylor was aware of the Texan attitude. While he needed the intelligence Hays might provide on Mexican movements, he seems to have been primarily interested in using the Rangers to cover the Indian frontier. They would serve a three-month enlistment, and if the war scare with Mexico subsided, could be mustered out by the end of the year. The first company was mustered into service in Victoria and Goliad counties in late September, under command of Capt. John T. Price. A few days later, on September 28, Ad Gillespie mustered a company in San Antonio. That, however, was as far as it went. The Indians were relatively quiet, and the Rangers hung around San Antonio, Victoria, and Goliad, while Taylor assembled and drilled his troops at Corpus Christi.[8]

If the Americans were complacent, the Texans were certain of war and used the idle time to prepare. Ranger Robert Hall, who joined a company mustered by Capt. Ben McCulloch, spent $25 for "the finest bowie knife I ever saw." He knew that Mexican *rancheros,* the irregular equivalents of Mustang Gray's "cow-boys," fought with lariats, roping an enemy around the neck, jerking him off his horse, and dragging and choking him to death.[9]

ON FEBRUARY 24, Taylor started marching overland toward the Rio Grande. Texas was now an integral part of the United States, and the new governor, J. Pinckney Henderson, had been notified to expect quotas of troops for federal service. Taylor himself was to enforce the Texas–U.S. claim of the Rio Grande as the boundary. On March 21, the troops reached the Arroyo Colorado, a northern channel of the river, driving off a small contingent of Mexicans that threatened them from the south bank.[10] The following day, Taylor took the bulk of his forces to Point Isabel (now Port Isabel) to seize the port facilities as a depot and erect an earthen defense work. Once that was done, he moved to the main channel of the Rio Grande, opposite Matamoros, about twenty miles above the mouth of the river, where work began on a second set of earthen fortifications.[11]

In San Antonio, meanwhile, Ranger enlistments had expired. Tired of the inactivity, Sam Walker took a large contingent south to join Taylor in hopes of finding some excitement. The timing was right. Although Taylor considered Texans an undisciplined rabble, he was in a bad spot. He was ignorant of the country, and one patrol that clashed with the Mexicans was unable even to relocate the scene of their fight, much less recover the body of an officer who had been killed in the skirmish. Taylor's quartermaster, Col. Truman Cross, had wandered away from camp and was captured and killed by *rancheros,* indicating a need for American irregulars who could function as scouts and counterguerrilla fighters. The situation was all the more acute because a shift in Mexican forces threatened his supply line.[12]

"There is no doubt the enemy are crossing the river, and that all communication with Point Isabel is extremely hazardous," one officer noted.[13]

About this time, Walker arrived in Point Isabel with seventy-seven men ready to serve as Rangers. The commanding officer, Maj. John Monroe, ordered him to gather intelligence and establish communications with General Taylor. They were formally mustered into federal service for a three-month enlistment on April 21. Three days later, a company of dragoons under Capt. Seth Thornton clashed with a large contingent of Mexican regulars in territory claimed by the United States. Sixteen were killed and the rest taken back to Matamoros as prisoners. Taylor considered this an act of war and called on Governor Henderson to send four regiments of troops—two mounted and two infantry—to augment Walker's Rangers.[14]

Samuel Hamilton Walker was the classic mercenary who, in another era, might have been a Swiss Guard or a Foreign Legionnaire. Sometimes called "Mad Walker" because of his reckless bravado, he enjoyed fighting and appeared to have a natural gift for logistics and command. A native of Maryland, he had served in the U.S. Army in the Seminole Wars and had written a monograph on the command system. As the fighting in Florida drew to a close, he left the army and went to Texas in hopes of finding further use for his talents on the frontier. His arrival in 1842 coincided with Woll's Raid on San Antonio, and he joined Somervell's expedition. He was among the Mier prisoners, drew a white bean, and was incarcerated in Perote. Upon being repatriated in 1843, he joined Jack Hays's company, and he had been a Ranger ever since.[15]

J. H. Kuykendall, who met the thirty-two-year-old Walker shortly after the latter's arrival in Texas, recalled:

> There was nothing in the personal appearance of Capt. Walker that denoted the hero. His intellect was mediocre and not much cultivated, but he was modest, moral, high-minded, and the "bravest of the brave."[16]

Despite such accolades, and his casual attitude and appearance, he had a well-earned reputation as a man who took few prisoners.[17]

ON APRIL 28, *rancheros* attacked Walker's camp on the plain between Point Isabel and Matamoros. Walker himself was scouting with his most experienced men, leaving the camp in the hands of recruits, who apparently grew careless. Of the fifteen Rangers in the fight, five were killed and five listed as missing. One of the missing men reportedly was lariated to death, a fate that unsettled the Americans, who had never seen the method.[18]

This attack, together with reports of a large force of Mexican regulars crossing the river below Matamoros, convinced Monroe that his depot was threatened. Late on the night of April 29, Walker and six Rangers slipped out of Point Isabel and started toward Taylor's camp on the Rio Grande. They were within eight miles of the river when they encountered Mexican troops stretched across the prairie in front. There was a quick conference to discuss the best means of going around them when, in the words of Nelson Lee, Walker "coolly announced he was going *through* them."

The Rangers started their horses toward the Mexican line at a walk. Because their attire was very similar to that of the *rancheros,* the Mexicans apparently mistook them and made no challenge. Then, at fifty yards, Walker ordered a charge. "Instantly the spurs were buried deep in the sides of our good horses, which bounded forward like the wind, and greeting them with a terrific yell, we dashed right through," Lee wrote. The Mexicans were so startled that the Rangers were a good 150 yards beyond before anyone had the presence of mind to shoot at them. The Texans rushed up toward Taylor's fortified camp, waving a white handkerchief to the American dragoons coming out to meet them.[19]

Concerned for his depot, Taylor took the bulk of his troops back to the coast. The nearly completed fort on the Rio Grande was left under command of Maj. Jacob Brown. The threat against Point Isabel proved to be a false alarm, but on May 3, the American troops camped by the bay heard cannon fire from the direction of the Rio Grande. After one unsuccessful attempt to communicate by courier and cavalry escort, Taylor sent Walker and his men. The Rangers slipped into the fort a little before 3 A.M., May 4, found it under bombardment from artillery emplacements in Matamoros, and returned to Point Isabel with a report from Brown. After strengthening his defenses at the depot, Taylor ordered his army back toward the river and prepared for battle.[20]

There is no record that Rangers were actively involved in the American victories at Palo Alto on May 8 or Resaca de la Palma the following day. The former was an artillery duel fought at long range, and the latter largely depended on infantry. The siege of the fort was lifted, the defeated Mexican army withdrew, and Taylor occupied Matamoros. The fort itself was designated Fort Brown, in honor of its commander, who was killed during the bombardment.

WHILE THE COUNTRY celebrated its victories, Taylor tackled the problem of conducting a war. He desperately needed troops. Price's Rangers had arrived from Victoria and Goliad, but so far his was the only state contingent besides Walker's.[21] Nevertheless, volunteers were coming, though not always with enthusiasm. James K. Holland, a member of a Ranger company recruited in Harrison County in east Texas, remembered the departure for the war zone on May 24.

> We left Elysian Field on this day about 11 o'clock—for the Rio Grande—women in tears, God bless them—their tears would make a recreant brave—we all felt gloomy of course for such a separation I look upon as worse if possible than death—for when

death comes upon us the grief subsides and now we are parting from our friends perchance never to meet again—which leaves them in miserable suspence as to our future fate but such is the call—let us respond like men—like Texians.[22]

Throughout July, Texans banded together to organize the First Texas Mounted Rifles as part of the state's quota for federal service. When the enlistments expired for Walker's and Price's Ranger companies, they were reenlisted into the new regiment. Jack Hays was named colonel and Sam Walker lieutenant colonel. Seven of the ten company captains were Rangers, and the regiment incorporated so many former Rangers that it remained essentially a Ranger unit.[23]

Weapons carried by these Ranger/soldiers appeared to be a mixture of personal property and arms and equipment drawn from U.S. ordnance officers when they reported for duty. In Walker's case, it included Colt's revolvers, because by now his belief in them was absolute. When mustered into federal service, he drew as many revolvers as he could get his hands on—thirty-two in all—for issue to his men.[24] Besides the Colt's revolver, an idea of Ranger weaponry can be formed by an inventory of federal arms and accessories provided by Walker's company in Matamoros on July 22, 1846:

9	Colts revolving carbines
3	Contract brown full stock rifles
6	Halls Carbines
9	Carbine or Rifle Cartridge boxes
3	do. do. waist belts
7	do. do. do. plates
4	Colts Bullet Moulds
3	do. Pistol Flasks
3	Colts wrenches & screwdrivers
2	Rifle Wipers
4	Capper Flask's
5	Rifle Pouches[25]

ONE OF THE most prominent units in the First Texas was a company commanded by Ben McCulloch and known as McCulloch's Rangers. Like so many Texans of his era, McCulloch was a Tennessean, born in Rutherford County, November 11, 1811. That part of the state was still a wilderness, and the McCulloch children received the rudiments of formal education augmented by good frontier sense. The family supplemented its farm diet by hunting, and the boys learned to be self-reliant. Frontiersman and congressman Davy Crockett was a neighbor, and Ben was a close friend of his sons, particularly William Crockett, who was about the same age.

In 1833, Ben McCulloch and his brothers began rafting logs down the Mississippi to New Orleans, as well as flatboating cargo. In 1835, McCulloch returned from one of his rafting ventures to find Crockett on the verge of losing his Congressional seat, and Old Davy mentioned the possibility of going to Texas. Crockett left for Texas in October of that year, and Ben and his brother Henry soon followed. They arrived as the War of Independence broke out.

McCulloch served with distinction in the war, and after the battle of San Jacinto received a field promotion to lieutenant of the artillery. After a brief stint in the army, he traveled back to Tennessee, but returned to Texas and served a term in Congress before joining the Rangers, where he distinguished himself against Comanches at Plum Creek and other fights. In the summer of 1846, he was thirty-four years old, six feet tall with light hair, but his fair skin and features were rough from long exposure to the Texas sun. One of his most striking traits was his clear blue eyes, which stand out even in the primitive photographs of the period.[26]

Samuel Reid, who resigned his appointment as adjutant of a Louisiana Volunteer regiment in hopes of finding more excitement with the Rangers, recorded his first impressions when he joined McCulloch's company in Matamoros on July 1, 1846.

> Here was a scene worthy of the pencil. Men in groups with long beards and moustaches, dressed in every variety of garment, with one exception, the slouched hat, the unmistakable uniform of a Texas Ranger, and a belt of pistols around their waists, were occupied drying their blankets, cleaning and fixing their guns, and some employed cooking at different fires, while others were grooming their horses. A rougher looking set we never saw. They were without tents, and a miserable shed afforded them the only shelter. . . . Notwithstanding their ferocious and outlaw look, there were among them doctors and lawyers, and many a college graduate.[27]

There was a casual informality about the group. As McCulloch introduced Reid around the camp, one Ranger arrived with two ducks he had killed on a hunt. Walking up to the company commander, he said, "Ben, if you hav'nt [*sic*] had dinner, you'd better mess with me, for I know none of the rest have fresh grub to-day."[28]

AS THE ARMY settled in for occupation, complaints against it began to mount. Volunteer troops from throughout the Union were arriving and, not subject to the same discipline as regulars, doubtless took their cue from the Texans. Commenting to his fiancée, Julia Dent, Lt. U. S. Grant wrote:

> Since we have been in Matamoras [*sic*] a great many murders have been committed, and what is strange there seems to be but very weak means made use of to prevent frequent repetitions. Some of the volunteers and about all the Texans seem to think it perfectly right to impose upon the people of a conquered City to any extent, and even to murder them where the act can be covered by the dark. And how much they seem to enjoy acts of violence too![29]

General Taylor shared that opinion. The Texans picked fights not only with the local population but also with U.S. regulars, and they had the annoying habit of shooting randomly at signboards and other attractive targets in the middle of town.[30] "On the day of battle, I am glad to have Texas soldiers with me, for they are brave and gallant," Taylor commented to one officer, "but I never want to see them before or afterwards, for they are too hard to control."[31] Many times during this war, the Texans would justify both aspects of the general's comment.

A MOVE TO Reynosa, almost seventy miles upriver from Matamoros, did little to calm the Texans. Ironically, the move had been requested by the *alcalde* of Reynosa, who was prepared to surrender the city in return for American protection against Mexican stragglers and *rancheros* left behind during the retreat to Monterrey. As a pledge of good faith, he delivered one of Price's Rangers who had been captured six months earlier. In response, Taylor sent four companies of infantry, a section of artillery, and Rangers to occupy the city and prepare a defense.[32] The Rangers, however, included former Mier prisoners with harsh memories of this city, where they had been stoned and spat upon as they were marched through town. They also regarded Reynosa as the headquarters of many of the gangs that raided into Texas. Most believed some sort of retribution was in order, and Sam Reid noted wryly:

> Our orders were most strict not to molest any unarmed Mexican, and if some of the most notorious of these villains were found shot, or hung up in the chaparral, during our visit to Reynoso [*sic*], the government was charitably found to suppose, that during some fit of remorse and desperation, tortured by conscience for the many evil deed they had committed, they had recklessly laid *violent hands upon their own lives!* "Quien sabe?" [Who knows?][33]

Very probably the Rangers knew how these men had been hanged or shot. Given the strong hold of the Roman Catholic Church at that time, along with the vehement Mexican nationalism that justifies all things, remorse and suicide were highly unlikely.

Even in lighthearted moments, the Texans lived up to their reputation for unruliness. Lt. Rankin Dilworth of the First U.S. Infantry noted in his diary that the Rangers were quartered in an abandoned cotton gin near one of the American camps. "At dark," he wrote, "hearing a great noise, I looked out in that direction and saw them all on top of [the gin] dancing a war dance to the infinite amusement of the natives who were collected below."[34]

When the Mexicans observed St. John's Day with displays of horsemanship, the Rangers mounted up to show what they could do. A race ensued, but according to one American officer, the Mexican ponies "stood no chance with Texas horses." Finally the Texans wheeled their heavy horses around and charged the Mexicans, slamming into their light ponies, knocking them down, and scattering them. Far from aggravating the existing ill-feeling, the stunt won a grudging admiration from the Mexicans, who were serious in matters of horsemanship.[35]

A week or so later, however, McCulloch's Rangers celebrated the Fourth of July with a barbecue, killing and eating every Mexican pig and chicken in the vicinity and washing it down with purloined whisky. They justified the slaughter of the local livestock by claiming that the animals wandered into the line of fire as they were discharging their guns to celebrate the holiday, and to keep the meat from going to waste it was cooked. Nobody seemed to care how this would affect the impoverished Mexican farmers, whose lifetime of hard work went onto the Texans' cooking fires.[36]

JAMES HOLLAND, THE Ranger from Harrison County in east Texas, was still downriver at Fort Brown, where his company had arrived on June 25, after a grueling march. These Rangers—assigned to a companion regiment, the Second Texas—were supposed to be in Point Isabel, but had taken the wrong road below the Arroyo Colorado and found themselves closer to Matamoros. Their commissary, meanwhile, had taken the right road and was in Point Isabel, so the east Texans set up camp miserable and hungry in a pouring rain. The following day, they continued on toward the Rio Grande, passing Palo Alto, where Holland noted "Mexican bodies lying here and there the victims of our arms." Some U.S. troops invited them to breakfast, and they finally rendezvoused with their commissary. The rain kept up all day and all night, so they slept outside Fort Brown in water and mud, albeit with full stomachs.[37]

The sun came out on the morning of June 26, and the Rangers occupied themselves doing their laundry and cleaning up. So far, the war had been only an abstract in Holland's mind. Now, however, they were in a strange and hostile environment. Many of the men were desperately ill from unknown tropical fevers, and there was a Mexican city in plain view just across the river. Reality sank in. "Never thot of dying before," he remarked in his diary, "scared to death." Later he added, "I wish the Mexicans would behave themselves and let us alone."[38]

That last statement seems incredibly naive, but unlike the Rangers from San Antonio and the frontier, these men had enlisted for purely patriotic reasons. Isolated in east Texas, they had minimal—if any—contact with Mexicans, and they felt little animosity toward Mexico. Holland expressed their view in his diary:

> All is dull and gloomy—becoming tired of a stationary life—
> want to be moving—if there is no fighting to be done—as there
> seems to be—we are all willing to go home.[39]

On July 2, after six weeks in the field, the Harrison County men were finally mustered into federal service as part of Col. George T. Wood's Regiment of Texas Rangers, the six-month term retroactive to the date of their arrival on the Rio Grande. In contrast to the rowdy Fourth of July celebration by McCulloch's Rangers, the east Texans listened to a reading of the Declaration of Independence and patriotic speeches.[40]

EVEN THE MEN who had spent much of their adult lives fighting Mexicans could occasionally put aside old grudges and join the Mexicans for a good time. For not only were the Texans and Mexicans locked in a war against each other, both had to struggle to survive against the Indians, and against the man-killing climate and terrain of the borderlands. The Mexicans, having lived there longer, had far more experience, and the Texans had acquired many of their survival skills. In the process, they had become much more Mexicanized than either side cared to admit. Many Rangers spoke Spanish, had the same likes and dislikes as the Mexicans, and enjoyed the same types of amusement and entertainment. Sometimes circumstances brought the two groups together.

One night Lt. John McMullen, who commanded McCulloch's company in Reynosa while the latter was in Matamoros on business, was told the *ranchero* leader Antonio Canales was attending a dance at a ranch six miles from Reynosa. Canales, who previously had joined with the Nueces "cow-boys" in a secession attempt, now was colonel of a Mexican militia regiment in Camargo. He coordinated the activities of the *rancheros* in the area and was believed to be responsible for the death of Colonel Cross, the murdered quartermaster. McMullen formed up the Rangers and started toward the ranch. About a mile away, they spotted lights coming from the ranch. As they crept up, they came on a scene that Sam Reid describes as "unique and beautiful."

> The dance was held in the open air; and the bright fires kindled at different points, the candles and torches moving to and fro, the animated groups of revellers clustered on every side, the white robes of the girls prettily contrasting in the fire-light with the dusky apparel of their partners; while gay forms, replete with life and motion, founded in the lively dance, or floated in the graceful waltz, in sweet accord with the spirit-stirring strains of music which the night-breeze wafted to our ears.[41]

"Halt!" McMullen commanded. "Dismount! Creep up cautiously, men, and surround the house—and when I call you, come up quickly and firmly at the charge."

With that, he loosened his pistols and strolled into the middle of the dance. Before the startled Mexicans could recover, they were surrounded by Texas riflemen. Women screamed, and the men tried to break through the line but were forced back at gunpoint. A quick search of the ranch house failed to turn up Canales, and the Rangers concluded they had been misinformed.

One drunken old man shouted, "We are poor honest people—what have we to fear from our enemies?" and the crowd began to calm down. Equally eager to avoid a confrontation, McMullen apologized for the intrusion and explained it by saying the Rangers had been out on patrol and had stopped by to investigate the gathering. The Mexicans then invited the Rangers to join the dance, and two or three of the best dancers in the company chose partners from among the girls. It was the first time in months they had been able to dance, and they intended to make the most of it. "We had seen some pretty *tall* dancing in our time, but we think the feats we witnessed that night, were a little ahead of anything in that line we ever saw before," Reid said.

Finally, McMullen intervened.

"Come, boys," he ordered, "this is enough fun for one night. Mount and return to quarters."

There was a last round of drinks and the Rangers rode back to their camp. Their only disappointment was that they had not found Canales.[42]

ABOVE REYNOSA, THE flat coastal plain gives way to rolling hills and semi-desert where, on a clear day, the northernmost spur of the Sierra Madre Oriental can be seen in the distance from the Texas side. This is one of two great mountain ranges that divide Mexico into thirds along a north-south line, the other being the Sierra Madre Occidental. Between these two ranges, a central valley leads hundreds of miles into the wealthy, populous Mexican interior. The city of Monterrey is on a plateau in the Sierra Oriental, guarding the pass into the valley. If he had any hope of advancing beyond the Rio Grande, General Taylor would have to take Monterrey, and the city was heavily fortified.[43]

Taylor determined to make his base at Camargo on the San Juan River, about a mile from its confluence with the Rio Grande and about fifty miles upriver from Reynosa. Already, Rangers had reconnoitered within eighty miles of Monterrey and determined that the most feasible route for the army was through Camargo rather than directly from Matamoros.

Water was scarce on the Camargo road, but it was closer than Matamoros by more than a hundred miles and could be readily supplied by steamer.[44]

While Taylor was consolidating his forces, he found himself confronted by an enemy that would become all too familiar to American soldiers over the next three decades—Comanches. As early as mid-June, rumors had reached Reynosa that some five hundred Indians were raiding on the Texas side of the Rio Grande, "robbing cornfields and taking some of the inhabitants," according to one officer.[45] On July 22, a runner reached the Ranger camp in Camargo with news that a large war party under the chief Buffalo Hump "had been scouring the country above us, on both sides of the Rio Grande, stealing horses, burning ranchos, murdering the Mexican *hombres,* and carrying off [into captivity] the most beautiful of the Mexican *Señoritas.*"

Already, they had raided Gillespie's Ranger camp about three miles away, on the Texas side of the Rio Grande, and made off with some of the horses.[46]

Gen. William J. Worth, commanding officer in Camargo, told McCulloch to take thirty men and hunt down the Indians. Knowing very little about Comanches at that time, the Americans apparently assumed reasoning might work, and McCulloch was instructed "to have a parley with them, if possible, and not engage them without absolute necessity."[47]

McCulloch started out at dawn the next morning. Reaching the Rio Grande, the Rangers hailed a heavily loaded steamer struggling against the swollen river and sent aboard their saddles, blankets, and arms to be ferried across. The boat, however, was too heavily laden to carry the extra weight of men and horses against the current, so the Rangers were told they would have to cross on their own. They stood for a while watching the five-mile-an-hour current sweeping past, carrying trees, driftwood, and other flotsam. The horses were beginning to grow nervous. Finally, McCulloch called out, "Now, boys, wade into it," and spurred his horse into the river.

McCulloch and about a dozen men and horses made it across, but the rest were forced back when their horses refused to swim out into midstream. The Rangers stranded on the south bank cut long poles and prodded their animals back into the river. Most made it across, but one young Ranger bringing up the rear went under, bobbed back to the surface, waved his arms, and went under again. Several companions searched the bank and found a dugout canoe and went after him. They had almost given up when he came to the surface, laughed, and swam ashore; it had been a prank. According to Reid, the young Ranger was reprimanded with "unvarnished and original cursing [that] would make a devil cross himself with fear."[48]

The Rangers paused and rested on a bluff where rancher and speculator Henry Clay Davis was already laying out town lots for what would become Rio Grande City on land belonging to his Mexican wife. Late that afternoon, they picked up a broad Indian war trail. Over the next several days, they came across deserted Mexican ranches, their people having fled across the river to escape the Indians. Lieutenant McMullen and several others took a dugout across the river and brought back several Mexicans, who described the raids and gave the route they believed the Indians had taken. Following it, they came to a ranch where the Comanches had killed the cattle, stolen horses, and carried off a young woman and several children.

Some of the local Mexicans informed the Rangers that the Indians had crossed the river nearby, so McCulloch led his men across and down to Mier, where they requisitioned rations from the local *alcalde*. For some of the Rangers, the city brought back memories. "All the most notable points of the battle-ground were pointed out to us by Lieut. McMullen, who was in the fight, and who . . . shared all the horrors of Mexican captivity," Reid wrote.

There seemed to be more nostalgia than bitterness. Now that they were conquerors rather than prisoners, the Texans found Mier to be a pleasant town, and the people seemed genuinely friendly. Learning that the Comanches had swept through the area and turned back toward the northwest, McCulloch decided it was useless to continue pursuit and ordered his men back to Camargo. "It was with not little reluctance that we were compelled to leave so pleasant a spot," Reid remarked.[49]

Chapter 6

Glory and Infamy

Throughout August 1846, Taylor assembled his forces at Ca-margo and started them by stages into the Mexican interior. By late in the month, the U.S. vanguard had occupied the sixteenth-century city of Cerralvo, where the Monterrey road enters the foothills of the sierras, and on September 5, it was joined by McCulloch's and Gillespie's Ranger companies. More Ranger units arrived, but often they were understrength, because the six-month enlistments had begun to expire among the companies recruited the previous spring. Nevertheless, those who remained were ready for a fight, and while they waited for orders to advance into the Mexican interior, they passed the time roasting coffee for the coming march, straightening their gear, arranging pack saddles, and cleaning their firearms. Off hours were spent bathing in the nearby river lined with ancient cypress trees or at dances in town.[1]

On September 11, Taylor began marching the army out of Cerralvo toward Monterrey in sections at one-day intervals. Pioneers went ahead to prepare the road through the rocky, broken country for wagons and artillery. The two Texas mounted regiments came together under command of Governor Henderson, who was serving as a volunteer major general, and rode parallel to the main column while individual Ranger units from the regiments scouted toward Monterrey.[2]

After three days on the march, McCulloch with a detachment of thirty-five men crossed the trail of about two hundred Mexican lancers. He divided his men and hit the Mexicans with fifteen men, while the other Rangers stirred up dust in the hills beyond, giving the impression that McCulloch's small group was the advance of a much larger force. After a few shots were exchanged, wounding one Texas horse, the Mexicans retreated.[3]

On September 18, the army halted at the town of Marin, only a short distance outside Monterrey. At sunrise the next morning, Taylor personally accompanied the two Texas regiments to have a look at the city. James Holland, whose diary indicated mutual animosity between the Texans and General Taylor, remarked, "Texas went ahead today—now that danger is expected old Taylor has put us in front."[4]

The Rangers were excited and hurried their horses forward. About 9 A.M., they came to a broad plain leading into the city only two miles from a massive citadel that the Americans dubbed "the Black Fort." Suddenly they saw the flash of a cannon from the citadel and heard the whistle of a ball that bounced onto the ground nearby.[5]

For the Texans this was a challenge, carried over from Indian fights in which Rangers and Comanches might ride against each other, breaking off at the last minute, each daring the other to respond. They rode up close to the citadel, zigzagging to avoid the shot, defying the gunners, and timing their moves to when the gunners were shifting their pieces to compensate for range or direction.[6]

"Many of their balls were directed very well—yet no one was hurt," Holland wrote. "It was cheering to see how The Texians greeted the Mexican Balls—Every fire was met with a hearty response of 3 cheers and such waving of hats and huzzaing Genl T says he never heard—The Texians proved their spunk by the utter carelessness with which the[y] Rec[eive]d the Enemy's shot—They whizzing by us in all directions. . . ."[7]

Taylor recalled the Texans and withdrew to a grove of trees that the Americans dubbed Walnut Springs, where the army bivouacked while Ad Gillespie accompanied engineers to reconnoiter the city. Monterrey was laid out in Hispano-Roman fashion with streets at right angles to each other, extending out in regular squares from a main plaza. The houses were of stone with flat roofs, making each a potential fort. Two real forts, the Teneria (Tannery) and the Diablo (Devil), covered the road Taylor would use, and the whole was dominated by the Black Fort.

Across the city were two heights, Independence Hill, defended by the fortified Bishop's Palace, and Federation Hill. These covered the road beyond Monterrey to Saltillo. The Mexicans, however, had made the mistake of fortifying all these strong points, so their forces were too strung out to support each other and, with careful planning by the Americans, could be cut off and reduced piecemeal.[8]

THE TEXANS RESUMED their games the next morning, September 20. This time, however, they added a new twist, actually riding up to the Mexican lines to see if they could take prisoners. An army surgeon, Dr. E. K. Chamberlain, remembered them as "very venturesome, and, advancing within the range of their [the Mexicans'] hottest fire, picked out, from under their forts and barricades, many prisoners."[9]

The struggle for Monterrey began at two o'clock that afternoon, when Taylor ordered General Worth's division to move on the city. Jack Hays and the First Texas took the lead, followed by U.S. troops. Pioneers had to hack a path through the dense brush for artillery, and progress was slow. They covered only seven miles before Worth ordered the main column to halt and went ahead with Hays and about fifty Rangers. A cornfield was off to one side, and Hays spotted a Mexican detachment working through the field trying to get behind them. He ordered most of his men to dismount in the corn, then sent McCulloch with another group to form a decoy. The Mexican cavalry chased them deep into the field.

Meanwhile, the batteries on Independence Hill opened fire, and the Texans' horses, unaccustomed to shell explosions, became unmanageable. Sam Reid was pitched out of his saddle and hung his foot in a stirrup, holding on to the horse's mane for dear life while the animal galloped blindly for about a hundred yards, until Reid could pull himself back up again. Another Ranger was thrown to the ground just as the Mexican cavalry came charging up. Lieutenant McMullen rode back, swung him onto his own horse, and dashed off just in time. The Mexicans were now on top of Hays's concealed men, who rose up and fired into them at point-blank range. The startled Mexicans milled about in confusion, and Hays and Worth began to retreat to the safety of the division. Night was falling, and Worth went into camp, poised for the assault on the city.[10]

He started at sunrise, with Hays again in the lead. The objective was Independence Hill and the fortified Bishop's Palace. The morning was foggy, and Gillespie and Big Foot Wallace took advantage of the cover to scout up close to the base of the hill under the walls. Before they could withdraw, the fog lifted and a Mexican sentry fired on them. The heavy musket ball struck the lock of Gillespie's pistol and split, one half going completely through him. Wallace carried him to the rear.[11]

The main body of Texans were almost to the hill when they encountered Mexican infantry and cavalry, and Hays deployed his men as skirmishers. As they moved ahead, Mexican gunners opened up from Federation Hill, and the shot fell in the midst of the American forces. A Ranger positioned in a tree with cannon balls flying around him reported that the Mexican infantry showed no sign of moving, then asked if he could come down.

"No, sir. Wait for orders," Hays replied and promptly forgot about the man.

Soon the Texans were ordered to withdraw. Reminded that the Ranger was still in the tree, Hays shouted, "Holloa, there—where are the Mexicans?"

"Going back up the hill," the Ranger reported, not knowing who had asked the question.

"Well, hadn't you better come down from there?"

"I don't know," the Ranger said. "I am waiting for orders!"

"Well, then, I *order* you down."

Realizing now that it was Hays, the Ranger came down without waiting to be told twice.[12]

THE FIGHT FOR the Bishop's Palace was long and bloody. One eyewitness remembered:

> The Texan Rangers are the most desperate men in battle that I ever heard of. They charged up to the breastworks, dismounted, and rushed over on foot, with sword in hand. . . . [Ranger Samuel W. Chambers] got over the breastworks, obtained a foothold on a thirteen-pounder, and deliberately took aim with his 'five-shooter,' firing with great effect and cursing the Mexicans, until the piece was taken by Gen. Worth and turned on the city. Chambers escaped without a wound.[13]

The Mexicans fought desperately as the Americans forced their way into the palace. In the great hall, fighting was hand-to-hand. "Steel clashed against steel, muskets came down on heads with a sickening 'thud,' scattering brains and blood," according to one account. Finally the Mexican defenders had enough. As their truce team approached, Big Foot Wallace aimed his gun at the officer carrying the white flag. "Lieutenant," a U.S. officer called, "don't you know a parley when you hear it blowed?"

"No!" Wallace snapped. "Not when I am in front of that man." He marched over to the Mexican officer and demanded to know if he would like to hold a bean lottery. Without giving the man time to answer, Big Foot held up his hand. "Look at that hand. Do you know it? Ever see it before?"

When the Mexican said he hadn't, Big Foot fumed, "Yes, you did, and called up others to look at it."

The officer now realized he was facing a survivor of the drawing he had supervised at Hacienda Salado. Wallace remembered that he hung his head "like a coyote."[14]

That night, the soldiers rested in the hard-won palace.

> There were many strange weird scenes in the old, gloomy building . . . groups of savage looking Rangers were gathered around the fires relating stirring tales of adventures with Commanches, Mexicans and wild animals, while others were engaged in gambling with the spoils obtained from the dead, while others were watching by the side of some wounded comrade, the fires throwing their shadders in gigantic proportions on the huge columns and walls.[15]

Among the wounded was Gillespie, his intestines torn open by the bullet fragment. He lived twenty-two hours in agony from pain and thirst. Finally morphine was administered and, in Wallace's words, "he died easy."[16]

THE BATTLE FOR Monterrey raged for three more days. By September 23 the defenses around the city had fallen and the veterans of Wood's Second Texas, accustomed to fighting in cities like San Antonio and Mier, led the assault into the center of town. A thunderstorm broke, and the dismounted Rangers ran up the streets in pouring rain, startling both the American regulars and the Mexican defenders.

"They did not understand such bold movement," Holland wrote. "When we got in possession of the houses—pick them from the housetop to housetop and such fun you never did see—the greatest danger we encountered was in crossing the streets—the hotest [*sic*] place you ever saw."[17]

Ranger James Buckner (Buck) Barry remembered using crowbars and sledgehammers to punch holes in stone walls to move from one house to the next.

> Often there was only a single wall between the Texans and Mexicans, so as soon as the Texans battered a hole through the wall the Mexicans would commence shooting at random through it. It was nothing strange for the muzzles of the Texans' and Mexicans' guns to clash together, both intending to shoot through the hole at the same time.[18]

The hand-to-hand fighting continued throughout the night and into the next morning, when Taylor ordered U.S. forces to withdraw so that he could bombard the city. The Ranger captains were outraged. They had already taken a good portion of Monterrey, and to them it was senseless to give it up now. They held their positions, keeping down to avoid the American shells falling into their midst. Amazingly, no Texan was hurt, and they remained in place until that night, when a cease-fire was arranged while the commanders of the two sides negotiated a truce.[19]

Monterrey was surrendered on the morning of September 25, and the Americans settled down for occupation. Despite the efforts of U.S. authorities, one officer noted "many riots and murders occurred, which were not only disgraceful to the participators, but to the American name." He blamed them on "a few evil-disposed volunteers, for whom the weak discipline of that arm had no terror." General Taylor found it convenient to blame the Texans because, although there is no evidence that they were particularly guilty, they were independent and insubordinate. Consequently, on October 2, when several more Ranger companies reached the end of their six-month enlistments, took their discharges, and began going home in small groups, Taylor was glad to see them go. Reporting to Adjutant General Jones in Washington, he wrote, "With their departure we may look for a restoration of quiet and order in Monterey [*sic*], for I regret to report that some shameful atrocities have been perpetrated by them since the capitulation of the town." To replace these Rangers, he authorized former Texas president Lamar, a veteran of the War of Independence, to raise a mounted company of eighty twelve-month Ranger volunteers.[20]

THE MEXICAN WAR was, perhaps, the first conflict reported in newspapers as it unfolded. In the United States, the public quickly found heroes, many of whom were from the new state of Texas. One of the most popular was Sam Walker, who always seemed to be in the thick of the fighting. He captured the American imagination, especially after it was learned he had been one of the Mier prisoners. This brought letters from relatives of missing prisoners, asking if he knew anything of the fate of their loved ones. "You would confer a lasting favor upon me and also on his Mother by making necessary inquiries," a despondent father wrote from Carlisle, Pennsylvania. From Baltimore came a letter expressing the "anxious feelings of a sister and widowed mother."[21]

There is no indication that Walker was able to fulfill these requests, because the federal government had other things for him to do. No longer a colonel of the Ranger-based First Texas Mounted Rifles, he had been taken into the regular army with the permanent rank of captain of the United States Regiment of Mounted Rifles, and on October 1, 1846, he was ordered to Washington. From there he was sent to Maryland to use his popularity to recruit troops. He had another piece of business to handle—the introduction of Samuel Colt's six-shot revolver.[22]

Despite the success of the original revolver in Texas, the United States government showed no interest in the weapon. Federal contracts were critical to the Colt company's survival, and the failure to procure a government contract, together with the lingering effects of the financial panic of 1837, had forced it into receivership in 1842. The same year, however, the government did grant Colt $50,000 for development of harbor defense systems, which at least kept him involved in the arms business. Nevertheless, his own priority was the revolving pistol, and the Mexican War revived hopes that the government might take interest.

It is not known exactly when Walker and Colt first discussed a new revolver. Colt was unaware that Walker planned to actually purchase arms during his trip east, and his initial effort was directed at getting an endorsement of what appears to have been the prototype.[23] On December 1, Colt wrote an associate in Washington, "Permit me to make your acquaintance with Captain Walker 'U.S. Rifles' & to request you to lend him the repeating Pistol you have of my construction for purposes of experiment & oblige. . . ."[24]

Walker, whose enthusiasm for the revolver was based on hard-won experience, was happy to oblige and endorsed the concept of an improved model. This enabled Colt to obtain an army contract almost immediately, and within two weeks he was urging Walker to meet him in New York "to determine on the exact model of the Pistols. It is important that this is done with as little delay as possible or I will not be able to complete them by the time they are wanted."[25]

Together, Walker and Colt worked out specifications, and tooling for the new pistol began in January 1847. It was a .44-caliber, six-shot weapon that, at four pounds nine ounces, was the heaviest production Colt's revolver ever made. Issued to the Rangers, it was formally designated the Walker Model, and to emphasize the point the cylinder was decorated with Ormsby's engraving of Walker's Indian fight sketch. The pistol's introduction during the Mexican War assured Colt's future success.[26]

Even the word "revolver" gave a psychological edge, for the Mexicans associated it with a nearly identical word in their own language but one that has substantially different meaning. The Spanish verb *revolver* is the root of the word *revuelta,* which describes any number of spinning or turning motions. In this instance, the Mexicans believed the Americans had devised a new technology that, in the words of one U.S. officer, allowed the bullet itself to "run around trees and turn corners, go into houses and climb stairs, and hunt up folks generally." Convinced there was no shelter from such a weapon, they already had defeat on their minds when they went into battle.[27]

GENERAL TAYLOR, MEANWHILE, was preparing his troops to meet a large Mexican army rumored to be heading north under the command of General Santa Anna, who had recently returned to power. Despite Taylor's ill feeling toward Rangers in general, he liked some of their leaders and apparently was pleased when McCulloch rejoined him in late January 1847. The needs of battle took priority over Taylor's personal opinions, and with the possibility of new hostilities, the recently discharged Mounted Volunteer companies of Rangers were recalled to active duty together with recently formed units from San Antonio. These new arrivals brought a particularly dangerous element, for among them was Mabry "Mustang" Gray, the "cow-boy" who had so blithely helped massacre the Mexican trading expedition near Victoria five years before.[28]

Mustang Gray was twenty-one years old when he arrived in Texas from South Carolina in January 1835. He listed his occupation as farmer, and it is known that he fought at San Jacinto. Beyond that and general knowledge of his depredations along the Nueces Strip, his life is largely a mystery. Nevertheless, he was now in Mexico at the head of a company of Rangers who took pride in being called the Mustangers or the Mustang Grays.[29] Gray found good company in John Glanton, a member of Walter P. Lane's new company of Rangers from San Antonio. Glanton was a cultured, affable man, but a vicious sociopath who later became a notorious scalp hunter, killing Indians of all ages and sexes for the bounty on their scalps paid by local jurisdictions in the southwestern United States and northwestern Mexico.[30]

Despite the valiant service of the Rangers in Taylor's victory over Santa Anna in the bloody two-day battle of Buena Vista in February 1847, the American regulars expressed only contempt for the likes of Gray and Glanton. Dr. S. Compton Smith, who served as acting surgeon for Taylor's division and considered Walker, McCulloch, and Hays to be "the genuine, brave, and hardy pioneers [of Texas]," nevertheless wrote:

> Some of the so-called Texas Rangers, who came into the country at a later period, were mostly made up of adventurers and vagabonds, whose whole object was plunder. . . .
>
> The gang of miscreants under the leadership of *"Mustang Grey"* [*sic*] were of this description. This party, in cold blood, murdered almost the entire male population of the rancho of Guadalupe,—where not a single weapon, offensive or defensive, could be found. . . .
>
> Others came after them, but were not mustered into service;— the General declaring that the American army should no longer be disgraced by such wretches.[31]

Taylor reacted to the Rancho de Guadalupe massacre and other atrocities apparently by packing Gray and his men back to Camargo, where they were mustered out on the expiration of their enlistments.[32] Nevertheless, the damage was done.

These incidents help bring a whole new aspect to the conflict—a bloody counterguerrilla struggle in which neither side showed mercy. The vicious fighting between the irregulars of two nations became a war within a war, especially after April 4, 1847, when Antonio Canales, himself far from squeamish about committing outrages, sent an order to Mexican commandants under his control.

> With the greatest indignation I have learned that the Americans have committed horrible murders on the Guadalupe Ranch, hanging twenty-five peaceful men in their own homes and by the side of their families, and shooting them almost immediately. Reprisal is the only recourse left to us to repel this warfare, which is not war, but atrocity in its greatest fury. . . . You will immediately proclaim martial law, with the stipulation that eight days after the publication of said law all individuals who are capable of bearing arms and do not do so will be considered traitors and will be shot immediately. . . .
>
> You are authorized to give no quarter to any Americans whom you may find, or who may present themselves to you, even though they be unarmed. You will make this known to all the towns in the State, informing them of the severe penalties which will be incurred in case of the least omission.[33]

Walter P. Lane's company had the loathsome job of hunting down the *rancheros,* matching Canales murder for murder. All too often, Lane's Rangers went about it with relish. Capturing the *ranchero* chief Juan Flores, Lane took him to Cerralvo, conducted a drumhead court-martial, and had him shot. A few days later, the company was scouting the interior beyond Monterrey and came to the city of Magdalena one night. In the moonlit street they spotted an armed Mexican, who shouted an obscenity and spurred his horse away. John Glanton gave chase and (according to Lane's version) ordered the man to halt. When the Mexican refused, Glanton shot him.

Taylor had already heard of the shooting by the time Lane reported back to him and, in Lane's words, "commenced abusing my command as a set of robbers and cut-throats." After a heated exchange between the Ranger and the general, Lane returned to his headquarters, where he sent for Glanton.

"Get away at once," Lane told him, because he was certain that "Taylor was bound to have his scalp." Nevertheless, Glanton eventually was exonerated for the Magdalena killing and the subsequent killing of a soldier of the Eighth Infantry. Soon after he transferred to Capt. J. M. Handley's company of the First Texas Mounted Rifles under Jack Hays and served in General Scott's army in central Mexico. He was mustered out in Veracruz, returned to San Antonio, and from there drifted west, where he began his career as a scalp hunter.[34]

TAYLOR, MEANWHILE, WAS disgusted by the whole business of Ranger vs. *ranchero*. Whatever their fighting abilities, he had had enough of the Texans. "There is scarcely a form of crime that has not been reported to me as committed by them," he wrote Adjutant General Jones. "The mounted men of Texas have scarcely made an expedition without unwarrantably killing a Mexican." Consequently, he requested that he be sent no more troops from Texas.[35]

Dr. Smith wholeheartedly agreed with his general's decision. Nevertheless, Mustang Gray or Glanton notwithstanding, the surgeon could not withhold his admiration for the Rangers as a whole. Writing of the units from Mississippi and Texas, he said:

> At Monterey [*sic*] and Buena Vista, these gallant troops were cruelly cut up. Hardly one-tenth of the members of those veteran regiments were returned to their homes,—and those with shattered constitutions.[36]

THE WAR IN northern Mexico was essentially over, and the fighting shifted to the central part of the country, where Maj. Gen. Winfield Scott landed in Veracruz in March 1847. McCulloch's men remained in the north, served out their latest six-month hitch, and returned home. Sam Walker now served as a regular soldier under General Scott. With his Ranger background, however, he and his men were assigned to keep the road open between Scott's troops advancing on Mexico City and the port at Veracruz. He established headquarters at the fortress of Perote, which he had last seen as a prisoner following the Mier expedition. One can only speculate on his feelings about returning as a conqueror to his former prison, for although there is a tightly spaced twelve-page letter to his brother Jonathan in Washington, "Castle of Perote" is mentioned only in the heading.[37]

Two days after Walker wrote the letter, on August 16, Mexico instituted a formal guerrilla warfare policy, its government-sanctioned packs of irregulars plundering American supply trains and cutting communications between the coast and Scott's troops nearing Mexico City. In response, President Polk ordered Hays to take as many men as he could gather to Veracruz and commence counterguerrilla operations. Hays was already recruiting men in the San Antonio–Austin area and had assembled a new regiment, many of whom had already served under General Taylor. Upon receiving Polk's orders, he took the regiment to the Rio Grande, and in September the Rangers boarded transports for Veracruz.[38]

Walker was pleased at developments. Scott had entered the Mexican capital on September 14, and now Hays was on his way, presumably with the new revolvers. On October 5, he wrote a last letter to Jonathan from Perote:

> I write in haste to inform you that I leave here tomorrow under command of Gen [Joseph] Lane in command of three other companies of Cavalry with the expectation of fighting Gen Santa Anna at the pass of Pinal about fifty miles from this place[.] He is said to have a force of eight thousand men But I must confess that I have some doubts about his meeting us voluntarily our force being upwards of three thousand men, we will move light with as few waggons [*sic*] as possible. . . .
>
> Jack Hays will soon be here with his Regt of Rangers and I have no doubt that Santa Anna will be in a tight place; if I had my Revolving Pistols I should feel strong hopes of capturing him or killing him. . . .
>
> I have just recd a pair of Colts pistols which he sent to me as a present, there is not an officer who has seen them but what speaks in the highest terms of them and all of the Cavalry officers are determined to get them if possible.[39]

Four days later, General Lane learned that Santa Anna was in the town of Huamantla, just north of the main road to Mexico City. Hoping to catch him there, he sent Walker's men ahead while he followed with infantry. At the edge of town, Walker's advance guard surprised a Mexican outpost, chasing the soldiers to the square, where the Americans suddenly found themselves confronted by five hundred lancers supported by artillery. In the ensuing fight, Walker was killed, and his men were saved only by the arrival of Lane's troops. Santa Anna escaped.[40]

HAYS ARRIVED IN Veracruz on October 17. Two days later the first consignment of Colt's Walker Model revolver were delivered and issued to the Rangers. Although the war was nearing its conclusion, the U.S. garrison at Puebla, a major city on the road between Mexico City and Veracruz, was under a virtual state of siege. Hays began a series of strikes against suspected guerrilla hideouts and strongpoints, clearing the path for Lane's troops to relieve Puebla. Ultimately Lane broke through, and Hays's Rangers reached Mexico City, where they clashed almost continually with the local population. They divided their time between the capital and counterguerrilla forays until they were demobilized and sent home.[41]

The Mexican War secured Mexican recognition of Texas as part of the United States with the Rio Grande as the boundary. The United States also gained all of California, most of New Mexico, Arizona, and Nevada, and parts of Colorado and Utah. For Texas, however, the war was costly. Great Rangers like Walker and Gillespie were dead. Less noble Rangers gave the service a reputation for brutality that still lingers. But the fame of the organization had spread beyond the boundaries of Texas. The Texas Rangers were becoming a legend.

PART 3
THE TORCH IS PASSED

Chapter 7

A New Era

During Texas's ten years as a sovereign republic, much of its resources had been devoted to a two-front war—against the Indians to the north and west, and against the threat of Mexican military intervention in the south. As a result, little could be done to develop the vast, trackless interior west of San Antonio and Austin. But the close of the Mexican War removed the danger from the south, and the federal government was responsible for defense against the Indians. Texans were eager to break out of the confines of their eastern settlements and move into the frontier regions.

Jack Hays led the way. Famous throughout the United States because of his exploits during the Mexican War, he traveled to Washington in June 1848. There he turned in his resignation from the army and took advantage of a hero's welcome in the federal capital to promote the opening of a road across the six hundred miles separating San Antonio and El Paso. Hays offered sound arguments. The government hoped that a practical way could be found to cut travel time to Santa Fe in the newly acquired territory of New Mexico.[1] Traditionally, trade between the United States and the New Mexico settlements followed a northern route through St. Louis, an expensive and uncertain process involving immense wagon trains traveling for months across the Plains. The western part of Texas was a void. Although Hays had been as far into that wilderness as anyone, he had never ventured more than about two hundred miles west of San Antonio. The area beyond was unknown country. Federal officials authorized him to enlist a detachment of Rangers and explore possible routes.

The El Paso expedition included seventy-two Rangers, civilians, federal soldiers, and Mexican and Indian scouts. They left San Antonio on August 27, 1848, traveling easily at first over familiar country. Striking out into the unknown beyond Las Moras Creek (near the present town of Brackettville), they followed crude Spanish maps, correcting many of the errors they found. The trip was brutal. Running low on food, they were forced to kill several of their horses, and water was always a problem. One man suffered a mental breakdown from the hardship, wandered off from camp, and was saved only by a band of Indians who found him and nursed him back to health. Eventually, Hays led them to Ben Leaton's fortified trading post in the Big Bend of the Rio Grande near what is now Presidio, Texas. El Paso was only 150 miles up the river. Here the expedition turned back toward San Antonio. The Rangers, who were provided by the state, were expected to be back at their post on the Llano River near Fredericksburg within a certain time, and could go no farther and remain on schedule. Many of the civilians were in bad physical condition from the trip. Because the stretch between Leaton's fort and El Paso was already known, Hays saw no point in continuing.

To avoid shortages on the return trip, he divided the expedition into three groups, theorizing that smaller parties traveling different routes would make less demand on local game, forage, and water holes. All eventually returned to civilization, and only one group suffered any particular hardship. Hays's own band reached San Antonio on December 10. He had mapped a suitable route to El Paso, explored a river they named Devil's because of the hellish country in which it was located, and corrected many errors on Spanish maps of the Pecos River.[2]

IT IS ONE of those quirks of fate that Hays determined a route to El Paso just as news was reaching the east of the discovery of gold in California, because the influx of westbound argonauts soon made the new road essential. Among those heading to the goldfields were Hays himself, Ben McCulloch, and other old Rangers. The Mexican War, the acquisition of vast new western territories, and the Gold Rush marked the end of one era and the birth of another for the Texas Rangers. The men were passing who had set the standard for all Rangers to come. Hays remained in California, becoming a lawman, businessman, and land developer and one of the state's leading citizens. McCulloch eventually returned to Texas, although he did not reenter the state's service until the eve of secession. Defense of the Texas frontier now devolved on new leaders. They faced a difficult situation because their status under the American regime was not clear, and the Rangers were hampered by competing authority with the military and conflicting policies between the state and federal governments.[3]

NOW THAT THE Mexican War had ended, the United States considered itself at peace, whereas the Texans viewed themselves as perpetually at war with the Plains Indian tribes. The Texas policy toward hostile Indians was simple—extermination. The federal government, on the other hand, was determined to pacify them through agencies and, in extreme cases, by removal to new locations. U.S. troops were sent to garrison the frontier, and it was assumed they would maintain the peace.

The problem with the federal policy was that annexation confronted the United States with a new and unfamiliar situation. In the past, by the time a territory attained statehood, the local Indian tribes had been subdued and reduced to the dependency of a federal reservation. The duty of the soldiers, therefore, was more the enforcement of laws governing white-Indian relations than protecting settlements from depredations. Thus when a string of military posts was established along a so-called frontier line of defense between Fort Worth on the Trinity River and Fort Duncan on the Rio Grande at Eagle Pass, they were situated at great distances from each other and garrisoned largely by infantry, a branch of service virtually useless against mounted Indian tribes. "With the exception of the 'mounted rifles' [in this case, federal cavalry], we have no force that pretends to meet the Indian on his own ground," one visitor commented. Even when cavalry was available, it was restricted to the federal policy of pacification.[4]

AS EARLY AS 1848, while the U.S. Army was still deployed in Mexico, the need for protection became obvious when a large band of Indians embarked on a prolonged raid through Texas. "Many were murdered, others robbed of all they possessed, and a general fear and alarm diffused throughout the whole extent of the frontier," according to a Congressional report concerning state claims against the federal government for frontier defense.[5]

In the absence of federal military protection, Governor Henderson's successor, George T. Wood, ordered six Ranger companies mustered not only for the immediate crisis but until a federal military presence could be established. He also directed an extension of the soon-to-expire enlistment of a frontier defense company near the headwaters of the Trinity River. The length of service of these companies is not clear, but they apparently were discharged once federal troops began settling into permanent garrison duty.[6]

Given their long experience with Indian raids, the Texans placed little confidence in the army, nor did they have any sympathy for the pacification policy. One California-bound goldseeker gave his opinion of the federal policy as his party reached Fort Worth.

> Here were stationed a company of, or companies of, U.S. Cavalry which had recently replaced the discharged, efficient Texas Rangers. Hostile, wild Indians visited the Station almost nightly. They stole animals, shot at the sentries and committed any deviltry their mischievous hands found to do.[7]

The situation was aggravated because the Plains Indians themselves did not understand the impact of annexation. The Texans always had been a people apart from the United States. The Plains tribes were at peace with the federal government and at war with the Texans, and could not comprehend why the newly appointed federal Indian agents objected to their depredations against the Texas settlements.[8]

In early 1849, extensive raiding broke out in the vicinity of Corpus Christi. Because the nearest federal troops were infantry stationed more than eighty miles away, Governor Wood ordered the formation of two Ranger companies totaling 150 men to patrol the area for three months at state expense. After laying out approximately $12,000 for these companies, Texas was no longer able to carry the burden, and the army agreed to requisition three full companies of Rangers for six months at federal expense in the Corpus Christi area.[9]

Even the vicinity of the capital was dangerous. One citizen recalled, "In those days a gentleman seldom rode into the country any distance [from Austin] without carrying arms. It was not safe to ramble in the suburbs of the town unarmed." A man who lived within the Austin city limits was attacked on his way to market.[10]

In May 1849, Indians struck settlements along the San Antonio River around Goliad, and even threatened Goliad itself. An ad hoc Ranger company attacked one band shortly before midnight on June 4, scattering the warriors and capturing their camp and equipment. Three days later, Governor Wood formally mustered the company into state service. Three additional companies were formed and taken into federal service for six months, beginning in August.[11]

Nevertheless, the raids continued through the end of the year, centering on an area running south from Goliad and across the Nueces Strip to the Rio Grande. On January 12, 1850, a prominent Corpus Christi citizen was ambushed and killed en route to Goliad, and between sixty and eighty horses were taken from a nearby ranch. News reached the Ranger station on the Nueces the following night, and on the morning of January 14, the men began pursuit. The Indians managed to stay ahead of the Rangers, lancing to death any of their horses that gave out and slowed their retreat. The trail finally led into the broken escarpment leading to the central Plains and the Rangers, who were running low on food, put in at Fort Inge near Uvalde to reprovision.

In the Rio Grande settlements downriver from Laredo, Indian depredations prompted the leading citizens to petition the new governor, Peter Hansford Bell (himself a former Jack Hays Ranger), for a company to be stationed on the Texas side of the river near its confluence with the Salado, about midway between Ringgold Barracks in Rio Grande City and Fort McIntosh in Laredo. The petition noted they were about sixty miles from either post and needed more immediate protection than the military could provide. Signed by forty-four of the leading Texan and *tejano* citizens, the appeal could not be ignored. Neither could their request that "Capt. John S. Ford. Be Commissioned to Command Such Company or force as may be stationed in accordance with the prayers of your petitioners." As a result of this public pressure, the Ranger companies were reorganized and their enlistments extended.[12]

IF THE REPUBLIC was the era of Jack Hays, the 1850s could well be called the Ford years, for John Salmon Ford distinguished himself on both the Indian frontier and the Mexican border. A native of South Carolina, Ford read medicine, which is to say that in an era of few medical schools he prepared for the profession by studying under the supervision of a trained physician. When news arrived in Tennessee of the Texas War of

Independence and the fall of the Alamo, he began recruiting a company for service in the new republic. Although the war ended before he could organize his company, Ford was determined to try his luck in Texas anyway. He crossed the Sabine in June 1836, a month past his twenty-first birthday, and established a medical practice in San Augustine. It is unclear whether he was divorced or separated at this time, but he had custody of a small daughter.

Ford spent the next ten years involved in community affairs and politics, and he served in the local militia when the Cherokees were expelled from east Texas. He was elected to the Texas Congress as a strong advocate of annexation. In 1845 he remarried and moved his family to Austin, where he was copublisher and editor of a newspaper. On May 10, 1847, he enlisted as a Mounted Volunteer for service in Mexico, rising to lieutenant and serving as Jack Hays's adjutant in General Scott's campaign. This began a career as a soldier and Ranger that Ford would follow for the next two decades. Besides a reputation as a competent officer, he also acquired a nickname; when a soldier or Ranger was killed, he habitually signed the condolence letter to the family "RIP [Rest in Peace]/Ford," and so became known as Rip Ford or Old Rip.[13]

Ford was different from many Ranger captains in that he emphasized drill. Writing in the third person, he said he

> never subscribed to the theory that Texas Rangers needed no drilling. He had seen enough service to convince him it was necessary for men to know how to perform simple evolutions to render them efficient in the presence of an enemy. He exercised the men in the manual of arms, wheeling, changing front, and other maneuvers.[14]

He was already known to the citizens of the Rio Grande area, having led Rangers in the vicinity the previous year. Perhaps the fact that virtually nothing happened during that initial assignment (the bulk of the trouble was along the Nueces and around Goliad) helped convince people that if he was in charge, they could sleep securely.[15]

FORD ESTABLISHED HIS base at an abandoned ranch called San Antonio Viejo, once the seat of a large stock raiser who had been driven off by Indians. In keeping with the petition of the citizens who sought his presence, the camp was located about forty-five miles upriver from Ringgold Barracks and seventy-five miles downriver from Fort McIntosh. The Rangers lived in tents pitched around a square, using the ranch buildings for storing their supplies. Several good wells and stone troughs provided water for men and animals.

Because the company's pistols were unserviceable, Ford decided to combine a requisition for new ones with a scouting expedition. He would take forty men upriver as far as Laredo, from there move north along the road toward the city of San Antonio, turning east to Corpus Christi, where he would draw new pistols, and finally cut southwest across the desert back toward the Rio Grande and San Antonio Viejo.

The expedition left camp in early May, stopping for a few days at Laredo to draw supplies and equipment from the army at Fort McIntosh, then patrolled about thirty more miles upriver before turning north. "We proceeded cautiously," Ford wrote, "keeping our men out of sight as well as we could." A few of the most cautious and trustworthy men were sent well ahead. Although they initially saw no signs of Indians, they believed them to be near, and soon began finding evidence of recent hunts to confirm their suspicions.

Ford ordered Lt. Andrew J. Walker to take half the men eastward toward the Nueces River, while he continued on slightly northwest to its headwaters. In doing this, he hoped the Indians would spot one group of Rangers and, trying to avoid it, would run into the other group. Walker was the first to encounter Indians and chased them until his horses gave out. Soon after, on May 12, Ford's detachment located the fresh trail of the same band. They followed it to the Nueces and found where the Indians had forded. Crossing after them, Ford's scouts noticed that the Indians were in no particular hurry, apparently assuming they had outdistanced the Rangers. In fact they were amusing themselves as they rode by slashing with their whips at the pads of the prickly pear cacti that grew in profusion in the region. Riding as hard as they could without exhausting their horses, the Rangers followed the trail some eight miles until they spotted the Indians emerging from some timber onto a prairie. They were Comanches.

"Here they are!" Ford yelled, galloping toward them. A Mexican scout whom Ford called Roque Maugricio (probably Mauricio) and Sgt. David M. Level joined him. Seeing only three men, the Comanches turned on them. About that time the other Rangers arrived, and both sides—each with sixteen men—formed up for a fight. Only Ford and Level had revolvers. The other Rangers had government-issue single-shot, muzzle-loading Mississippi rifles, and Ford cautioned them to alternate, half firing while the others reloaded.

The Comanche chief rode out toward the Rangers as if daring them to shoot him.

"Be steady, boys!" Ford cautioned. "He wants to draw your fire and then charge you with the lance!"

The chief came at Sergeant Level, who wounded him in the arm with a shot from his revolver. As he turned and rode back toward the other Comanches, Ford ordered the Rangers to charge. The Comanches divided up, half moving to the left and half to the right. The Rangers, staying together, rushed around the flank of the left, firing as they passed. The Indians let out a wail, signifying prominent warriors had been killed. The right line of Comanches cut loose with a volley of arrows, and Ford ordered each Ranger to move in close to a warrior so the Indian's companions could not fire at them. After several minutes of vicious hand-to-hand fighting, the Comanches broke off, unwilling to take any more losses. The Rangers chased them four or five miles before giving up.

Following custom, the Indians retrieved their dead and wounded, but Ford estimated they had lost four killed and seven wounded. One Ranger was wounded, and a horse was killed. Ford himself received what appeared to be a scratch on the back of his right hand, which, while unusually painful, did not appear serious. It never stopped troubling him, however, and within six years, his right arm was completely paralyzed. As these were also the symptoms of an untreated snakebite, he speculated the scratch came from an arrow poisoned with rattlesnake venom.[16]

THE MISSISSIPPI RIFLES carried by Ford's men were efficient long-range weapons that contributed substantially to the American victory during the Mexican War. They were totally unsuited, however, for Ranger service. A Ranger customarily fought at close quarters, and chose his weapons accordingly. By the mid-1850s, most provided their own horses, saddles, arms, and equipment, except for rifles, which were supplied by the state.[17] When equipment was lost, company commanders filed claims against the state, and these documents, preserved in the State Library and Archive in Austin, give an idea of the arms preferred by the Rangers. The handgun of choice appears to have been Colt's

.44-caliber Dragoon Model revolver, along with a double-barreled shotgun, both suited for close-in fighting. A subsequent requisition from the Executive Department of Texas to the U.S. Bureau of Ordnance indicated a preference for the Colt's repeating rifle, which had a revolving cylinder, like the Colt's pistol, and was deemed the rifle "peculiarly adapted to our border warfare."[18]

Derived from the Walker Model, the Colt's Dragoon pistol was a better-built, more streamlined, and more efficient weapon. It was the same caliber as the Walker and, at four pounds two ounces, was lighter, if not by much. It was produced with slight variations from 1848 to 1862 and, like the Walker, had the Indian fight scene engraved on the cylinder.[19]

The Colt's Dragoon was the first revolver formally adopted by the regular U.S. Army after a reluctant Bureau of Ordnance was forced by the realities of frontier warfare to purchase them for the U.S. Regiment of Mounted Rifles. By the end of the 1850s, virtually every U.S. mounted unit on the frontier carried Colt's revolvers. Federal cavalry often operated in conjunction with Rangers during that period, and the Texas influence became evident as the army also adopted the broad-brimmed hat to replace the shako and kepi for field service, and went to a horse more suited for the rigors of frontier service than the Eastern thoroughbreds. Soldiers also employed the Ranger tactic of slipping quietly up on the Indians and catching them unawares.[20]

IN 1852, FORD dropped out of the Rangers for the time being, assuming a seat in the state senate and returning to the newspaper business in Austin.[21] Throughout the 1850s, however, Indian raids were common along the frontier, and Ranger units were almost continually in service. People on the Rio Grande, left without Ranger protection following the disbanding of Ford's company, complained that federal troops at Ringgold Barracks and Fort McIntosh "are totally inadequate to protect the lives and property of our citizens."[22]

One problem facing Texas was that its citizens were expanding and settling the frontier faster than either the state or federal government could secure it. Whereas in 1848 the line of defense ran north-south from Fort Worth to Fort Duncan at Eagle Pass, within seven years it had extended as much as 150 miles westward. Fort Worth itself no longer had any military value and was abandoned, its name preserved in the community that had grown up around it. It was replaced by Fort Belknap some hundred miles farther west, and Camp Cooper about fifty miles beyond Belknap. Military posts were also erected along the new road running between San Antonio and El Paso.[23]

Nevertheless, the Rangers remained the premier defenders of the frontier. Frederick Law Olmsted, later famous as the architect of Central Park in New York, visited Texas in 1854 and described Rangers returning to San Antonio from six months in the field. "They had only a few rags tied together and drawn round them for decency," he wrote. But on dismounting, they headed for the local merchants, emerging "in fine cloth, stove-pipe hats, and all the etceteras."

Olmsted was impressed by their casual attitude.

> Men and officers were on terms of perfect equality, calling each other by their Christian or nick-names. Their time, when not in actual service, was spent in hunting, riding, and playing cards. The only duty was for four (out of seventy) to stand guard. Men were often absent, without leave, three or four days, without being reprimanded. They fought, when engaged, quite independently, the only order from the commander usually being—"All ready, boys? Go ahead."
>
> Their principal occupation has always been Indian fighting, but two or three regiments of them were employed, during the Mexican war, with great advantage, mainly as scouts, pioneers, and foragers.[24]

The Rangers continued to be a volunteer service called up when needed. The American people (and, by extension, the people of Texas) still distrusted a permanent, regular military force, preferring to place confidence in citizen-soldiers, minutemen, and short-term volunteers. Neither the state nor the federal government seemed to have much foresight, and the possibility that frontier defense would be a long-term proposition apparently never occurred to anyone. Thus frontier defense laws were for specific time periods, and the legislature frequently had to approve new bills in order to keep Rangers in the field. Often Ranger companies were mustered at the behest of military authorities to serve together with U.S. regular troops.[25]

The situation was aggravated because the legislature did not always approve a new defense bill when the old one expired, leaving the frontier virtually unprotected. During one such lapse in 1856, marauders struck the settlements west of Austin, and the governor had to tell the citizens that there was "not means . . . placed at my disposal for the protection of the frontier." He advised them to form "a Company of Minute Men" for their own protection, and said he would urge the legislature to reimburse them for their expenses.[26]

In 1854, the U.S. Congress sought to resolve the Indian crisis by establishing two reservations, which were occupied the following year.[27] The state's willingness to allow these reservations was a complete reversal of its previous policy, which had denied Indians the right to any land for settlement. It came at the behest of Secretary of War Jefferson Davis, who reasoned that as long as the Indians had no land of their own, they had a right to go anywhere they pleased and the army could do nothing until they actually committed depredations. If, on the other hand, they were given a specific territory and required to remain there, the army could intervene anytime they were off their reserve.[28]

One of the new reservations, on the main stream of the Brazos twenty miles below Fort Belknap, was for the Anadarkos, Tawakonis, Wacos, Tonkawas, and Caddos. The second, at Camp Cooper on the Clear Fork of the Brazos, was allocated for the more tractable southern bands of Comanches. Here the tribes were expected to establish permanent homes and support themselves with farms and ranches.[29]

Though the Southern Comanches were willing to try their hand at agriculture and stock raising, the Northern Comanches and Kiowas were determined to continue their raids into Texas from Oklahoma. Despite Davis's optimism, the northwest frontier became a bloody battleground, particularly during the period of 1858 to 1860. Not only did the Northern Comanches and Kiowas attack whites, but they also remembered that the various tribes congregated around Fort Belknap had scouted for soldiers and Rangers, and so raided that reservation as well. The hostile tribes were armed with rifles provided by the federal government. Ostensibly the rifles were for hunting, but in fact they gave them an edge for their forays into Texas, where they would steal livestock, then drive the stolen animals north to the Arkansas River and sell them to white traders.[30]

Indian Superintendent Robert Simpson Neighbors was convinced that the raiders were "Indians who do not properly belong to the State, but intruders from the United States Indian Territories [i.e., Oklahoma]."[31] Rip

Ford was not so certain and decided to investigate any possibility. Ford had reentered state service after the legislature authorized Governor H. R. Runnels to enlist a hundred men for six months' service in the Rangers and appropriate $70,000 for their expenses. In his instructions to Ford, Runnels wrote, "I impress upon you the necessity of action and energy. Follow any trail and all trails of hostile or suspected hostile Indians you may discover, and if possible, overtake and chastise them, if unfriendly."[32]

Ford wasted no time taking to the field. He met with former Ranger captain Shapley Ross, who now served as agent for the Lower Brazos near Belknap and recruited warriors to serve as scouts for an expedition along the Canadian River. The expedition set out on April 22 and included 102 Rangers with 113 Indians commanded by Ross. A week later they reached the Red River, where the Indians guided them across the treacherous quicksands and into the Indian Territory of Oklahoma. Indian scouts and flankers moved as much as twenty miles ahead of the main force, looking for signs of hostiles. On May 10, they returned with Comanche arrowheads. They had happened on some wounded buffalo, and after killing them, extracted the hostile points from the carcasses. The following day, the Indians reported they had spotted Comanches chasing buffalo.

Ford left a small guard at camp, and at 2 P.M. set out with his main force of Rangers and Indians to find the Comanches. They had hoped to locate the hostile camp and attack it at daylight on May 12, but it was 7 A.M. before they discovered and overran a small camp of five lodges. A band of Tonkawas was left behind to destroy the camp, while the rest of the force moved on, locating the main camp several miles away on the Canadian River. Ross's Indians rode between the camp and the river and charged from that direction while Ford took the Rangers straight in.[33]

"The head chief, Iron Jacket, had ridden out in gorgeous array—clad in a coat of mail—and bore down upon our red allies," Ford reported to Governor Runnels.

> He was followed by warriors and trusted for safety to his armor. The sharp crack of fire of six rifles brought his horse to the ground, and in a few moments the chief fell riddled with balls. . . . The fight was now general, and extended very soon over a circuit of six miles in length and more than three in

breadth. It was in fact, almost a series of single combats. Squads of Rangers and [government] Indians were pursuing the enemy in every direction. The Comanches would occasionally halt and endeavor to make a stand, however, their efforts were unavailing and they were forced to yield the ground to our men in every instance. The din of the battle had rolled back from the river—the groans of the dying, cries of frightened women and children, mingled with the reports of fire arms, and the shouts of men as they rose from hill top, from thicket and from ravine.

The noise attracted Comanches from another large camp several miles upriver, and they came into the fight. The Rangers and their Indian allies were now in control of the first big camp, and the two sides faced off, each daring the other to move. Occasionally one side would rush the other and break off at the last moment. "Half an hour was spent in this without much damage to either party. A detachment of Rangers advanced to reinforce the friendly Indians, and the Comanches quited [*sic*] the field. . . ."

The Rangers pursued, but eventually broke off. It was growing late, and Ford wanted to get back to his own camp with its skeleton guard detail before the Comanches discovered it. He was particularly concerned when one of the captured Comanche women said that Buffalo Hump was camped twelve miles downriver "with a considerable body of warriors." Texas casualities that day were two killed and three wounded. Based on the number of bodies that the Comanches had been forced to leave behind, Ford estimated their losses at seventy-six killed and a large but indeterminate number wounded. There were eighteen prisoners, mostly women and children.[34]

THE VALIANT SERVICE of the Indians from Fort Belknap did them little good against the white tide that was rapidly overwhelming them. The reservation was on prime land, and although the newly established town of Belknap was economically dependent on the soldiers at the fort and the Indians from the reserve, a flood of newcomers intended to open the Indian land to settlement. Incidents flared up and spread to the Comanche reserve at Camp Cooper. Settlers alleged that reservation Indians were joining in on the raids, and while Ford was willing to concede the probability that some reservation Comanches were involved, he was not willing to move against the reservation tribes as a whole.[35]

During one officers' conference, Ford proposed sending patrols through the vicinity of the Comanche reservation. One officer remarked that a trail leading from the scene of an attack to the reservation would be enough evidence of guilt. To that, Lt. Allison Nelson added, "The thing can be managed; the trail can be made."

Jerking Nelson up by the collar, Ford thundered, "No, Sir, that will not do, I am responsible to the state, and to public opinion, and I will take no step in the matter, unless I am backed by the facts, and of such a character as to justify me before the public. I am willing to punish the [reserve] Comanches, if they are found guilty; but I am not disposed to do so unjustly and improperly."[36]

Nelson walked out of the meeting and soon found an ally in John R. Baylor, whom Superintendent Neighbors had discharged as Comanche agent because his overbearing attitude had alienated the chiefs. Baylor issued public statements accusing the Comanches of depredations, while Nelson, hoping to obtain Neighbors's position, began inciting the local population against the superintendent. On the night of December 27, 1858, while Agent Ross was in Waco, a band of whites slipped onto the reserve by Belknap and attacked an Indian camp. Four men and three women were killed while they slept. The Rangers identified the assailants and Ford was ordered to arrest them, but refused on the grounds that as a military officer he could not enforce the orders of a civil court. Legally he was correct, because the Rangers (technically at least) were state auxiliaries to the army, but Neighbors never forgave him. The killing of the sleeping Indians was explained away by stating that the whites simply could not distinguish between friendly Indian and hostile.

Although Governor Runnels appointed a peace commission "with power and authority to repair to said Brazos Agency and represent the State of Texas, in the peacable [sic] and lawful adjustment of said difficulties," confrontations and killings continued into the next year. The climate of violence probably was responsible, at least in part, for the increasing number of depredations in 1858 and 1859, for when raids against the Indians on the reserves stepped up, so did raids against the white settlements as the reserve Indians began to retaliate. Rangers and even federal troops from Fort Belknap were called out to protect the Indians from the whites, occasionally forcing the settlers back at gunpoint. Neighbors realized that to avoid a full-scale war, he would have to close the agencies and move his charges to Oklahoma. The relocation began on

June 11, 1859, and continued through the summer. As the Indians attempted to round up their livestock, Rangers patrolling the edge of the
reserve refused to allow them to leave to search for strays. Stock losses
during those roundups and during the trek northward left the tribes impoverished when they arrived at their new homes.

On September 1, Neighbors officially turned the Indians over to the
Wichita Agency. Upon his return to Belknap, he was gunned down on the
street. The murder infuriated the Rangers, who respected Neighbors as a
man even if they did not approve of his ideals. When his killer's body
was found out on the prairie, it was presumed the Rangers had inflicted
their own justice.[37]

NEIGHBORS WAS DEAD but Shapley Ross remained, hated by the pro-Baylor
faction for standing by his beliefs. Ross's courage and convictions carried over to his son, Lawrence Sullivan (Sul) Ross, who at twenty-one
years of age became the last great Ranger leader of antebellum Texas.
Like his father, he was faithful to any man—red or white—who stood by
him, and ferocious to any man who opposed him.

Although Sul Ross ultimately became a Confederate general, he dif-
fered from most Ranger leaders of the era by the fact that he was not a
Southerner. Born in Iowa Territory, he was not quite a year old when his
family emigrated, and so was the equally rare case of a man who had
been in Texas since infancy and knew no other home. His first experience with Indians came as a toddler when he and his father were walking
home from a neighbor's and encountered fifteen Comanche warriors.
Shapley thrust young Sul up on his back and dashed for his cabin, barely
making it to the door before a shower of arrows rained down. He was still
young when a band of Comanches caught him near the cabin. Between
his own nerve and Shapley's offer to barter part of his crop for the boy,
Sul was released after being whipped on his bare legs with arrows.

In 1845, Shapley Ross moved the family to Austin, and again in 1849
to the newly surveyed site of Waco, where they operated a farm on the
south side of the prospective town. Sul entered Baylor University, then
located in Independence, Texas, in 1856. Although Baylor provided a
reasonably good education at the time, Ross, for reasons lost to history,
transferred to Florence Wesleyan University in Alabama. Returning to
Texas on holiday in 1858, he assisted his father on the Lower Brazos
Reservation at Fort Belknap and led a group of Indian auxiliaries in an

army expedition commanded by Bvt. Maj. Earl Van Dorn against Buffalo Hump's Comanches. He and Van Dorn were both badly wounded in a fight on Otter Creek in the Indian Territory, and it was five days before he was well enough to be moved.

Eventually Ross recovered, and he graduated from Florence Wesleyan in 1859. Still weak from his wound, he spent much of the remainder of the year recovering. During that time, he adopted a little white captive girl recovered in the Otter Creek fight, whose identity could not be established. In March 1860, he joined a company of Rangers from Waco, one of several units raised on order of Governor Sam Houston in response to stepped-up Indian raids. He soon became lieutenant, and when the company captain was promoted to major, Sul Ross succeeded him.[38]

Ross distinguished himself as company commander, and Houston had further use for him after the enlistments of the Waco Rangers expired. On September 11, 1860, the governor authorized him to raise a Ranger company for service in the vicinity of Fort Belknap, known as a route toward Texas for marauding Indian bands from Oklahoma and the Plains. Resentment of his father—and by extension of him—still ran strong among the anti-Neighbors faction in the area, but he ignored it as he prepared to carry the war out onto the Plains and into the Comanche homeland.[39]

THE CASE OF the little captive girl adopted by Ross was not unusual. For more than two centuries, from the beginning of British settlement on the Atlantic seaboard, white children almost routinely had disappeared into Indian captivity. Some were later located and recovered; others were never seen again. Among those recovered, many were reunited with family members, but often the children were essentially displaced orphans. The great mystery of the era, however, was Cynthia Ann Parker, who was taken in the massacre of Parker's Fort in 1836 and whose surviving relatives never ceased looking for her.

She reportedly had been seen four years after the raid, when she was thirteen years old. According to the story, two white traders and a Delaware guide found her in a Comanche village, but the Indian family into which she was adopted refused to ransom her, and she expressed no particular interest in the whites, nor did she indicate any understanding of English. Several years later, when she was about twenty-four, she supposedly was located in a Comanche camp on the Upper Canadian River.

By that time, however, she was married with children and fully assimilated into Comanche life.[40]

Cynthia Ann Parker would have been about thirty-three in the fall of 1860, when Indian forays into the northwest frontier became especially bad. The depredations began as horse-stealing expeditions in October and culminated in a string of murder raids toward the end of November. A pregnant woman identified as "Mrs. Sherman" reportedly was tortured, raped, scalped, and left to die when the Indians rode on, creating an uproar on the frontier.

Sul Ross had been out scouting with his company when the raids occurred, and upon returning to his base he learned that local citizens had managed to trace the raiders to camps on the Pease River in northwest Texas. Faced with the prospect of attacking a large village, he asked for support from the army at Camp Cooper, and was given a twenty-one-man detachment of the Second Cavalry. The addition of a company of volunteers from Bosque County brought the total up to about 150 men.[41]

An Indian camp was located on December 18, but from that point, the record is clouded with various conflicting accounts. One Ranger on the expedition, Benjamin Franklin Gholson, recalled more than seventy years later that they located the village about daylight. It was a hunting camp and the Indians were drying meat. Gholson said that "women and children and all, there was between five and six hundred Indians," perhaps two hundred of whom were warriors under the renowned war chief Peta Nacona. Other sources place the total number of Indians as low as fifteen.[42]

The truth is probably near to the lower figure, for the whites made quick work of the camp, prompting one Ranger later to admit that he was ashamed of the fight because it amounted to killing women and children. Some, including Gholson, contend that Peta Nacona was killed, while other witnesses say they saw him very much alive years later. Whatever the case, the few prisoners included a woman with an infant girl, captured by Lt. Tom Kelliher, who nearly ruined his exhausted horse chasing them.[43] As Gholson remembered it:

> She . . . looked at [Ross] with a wild glare, and Sull [*sic*]
> hollers out to Callahaw [Kelliher], "Tom, this is a white woman!"
> Tom said, "Hell, no, that ain't no white woman!" for he was

mad, and cussing, and was an Irishman, and he said, "Damn that squaw! If I have to worry with her any more I will shoot her."

Sull contended she was a white woman and he stayed in front of her and finally laid hold of her horse's bridle.

About that time Antonio Martínez, a scout who knew the Comanches, came up, and Ross asked, "Who is she, Anton?"

"Oh, she is Nacona's wife," Martínez replied.[44]

Beyond that, the Rangers could determine nothing about her, and finally they took her to Camp Cooper and turned her over to the army, which made inquiries among white families known to be seeking missing relatives. Among those contacted was Isaac Parker, who arrived at Camp Cooper and began questioning the woman through the post interpreter. Her recollections were hazy, but, speaking Comanche, she described a childhood home that fit Parker's Fort. Parker then spoke to her in English, but she obviously did not understand him.

Finally, Parker turned to the interpreter and said, "If this is my niece, her name is Cynthia Ann."

The name caught her attention. Without waiting for the translation, she slapped herself on the chest and said, "Cynthia Ann!"[45]

Cynthia Ann Parker was restored to her family after twenty-four years of Indian captivity. The tragedy was that she had become completely Comanchefied and no longer belonged in white society. She was, in effect, more a prisoner among her own race than she had been with the Indians. If her husband was still alive, she would never see him again, nor would she see her two sons, who were growing to manhood somewhere out on the Plains. Her daughter died at the age of five, and she became indifferent to life. In 1870, her health already undermined by self-starvation, she died of influenza.[46]

Chapter 8

The Cortina War

By the late 1850s, Rangers were accustomed to fighting bandits along the Mexican border. But the depredations of Juan Nepumoceno Cortina created an entirely new situation.[1] These were no ordinary robber raids, but a carefully crafted campaign of terror and harassment by a man who carried a strong sense of personal grievance, and whose name would become familiar to the Rangers for almost two decades.

To use the word "bandit" for someone like Cortina is to invite controversy, because whether or not a person was a bandit on the Mexican border often depended on his language and ethnic origin. Border people made their own rules, and law and justice were the exclusive domain of the high and the mighty. Initially, Cortina was allied with at least some of Brownsville's power brokers of Anglo-Saxon or European origin, but after he split with them, his Mexican background made it easy to outlaw him.[2] Once Cortina was declared a bandit, however, he was not as easily suppressed as most of his Hispanic compatriots. He remained powerful and influential, with ample capacity to fight back.

Cortina was a son from the second marriage of doña María Estefana Gosceascochea de Cavazos y de Cortina, a prominent landholder and a descendant of the original Spanish settlers of the area.[3] Rip

Ford, who seems to have spent an equal amount of time either hunting Cortina or protecting him, described him as

> of medium size, with regular features, and a rather pleasing continence [*sic*]. He was rather fairer than most men of his nationality. He was fearless, self-possessed, and cunning. In some cases he has acted towards personal and political enemies with a clemency worthy of imitation. When he thought he was being pushed to the wall and in hazard of his life, he acted decisively and promptly.[4]

Cheno, as his family called him, appears to have been a prodigal son. Although his mother's other children from both marriages became well educated, he rejected schooling and was illiterate, not learning to read or write until well into middle age. He rode with the rough-and-tumble Mexican stock herders of the region, and soon was respected among them as a leader. He also had a reputation as a brawler. Nevertheless, after serving as a mule skinner during the Mexican War, he was discharged at Fort Brown with credit for faithful service. Over the next few years, he ran cattle, got into fights, and dabbled in local politics.[5]

The change of sovereignty on the Lower Rio Grande boded ill for the local Hispanic population. The rank and file were lower-class, and the Americans viewed them with undisguised contempt except at election time, when their votes were needed. Among the leading families, resentment flared when some lost their land to American squatters or in title disputes as the Spanish-Mexican property laws were replaced by those of Texas. By the summer of 1859, after thirteen years of American rule, many were ready to rise up against their English-speaking leaders. The time was ripe for reprisal, because earlier in the year, Fort Brown had been deactivated and the troops withdrawn. All they needed was someone to stand up for them. Cortina was the likely candidate. He was already under indictment for cattle theft, a charge commonly used by south Texas power brokers to rid themselves of political opponents, and was widely known for his determination.[6]

The trouble began on July 13, 1859, when Cortina shot and wounded Brownsville town marshal Robert Shears for pistol-whipping an old man named Cabrera, who had once worked for Cortina's mother. Over the next two months, Cortina and Shears exchanged recriminations, until in September Cortina decided to settle the matter by killing the marshal. He also wanted the blood of Adolphus Glaevecke, the man responsible for the indictment against him.[7]

The Cortina War broke out shortly before dawn on September 28, 1859, when Cortina led seventy-five men into town. Shouting "Viva Cheno Cortina! Mueran los gringos! Viva la República de México!"[8] they rode down Elizabeth Street, Brownsville's main thoroughfare. After taking control of the town, Cortina divided his men into squads to hunt down Glaevecke, Shears, and several others, among them William Neale and George Morris, whom Cortina contended (and a U.S. government official later agreed) had wantonly killed several Mexicans.[9] They shot Neale through the window of his home, mortally wounding him as he lay asleep. Morris was found under his house and, according to one account, killed three of Cortina's men from that hiding place. Glaevecke had taken refuge in a nearby office, where he prepared for a fight. Cortina wandered up and glanced in the window as Glaevecke drew a bead on him. But Cortina had seen nothing in his quick glance, and he moved on before Glaevecke could fire.[10]

A delegation of dignitaries from Matamoros persuaded Cortina to leave Brownsville. Once he was gone, local officials requested protection from Mexican troops, who crossed the river and occupied the city for several days until Cortina shifted into Mexico. On October 12, a sheriff's posse from Brownsville rode upriver to the Cortina ranch, where they caught his sixty-five-year-old lieutenant, Tomás Cabrera (probably the same Cabrera pistol-whipped by Marshal Shears), and brought him back to town as a prisoner. Cortina, who was in Matamoros, sent word to release Cabrera immediately or he would "lay the town in ashes, &c." That night, he recrossed the river into Texas.

A local militia unit was formed and, together with *tejano* citizens and seventy-five Mexican national guardsmen from Matamoros, started upriver. They had two cannon, one left by the army at Fort Brown and another brought by the Mexicans. The expedition left Brownsville on October 22. Two days later, Cortina ambushed the column and sent it fleeing back to Brownsville, abandoning both guns, which Cortina quickly recovered and took to his camp. Meanwhile, citizens sent a letter to the influential New Orleans *Picayune* pleading, "For God's sake, urge the government to send us relief. Let . . . the soldiers of Uncle Samuel keep marauders here in check, or practically the line of boundary between the United States and Mexico must be moved back to the Nueces."[11]

THE FIRST HELP from the outside was a company of Rangers commanded by Capt. William G. Tobin of San Antonio, who had been authorized by Governor Runnels to raise a company of one hundred men to "quell the lawlessness and bloody disturbances at the City of Brownsville." The governor's instructions were explicit:

> You will be prudent and refrain from disturbing Mexican or American Citizens or encroaching upon Mexican soil, the sole object of your mission being to arrest offenders and prevent further violent and lawless assaults upon the Citizens in that vicinity and their property.[12]

Cortina, however, intercepted the mail to Brownsville, and learning that the Rangers had been sent, made plans to ambush them. Glaevecke apparently got wind of it, for on the night of November 10, he rode out to meet them on the road and guide them into town. The Rangers, as it turned out, had more to fear from the nervous citizens of Brownsville, who fired at them with a cannon loaded with grapeshot before they were identified.

Tobin wasted no time. Cortina's planned ambush and the near-panic in Brownsville seemed to convince him that an immediate example was necessary, the governor's orders notwithstanding. The night after the Rangers arrived, Tomás Cabrera was taken from jail and lynched, and it is generally agreed that Tobin's men were responsible. In patrols of the surrounding vicinity, the company made almost as much trouble as Cortina himself; a local story holds that Tobin had one good man in his company, but that individual fell and broke his neck soon after arriving in Brownsville.[13]

Cortina lost little time retaliating. Eight days after Tobin's arrival, a detachment of thirty men was ambushed near the old Palo Alto battlefield. Three Rangers were killed, four badly wounded, and one captured. The others fled back to Brownsville. The following day, the Rangers went out to retrieve and bury the bodies; they found them mutilated and the captured Ranger dead. They continued on to Cortina's headquarters at Santa Rita but, knowing he had artillery, withdrew after making "a demonstration." This was the first of several "demonstrations" Tobin would make without actually attacking Cortina, in part because of his growing strength and in part because no one among either the Rangers or the citizens seemed sure what to do. "Tobin does well," one citizen wrote to a friend, "but has not the confidence of the men as Jack [Hays] had." The Mexicans, on the other hand, were particularly confident because the deactivation of Fort Brown and Fort Ringgold (then known as Ringgold Barracks) convinced them that the federal government had abandoned Texas.[14]

As the situation deteriorated, Brig. Gen. David E. Twiggs, commander of the Department of Texas, ordered Maj. Samuel P. Heintzelman to the Rio Grande with five officers and 117 men to investigate and report on the situation.[15]

"Cortinas [*sic*]," Heintzelman noted, "was now a great man; he had defeated the 'G[r]ingos,' and his position was impregnable; he had the Mexican flag flying in his camp, and numbers were flocking to his standard. When he visited Matamoras [*sic*] he was received as the champion of his race—as the man who would right the wrongs the Mexicans had received; that he would drive back the hated Americans to the Nueces, and some even spoke of the Sabine as the future boundary."

One problem the soldiers faced was the lack of accurate intelligence. The overbearing attitude of the Americans had earned them enemies among all classes of Mexicans, and although Cortina's movements were well known in Matamoros, "we were answered with vague and exaggerated accounts." Even Americans who had lived in the area for years and were married to Mexican women, a situation that usually would make them privy to anything, could not get reliable information.

Under normal circumstances, Rangers would fill in the gap by scouting and observing, but Heintzelman, who did not care for Rangers in the first place, found them virtually useless. The Rangers, he noted in his diary, were on the verge of mutiny, and Tobin seemed to have little control over them. Tobin placed himself under the major's command, and Heintzelman asked him to reconnoiter Cortina's position. He later commented in his official report, "Several went, but none of them ever got near enough to give me any information."[16]

IN THE ABSENCE of reliable information, hearsay abounded. In Austin it was reported that Cortina had burned Corpus Christi. The legislature was in session, and when former Ranger Rip Ford ran into Gen. Forbes Britton, Corpus Christi's senator, on Congress Avenue, he found Britton "uneasy, if nothing more." Ford discounted the rumor and had nearly succeeded in calming the senator when Governor Runnels strolled up. With the governor present, Britton went into near-hysterics and, as Ford recalled,

> portrayed the conditions of things at Corpus Christi: the town sacked by a dissolute crowd of barbarous marauders, the houses burned to the ground, his family depending for the necessities of life upon the charities of a cold world. The general's eyes danced wildly in their sockets, his chin trembled, and his voice quivered with emotion.

Runnels turned to Ford and said, "Ford you must go; you must start tonight, and move swiftly."

Knowing full well that Cortina was nowhere within a hundred miles of Corpus Christi, Ford nevertheless agreed, although he personally believed that Britton "either felt very intensely on the subject, or he was a first class actor. Opinion leaned rather in the latter direction."

Regardless of his feelings about Britton's histrionics, Ford realized that a Cortina raid on Corpus Christi was not impossible, and he immediately began preparing for the mission. He contacted S. B. Highsmith, one of his old lieutenants, "begging him in the name of old companionship to enlist his men and move at once without waiting for further orders." On November 17, the governor commissioned Ford a lieutenant colonel, giving him command of the state troops, including Tobin's men and Ranger companies raised in other counties, with authority to purchase provisions and mules. The governor, however, had violated tradition by designating Ford as a lieutenant colonel, because during the years since Jack Hays, militia and Rangers had become accustomed to electing officers. Consequently, he modified the order, reducing Ford to major and throwing the command open to election. That suited Ford; he knew his men and believed he would have a better chance at leading them if they believed it was their idea.[17]

On November 18, Ford left Austin with eight men, picking up more on the road to Goliad, where he made arrangements with local community leaders to underwrite the expedition pending appropriation of funds by the state. At Banquete, twenty-five miles west of Corpus Christi, they were joined by Highsmith and the main force, bringing the command to fifty-three. "They were quite well armed, mounted on serviceable horses, and gave evidence of possessing good fighting qualities," Ford observed.

About December 1, the detachment reached King Ranch, established several years before by Capt. Richard King, who, together with Mifflin Kenedy, operated a steamboat line between Point Isabel and Roma via Brownsville. From there they started on the 125-mile trek almost due south to Brownsville.

Ford struck the Rio Grande at Los Indios, about twenty-five miles upriver from Brownsville. As they neared the river, they saw smoke signals "and felt assured we were closely watched by Cortina's spies." That night, they camped in a circle with their horses and mules inside and sentinels beyond the perimeter. The company elected Joseph Walker captain, William H. Fry first lieutenant, and William Howard second lieutenant.[18]

MAJOR HEINTZELMAN, MEANWHILE, marched out of Brownsville on December 14, with 165 soldiers, including artillerymen, and 120 Rangers. He intended to attack one of Cortina's camps at Ebonal Ranch, a few miles north of town, where his men may have been waiting to intercept Ford. Less than two miles from Cortina's position, the major asked the Rangers to make a reconnaissance, but they were "so thoroughly stampeded" that they agreed to go only after Judge Edmund J. Davis offered to accompany them. Cortina's entrenchments and breastworks, as it turned out, had been abandoned for about a week. Heintzelman ordered a road cleared around the obstructions and continued the march. About three miles farther, the column was marching through a dense grove of ebony when the soldiers saw several men gathered around a flag a few hundred yards ahead. At that moment, a cannon fired and the shot fell onto the road.

Heintzelman ordered his artillery into position and returned fire. "The rangers seeing with how much coolness the regular troops stood off the fire of the enemy regained confidence, and were finally enduced to attack," he reported.

The position, which proved to be one of Cortina's main camps, was overrun and arms and provisions were captured. The soldiers and Rangers chased the Cortinistas about two more miles through dense brush before finally breaking off and returning to the column. Heintzelman estimated there had been about sixty men in the camp, although Cortina himself was not present. The bodies of six Cortinistas were found. One Ranger was mortally wounded and two American artillerymen slightly wounded. Cortina had suffered his first setback, although he also showed that he was prepared to fire on United States regular troops, something that, until now, no one had believed he would dare.[19]

Elsewhere, Ford heard the artillery and, unfamiliar with the immediate terrain, presumed Brownsville to be under attack. Galloping into town, the Rangers were met by a citizens' company formed by Mifflin Kenedy, who directed them back toward Heintzelman's column. They reached the scene of the fight, where the major was resting his men and animals. The soldiers and Rangers camped at Ebonal that night, and were caught in a heavy rain that ruined the paper cartridges for their firearms. The following morning, they heard Cortina's bugles but, finding most of their ammunition virtually useless, decided against attacking "an enemy fully prepared and occupying a position chosen by himself."

After trying unsuccessfully to lure Cortina into attacking the column, the soldiers and Rangers returned to Brownsville. During the march, the Rangers set fire to several houses along the road until Heintzelman issued a directive forbidding any more burning without his express order. "This sets a very bad example to Cortinas [sic] & the Rangers were burning all—friends and foes," he commented.[20]

DESPITE THE SETBACK, Cortina could no longer be regarded simply as a border bandit. He now had some four or five hundred men under his command, and his depredations had assumed the character of an insurrection. General Twiggs in San Antonio reacted accordingly. On December 16, he ordered two companies of cavalry, a light battery of artillery, and four companies of infantry to the Rio Grande. He was none too soon, because Cortina was expanding his operations farther up the river, raiding ranches and burning and sacking houses as he went. "The inhabitants had fled for their lives," Ford noted. "Cortina had committed these outrages upon citizens of the United States regardless of race and upon Mexicans suspected of being friendly to Americans."

Heintzelman was hard on his trail, but the elusive chieftain always seemed to manage to stay just ahead of him. The major was also having trouble with the Rangers, who were squabbling among themselves. Governor Runnels had instructed Ford upon his arrival in Brownsville to hold elections for major of the Ranger battalion, but Heintzelman hoped it could be forestalled. Both Ford and Tobin were under his command, and he had little patience with Ranger politics. All mounted units were needed as scouts in the field, and there was no time for elections. Privately, Heintzelman also wanted to give Ford time to build support and win the election.

"He is by all odds the better man," the major confided to his diary. "He controls his men & Tobin is controlled by his. I would rather have Ford with 50 men than Tobin with all his men."

Heintzelman had ample reason to resent Tobin, because his men committed atrocities against the local population that undoubtedly prompted many to join the Cortinistas. In one instance, an army patrol discovered the body of a loyal and respected *tejano* who had been lynched. Tobin later admitted some of his men were responsible.[21]

ON CHRISTMAS DAY, the soldiers and Rangers arrived in Edinburg, some sixty miles upriver from Brownsville, to find Cortina had departed after robbing the customs house, post office, and other government buildings. The next day, Heintzelman learned Cortina was occupying Fort Ringgold and the adjacent town of Rio Grande City, about fifty miles beyond Edinburg. He decided to surprise Cortina by a forced night march. Because the road was in full view of the Mexican side of the river, the soldiers moved out according to their usual routine during the day, and went into camp at their regular time at Las Cuevas Ranch, about eighteen miles below Rio Grande City. After dark, Heintzelmen called the army and Ranger commanders together and told the Rangers to circle around Rio Grande City and block the road upriver to Roma, while the troops attacked from the front. They would hit Cortina at daylight.

"You must be extremely cautious," he said. "Do not stir up Cortina tonight."[22]

The command moved out at midnight, with orders for complete silence. Ford had ninety Rangers, many of whom were veterans of his earlier campaigns. They were accompanied by Henry Clay Davis, the developer of Rio Grande City, who was familiar with the countryside, and James B. McClusky, the former post trader at Ford Ringgold. After about an hour's slow ride, the Rangers' guide spotted a party of men ahead and issued the Mexican challenge, *"Quién vive?"* A shot rang out in reply, and the guide returned fire. The Rangers charged and drove the strangers into the brush. They surmised it was a Cortinista scouting party, but Davis discounted them as a possible threat. Now that the Rangers had seen them, the Cortinistas would not dare take the road back to Rio Grande City, and it would be impossible for them to make their way back through the brush at night.[23]

About an hour before daylight, the column was within three miles of Rio Grande City. Davis suggested the Rangers halt about a mile and a half short of Fort Ringgold, at the home of a Mexican friend who would have reliable information. As they approached, they passed several houses, and some of the Rangers fluent in Spanish stopped and assured early risers that they were reinforcements for Cortina. Davis's Mexican friend advised that Cortina was camped on the main street of Rio Grande City, with his line thrown across the town from the river to a hill over-looking the town. With his flanks secured by the terrain, the Rangers would be unable to circle around, and the command could only approach on the plain in front of Fort Ringgold. The Texans also learned Cortina's forces were stronger than they originally had believed. Ford threw up a picket across the road less than two hundred yards from Cortina's line and rested his men while they waited for Heintzelman. The Rangers, ac-customed to grabbing whatever sleep they could in the field, wrapped their horses' reins around one arm and dozed off on the cold, bare ground.

Heintzelman, meanwhile, had sent Tobin with two companies in ad-vance of his right. Not familiar with the layout of the town, he planned to give the Rangers half an hour to circle around behind, after which the regulars would attack with artillery cover. What happened next is uncer-tain. In his memoirs, Ford wrote that upon hearing Heintzelman's ar-tillery carriages approaching, he rode up to the column and made a verbal report of the situation, which the exhausted major only vaguely understood. He said that he suggested continuing the effort to turn Cortina's left flank on the hill, and Heintzelman agreed. Heintzelman, however, reported that his column had just reached Fort Ringgold when a Ranger rode up and reported that Ford, supported by Ranger companies under Tobin, Capt. Peter Tumlinson, and Capt. Wade Hampton, had at-tacked Cortina's line from the front.[24]

Ford moved up the road and attacked the picket line, driving it back and meeting a Cortinista scouting party in Ringgold just as the sun was coming up. The daylight did little good, because a heavy winter fog had set in. Nevertheless, the Rangers fired into the Cortinistas, forcing them into town. Here the Rangers were met with gunfire from the housetops, which Ford called "ineffective" and Heintzelman said was "a vigorous resistance." The Rangers gained the hill overlooking the town. To the right toward the river was the cemetery, and beyond, the Roma Road. Believing that Heintzelman would arrive at any moment with artillery, Ford sent Tobin to attack Cortina's left at the cemetery and gain the Roma Road. While Tobin was busy with the left flank, Ford moved against the right, down by the river where Cortina had his artillery. Because of the dense fog, Ford was within two hundred yards before he knew where the guns were. Cortina's gunners opened fire.

Elsewhere, everything was going wrong. Tobin, for some reason, did not attack the cemetery, allowing the Cortinistas to turn all their attentions on Ford and retake the guns. Heintzelman, meanwhile, had overrun Cortina's camp, forcing him to abandon provisions, a baggage cart, and half-cooked meals, but his men were too exhausted from their long night march to push on, and many of the Cortinistas took advantage of the fog to escape into the brush.

Ford sent Lieutenant Fry with a small detachment of mounted riflemen "to pay his respects entirely to the [Cortinista] artillerymen." Fry's Rangers rode up to within forty yards of the guns and opened fire, and the Cortinistas moved out to meet them. "The opposing forces were within a few yards of each other," Ford remembered. "The very heavy fog rendered it difficult to distinguish a Mexican from an American at the distance of twenty yards."

The guns were silenced, but the Cortinistas made a mounted charge, and Ford ordered his men to take their horses into the brush. About that time, Tobin came up and the charge was thrown back, but the Cortinistas had taken advantage of the confusion to carry off their cannon. About this time, Heintzelmen arrived and found the Ranger companies "all broken up, and strewed along the road, with most of their officers in advance." He caught up with Ford and told him to push on because "our victory would not be complete if they succeeded in carrying off their guns."

After a chase of about nine miles, the Cortinistas were forced to abandon the guns. The Rangers found cartridges filled with grape and canister, with buckshot stuffed in between. They also had solid cartridges with slugs of iron.

Heintzelman was pleased. "The defeat was complete," he reported. "We captured [Cortina's] guns, ammunition and baggage carts, provisions, everything he could throw away to lighten his flight, and entirely dispersed his force." Sixteen Rangers were wounded, most of whom were caught in a single blast of grapeshot from Cortina's guns. Three were listed as "severe," and the others were only slightly wounded. Ford himself reported "two contusions from grapeshot." Heintzelman estimated Cortina had lost about sixty killed in the fight or drowned trying to cross the river, although Ford later heard from Mexicans that the number might have been as high as two hundred. Cortina himself escaped into Mexico, and reappeared opposite Roma, about eighteen miles upriver, threatening to burn the town. A detachment of troops under Capt. George Stoneman was sent to protect Roma. One company of artillery was detailed to Fort Ringgold, and two companies of artillery were sent downriver to garrison Fort Brown. Heintzelman urged the War Department to regarrison the military posts from Fort Duncan at Eagle Pass on down to Fort Brown.[25]

WITH CORTINA NEUTRALIZED for the time being, the Rangers again fell to quarreling among themselves. There was no reason to further postpone the long-delayed election for battalion major, and Ford had no choice but to call it. Tobin's own correspondence indicates a certain amount of resentment at the delay, and Ford later accused him of "working more to secure his election than to assure the success of the operations." Additionally, Lt. John Littleton's only chance for election to captain would come if Tobin replaced Ford as major, and he was working to undercut Ford. Pete Tumlinson felt Rangers should be allowed full freedom of action, particularly in a fight, and resented the discipline Ford imposed. Tobin was elected major, and Littleton received his captaincy. The men of Joe Walker's company refused to serve under Tobin, and he ordered them mustered out along with the companies of Wade Hampton and a captain named Herron.

Heintzelman, who was busy trying to organize the defense of the Rio Grande frontier on the 150-mile stretch between Roma and Brownsville, was disgusted by the whole affair, maintaining that Ranger squabbling "created much embarrassment and delay." The election of Tobin particularly infuriated him because, only a day before, there had been another lynching, and the Rangers were killing all the dogs and chickens in Rio Grande City and the surrounding ranches. "If he dont [sic] keep better order & do something I will write to the Governor to have the Rangers recalled," he remarked in his diary. "They are doing no service and only bringing disgrace upon the country."[26]

Whatever differences they might have had, Ford and Tobin both realized that the Cortina War was far from over. Shortly after the December
14 fight at Ebonal, Tobin had reported to Governor Runnels that the
heavy, thorny brush worked to the advantage of the Cortinistas, and
added, "the numbers, skill, and courage of the marauders have been
greatly underrated." Cortina, he said, preferred hit-and-run attacks, was
familiar with paths through the brush, and his men wore heavy leather
clothing "which enables them to traverse the woods without a scratch
while we in following bleed at every pore." Consequently, he said, the
capture or destruction of Cortina's band would be "the work of time."[27]

Ford was in complete accord. He warned Governor Sam Houston,
who had succeeded Runnels in late December, not to consider the fight
at Rio Grande City as the end of the Cortina trouble.

> The defeat and dispersion of Cortinistas' [*sic*] troops will change
> the character of operations. In small parties they will now beset the
> roads, wage a guerrilla warfare and murder and plunder. . . . It is
> probable they will return to the neighborhood of Brownsville and
> levy blackmail on all the defenseless they may fall in with.[28]

For the time being, however, the Rangers were too divided among
themselves to be of any value against Cortina. Ford traveled with
Walker's company back to Brownsville, where they intended to take their
discharges and go home. Heintzelman, meanwhile, tried to distribute the
Rangers along the river in small parties to prevent the Cortinistas from
reorganizing. Despite assurances of mutual cooperation, however, Tobin
did not appear inclined to carry out his orders.[29]

Tobin had little time to enjoy his new position or create further problems for the military. Two state commissioners, Angel Navarro and
Robert H. Taylor, had arrived in Brownsville under instructions from
Houston to investigate the entire Cortina affair and take whatever action
they deemed appropriate. They found the Rangers under Tobin "without
organization, muster-rolls, or anything like discipline." In fact, the commissioners soon learned that Tobin was more unpopular in some quarters
than Cortina. Businessman and rancher F. M. Campbell had firsthand experience with both, having been held prisoner by Cortina for about ten
days in Rio Grande City, while Tobin and his men requisitioned his ranch
near Brownsville for headquarters without compensation. In filing a

claim for damages, Campbell commented, "I estimate the value of the property taken by Cortinas as fully two hundred dollars, and the value of property destroyed by Tobin's command at fully one thousand dollars."

After sacking Tobin, Taylor and Navarro named Ford senior officer on the Rio Grande "under instructions from the United States officer commanding that frontier."[30] Heintzelman himself believed the two Ranger companies then forming under Ford and Littleton would be adequate. He noted that the one unit of federal cavalry at his disposal was inadequate. Besides, as a federal officer, he was not empowered to take these troops across the Rio Grande into Mexico, which would "make it exceedingly difficult to give protection, unless the troops are authorized to occupy the opposite side of the river."

It is hard to imagine why Heintzelman would discuss the limitations of federal troops in the same paragraph as his need of Rangers unless he was hinting that the Rangers could cross into Mexico whereas his own men could not. Whatever his reasoning, Navarro and Taylor were prompt to accommodate; the same day, February 2, they instructed Ford that henceforth "your movements and the troops under your command will be directed by Major Heintzelman, or other commanding officer of the U.S. army on this frontier."[31]

WHILE THE BUREAUCRATS, soldiers, and Rangers worked out authority, the steamer *Ranchero* was heading downriver from Rio Grande City, shadowed along the bank by Major Tobin's Rangers, who were returning to Brownsville for their discharges. River traffic had come to a complete halt since the outbreak of the Cortina War, and this was the boat's first trip since September. The value of the accumulated cargo was estimated at $200,000. Cortina was camped about thirty-five miles upriver from Brownsville, on the Mexican side at a place called La Bolsa ("the Purse"), so named because the river looped back on itself, forming a bend that Mexicans compare to a leather purse and the Americans call a horseshoe. He knew the steamer was coming, and his camp was alive with talk about taking it.

Ford had left Brownsville on February 1, with two companies of Rangers and the federal cavalry under Captain Stoneman. The cavalry took the road upriver with the wagons while the Rangers worked the bends in the river, meeting that night at a predetermined campsite. The next day, Ford and a small group stopped by the Cortina ranch for a social call on the aging dõna María Estefana, Cheno's mother, one of those courtesies of border warfare that was always remembered whenever the guerrilla chief was in a position to help the Ranger's family.

Two days later, on February 4, the wagons and pack mules arrived at Zacatal Ranch, just opposite La Bolsa, at about 1 P.M., when the guard detail under Cpl. Milton A. Duty spotted about thirty armed Cortinistas crossing the river with stolen horses and other plunder. The guards opened fire, forcing the Cortinistas to abandon most of the horses and plunder, and a fusillade opened up from the Mexican side. The Rangers retreated back to their wagons without suffering any injury. At that moment, Tobin's company rode up and fighting broke out again. Ranger Fountain B. Woodruff was mortally wounded and handed his revolver to a friend, saying, "Take it. I shall never be able to use it again."

The two sides were exchanging gunfire across the river when the *Ranchero* arrived and entered the narrow bend at La Bolsa. Everyone's attention turned to the steamer, and the Cortinistas opened fire. The boat carried a detachment of soldiers under Lt. Loomis Langdon, and manning the two artillery pieces captured from Cortina in Rio Grande City, they drove the Cortinistas back into the brush. The *Ranchero* was safe for the time being, but could not round the bend without more support.[32]

A courier reached Ford, who came on the scene with the main body of Rangers. Cortina's men had occupied a group of houses, fence lines, and undergrowth, giving them cover to take the steamer as it emerged from the bend. Here the river was only 150 yards bank to bank. As Ford looked over the situation, Lieutenant Langdon asked, "Captain, are you going to cross into Mexico?"

"Certainly, sir," Ford replied,[33] then penned a note to Major Heintzelman:

> There is a numerous force lying in wait along the river on the Mexican side to capture the boat, or at least attempt it. I do not think that it is practicable to protect the steamer with forces on one side of the river only. I shall pass over this evening afoot, and beat the bush in the neighborhood. To-morrow morning I will pass over my horses, and, with the whole force under my command, go down upon the Mexican side, keeping as near as possible even pace with the boat. I would suggest that you detach a force to come up on the Texas side to escort her down. I think

that by this co-operation only can the life and property on her be secured.

The note passed through Stoneman's camp downriver, and upon examining it, he forwarded it on to Heintzelman with the addendum "I leave here immediately for . . . wherever the boat may be. I shall not cross the river without instructions, except to repel an attack on the boat."[34]

Back at La Bolsa, it began to appear that the two-day operation imagined by Ford would not be necessary. Tobin and Pete Tumlinson took ten Rangers across the river and scouted Cortina's position. Ford followed with another thirty-five Rangers and met Tobin as he was returning to the steamer.

"We found nobody," Tobin remarked, "they have gone."

Ford observed that Cortina had probably shifted the bulk of his forces to strengthen his weak points. "I do not think they have gone," he said. "I see a large number near the houses and behind the fence."

The Rangers formed in line and hit Cortina's right flank, gaining the riverbank and using it for cover. From here they could work around the Cortinistas, forcing them to keep their horsemen under cover. The Mexicans poured fire on the Ranger lines, while the Texans, under orders to save ammunition, fired slowly with deliberate aim. When someone remarked on the heavy Cortinista fire, Ford replied, "Don't mind that. They will soon need the ammunition they are wasting."

The *Ranchero* began moving into the bend so that Langdon could use the artillery, while a lieutenant took a lance corporal and a detail of soldiers from the steamer to the U.S. bank and fired across the river into Cortina's camp. The Cortinista cavalry, meanwhile, had abandoned its position, and the Rangers moved in on foot to fill the gap. Gaining the Cortinista palisade, the Texans rushed the defenders, scattering them.

"Cortina was the last to leave the field," Ford remembered. "He faced his pursuers, emptied his revolver, and tried to halt his panic-stricken men. . . . One shot struck the cantle of his saddle, one cut a lock of hair from his head, a third cut his bridle rein, a fourth passed through his horse's ear, and a fifth struck his belt. He galloped off unhurt."[35]

THE ATTACK ON the steamer was the last major fight of the Cortina War. The Mexican government, beset with far more serious internal problems, found this border conflict with the United States embarrassing and directed its authorities along the Rio Grande to assist in breaking up Cortina's band and others like it. On February 5, Heintzelman sent a note to Gen. Guadalupe García in Matamoros, formally notifying him that Ford had found it necessary to cross into Mexican territory and politely but firmly inquiring as to when his troops would be available to police the Mexican side of the river.[36]

Lest General García believe Heintzelman and Ford were acting alone, a more prominent soldier soon arrived on the Rio Grande to reiterate the United States position. In San Antonio, illness forced General Twiggs to take extended leave, and on February 20, Bvt. Col. Robert E. Lee assumed temporary command of the department, with orders to use all the troops he could spare and bring the Cortina War to a close.[37]

Lee departed San Antonio for the Rio Grande on March 15. After checking Fort Duncan at Eagle Pass and Fort McIntosh at Laredo, he arrived at Fort Ringgold, where he sent a letter to Tamaulipas governor Andrés Trevino, notifying him that Mexican authorities would be held responsible for failure to break up any bands of outlaws taking refuge in that country. At Edinburg, he notified authorities in Reynosa that he expected known Cortinistas to be expelled from the city. It had the desired effect. From there, Lee continued on toward Brownsville, noting in his diary that "nearly all the ranches on the road have been burned—those spared by Cortinas [*sic*] burned by the Rangers."[38]

EARLY DEFENDERS OF A RUGGED LAND

Stephen S. Austin was the father of American colonization in Texas. By combining the minuteman ranger concept of the southeastern United States with the existing Spanish-Mexican frontier militia system, he helped create a uniquely Texan institution.

Edward Burleson was a competent commander of the early volunteer Rangers, but his shoot-first-ask-questions-later attitude toward Indians helped spark a general uprising in 1836.

Sam Houston greatly influenced the development of the Rangers, first as president of independent Texas and later as governor of the state.

Those who knew Capt. John Coffee Hays by reputation alone were startled when they first met him. Young and small, with boyish features, Hays nevertheless was a superb leader and outstanding frontiersman. His Rangers, many of whom were older than he, respectfully called him "Captain Jack."

GLORY AND INFAMY IN THE MEXICAN WAR

Gen. Zachary Taylor, commander of U.S. forces in northern Mexico, appreciated the Rangers as scouts and fighters but detested them for their tendencies to murder and plunder.

Capt. Samuel H. Walker, shown here in the uniform of the U.S. Mounted Rifles, introduced the first specifically military revolver, based on his experiences as a Ranger. Walker's reputation helped make the Rangers famous throughout the United States.

INDIAN FIGHTS AND BORDER RAIDS

Affectionately known as "Sul," Capt. Lawrence Sullivan Ross was one of the most intellectually gifted Rangers. A noted Indian fighter, he also served as a Confederate general, member of the committee that drafted the present state constitution, governor of Texas, and president of Texas A&M. Sul Ross State University in Alpine was named in his honor.

A Tonkawa chief known variously as "Johnson" and "Charley Johnson" typified the friendly Indians who scouted for Rangers and soldiers against their ancient enemies, the Comanches, from the 1830s through the 1870s. He holds one of the early cap and ball Colt's, probably the Army model.

Capt. John Salmon Ford, shown here later in life, served under Jack Hays in the Mexican War and later gained fame for pacifying the Lower Rio Grande frontier.

An old man with a young wife in this photo, Juan N. Cortina still shows the stubborn determination that made him the terror of the Texas-Mexico border for more than two decades.

CONFEDERATE RANGERS

Capt. Ben McCulloch gained fame fighting for the Republic of Texas and, later, during the Mexican War. After trying his luck in California during the Gold Rush, he returned to Texas on the eve of the Civil War and was instrumental in organizing the state's defense following secession.

The Alamo, then a U.S. military installation, flies the Texas flag after its surrender to Ben McCulloch's Rangers in 1861. The drawing erroneously depicts the white bar as at the bottom of the flag.

A TEXAN RANGER.

We publish above a sketch, by one of our most reliable artists, of a TEXAN RANGER. A gentleman, just from Richmond, gave the following account of these redoubtable warriors:

Ben M'Cullough's Texan Rangers are described as a desperate set of fellows. They number one thousand half savages, each of whom is mounted upon a mustang horse. Each is armed with a pair of Colt's navy revolvers, a rifle, a tomahawk, a Texan bowie-knife, and a lasso. They are described as being very dexterous in the use of the latter. These men are to be pitted against Wilson's Zouaves and M'Mullin's Rangers.

"A Texan Ranger," an unidentified newspaper clipping that satirizes McCulloch's Rangers. The tone indicates it probably came from a Union-held border state early in the Civil War. Even so, the description of Ranger equipment is detailed and accurate.

THE FRONTIER BATTALION

Reconstruction governor Edmund J. Davis is often accused of abolishing the Rangers and replacing them with a state police to enforce federal edicts. Ironically, he worried about Indian depredations and authorized Ranger companies to deal with them. His state police demonstrated the need for a permanent constabulary, which led to the creation of the Ranger Frontier Battalion.

John B. Jones elevated Ranger command to strategic levels in policing the state, first as commander of the Frontier Battalion, then as adjutant general.

Captain J. B. Gillett, Texas Ranger, mounted on "Dusty," in 1879, who says: "Original picture was taken on tin-type, which made it appear backwards." It is here reversed to show gun and pistol on his right side, as he actually wore them. (• • by N.H.Rose)

A portrait of Sgt. James B. Gillett shows him with field equipment, including Winchester rifle, Colt's revolver, and two sheath knives.

Heavily armed Rangers of Capt. Dan Roberts's company gather for a meal near Fort McKavett in west Texas in the 1880s.

THE WAR AGAINST BADMEN

The frail, tubercular Capt. Leander H. McNelly spent the last two years of his life trying to control blood feuds and border stock raids in south Texas.

John Wesley Hardin
Copyrighted by N.H. Rose

John Wesley Hardin's long string of killings made him the object of a manhunt that took Texas Rangers all the way to Florida.

Sgt. John Barkley Armstrong
captured John Wesley Hardin
and returned him to Texas.

At the height of their often
ludicrous careers as badmen,
Sam Bass (*standing, left*) and
three members of his gang took
time for this studio photograph.
Others include (*seated, left to
right*) Joe and Joel Collins and
(*standing, right*) J. E. Gardner.

KING FISHER,

JOHN H. CULP

From old tin type made 1873.

Badman John King Fisher (*left*) poses with friend John H. Culp in a tintype made in 1873. Note the heavy Smith & Wesson No. 3 revolver across Culp's leg. Introduced in 1870, the Smith & Wesson No. 3 was the first practical heavy-caliber cartridge revolver and as such was the weapon of choice until Colt's responded with the Single Action Army, or "Peacemaker," in 1873. Even after the advent of the Colt, the Smith & Wesson remained popular on the frontier.

DAN STUART'S FISTIC CARNIVAL

Fight promoter Dan Stuart planned to stage a world heavyweight championship bout in Texas, despite growing opposition to prizefighting.

The youthful governor, Charles Culberson, matched Stuart in determination and was intent on stopping the fight.

PICK THE WINNER OF THE BIG FIGHT.

A New York cartoonist's view of a Texas Ranger holding Fitzsimmons and Maher apart at gunpoint with revolvers that look suspiciously like the heavy Colt's Walker model.

The state flexed its muscles by sending every available Ranger to El Paso to stop the fight. While there, they posed for this group photo, which included (*front, left to right*) Adjutant General W. H. Mabry and the four Ranger captains, John R. Hughes, J. A. Brooks, William J. McDonald, and J. M. Rogers.

Judge Roy Bean (*center, with white beard*) stands with friends in front of the Jersey Lilly Saloon, which served as his courthouse. If there was a way to get around the law and hold the fight, the shifty old judge would find it.

REVOLUTION ON THE RIO GRANDE

Capt. Monroe Fox and two Rangers drag the bodies of radical leader Luis de la Rosa's men, who had been killed in a fight at Norias during the border disturbances that accompanied the Mexican Revolution of 1910–1917. Fox desecrated corpses as a terror tactic against bandits and revolutionaries but succeeded only in alienating much of the staunchly Catholic *tejano* community.

The destruction of a train by radicals at Olmito resulted in the Rangers killing innocent people.

HOLLYWOOD AND THE RANGERS

Good luck always
The Lone Ranger
& Tonto

The entertainment world's most durable Ranger is the Lone Ranger (*left*), portrayed by Clayton Moore in this giveaway premium photograph from the 1950s. According to the storyline, he was the sole survivor of a company of Texas Rangers ambushed and massacred by badmen.

Actor Joel McCrea portrays Ranger Jace Pearson on the cover of a Dell comic book based on the radio and television series *Tales of the Texas Rangers*. Although the programs were based on actual cases, the comic-book plots were imaginary.

Chapter 9

Confederate Frontier

Soon after his encounter with Ranger methods on the Rio Grande, Robert E. Lee was assigned to command Fort Mason, forty miles northwest of Fredericksburg. Lee found secession sentiment to be strong, not only because of the Texans' Southern ties, but because they believed the federal government was indifferent to Indian raids on the frontier. The weaknesses were twofold, one being the Kiowa and Comanche range along the north-south line between the Red and Nueces rivers and the other along the Rio Grande, where, in addition to Cortina's assaults, citizens had to contend with depredations from Indians who took refuge in Mexico.[1]

The situation along the Rio Grande, however, was far less serious than that along the north-south line. Raids were particularly bad in the vicinity of Fort Belknap, where, despite assurances by John R. Baylor and his adherents that peace would reign once the agencies were closed and the Indians removed, the situation was worse than ever. Some blamed the situation on the murder of Robert Simpson Neighbors, who, it was belatedly realized, had exercised a calming influence on the tribes. And there were those who contended the Neighbors assassination had alienated the federal government to Texas's Indian problems. Conditions around Belknap and Camp Cooper were aggravated by "some white men around the agencies," who were encouraging the Indian raids and profiting from the plunder.[2]

In response, Governor Houston ordered the organization of a new Ranger battalion in the region, with orders to treat "every Indian caught this side of Red River as an enemy to Texas." Col. William C. Dalrymple was placed in overall command on the frontier and established his headquarters at the Clear Fork of the Brazos River about midway between the old Camp Cooper and Fort Belknap Indian reservations. He tightened discipline among existing Ranger units, prohibiting horse racing, gambling, and liquor in the camps, and positioned the six companies of his battalion on a north-south line of defense with his headquarters in the center. Scouting parties were constantly in the field, and a special "Indian Spy Company" consisting primarily of Tonkawas under Sul Ross's brother Peter Fulkerson Ross was attached to the battalion.[3]

WHILE DALRYMPLE WORKED to establish a frontier line of defense, secession sentiment was growing. A state convention had been called to consider the issue, and rumors reached San Antonio that Baylor was organizing a thousand men for a "buffalo hunt." Because he was a known secessionist, locals believed this was a pretense to assemble enough men to seize the federal arsenal. General Twiggs, who had recovered from his illness, called up several state militia companies to strengthen the force around San Antonio. These, however, were soon disbanded, and local Unionists began questioning the Southern-born Twiggs's own loyalty.

On February 1, 1861, the convention adopted a resolution declaring Texas a sovereign state. The resolution was submitted for a public referendum set for February 23. Houston reminded the legislature that the withdrawal of federal troops would leave the frontier completely exposed, and in response, the state ordered all frontier counties to form minuteman Ranger companies not to exceed forty men each. Each man was expected "to keep himself furnished with a suitable horse, gun [i.e., rifle], [Colt's] navy revolver, at least one hundred rounds of ammunition, ten days' provisions, and all necessary equipments, to be ready at any moment when called on to take the field." The legislature appropriated $25,000 to supply Colonel Dalrymple.

The Secession Convention appointed a Committee of Public Safety to take over U.S. military installations from federal troops, secure public property on the posts before it was destroyed, and assume responsibility for frontier defense. McCulloch was designated to command the state military forces around San Antonio and assume control of military installations there. His brother Henry McCulloch, who had earned a reputation as a Ranger leader in his own right, was placed in charge of forces on the northwest frontier, and Rip Ford was named commander of the forces on the Rio Grande. Henry McCulloch was also to take possession of federal posts on the frontier.[4]

On the morning of February 16, Ben McCulloch led over a thousand state troops and Rangers into the city and demanded the surrender of all public property. As one Unionist remarked, "Captain Baylor's buffalo-hunt had at last assumed a tangible shape." Faced with this force and swayed, no doubt, by his own loyalties, Twiggs assented and sent a general order to all commanding officers in Texas to evacuate their garrisons and prepare to leave the state.[5]

Robert E. Lee arrived in San Antonio the afternoon of February 16, en route from Fort Mason to Washington, where he had been ordered to confer with General Scott. As he came into town, he was surrounded by Rangers. Caroline Darrow, a Union sympathizer, went to meet him and advised him the secessionists controlled the city. Lee, who at that juncture was still a federal officer, eventually was paroled and allowed to continue his journey.

Secession now was a foregone conclusion, and the Rangers were barely controllable. Mrs. Darrow remembered:

> During the next two days the Rangers were drinking and shouting about the streets, recklessly shooting any one who happened to displease them. From this time on, Union men were in danger, and Northerners sent their families away. Some who were outspoken were imprisoned and barely escaped with their lives; among them, Charles Anderson, brother of Robert Anderson [the Union defender of Fort Sumter].[6]

In the confusion, Ranger officers in the field began receiving conflicting orders. Lt. Buck Barry had spent most of January scouting for Indians. Upon returning to his main camp, he gave his men five days' furlough and returned home. Here he found an order from Houston countermanding any further scouts, and another order from the Committee of Public Safety instructing him to raise a hundred men to assist in taking control of federal frontier forts.

> Thus I found myself with two commissions, from two governments, without a precedent to be governed by. But the only con-

clusion I could arrive at was to stand by the voice of the people of Texas, who had voted by a large majority to secede. So I paraded my old company and explained the whole proceedings of the convention to them and told them that they were discharged. But I told them that if they wanted to they could help make up the company the convention had commissioned me to raise. About half of my old company went home as they said they did not care to fight their own government, and the other half stayed with me.[7]

One by one the military posts in Texas surrendered. Although some military commanders disabled equipment to keep the state forces from using it, there was little inclination to resist except at Camp Cooper, where Capt. S. D. Carpenter of the First Infantry put his troops on notice that he intended to defend the post.[8]

That done, Carpenter sent a letter "to the Commanding Officer of the State Troops of Texas, and other armed bodies of citizens, encamped in the vicinity of this post." In it he said he had been advised of "a hostile movement against this camp" and demanded to know the state's intentions. On February 18, Colonel Dalrymple replied that within twenty-four hours he would demand surrender of the post.

Carpenter was fully aware that Fort Sumter, South Carolina, and Fort Pickens, Florida, were still holding out, and when Twiggs's order arrived, he was sorely tempted to disobey and stand his ground. He knew that this would mean "the inauguration of a civil war that must eventually involve all the States in fraternal strife," but was willing to take that responsibility. Carpenter, however, was a soldier, subject to the orders of his commanding officer, and that commanding officer had ordered him to surrender. After consultation with his own officers, he agreed to turn the post over to Dalrymple.[9]

In March, McCulloch assumed command from Dalrymple, who, as a Houston appointee, no longer had jurisdiction. Houston himself had been removed from office for refusing to take an oath of allegiance to the Confederacy, and Lieutenant Governor Edward Clark was installed to finish the term. Buck Barry was placed in command of Camp Cooper, and Ranger companies also were sent to garrison Camp Colorado and Fort Chadbourne on the line of defense running south from Cooper, a line they held until May. "We were not able to keep the Indians from doing any mischief but broke up their camps and prevented them from doing serious injury at this time," Barry observed. In San Antonio, meanwhile, the remaining army officers maintaining a federal presence in Texas were "seized by an armed force, acting under what they term the Confederate States of America," and informed they would be confined until paroled or exchanged. They took their paroles and returned north. The breach with the United States was complete.[10]

AS TEXAS AND the Confederacy prepared their respective defenses, the lines between a purely state ranger force and the army of a national government sometimes became blurred, making the Civil War a confusing period in Ranger history. The problem of identity is complicated by several factors. First, famous Rangers like Rip Ford, Sul Ross, and Ben McCulloch began the war commanding local Ranger units, prompting some historians to continue referring to them as Rangers even after they were transferred to the Confederate Army. Additionally, throughout the war, frontier Ranger units created by the state were called into regular military service by the Confederate government and reassigned to duties as soldiers.

And finally, many Texas units serving with the Confederate forces in the East styled themselves "rangers." Among the most famous was the Eighth Texas Cavalry, known as Terry's Texas Rangers in honor of their first commander, Col. Benjamin F. Terry, who was killed in the battle of Woodsonville, Kentucky, in December 1861. Despite their heroic service, Terry's Texas Rangers were soldiers who served in a war totally unrelated to traditional Ranger conflicts, and for that reason they are beyond the scope of this work. The genuine Ranger was still the citizen volunteer called into service to defend the frontiers of the state.[11]

Ultimately, protection of the Confederate frontier devolved on three different Ranger units during different periods of the war. The first, known as the Mounted Riflemen, was raised by Henry McCulloch almost immediately after secession. It was replaced in early 1862 by the Frontier Regiment. When that regiment was incorporated into the Confederate Army in the spring of 1864, its role as a Ranger force was assumed by the Border Regiment. Often the same people served in each of these regiments, simply transferring from one to the other; Indian fighting was a highly specialized profession, and men who knew the frontier were always in demand. And regardless of what they were called, they were Rangers in the truest sense of ideal, organization, and mission.[12]

As always, the Rangers existed because of need, and with the expulsion of the last federal troops in the spring of 1861, some sort of immediate protection for the frontier became imperative. As early as March 4, Confederate secretary of war Leroy Pope Walker wrote Ben McCulloch, acknowledging that although the Confederate government itself was in the process of organizing and would be unable to field a regular army in the immediate future, "the necessities of your defenseless frontier demand instant action." In view of the emergency, Walker and Confederate president Jefferson Davis requested McCulloch to raise the regiment of Mounted Riflemen for frontier defense. It consisted of ten companies, composed of sixty to eighty men each. Later that month, Henry McCulloch, to whom Ben had given the task of organizing the regiment, ordered Buck Barry to enlist a mounted Ranger company that would be "entitled to the same pay and allowances allowed volunteers in the army of the 'Confederate States' and subject to the same rules and government." He was ordered to report to Camp Cooper on May 4, where it would be mustered into Confederate service for twelve months.[13]

Camp Cooper was a key link in the badly deteriorated line of defense between the Red River and the Rio Grande. To the west were the Mexicans, who, in the words of Governor Clark, "bear no love to us," and to the north and west were the Indians, "who are our perpetual foes." Rip Ford was managing to hold down the area along the Rio Grande with five makeshift companies, while Henry McCulloch's regiment had responsibility for the entire north-south line and was completely inadequate for the job.

"The people of this State have been positively assured that their protection would be far more perfect under the Government of the Confederate States than it was under that of the old United States," Clark advised President Davis, adding, "Our protection properly devolves upon you. . . ." If Texas received that protection, the Confederacy could depend on its steadfast support. Otherwise, Clark warned, the pro-Houston faction stood a good chance of getting enough support to break away from the Confederacy and form an independent republic.

Having dealt with the Indian crisis as U.S. secretary of war, Davis was not blind to the situation, but the difficulties of organizing, leading, and defending a new nation took priority over the frontier problems of one state. Secretary Walker, meanwhile, had no better grasp of the true nature of Texas's plight than had many of his Union predecessors. Despite previous expressions of concern, he soon decided the raids were "merely predatory and incursional, and carried on only by roving tribes of Indians." The secretary of war had absolutely no understanding of the devastation these "roving tribes of Indians" could inflict; one fourth of the United States Army had been unable to control them in the 1850s, and the single regiment of mounted rifles he envisioned had no chance whatever. His assurances that the Confederate government would defend the state "at whatever cost" rang hollow. The situation that had helped prompt secession from the Union was no better under the Confederacy.[14]

Slowly, however, some effort was made to establish order out of the chaos. In May, two western lines of defense were established, with Henry McCulloch having the north line from the Red River south to the junction of the two branches of the Concho River (the site of modern San Angelo). The second line, under Rip Ford, covered the San Antonio–El Paso Road from Fort Bliss at El Paso to Camp Wood east of Uvalde.

The situation was less serious on the far western frontier, beyond the Pecos River, partly because few settlers had ventured to that extent, but largely because intertribal warfare kept the Comanches and Apaches too busy fighting each other to concern themselves with the whites. Although the specter of Cortina still loomed along the Rio Grande, the region remained relatively quiet.[15] The critical area was the northwest frontier, where, according to Buck Barry,

> [t]he settlements . . . had been moving westward a few miles each year but were subjected to constant depredations from the wild Indians of the plains. . . . Because of the very nature of the incursions of the Indians, their superb horsemanship, and rapid movements they could only be overtaken if immediately pursued. Even then when a pursuit was about to overtake them, they would often scatter and hide themselves.[16]

To counter this, McCulloch looked for horsemen of proven courage and physical stamina who were familiar with the country and with the Indians and who could take to the field at a moment's notice. They not only were expected to patrol the line of defense, but to range far to the north, hunting out the Indians responsible for the depredations. Over the ensuing months, the different Ranger units made weekly scouts, overlapping and linking up with the scouting parties from other companies. They also furnished guards for wagon trains carrying supplies to other Ranger stations, and in July 1861, a ten-man detail returning to Camp Cooper from escorting a train to the Red River Station had a fight with almost fifty Indians on the Little Wichita River, some fifty miles north of Cooper. Seven Rangers were wounded, four seriously and one mortally, and five horses were killed during the fight, which lasted several hours.

Three days later, on July 29, Buck Barry and thirty-two Rangers got into a running battle with about seventy Indians. Over the fifteen-mile course of the fight, three Rangers died and, Barry estimated, at least a dozen Indians were killed. The Indians broke off and fled when their chief fell, and Barry followed them beyond the Wichita Mountains, where he lost the trail among the numerous buffalo herds.[17]

DESPITE SPORADIC OUTBURSTS, raids were light during the opening months of 1862, because a smallpox epidemic had broken out among the Plains tribes. Thus Texas got a reprieve, although it was short-lived.[18] By the middle of the year, raiding resumed. Both Union and Confederate agents attempted to keep the Indians stirred up, each hoping that Indian depredations on the frontier would harm the war effort of the other. As one Kiowa chief later observed, "Our people . . . carried war against Texas. We thought the Great Father would not be offended for the Texans had gone out from among his people and become his enemies."[19] Cattleman Oliver Loving reported to Governor Francis Lubbock that during a trip to Colorado in 1862,

> I saw a large number of Comanche with some four or five thousand horses that have be[e]n stolen from Texas. These Indians are fed by the U.S. Posts at Fort Adams on the Arkansas and Fort Bent, and the Indians are paid by the U.S. Troops occupying these parts for all the scalps taken from Texas. They are perfectly friendly with the U.S. Troops an[d] in fact with all except Texans. I am satisfied that we will not have any rest from these Indians until we go to their general rendezvous and destroy them.

Loving recommended raising "three or four companies" of volunteer Rangers to augment the existing Frontier Regiment, not only to strike back at the Indians but to stop the raids at what he considered their source by capturing the U.S. posts in the area.[20]

The allegation that the United States was buying hair no doubt was an exaggeration, but there is no question that federal authorities did encourage raids—as did Confederates—as much to draw the Indians away from their own respective frontiers as to harass the enemy. And Loving's belief that Texas frontier forces could take U.S. military installations, while overly optimistic, indicated that the people had far more faith in their Rangers than in the general government in faraway Richmond.

The Frontier Regiment that Loving's hypothetical companies would augment had been authorized by the legislature at Governor Lubbock's behest on December 21, 1861. It had two purposes: to carry the war to the Indians, and to make sure that these troops would remain under state control. The governor realized that McCulloch's troops, attached as they were to the Confederate Army, were subject to Confederate authority and could be redeployed according to the military needs of the South. The Frontier Regiment, begun essentially as a Ranger outfit, would answer exclusively to the state. The act called for ten companies, nine of which would be raised from a list of specific counties on the northwest and western frontiers and one from throughout the state. They would be divided into detachments of twenty-five men, with each detachment maintaining a post one day's ride from the next. In that fashion, the legislature hoped to secure the entire line from the Red River south and west to the Rio Grande.

The problem was supply and equipment. The state did not have the resources to equip this force of Rangers, any more than it had been able to provide for them under U.S. jurisdiction. Just as the Texans had hoped that the federal government would pay and provision the Rangers for assisting the army, so they now appealed to Richmond, and the Confederate Congress responded with appropriate legislation. The bill, however, was vetoed by President Davis on the grounds that the general government could not support an armed force that was under the exclusive jurisdiction of the state. During the two years of its existence as a state Ranger unit, the Frontier Regiment subsisted as best it could, while the politicians in Austin and Richmond argued over responsibility.[21]

THE FRONTIER REGIMENT began organizing in January 1862. Col. James Norris was appointed commanding officer, with Lt. Col. Alfred J. Obenchain and Maj. James E. McCord subordinates. They would replace McCulloch's Mounted Rifles, who, to their disgust, found their own enlistments extended on the Confederate draft and were reorganized into what later became the First Texas Cavalry. As McCulloch's citizens-turned-soldiers reported to Fort Mason for reorganization, their places on the frontier were taken by Colonel Norris's Rangers.[22]

Colonel Obenchain took direct command of Capt. J. J. Cureton's Company B at Fort Belknap. Although he wanted to fight and his intentions were honorable, Obenchain was singularly unqualified for field command.

"He must have got the command because there was nobody else to get for an officer," Ranger Charles Goodnight remarked. "He had no idea of frontier service and would give the scout enough work in one day to do for two. We did not pretend to obey orders. We would get out of his sight and do the best we could."[23]

Obenchain's spit-and-polish attitude and his insistence that officers should not associate with rank and file did not fit with the casual structure of Ranger units, nor with the close-knit society of the frontier. The colonel further infuriated them on scouting expeditions when he camped apart from the others in a tent. "Some of us scarcely had shirts," Goodnight complained.

Cureton, on the other hand, was a frontiersman who was close to the men. Given the different backgrounds and personalities, trouble was bound to develop. Cureton openly defied orders he considered unnecessary and unreasonable, and he was supported by the men. Relations continued to deteriorate until June, when Obenchain placed Cureton under arrest for insubordination.

With Cureton confined to post, Obenchain alone led the next expedition against Indians. Knowing little about the terrain, he took his men out toward the waterless country of the Staked Plains, exhausting both Rangers and horses. After wandering through the area for several days, he decided to take a small party of volunteers and scout Blanco Canyon, leaving the main body in camp. About ten miles out, Obenchain and his volunteers—almost all of whom were raw recruits—were jumped by Indians. As the others held off the attack, Ranger Sid Davidson took a fast horse and rode for help. Several warriors chased him but could not catch him, and knowing Davidson had ridden for help, they broke off the fight and retreated. Upon arriving, the main company of Rangers took up the chase, finally losing the Indians in the rough country around Quitaque Canyon, about forty miles beyond.

When the company finally returned to the settlements, Obenchain filed formal charges against Captain Cureton. The men were now thoroughly disgusted, and there were murmurings in the ranks. Although technically Obenchain was in the right because of Cureton's defiance, such discipline hardly applied in a Ranger company, where leadership was based on judgment, skill, valor, and confidence of the men.

Several weeks later, Obenchain started toward regimental headquarters at Camp Colorado accompanied by two Rangers who openly despised him. He never arrived, and a search party found his remains several days later. One of the two Rangers fled to Colorado Territory and the other was captured and died in the penitentiary. Two weeks later, Cureton was found guilty of the charges against him, and was suspended from rank and pay for three months and publicly reprimanded.[24]

AS THE WAR progressed, recruitment for the frontier became increasingly difficult. Not that the Texans were adverse to Indian fighting—that was part of their character. But with the military situation in the East requiring more and more manpower, many were afraid that if they volunteered for Ranger service they ultimately would be drafted into the army "to leave homes and families unprotected." After a particularly bad raid in Tarrant County in the summer of 1863, local Ranger companies were mustered only after Confederate officers gave assurances that they would be allowed to remain near their homes because the government "intended to defend every portion of the State." Equally concerned, Governor Lubbock wrote Rip Ford, now commandant of conscripts in Texas, recommending that able-bodied men who joined the frontier defense force be exempted from the Confederate draft on the grounds "that they are necessary for the protection of the Frontier Counties, and that the time has come that their services are necessary for the purpose. . . ."[25]

The crisis was not due to lack of effort on the part of the Frontier Regiment. It was doing the best it could against an impossible situation. The problem was simply that a single regiment of six hundred to eight hundred Rangers was being expected to do what one quarter of the United States Army had been unable to do in the 1850s—maintain peace on the Texas frontier. And the military resources of the Confederacy were far less than those of the United States.

AS FAR AS Indian raids were concerned, the closing days of 1863 and the year of 1864 were among the worst in the history of Texas. During the final weeks of December 1863, Indians crossed the Red River from Oklahoma and rampaged through the adjacent counties, burning and killing. This, however, was a portent of things to come in the long, bloody year of 1864 as the tribes took advantage of the chaotic conditions that the Civil War brought to the frontier. Both North and South had courted the Plains tribes, each attempting to make treaties to secure their own frontiers while directing the Indians against the other. By now, however, the tribes were entirely out of hand.

The situation in Texas was so bad that many families on the northwest frontier along the Clear Fork of the Brazos River abandoned their homes, moving to the comparative safety of the interior settlements. Several northern counties were almost completely deserted, and on March 26, Governor Pendleton Murrah, who succeeded Lubbock, issued a proclamation "forbidding the immigration to, and settlement in, any of the unorganized counties of this State" for the duration of the war. Anyone attempting to settle would be subject to military conscription, and the "officers of the frontier organization" were ordered to arrest offenders and turn them over to Confederate military authorities.[26]

Despite the best intentions of the Ranger forces, neither Texas nor the Confederacy had the military capacity to carry the war to the Indians. The federal government, however, did have that capacity, and with the Indians now raiding along the Santa Fe Trail as well as in Texas, U.S. troops in New Mexico prepared retaliatory expeditions against the Kiowas and Comanches. Throughout August and September, federal scouting expeditions reported the two tribes were assembling in large camps in remote areas of the Staked Plains of Texas and northeastern New Mexico and laying in substantial amounts of food and water. It was obvious they were planning some sort of major undertaking.[27]

The Indians in fact were preparing for what probably was the worst single raid in the history of Texas, a sweep through Young County in the vicinity of Fort Belknap. Most of the Rangers posted to Belknap were out on patrol, although a small detachment under Lt. N. Carson occupied Fort Murrah, a blockhouse outpost about thirteen miles west of Belknap. The first indication of trouble came about 11 A.M., October 13, when smoke signals were spotted in the distance. Peter and Perry Harmonson were herding their cattle near Fort Murrah as the Indians rode in from the north. Seeing them, the Harmonsons spurred their horses into a grove of timber and prepared to defend themselves. A small group of Indians broke away from the main band and charged the grove, but Perry shot one and the others paused to tend to him. Taking advantage of the delay, the Harmonsons dashed to a heavy thicket where they had more protection, and the exposed Indians returned to the main band.

Altogether there were more than six hundred Indians, who now split into two groups, one moving down each side of Elm Creek. Two warriors came on the Fort Murrah horse herd and were trying to drive it off when a pair of Rangers spotted them. The Rangers rode after them but, judging from the way the warriors maneuvered, concluded they were part of a much larger party. One of the Rangers rode back to Fort Murrah for help, and Lieutenant Carson took fourteen men in pursuit, unaware that the two warriors were leading them into an ambush. Just before riding into the trap, however, Carson saw the main body of about three hundred warriors concealed about fifty yards ahead. Ordering a slow retreat, he managed to reach Murrah, losing five of his men.[28]

ELSEWHERE, THE TEXANS were taken completely by surprise. The Indians caught and killed settler Joel Myers at the confluence of Elm Creek and the Brazos River, then devastated the nearby Fitzpatrick Ranch, catching the women alone. Elizabeth Fitzpatrick and her two grandchildren were taken captive, and her daughter, Sue Durgan (or Durkin), was killed. Many barely escaped ahead of the raiders and fled toward the George Bragg Ranch with its well-built main house and outbuildings. Some arrived too late and were cut off by the Indians. They fled down the bank of Elm Creek and lay flat under a projecting rock shelter concealed by brush, listening to the six-hour battle that raged only a few yards away.

On several ranches, the men were away, and the warriors killed or carried off the defenseless women and children. The badly battered Rangers at Fort Murrah were no match for the Indians and dared not venture beyond their blockhouse. Families at Belknap retreated into the heavy two-story stone commissary building of the abandoned fort and prepared a defense, although the Indians eventually bypassed it. Finally, after dark, the Indians retreated north, leaving behind burning ranches and eleven dead. With their plunder, they had seven women and children as prisoners, not only whites, but blacks from among the families of freedmen and semiliberated slaves who ranched in the area. Over a thousand head of cattle were also taken.[29]

That night, young Francis Peveler took a fast horse and made the seventy-five-mile ride to Weatherford for help. Reinforcements arrived the following day. Among them was Ranger Charles Goodnight, who found Fort Belknap "in great turmoil and excitement." Continuing on through the county, the relief force arrived at the burned-out Fitzpatrick Ranch. The feather beds and pillows had been ripped open and the windblown feathers covered "an acre or more." To Goodnight, they looked almost like snow. Farther along, he saw equal devastation at the Hamby Ranch. The Hambys, whose home was the first attacked, had survived but lost everything except the clothes on their backs. Goodnight gave Thomas Hamby an Indian blanket.

"The Indians took away all their dead [except one killed in the doorway of the Bragg house], and it will never be known how many were killed, but their loss must have been considerable," Goodnight recalled. "A day or two later some of us followed the trail about forty miles, and we found several who had died of wounds." The Indians, however, had a two-day head start, and further pursuit was useless.[30]

THERE WERE MANY Indian fights along the frontier during the Civil War. In the early years of statehood during the antebellum period, the combined resources of the U.S. Army and the Rangers had provided substantial protection but were still unable to completely halt the forays. The strained resources of the Confederacy—fighting for its existence—were totally unequal to the task, and the defense of the Texas frontier was left to a single regiment of Rangers who were classified as Texas state troops.

It is estimated that over four hundred Texans were killed, wounded, or carried into captivity by Indians from the early raids of 1862 to the last major Indian fight of the Civil War at Dove Creek, near what is now San Angelo, in January 1865. Although these losses were devastating to the frontier, they were insignificant compared with the hundreds or even thousands of irreplaceable soldiers the Confederacy might lose in a single battle in the East. The Confederate government did not take the frontier depredations seriously, and, indeed, it scarcely could afford to.[31]

The best efforts of the Texans themselves were not enough. The state simply did not have the manpower. Nevertheless, the situation would have been far worse if these men had not been available to take on the odds, had been unwilling, or had chosen the more prestigious war against the Union instead of the forgotten, unglamorous war on the Plains.

Now it was over. Texas was an occupied province, and the priorities of its Northern conquerors were far different from the needs of its people on the frontier.

PART 4
THE TEXAS RANGERS

Chapter 10

Reconstruction

The Civil War was costly for Texas. Ben McCulloch was dead, killed at Pea Ridge in Arkansas. Albert Sidney Johnston—secretary of war for the Republic of Texas, colonel of the United States Army, general of the Confederate States Army—died at Shiloh. Although the state was spared the devastation of modern war inflicted on so much of the South, its frontier was ablaze. The border had been pushed back as much as 150 miles, almost to Fort Worth itself. For years afterward, travelers on the Plains beyond would remark on ruined houses and abandoned ranches in what had been, before the war, a prosperous and well-populated country.[1]

Like many Southern states, Texas was in economic and social chaos, the conditions all the more serious because of its position on the frontier. Most counties did not have the money for sheriff's deputies, courthouses, or jails. Such jails as did exist often were so flimsy that prisoners could simply walk out. Judges rarely leveled fines because the defendants usually couldn't afford to pay them, and juries often could not be empaneled because few qualified male residents had taken the loyalty oath required of former Confederate citizens. In some areas, outlaws and badmen made up such a large percentage of the population that they could operate with impunity.[2]

For lack of an immediate federal plan to restore civil authority following the surrender, Governor Murrah continued in office until June 17, 1865, when President Andrew Johnson replaced him with A. J. Hamilton. As provisional governor, Hamilton was empowered to call a constitutional convention composed of those who qualified for federal amnesty by taking the loyalty oath. The Hamilton administration drew widespread opposition, and the governor was often forced to call on Maj. Gen. Philip H. Sheridan, whose command included Texas, to maintain law and order with troops. Nevertheless, civil government was reestablished and moderate Unionist J. W. Throckmorton assumed office as elected governor on August 9, 1866.

One of Throckmorton's first acts was to call for the "withdrawal or non-interference of the military," which essentially meant relocation of the troops from the population centers of the state to the frontier area. Although the federal government was unwilling to relocate troops, President Johnson directed that the army not interfere with civil matters.[3]

Now that the state had control of its own affairs—for the time being, at least—it once again turned its attention to frontier defense. The demands for some sort of action were vehement, because the people felt—with reason—that they had been abandoned to their fate by the federal government. Typical was a petition to the governor, signed by fifty-nine leading residents of Lampasas County in July 1866, more than a year after the war ended:

> Whole Settlements have been broken up, families reduced from affluence to want, the rewards of a lifetime of industry have passed off before their eyes[,] the scalping knife not unfrequently used, and . . . to the present time the Cries of Suffering humanity have not been heard by the [federal] Government.

Similar petitions and complaints came from other citizens' groups and individuals in many frontier counties. In every case, the message was the same—they wanted the state to raise Ranger companies, and were prepared to serve if only the governor would allow them. Some correspondence in the Indian Papers of the Texas State Archives indicates ad hoc companies were formed without waiting for official authorization.[4]

The state was prepared to help. On September 21, 1866, the legislature enacted a law stating:

That there may be raised three battalions of Texas Rangers for the protection of the northern and western frontier of the State of Texas, to consist of ten companies, giving two battalions three, and one battalion four companies . . . to consist of one captain, two lieutenants, four sergeants, four corporals, one bugler, one farrier and eighty-seven privates each. . . .

Said men shall furnish themselves with horses, arms and accoutrements, and shall be furnished with ammunition, and shall be enlisted for twelve months unless sooner discharged.

As far as can be determined, this is the first time in history that the designation "Texas Rangers" appears in legislation. The new law expected the border counties to provide "the requisite number of men" whenever possible, because they were the counties that would be defended by the new battalions. They would be subject to the rules and regulations of the United States Army but always subject to the authority of the state for frontier service. They were not to venture beyond the limits of the state "except for the purpose of following and chastising marauding bands of Indians whenever found."[5]

Despite the nominal significance of this law, it is difficult to determine whether any sort of Ranger force actually was created. The bill to finance the new companies failed. There are virtually no records of the immediate postwar years in the Texas Adjutant General's files in Austin, nor are there accounts from other sources to indicate that Ranger units were organized under state authority.

Meanwhile, many Texans remained defiant of the Union. In Bonham and Weatherford, mobs destroyed the U.S. flag, and newly freed slaves were in danger of violence. The passage of black codes to restrict the movement of the freedmen and the general resistance by reenfranchised Democrats and even by Texas Unionists and conservative Republicans to changes wrought by the war brought the onus of Congressional Reconstruction onto the state. This allowed military authorities to remove Governor Throckmorton in 1867, on the grounds that he was impeding Reconstruction. The following year, a delegation from Texas requested the federal Congress to authorize a regiment of state cavalry for one year's service on the frontier, but there is no indication that Congress acted. As the Radical Reconstructionists in Congress saw it, any Texan under arms was a potential rebel, and the federal government did not intend to permit organized bodies of armed Texans to function under state jurisdiction. Frontier defense—if any—was the responsibility of the federal military. The military, however, was less inclined to defend the frontier than enforce Reconstruction edicts.[6]

WITH THE INSTALLATION of Radical Republican Edmund J. Davis as governor, the full force of Reconstruction fell on Texas. He and other Radicals were elected through the intervention of the military, and placed in office on January 8, 1870, by order of Col. Joseph J. Reynolds, commander of the Department of Texas. The Florida-born Davis was no carpetbagger, having already spent more than two decades in Texas and achieved distinction as customs collector, district attorney, and district court judge on the antebellum Rio Grande. In 1852, his name had been put forward as a candidate to command a Ranger company, although nothing came of it. Two years later, he chaired a public meeting in Laredo where citizens of Webb County enumerated raids by Lipans, demanded protection, and castigated the federal government for issuing provisions to the same Indians at Fort Inge. During the Cortina War he had bolstered the morale of Tobin's Rangers by personally accompanying them on their scout for Heintzelman's troops at Ebonal Ranch.

Davis had opted for the Union during the war and commanded a regiment of pro-Union Texas cavalry that spent the war skirmishing with Confederate Texas cavalry along the Mexican border. But it was his politics rather than his war record that made him attractive to the state's military rulers.

Personally honest, Davis acted as a watchdog against legislative corruption, and as a result used the power of his office to spare Texas much of the crushing debt imposed on other Southern states by freewheeling carpetbag legislatures. Nevertheless, he was not averse to patronage, abuses were widespread, and that, together with the governor's determination to impose his Radicalism on the state, earned him the contempt of much of its citizenry. Consequently, and despite his prewar record, he is called the carpetbag governor, and "the governor Texans love to hate."[7]

But the action that brought Davis more denunciation than perhaps any other was his creation of a state police that was viewed by many as nothing more than a means of protection for the Radicals and punishment of their opponents. Texas historian Walter Prescott Webb went so far as to call the Texas State Police an instrument of "official murder and legalized oppression." During its three-year existence, its members often were accused of fabricating "escapes" so that they could kill prisoners. The fact that more than a third of its personnel at any given time were freedmen did little to enhance its image, and many people regarded the killing of a state policeman as a patriotic act. The record of the Texas State Police is beyond the scope of this work. Suffice it to say that although abuses did exist, the police performed the function of a constabulary that Texas had long needed and, when viewed dispassionately, its overall record was reasonably good. But its mere existence, particularly with the large number of blacks in its ranks, brought the governor scorn that became increasingly open and vocal as time passed.[8]

THE DIVISIONS AMONG the whites continued to work in favor of the Indians. On June 27, 1870, twenty-five raiders swept through Wise County in north Texas, stealing "60 or 70 horses," and the following night entered the town of Decatur itself, taking another six horses. "No person killed yet. [A] great many Indians in the country," District Clerk G. Salmon reported to Secretary of State James P. Newcomb.[9]

Writing of a raid in Kendall County, in the Hill Country west of Austin, one local citizen told Governor Davis:

> I am requested by my neighbors to post you of these occurrences
> & request you put the Rangers on the war path as soon as it is in
> your power to do so—We know the difficulties that lie in your way
> and hope they will be moved as speedily as possible—It looks as
> if all the Indians on the Plains had found out that there was a good
> place in Texas for their business & had gathered here.[10]

Davis was not indifferent to conditions on the frontier. Already, on June 13, the legislature had approved a bill calling for "the protection of the northern and western Frontier [by] twenty companies of Texas Rangers. . . ." Amazingly, the bill and the proposed bond issue to finance it came under attack from all sides. Many honest citizens of Texas viewed the new Rangers as extensions of the State Police and enforcers of Radicalism. In Washington, a group of corrupt businessmen and politicians known as the Indian Ring, who profited from Indian warfare and the resultant military contracts, saw Rangers as a potential threat to their lucrative transactions. And the estimated cost—at $750,000 one of the state's largest single expenses—was more than the taxpayers of Texas believed they could afford. The bond issue failed, and the size and scope of the new Ranger service was reduced. There was an additional restriction besides funding; the War Department still did not trust an independent unit of armed Texans and insisted that the Rangers serve as auxiliaries to the army. The military would provide subsistence while the state paid the salaries. Under these conditions, fourteen companies were in the field by the end of the year.[11]

Despite the shaky start, these Texas Rangers (formally designated Frontier Forces) were the men who created the lasting image that has inspired so many motion pictures, television series, and pulp novels. The ever-observant A. J. Sowell, who served in Capt. David P. Baker's Company F, gave a description that largely supports the image, at least as far as appearance and outlook:

> In the first place he wants a good horse, strong saddle, double-girted, a good carbine, pistol, and plenty of ammunition. He generally wears rough clothing, either buckskin or strong, durable cloth, and generally a broad-brimmed hat, on the Mexican style, thick overshirt, top boots and spurs, and a jacket or short coat, so that he can use himself with ease in the saddle.
>
> A genuine Texas ranger will endure cold, hunger and fatigue, almost without a murmur, and will stand by a friend and comrade in the hour of danger, and divide anything he has got, from a blanket to his last crumb of tobacco.[12]

One thing he did not have was a badge, at least not officially; not until 1900 did the state issue a badge—a five-pointed star with the words "Texas State Ranger." Any shield or star carried by nineteenth-century Rangers generally was homemade, carved from the dollar-size Mexican silver eight-real coin or cut from a piece of tin (the latter giving rise to the Western expression "tin star" for a lawman). Rangers who did not want to fashion their own badges bought whatever was commercially available. These self-awarded badges generally were carried out of sight until the Rangers needed to show them.[13]

THE RANGERS MUSTERED under the 1870 frontier defense act included, for the first time, a contingent from El Paso. Although El Paso County was among the jurisdictions entitled to protection and expected to provide volunteers under earlier militia laws, it apparently was so far removed from the mainstream that no effort was made to organize units from that area. Residents themselves had been slow to react to the frequent Apache raids, probably in part because the area was so sparsely populated. The only towns of any importance on the Texas side were Ysleta, Socorro, and San Elizario (the former is now incorporated into El Paso, and the latter two are suburbs slightly downriver). In the middle nineteenth century, however, the lone semblance of community in what is now El Paso proper was the four small American settlements of Hart's Mill, Coone's Ranch, Magoffinsville, and Stephenson's Ranch. During the antebellum period, citizens petitioned Governor Bell for military protection, and Bell urged the government in Washington for some sort of action. Eventually the War Department established Fort Bliss near the American settlements, but the outbreak of the Civil War once again left the local population to its own devices.[14]

By the late 1860s, Apache depredations forced citizens to take some sort of action. In the three years between February 1864 and the spring of 1867, more than a dozen people were killed and thousands of dollars' worth of livestock taken. After a particularly vicious raid on January 30, 1867, San Elizario justice of the peace Gregorio N. García gathered eighty volunteers and chased the Apaches for twelve days before losing them in the Guadalupe Mountains to the east. García's effort ultimately led to the formal establishment, on August 26, 1870, of Company N, El Paso's first Ranger unit, with García as captain. Representative of the population as a whole, all but two of its seventy men were drawn from the *tejano* community.

García's Rangers first centered their activities near Fort Quitman, in the desert downriver from El Paso near what is now Sierra Blanca, apparently to be closer to the Apaches' mountain strongholds. Within a few months, however, they moved their headquarters back to San Elizario. Records of the company are obscure, and the only action appears to have been an incursion into New Mexico in February 1871, in pursuit of Apache raiders. A month later, the company was redesignated Company D, as which it was disbanded on June 15, 1871. Whatever its service record might have been, García's company was a portent of the key role Rangers would play in the Trans-Pecos well into the next century.[15]

AS EACH NEW company was organized, it took to the field, and the impact was felt immediately. After three scouts through the often harried Hill Country in November 1870, Capt. John W. Sansom of Company C wrote to Adjutant General James Davidson:

> I am very glad as yet that I can report to you that there has been no horses stolen from the district . . . that I am assigned to Guard. And I assure you that ever since the War among our selves closed say *1865* the Indians have been very bad, in Kendall, Kerr, Blanco & Bandera Counties. And not a horse has been taken from the above counties since my Co. Has been in the field. They may come; but I will try to beat them at their game when they start out.[16]

On the Lower Rio Grande, where horses and cattle had been stolen and driven into Mexico, Lt. John Heineman of Company G made a scout through Hidalgo, Starr, and Zapata counties, after which he reported to Capt. C. G. Falcón, "At all of the . . . *ranchos* I made carefull inquiries concerning the illegal driving of Stock and learned that although the practice has been carried on largely in times past, yet that in the last few weeks or since our arrival in this section, settlers have had less reason to complain."[17]

The real trouble, however, remained on the northwest frontier, which was the jurisdiction of Captain Baker's Company F. Local citizens long since had taken steps to protect themselves, and as early as 1868 had formed ad hoc Ranger units that rode together with military scouting parties from newly established Fort Richardson at Jacksboro, some seventy-five miles west of Fort Worth. Now the state was making a concerted effort to provide regular defense for the northwestern counties.

Company F was mustered into service in San Antonio on November 5, 1870, and assigned to scout the Wichita Mountains up near the Red River. The Rangers furnished their own horses, clothing, and revolvers, while the state furnished carbines, cartridges, and provisions. The thorough Captain Baker's first act was to send Sgt. Joel Payne with a procurement detail to Austin for wagons, mules, carbines, and other equipment the state was obligated to provide. When Payne returned on November 18, each man was issued a new Winchester carbine, and the following day, in high spirits, the company started on the five-hundred-mile trek to the north. Above Fort Mason they set up strict watches at night, because they now were in the country routinely traversed by the Indians. Scouting details were sent ahead during each day's march to look for Indian trails, and one group reported they had surprised and chased three Indians but lost them in a thicket. The Rangers had several other minor scrapes before they finally reached their station and spread out into several camps.[18]

The raids were bold, vicious, and consistent. "It was impossible for us to keep the Indians from coming into the settlements," Sowell wrote, "for they were constantly doing so, in spite of all we could do to prevent them. There was such a large scope of country for the rangers to protect that we could not watch all points at once."[19]

The Indians also had weapons comparable to anything in the Ranger arsenal, as Sgt. E. H. Cobb learned on February 7, 1871, when he and eight other men engaged a party of forty warriors "well armed with Henry rifles, needle guns, six-shooters, bows and arrows."[20]

That morning, Cobb had received word that the Indians were heading toward the settlements, and he followed their trail some thirty miles until he found them on the prairie near the "four corners" junction of Wise, Cooke, Denton, and Montague counties. The Indians retreated over a rise to a stand of tall grass. About half the warriors were dismounted and concealed in the grass, with the mounted men to the left and right. As the Rangers came over the rise, the Indians rose up and tried to surround them.

The Rangers opened fire, killing the chief in the first volley. His horse bolted, carrying the body through the Ranger lines before it fell off. Some of the Rangers recovered the horse "with his very fine Silver bridle worth forty dollars, his extra fine bow and quiver, and his richly adorned Cap with plumes and was about to lift his Scalp when the enemy dashed up to rescue the body of their chief which brought them again in close combat."

Ranger Gus Hasroot was cut off from the others by a warrior who attempted to lance him. "The boys all thought, Gus was gone up, but he made the lucky shot that droped [*sic*] the Indian dead before him, but a few steps."

Sergeant Cobb ordered the men to withdraw to a better position. According to a report to Adjutant General Davidson, "The Sergent [*sic*] came out bloody all over, but could not give a satisfactory account of it."

The Indians recovered the body of their chief and the warrior killed by Hasroot. Several others were believed to have been wounded. Ranger "Little Billy" Sorrells was shot in the hip with a revolver. His companions took him to the nearest home, summoned a physician, and left two Rangers with him.

The following morning, Sergeant Cobb took his remaining men and a band of local citizens to follow the trail, but the Indians had scattered in different directions. The citizens returned to their homes, and Cobb started back for his station. The Indians, meanwhile, had reassembled, and late that night Cobb ran into them, but apparently neither side was prepared for a fight. As soon as he got back to his station, he sent a courier to Captain Baker, who organized another search. Near Decatur, Baker found where a party of about twelve Indians had slaughtered some beeves, apparently eating the meat raw because they left no trace of a fire. This party, likewise, scattered.[21]

THE FRONTIER COUNTIES were in an uproar. These were more than ordinary stock raids. Each new onslaught left a trail of murder, and the settlers dreaded the bright "Comanche moon" of the spring that allowed the Indians to travel long distances at night. "Every new moon makes the number less of both men and horse, in this unfortunate part of our noble, lone Star State," Lt. A. C. Hill of Company F wrote Adjutant General Davidson. An army officer stationed at Fort Richardson commented, "The entire border was ablaze, and the stories that these wretched settlers brought in from time to time of murder, rapine, burning, pillaging and plundering was almost heartrending." Although the settlers praised the Rangers for taking on vastly superior bands of Indians, bravery alone was not enough to stop the depredations. There simply were too few Rangers and too many Indians.[22]

The dismal record for 1871 had begun on January 24, when a large band of Kiowas and Comanches massacred four black teamsters on the Salt Creek Prairie between Fort Richardson and Fort Griffin. One of these teamsters was Britt Johnson, a freedman who had become a local hero when he arranged the ransom and recovery of almost all the prisoners taken by the Indians in the brutal Elm Creek Raid of 1864. On February 10, a settler named Steve Hampton was killed. Indians also attacked a ranch on the line between Montague and Wise counties. The owner was gone at the time but the raiders forced their way into the house and killed his wife, a widow who lived with the family, and all the children except an eight-year-old boy, who managed to escape, and an infant girl, who had been left for dead but was revived by the boy, who returned after the raid.[23]

To bolster the forces in the northwest, Capt. A. H. Cox was ordered to bring Company B to the Brazos, and Captain Sansom's Company C was sent from the Hill Country to Fort Griffin, where Sansom became senior captain with jurisdiction over Cox and Baker. The settlers understood that whenever Indians attacked, a messenger would immediately take word to the nearest Ranger camp. Then settlers and Rangers would join together in pursuit. The problem was isolation. Sowell pointed out:

> Sometimes the nearest neighbor being ten to twelve miles distant; and as the Indians generally raided in bands, from ten to three hundred in number, it would take some time, and a great deal of rapid riding to collect men enough to make a successful fight, if the raiding band was large. And often, the brave and hardy pioneers, would follow them, with an insufficient force, and suffer defeat, and sometimes massacre, then homes would become desolate along the border.[24]

Despite the odds, the Rangers were willing to try. Almost immediately upon arrival on the Brazos, Cox's men had gotten into a running fight with a band of Indians, killing eight. Three Rangers were wounded because they were unfamiliar with Indian endurance—shooting down a warrior did not necessarily disable him unless he was actually dead. In each case, the Ranger had run up to a fallen Indian, only to find that he still had enough fight in him to inflict serious injury.

Dr. J. C. Nowlin, surgeon for Captain Sansom's company, saw firsthand evidence of how much an Indian could take when he examined the body of a warrior killed in a fight near the head of the Big Wichita River. His horse shot from under him, the warrior had charged the Rangers on foot with his bow, sending arrow after arrow at the whites until he finally was killed and scalped. Dr. Nowlin noted he had been shot three times before he fell, and had an old wound that had made one leg shorter than the other.[25]

The efforts of these Rangers were all the more remarkable because they experienced constant shortages of even the most basic essentials, primarily because of the state's failure to provide adequate funding. Typical is a series of letters from Captain Cox of Company B to Adjutant General Davidson:

On October 4, 1870, he wrote from Fort Richardson that his company's horses and mules "need shoeing badly and I have neither Forge nor Tools." The animals suffered from salt deficiency because no provision had been made for them. He also needed a supply of U.S. Army–size Colt .44 ammunition for his pistols and six thousand rounds of ammunition for Winchester rifles.[26]

On November 3, Cox wrote from Fort Griffin that he had borrowed subsistence rations from the military, but that he would probably have to relocate to Stephenville, ninety miles to the southeast, or perhaps even to Waco, in order to obtain provisions.[27]

On November 22, he again wrote, this time from Stephenville, "My Medical Officer reports to Me that he is without Medicines. I would respectfully request that Medical Supplies and Surgical Instruments for this company be forwarded as early as practicable as they are absolutely necessary."[28]

DESPITE THE SHORTAGES and the taint of the governor's Radicalism, Davis's Rangers were giving a good account of themselves. Company F's Lieutenant Hill apparently was prepared to face down anyone who denigrated the Frontier Forces, because on May 17, 1871, he wrote to Davis that those who had opposed the Ranger bonds the year before "deny having done any thing to hinder the negotiation of the *bonds*." The withdrawal of Rangers from the western part of Coryell County brought an immediate protest from its representative in the legislature.[29]

It is an interesting coincidence that Lieutenant Hill dated his letter to the governor May 17, for on that day, Gen. W. T. Sherman, general-in-chief of the United States Army, arrived at Fort Richardson on a visit that would change the entire focus of federal military policy in Texas.

Sherman discounted the hue and cry over Indians, believing that the Texans simply were trying to draw federal troops away from Reconstruction duty. The army had a vague western defense line of posts constructed after the war, including Fort Richardson, Fort Griffin, and Fort Concho, but Indian fighting had not been a priority. Despite his skepticism, Sherman had included the Texas forts on a general inspection tour, although upon his arrival at Fort Richardson, after a broad, circular trip through the state, he had seen nothing to convince him the Indian problem was more than hysteria.[30]

The general-in-chief was blissfully unaware that as he crossed the dangerous Salt Creek Prairie the last few miles before Fort Richardson, he had been watched by a war party of some 150 Kiowas and Comanches from Oklahoma. They easily could have overwhelmed his train, but had been restrained by their leader, the *do-ha-te,* or medicine man, Maman-ti, architect of many of the raids, who told them the oracles were against it. Wait one more day, Maman-ti advised, and a second party of whites would appear that would be easy plunder.

Maman-ti's vision proved correct, because the following morning, a wagon train appeared, carrying corn to Fort Griffin on a government contract. The Indians attacked, killed seven teamsters, ransacked the wagons, and rode back to Oklahoma with the loot from the train and forty mules. Five whites managed to escape because they had run for the cover of some timber and the Indians were more interested in the wagons than in chasing them. That night two of the survivors, one badly wounded, managed to reach Fort Richardson, where Sherman personally listened to their account.

The general's reaction was immediate. Troops were sent out in pursuit, and ultimately followed the Indians to the Kiowa-Comanche Reservation near Fort Sill. Upon arriving at Sill, Sherman arranged with the Indian agent to arrest three of the chiefs involved in the raid and send them to Texas for trial. One of the chiefs, an old warrior named Satank, jumped a guard and was killed at Fort Sill, but the others, Satanta and Big Tree, were tried and convicted of murder and sent to the penitentiary.

Now that Sherman had personally seen the result of Indian depredations, he was ready to assume responsibility for frontier defense. In Texas, the army's priority shifted from Reconstruction to Indian fighting, relieving the Texas Rangers of much of their heavy burden.[31]

Meanwhile, throughout Texas, reaction was building against Davis and his Radical regime, and in a hotly contested election in the fall of 1873, voters elected Richard Coke governor. On January 17, 1874, Coke moved into the executive offices. Reconstruction in Texas was truly over and the state, once again, was in the hands of its own people.[32]

For the Texas Rangers, this was a turning point. The need for a militia or minuteman type of Ranger to defend the frontier was drawing to a close, and the era of the professional lawman was dawning.

Chapter 11

The Frontier Battalion

Texas in 1874 was changing, whether or not anyone consciously
recognized the fact. Rangers still fought Indians, but the U.S. Army
had assumed the bulk of that responsibility. Although the Mexican
border continued to simmer, the frontier as a whole was evolving into
a less fluid, more stable society that needed law and order. Even if
Texans did not want to admit it, Governor Davis's State Police had
demonstrated the value of a permanent constabulary, and his successor, Richard Coke, was ready to provide one, albeit more in keeping
with the traditional guardians of the Texas frontier. On April 10, the
legislature responded by creating the Frontier Battalion, Texas
Rangers. In theory, the battalion served at the will and pleasure of the
governor; in fact, it established the Rangers as a permanent, professional statewide gendarmerie. The era of the citizen-Ranger was over.
For the duration of their enlistments, the men of the Frontier Battalion
had no occupation in life save as Rangers.[1]

Another significant difference was that for the first time in their
history, the Rangers had civil police powers. This, according to Adjutant General Wilburn Hill King in his 1898 history of the service, "did
not modify nor lessen their duties as soldiers, [but] it greatly widened
their field of usefulness in another direction and brought them into
closer touch with law-abiding people by giving them authority to act

as peace officers."[2] The authority was desperately needed because the state was rampant with stagecoach and train robbers, cattle and horse thieves, and fence cutters. The shift in priorities is demonstrated by the fact that during the first year of the Frontier Battalion's existence, and despite many Indian fights during that year, the Rangers recovered twice as much stolen property from civil lawbreakers as from Indians.[3]

"This new work was less romantic than the old Indian warfare," Ranger sergeant James B. Gillett later wrote, "but it was every bit as dangerous and as necessary in the building up of the fast developing state."[4]

Coming largely from common backgrounds, familiar with the hardships of the frontier, and bound together in what they felt was a unique organization, the Rangers developed a sense of elitism. Describing his enlistment as a member of Capt. Dan W. Roberts's Company D, Gillett recalled, "At ten o'clock we were formed in line, mounted, and the oath of allegiance to the state of Texas was read to us by Captain Roberts. When we had all signed this oath we were pronounced Texas Rangers. This was probably the happiest day of my life, for in joining the rangers I had realized one of my greatest ambitions."[5]

Company D was one of six companies, designated A through F, established on May 6, 1874, when Adjutant General William Steele ordered the Frontier Battalion formally organized. Each company consisted of seventy-five men commanded by a captain and two lieutenants enlisted for a period of twelve months. "As it is expected that this force will be kept actively employed during their term of service," Steele wrote, "only sound young men without families and with good horses will be received. Persons under indictment or of known bad character or habitual drunkards will be rejected."

Captains received $100 a month; lieutenants, $75; sergeants, $50; and corporals and privates initially $40 each. Later, however, the parsimonious legislature reduced the pay for privates to $30 a month, "a mere pittance for the hazardous service demanded of them," Gillett complained.[6]

THE FRONTIER BATTALION was probably the best-organized and best-disciplined Ranger unit of the nineteenth century, and credit for this belongs to the battalion commander, thirty-nine-year-old Maj. John B. Jones of Corsicana. Captain Roberts of Company D called him "the right man in the right place."[7] Although he was soft-spoken and sparely built (he was about five feet eight inches tall and weighed about 135 pounds),

Jones's dignified bearing automatically won respect. Moreover, he was unique among the Rangers as an administrator and strategist. Where Ford, McCulloch, Hays, and other leaders had been tacticians and field officers, Jones was a supreme commander, viewing the frontier as a whole and placing entire companies where they would be most useful.[8]

A native of South Carolina, Jones was brought to Texas by his family in 1838. He enlisted as a private with Texas forces in the Confederate Army, ending the war as a major and brigade assistant adjutant general. After the war, a group of disgruntled Confederates who detested the idea of Republican rule sent Jones to Latin America to investigate the possibility of expatriate settlements. His grim report on conditions there influenced most of them to remain in Texas. He was elected to the legislature in 1868, but was denied his seat by the Radical Republicans. In short, he was the perfect man to restore public confidence in state law enforcement in the wake of Davis's State Police.

Personally, the new major was abstentious. He neither smoked nor drank. His only vice appears to have been an addiction to coffee, developed in the field, where the stagnant, gypsum-saturated water was unsafe to drink straight from the pools. He was an active Freemason, ultimately becoming grand master of Texas.[9]

Jones did not tolerate the traditional casual attitude that heretofore had characterized the Rangers when they were not actually engaged in a fight. Inspecting Capt. W. J. Maltby's Company E, he found "the men in good health and the horses in good order, but doing nothing at this time; the men are all in camp idle, their officers all absent." Detailing the problem to Adjutant General Steele, he wrote:

> I find it the most dificult [sic] thing to make the men of this command and some of the officers, understand that they are not at liberty to go home when they please or get substitutes or have their brother or friend take their place for a while. I have established the rule however and am determined to maintain it, hoping that I will be sustained by the Governor and yourself, otherwise I can have no system or discipline in the command.[10]

By contrast, he was pleased with Company F, where Capt. Neal Coldwell had relieved a private and broken the first sergeant to the ranks for insubordination. Jones dishonorably discharged the private and upheld the sergeant's reduction. He also encouraged Lt. F. H. Nelson to resign from the service because the lieutenant apparently had no confidence among the men; he actually feared them, although Jones noted that Coldwell and the other lieutenant had no trouble controlling them.[11]

In short, the Texas Rangers were now subject to a discipline and organization that they never before had known. No longer were they citizen volunteers, minutemen coming together at their own need or convenience or that of their immediate friends and neighbors. Henceforth they would be professionals, obeying orders, serving where ordered and when ordered.

Despite his adherence to discipline, however, Jones would not allow procedure to interfere with efficiency. Considering it "unnecessary and indeed a waster of time and money" to assemble the Frontier Battalion as a unit, he ordered each company into the field as soon as it was ready. By June 1, five of the six companies were in service, and the sixth followed only ten days later.[12]

AS THE BATTALION organized, the various companies were posted to base camps that often were located conveniently to nearby towns. The camps themselves became small communities as the Rangers worked to establish such amenities as were available on the frontier. Lou Conway, who married Capt. Dan Roberts, recalled arriving at her new home in the Company D base camp near Menard.

> The Rangers required only a few days to prepare quarters for us. About fifty yards from their camp stood a portion of a camp house. It had a shingle roof and a rock floor. It was converted into a kitchen, size twenty feet by twenty feet. Gunny sacks were tacked upon the walls. For our bedroom the Rangers built a room of logs with walls three feet high, on top of which they put a tent. It was provided with a fireplace built of stone. The floor was carpeted with gunny sacks. The kitchen also served as a storeroom. It was all so cozy.[13]

Not everyone was impressed with the Rangers, however. H. H. McConnell, a federal cavalryman posted to Fort Richardson near Jacksboro, wrote:

> These Rangers were tolerable Indian fighters, but most of their time was occupied in terrorizing the citizens and "taking in the

town." Shooting scrapes and rows between citizens, soldiers and Rangers in this year (1874) were so frequent that the long suffering citizens by their votes "incorporated." . . .

The act of incorporation removed Jacksboro's law enforcement from state responsibility, and a municipal marshal was appointed to police the town and—presumably—police the Rangers when they came in.[14] This notwithstanding the fact that the vicinity around Jacksboro was the scene of some of the worst Indian depredations.

No doubt Rangers sometimes were a nuisance, but when commanded by a disciplinarian, they behaved well enough to attract the admiration of the communities. Citizens of nearby towns frequently visited, and if there was a military post nearby, the families of army officers exchanged courtesies with those of Ranger officers. The men kept pets, and those who played musical instruments often gave concerts. In some camps, the men laid out racetracks, because betting on horse races was permitted whereas cardplaying had to be done in secret. Some companies even had croquet sets.[15]

For all the amenities offered by local citizens, the Texas Ranger was first and foremost a law enforcement officer and an Indian fighter. A sampling of activities during the Frontier Battalion's first three months of existence in 1874 illustrates some of its activities:

> **May 7**   Capt. E. F. Ikard Co. 'C' frontier [*sic*] Battalion, with 6 men, attacked a party of 10 Indians, driving toward Indian nation a herd of some 150 head of cattle. Drove the Indians (fighting) about 15 miles. . . .

> **Company "D"**   July 29th. Capt. C. R. Perry's command [Perry preceded Dan Roberts as company commander] assisted civil authorities in bringing Felix Mann and accomplices to justice. . . .

> **Company E**   May 10th. Capt. W. J. Maltby and Lt. J. G. Connell captured 2 horses, bridles, & saddles from horse thieves—Property returned to owners. . . .

> **Company "F"**   Aug 31st Capt. Neal Coldwell arrested Wm. Hobbs, burglar & thief from Wood County, turned him over to sheriff of Kerr County. . . .[16]

On scouting expeditions, the Rangers relied on knowledge of astronomy and terrain, not bothering with maps or compasses. "Their reckonings were made by the sun, and the North star, taking into consideration the main rivers that run through the state, from north to south and the relative distance between them," Captain Roberts commented.[17]

"Due to the outdoor life we followed, we were seldom ill," Ranger G. W. Ellington of Company E remembered. "Remedies resorted to by the men themselves were sometimes extremely crude but effective." In one instance, Ellington returned to camp after riding all day in a heavy wind with a terrible toothache. "When I reached camp I was in a mood to try anything for relief." No one had pliers to pull the tooth, but one man heated an awl red-hot and thrust it into the cavity of the tooth to kill the nerve. "It sizzled and burned, but cured the ache," Ellington wrote.[18]

As always, the Rangers paid close attention to weapons. The legislation creating the battalion specified that the state would provide each officer and enlisted man with a breech-loading cavalry carbine, but that every Ranger was required to furnish for himself "one six-shooting pistol (army size)," specifically the Colt's Model 1873 Single Action Army revolver. Apparently, however, individual Rangers had difficulty procuring the new handgun, because three months after the battalion was organized, the Rangers of Company E petitioned Captain Maltby "to procure for us Colt's improved Breech Loading Pistol of the latest and best improved quality; For which we will pay cash price out of the first money we draw from the State for our services" (Rangers were paid quarterly). The Single Action Army, called the Peacemaker in its civilian form, was a cartridge weapon in various calibers and barrel lengths. Rangers seemed to prefer the version known as the Classic Peacemaker in .45 caliber with a seven-and-a-half-inch barrel.[19]

ALTHOUGH THE STATE was plagued by banditry and vicious blood feuds were either brewing or already under way, the most immediate concern was the northwest frontier. Across the Red River in the Indian Territory of Oklahoma, the Southern Plains tribes were preparing for one last stand against the white tide, an outbreak known to history as the Red River War. Their grievances were many, but the symbol of the conflict became the buffalo, exterminated for their hides in answer to the Eastern demand for industrial leather—a slaughter that threatened the entire economic existence of Southern Plains tribes like the Comanches, Kiowas, Arapahos, and Southern Cheyennes. The war began in earnest on June 27, 1874, when massed warriors under Comanche leadership mounted a daylong siege against a group of buffalo hunters at Adobe Walls in the Texas Panhandle. Troops were mobilized from four states and federal territories, and the Indian agencies were placed under military rule while the army hunted down the Indian bands in the field.[20]

While the army waged a general war throughout the Southern Plains, the Rangers were charged by the state with protecting citizens within the boundaries of Texas. One of Jones's first acts on taking command of the battalion was to make a tour of the northwest frontier. As they rode through the countryside, the Rangers saw hundreds of carcasses of buffalo. "There were so many that the wolves and buzzards could not eat them and they were left to rot and dry up," one Ranger recalled. Jones, with an escort of about twenty-five men, arrived at the headquarters of Capt. G. W. Stevens's Company B, at the old Ranger post of Fort Murrah, on June 10. The following day he ordered the entire company to move about ten miles east to Salt Creek, where the grass and water were better. There they received word that a band of Comanches had attacked and killed a cowboy named Heath at Oliver Loving's corral, and tracks were plainly visible.

The next morning Jones sent a scouting detail consisting of two men from his own escort along with two from Stevens's company under the command of Lt. Tom Wilson. They reported a large trail heading southeast, out toward the dangerous Salt Creek Prairie. Jones broke camp immediately, taking Stevens, Wilson, and thirty-three members of the battalion to follow the trail. The group also probably included several volunteers drawn from Loving's cowboys. Unknown to the Rangers, however, this was not the trail of the Comanches who had hit Loving's corral—it belonged to a much larger party of about fifty Kiowas, including some of that nation's greatest warriors. It was a murder raid, organized by Paramount Chief Lone Wolf to avenge the deaths of his favorite son and nephew, both killed the year before in a fight with federal cavalry in south Texas. The party was led by Maman-ti, the wily and gifted medicine man responsible for the most successful Kiowa raids. Before leaving the Indian Territory, Maman-ti had consulted his oracles and predicted a successful expedition in which at least one white would die without any losses to the Kiowas. None of the warriors had any reason to doubt him.[21]

The Salt Creek Prairie, isolated but well traveled, had always been good raiding ground for the Kiowas. Almost as soon as they came out onto the prairie, they jumped four cowboys, but the cowboys, mounted on fresh horses, escaped; the Kiowa ponies, exhausted by the long trip from Oklahoma, were unable to keep up. The failure to take the cowboys, along with the incredible, windswept loneliness of the prairie, discouraged some of the younger warriors. Sitting on a hill overlooking the valley, they began muttering among themselves, and Lone Wolf gave them a dressing-down.

"Don't be scared," he commanded. "If any Texans come and chase us, don't be afraid. Be brave. Let's try and kill some of them. That's what we came here for."

At that moment, one warrior spotted the glint of the sun on metal off in the distance, a sign more whites were coming. Maman-ti led them along the ridge where they could get a better view and saw a large party of well-armed men, all wearing white hats.[22]

THE RANGERS HAD already followed the trail some fifteen miles. Now it was very fresh, and they estimated at least fifty warriors. They found where the Indians had stopped to water their horses, and where they had killed and roasted some cattle. They rode past the rough monument that soldiers had erected over the mass grave of the teamsters massacred during Sherman's 1871 visit, and but lost the trail as it led into rough and rocky ground approaching the hill. Some of the younger, more inexperienced men rode ahead to find it again.

As the Rangers continued into Lost Valley, expecting to see the Indians ahead on the open plain, the Kiowas backtracked, crossing the Ranger trail and circling around above them, keeping under the cover of the hills. Maman-ti had worked out a trap. He concealed most of the Kiowas in a gorge in the hills, then he and another warrior rode down into the valley and dismounted to lead their horses where they would be in plain view. Spotting them, Jones led his men straight into the snare as the other warriors charged out from among the boulders and mesquite thickets. The major held his men together as the Indians circled. Ranger Lee Corn received a gunshot wound that broke his shoulder and nearly took off his arm. Separated from the rest, he managed to crawl into the brush and hide. Another Ranger named Wheeler stayed with him and helped bandage the arm. Most of the Rangers were caught in the open, and Stevens told Jones, "Major, we will have to get to cover somewhere or all be killed."

Jones ordered a charge that broke through the Indian line, and the Rangers managed to get into a thicket in a gully but were cut off from water. Several had lost their horses in the charge, and Ranger George Moore had a flesh wound in the lower leg. William "Billy" Glass was shot down and left for dead. The Indians, Jones noted, "are all well armed with improved breech loading guns (they used no arrows in the fight) all well mounted, and painted, and deck [*sic*] out in gay and fantastic style." There was no question in his mind that they were out for blood.[23]

The two sides began sniping at each other, with Billy Glass lying out on the plain between them. Terrified of what would happen if he was captured alive, he called out, "Don't let them get me. Won't some of you fellows help?" The Rangers responded with a heavy covering fire while three men dashed out and brought him in.

The Indians were making trouble along a ridge to the rear, and Rangers William Lewis and Walter Robertson volunteered to hold that position while the others held the front. Jones took them to find the best spot, and as they settled down he told them, "Boys, stay here until they get you or until the fight is over."

Later, during a lull in the shooting, Lieutenant Wilson went to see how they were doing. He was sitting under a tree fanning himself with his hat and describing the Kiowas in the strongest Anglo-Saxon terms when Lewis said, "Lieutenant you ought not to swear like that. Don't you know that you might be killed at any minute?"

"That is just so, boys," Wilson agreed and became quiet. A few minutes later, a Kiowa bullet cut a limb overhead, bringing it down on the lieutenant's bare head. As the blood poured down, he momentarily thought he had been shot. A later examination of the tree showed it had been shot to pieces on the side facing the Indians.[24]

THE KIOWAS, MEANWHILE, were settling down for a siege. In a murder raid, the purpose was enemy scalps with no losses to their own side, and they were taking no unnecessary chances. The day was hot and the Rangers were about a mile from the nearest water. The Indians decided to wait them out. None of their own had been hurt. The wounded whites were calling for water, but Jones had forbidden anyone to try to reach the creek. Finally, as the sun began to go down and the firing slacked, Ranger Mel Porter said, "I'm going for water, if I get killed."

"And I'm with you," David Bailey replied.

They mounted and dashed for the creek. The others could see Bailey sitting on his horse by the bank keeping lookout while Porter filled the canteens. Suddenly, about twenty-five Indians moved in on them. The Rangers in the gully tried to signal by firing their guns, and Bailey shouted for Porter to flee. The two men took off in different directions.

Porter was caught by two warriors near the water hole. Keeping his nerve, he fired at them until his pistol was empty, then threw it at one of the warriors. Using his lance, the warrior levered Porter off his horse, but before he could kill him, firing from the injured Lee Corn and Wheeler drove off the two Indians. They were content to take Porter's horse, while the Ranger dove into the creek and swam underwater until he came up by Corn and Wheeler. They stayed together until after dark, when they made their way to Loving's ranch. Bailey was cut off, surrounded, and levered off his horse with a lance. Lone Wolf himself chopped his head to pieces with his brass hatchet-pipe, then disemboweled him.

The Kiowas were satisfied. They had killed at least one Ranger (actually two, because Billy Glass had died), and they began to leave. The badly mauled Rangers tied Glass's body to a horse and rode back to Loving's ranch. The Kiowas did not admit to any losses, although Jones claimed at least three had been killed. Glass was buried at Loving's ranch. About 3 A.M. the next day, they returned to Lost Valley under cover of darkness and recovered Bailey's horribly mutilated body. At sunup, a detachment of cavalry arrived from Fort Richardson, and the Rangers and soldiers spent the rest of the day looking for the Indian trail before the Rangers returned to camp.[25]

Continuing his inspection tour after the Lost Valley fight, Jones came to Camp Eureka on the Big Wichita River, where he found Capt. E. F. Ikard's Company C "too far out to render the most effective service" and ordered it into closer proximity to Stevens, so the two companies could come together in an emergency. Meanwhile, scouting parties from both Ikard's and Stevens's companies were in the field, keeping pressure on the Indians, and a party from Company C had actually raided a camp and captured forty-three horses and mules, some of which were claimed by citizens from whom they had been stolen.[26]

THE RED RIVER War, which permanently broke the power of the Southern Plains tribes, was almost exclusively a military affair. The army relied on its own scouts, usually Tonkawas from Fort Griffin, Seminole-Negro soldiers from Forts Clark and Duncan, and buffalo hunters familiar with the region; the Rangers had very little role in the actual military operations. Sporadic raiding did continue, however, through the remainder of 1874 and into 1875, and Major Jones was determined that his battalion would be in a position to handle Indians or any other problem that arose.

"During the first six months of service," Sergeant Gillett recalled, "nearly every company in the battalion had an Indian fight, and some of them two or three."[27]

By December 1, Jones could report fourteen Indian fights, with fifteen warriors known dead, ten wounded, and one captured. "Twenty-eight trails [were] followed, on some of which the Indians were seen, but could not be overtaken, besides small trails found that were too old to follow," he said.[28]

BESIDES FIGHTING INDIANS and hunting badmen, one of the main duties of the Texas Rangers during the 1870s was handling "difficulties." In a state where the gift for profound understatement is equal to the talent for gross exaggeration, the term describes differences of opinion or conflicts of interest that will not be resolved until somebody dies. During the nineteenth century, "difficulty" often meant a blood feud as bitter and vicious as any fought in the mountains of West Virginia or Kentucky. And in the decade after the Civil War, Texas abounded in such "difficulties."

Blood feuds started for many reasons, but the most common was the bitterness caused by the war. As the eminent Texas historian and self-proclaimed "feud collector" C. L. Sonnichsen once noted, the only great outbreak of coordinated bloodshed during the antebellum period was the Regular-Moderator Feud in east Texas in the 1840s. Yet after the war, no sooner had the defeated Confederates returned home than the killing began. Whether the cause was Southerner vs. Northerner, Republican vs. Democrat, Unionist vs. secessionist, or citizen vs. carpetbagger, all had their roots in the great conflict. Throughout the 1870s, the Rangers not only defended the frontier but had to keep otherwise law-abiding Texans from murdering each other in spasms of organized hate.[29]

Rangers did not look for feuds, but handled them when ordered to do so. In at least one incident, the Mason County War, they became involved because they happened to be on the scene at the time. The violence in Mason County during the summer and fall of 1875 was a classic Texas communal feud. On one side were German settlers who had been predominantly Unionist during the Civil War and were prosperous stock raisers. On the other were the Anglo-Saxons, resentful former Confederates whom the Germans blamed for an upsurge of cattle thefts in the area.

The killing began in earnest after Sheriff John Clark, a member of the German faction, arrested an Anglo-Saxon rancher named Lige Baccus, his cousin, and three employees, jailing them in the town of Mason on charges of cattle theft. That night a mob formed, and Clark, fearing a lynching, enlisted the aid of Capt. Dan Roberts and Ranger James Trainer, who were in town to buy grain for the Company D horses. The mob, however, stormed into the courthouse, pushed past Roberts and Trainer, rushed upstairs, and cornered Clark in his office. The invading men told the sheriff they meant no harm to him or the Rangers, but demanded that they stay out of the way. Seeing they were outnumbered, Clark told Roberts and Trainer to stand back while he went for help. The mob broke down the door of the jail, took the prisoners about half a mile down the Fredericksburg Road, and began stringing them up from a tree.

About that time, Clark arrived with the Rangers and five or six volunteers. Hearing gunshots, they opened fire and scattered the mob. Baccus, his cousin, and a cowhand were dangling from tree limbs. A fourth prisoner was lying dead "with his brains shot out," accounting for the gunshots the lawmen had heard. The fifth victim, a man named Johnson, had managed to slip his noose in the confusion and had jumped a fence and fled. The cowhand was still breathing when cut down from the tree. Roberts threw some water on him and rubbed him until he regained consciousness. He could not talk until the next morning. A couple of days later, Johnson staggered into the Ranger camp asking for protection. He later fled the area, and since his departure coincided with the violent death of one prominent citizen and disappearance of another, Roberts suspected Johnson had evened the score on his way out of the country.[30]

The lynching set off a series of killings that polarized the Anglo-Saxon and German communities. Among those lending their guns to the Anglo-Saxon faction were Scott Cooley, a former Ranger with Company D, and famed gunman Johnny Ringo. They had a list of people they considered responsible for the deaths of prominent Anglo-Saxons, and they began a campaign of retribution. "No one could tell who would be the next victim of the unerring aim of Scott Cooley's rifle," one Ranger observed, "The people of the whole country rose in arms to protect themselves."[31]

MAJOR JONES WAS inspecting Captain Roberts's camp on the San Saba, about forty miles to the west, in late September when a special courier arrived from Austin with instructions to send a detachment to quell the violence in Mason County. Cutting his visit short, Jones personally took charge of ten men from Roberts's Company D and, together with thirty from Lt. Ira Long's Company A, rode toward Mason. At a place called Kellar's Store, fifteen miles south of town, they encountered fifteen or twenty members of the German faction, armed with Winchesters, carbines, and revolvers. Upon learning that the Anglo-Saxons were supposedly also in the neighborhood, Jones decided to spend the night at Kellar's Store, hoping to resolve the grievances by discussing the matter with both sides. If that failed, he advised Adjutant General Steele, "I shall resort to other means to quiet the disturbance."[32]

Jones's subsequent investigation determined his Rangers were too closely involved with the Anglo-Saxon faction to render an effective deterrent to the feud. Mason County was within the normal jurisdiction of Company D, and members of the company had friends among local citizens. Many Rangers had served with Scott Cooley, who was now wanted for several murders. A member of the company later admitted:

> The Company D boys who had ranged with Cooley [were] in sympathy with the outlaw and . . . making no serious attempt to locate or imperil him. It was even charged that some of the Company D rangers met Cooley at night on the outskirts of Mason and told him they did not care if he killed every damned Dutchman [*sic*] in Mason County [involved in the feud].[33]

Jones responded by discharging three members of Company D and sending the remainder back to camp. Henceforth, he relied on Long's Company A. The shake-up in the Rangers was the beginning of the end of the Mason County War. Most of Long's men were from the interior of the state and had no friends or associates on either side. Unable to depend on Long's Rangers for cover, Scott Cooley moved to Blanco

County, where he died a few years later from a cerebral hemorrhage. Johnny Ringo was arrested for one of the killings, but charges were later dismissed.

Major Jones himself left Mason County on October 28, to continue his disrupted inspection tour. He had been in the county exactly one month. He left Lieutenant Long behind to maintain the peace, and the presence of these Rangers had a calming influence. The Mason County War was over.[34]

Chapter 12

The Rise of McNelly's Rangers

The Mason County War was just one of the "difficulties" that caused the decade of the 1870s to be known in Texas as "the Terrible Seventies." There were many others, such as the Jaybird-Woodpecker Feud in Fort Bend County just south of Houston, the Horrell-Higgins Feud in Lampasas County northwest of Austin, and the Shackelford County Feud northeast of Abilene. They left in their wake broken families and painful memories. Most terrible of all was DeWitt County's notorious Taylor-Sutton Feud, which, over the course of thirty years, left scores of people dead and prompted the legislature to create a special unit of peace officers "to assist the civil officers of DeWitt county in enforcing quiet and obedience to the law in that desperado ridden section."[1]

Although the new unit ultimately was absorbed into the regular Ranger Service, initially it was designated Washington County Volunteer Militia Company A. Informally, it was known as the Special Force, Texas State Troops, and McNelly's Rangers after its commanding officer, Capt. Leander H. McNelly. Whatever its name, the special unit functioned as a ranging company that answered to Adjutant General Steele, and the men of the Washington County Volunteer Militia considered themselves Rangers. Like those of the Frontier Battalion, they were professional, full-time lawmen, and Captain McNelly was an experienced peace officer.[2]

A Virginian, Leander McNelly was about sixteen years old when he came with his family to Texas in 1860. During the war he served with Confederate forces in New Mexico and Texas and as a captain of scouts in Louisiana, where he gained a reputation as a tenacious fighter. George Durham, who served under McNelly as a Ranger, and whose father had served under him as a Confederate, described the tactics that were his hallmark: "General [Robert E.] Lee made his plans first and then fought. . . . Captain McNelly made his plans like a chicken hawk—after he had located his target and was coming in for the kill."[3]

When the war ended, McNelly married and farmed near Brenham in Washington County, about midway between Austin and Houston. On July 1, 1870, he became one of four captains in Davis's Texas State Police, despite his hatred of the governor's Reconstruction regime. His reasons were obscure, but it has been suggested he accepted the position at the urging of friends, who perhaps believed that the best way to protect themselves was to have one of their own in command of a force that might oppress them. Whatever the motive, he soon established a reputation for integrity, although his determination to enforce the law—including the Reconstruction edicts—cost him some public confidence. Nevertheless, when the time came to appoint an officer to handle the trouble in DeWitt County, McNelly's experience and character made him the logical choice.[4]

Physically, McNelly was thin and frail, his naturally slight build wasted by tuberculosis. When he took command of the new unit he already was a dying man, which makes his career all the more remarkable. Soft-spoken and a sometime lay preacher, he nevertheless resorted to throat-cutting, lynching, and confessions through torture when they served his purposes.[5]

THE TAYLOR AND Sutton factions had been fighting each other for almost seven years by the time McNelly's men were sent to DeWitt County. The conflict erupted shortly after the end of the Civil War as a power struggle between the anti-Reconstruction Taylors and the pro-Reconstruction Sutton faction. Both groups had an extensive network of blood kin, in-laws, and close friends who rallied to their cause. The bloodshed outlasted Reconstruction, and by the time it ended, much of the prairie between San Antonio and the Gulf Coast was aflame with violence. DeWitt County, center of the storm, was virtually depopulated of decent citizens. As one Ranger noted, "It takes five large counties to bound De-Witt, and it is an awful strain on them to hold it all."[6]

The Taylor-Sutton Feud gave rise to a young tough whose name would become all too familiar to Rangers and other lawmen throughout the West—John Wesley Hardin. Known variously as John Hardin, Wes Hardin, or Jack Hardin, he was nineteen years old with several killings to his credit when he allied himself with the Taylors in the spring of 1873. A year later, on March 11, 1874, he orchestrated the murder of Bill Sutton, one of the leaders of the opposing faction, then fled to his family seat in Comanche, some two hundred miles to the northwest.

The Sutton murder and ensuing reprisals prompted District Judge H. Clay Pleasants, who presided in DeWitt County, to call for state intervention. At Pleasants's insistence, Adjutant General Steele came down from Austin, and he spent the first week of July interviewing citizens of the area. Steele's grim report, reprinted in the July 15 issue of the San Antonio *Daily Express,* brought statewide attention to the feud.[7]

MCNELLY AND FORTY Rangers arrived in DeWitt County at the end of July. Court was ready to convene in Clinton, the county seat. The ordinary citizens took comfort in the presence of the Rangers, hoping that for once some indictments would be returned and put a stop to all the killings. As things stood, both factions were armed to the teeth, and terror reigned every day after sunset. The situation wasn't lost on Ranger T. C. Robinson, who supplemented his state salary by writing dispatches to the Austin papers under the pseudonym "Pidge."[8]

"They have a cute way to carry their six-shooters without breaking the law," Pidge commented. "Every man carries his coat tied behind his saddle, and in its folds is a peace preserver of the Smith & Wesson persuasion, ready at all times to demonstrate to any officious individual that his views on certain questions are not sound, and his argumentative position untenable unless he is behind a tree."[9]

Assessing some of the leaders of the feud, he wrote that Joe Tumlinson of the Sutton faction "goes about like Robinson Cruso [*sic*] with a gun on each shoulder and two Smith & Wesson's (No. 3) in his belt . . . he has the frosts of sixty winters on his head, and green spectacles on his nose, and, it is said, can see with his naked eye farther than any hawk on this side of the Rio Grande." On the opposing side, Pidge noted John Taylor, who, "when on foot, reminds one strongly of an old sundried bucket about to fall to pieces; when on horseback his powers of endurance are almost incredible."[10]

McNelly realized these men were not impressed by conventional law enforcement or by the courts. Although the grand jury was in session and he believed the jurors would return indictments against both the Taylor and Sutton factions, he doubted the indictments would have any impact. In a report to Steele, McNelly said he personally had seen Tumlinson "at the head of seventy five well armed men," and speculated he could muster as many as 150, all loyal exclusively to him. Tumlinson would not appear in court without armed support from the Suttons, and the Taylors were equally determined. Both sides handled unpleasant legal cases by murdering witnesses.

"They are all alike Taylor & Sutton equally turbulent, treacherous and reckless," McNelly commented. "I need Winchester rifles[;] these people are all armed with them . . . and if I am compelled to fight I don[']t want to get whipped."

McNelly's assessment was correct. When court convened in Clinton to hear a case against Tumlinson, the room was crowded with his heavily armed supporters; witnesses suddenly suffered memory loss. "Court has adjourned, and Tomlinson's [sic] trial is postponed till next term," Pidge Robinson observed.[11]

THE TAYLOR-SUTTON Feud continued, but by the fall of 1874 the rate of killing on both sides was beginning to drop. Many of the leaders were dead, and the survivors had exhausted themselves, each other, and the people of DeWitt County. It was particularly evident in public gatherings. Pidge told his readers about a church service in Clinton.

> Not an old man was seen in church, not a silverhead could be observed, and I suppose that old people are never seen in DeWitt. If they are not killed they hide out in a country above here called "the brush," where the words of the gospel will never reach them unless used as wads for a double-barreled shotgun.[12]

One of the few old men left to attend church was Sutton leader Joe Tumlinson, and he had become regular about it. Perhaps sensing his own approaching end and conscious of all the blood on his hands, he was baptized and spent the final weeks of his life in prayer and penance. Some of the Taylors questioned his sincerity, but were willing to let the matter go. Joe died in late fall 1874, and with his death the feud lost much of its steam—at least for the time being.

The district court convened again in December and, as usual, took no action against any of the feudists. The remarkable thing was that the session was quiet. McNelly's men departed for the Mexican border, where their presence was deemed more necessary, and an uneasy calm settled in DeWitt County.[13]

For almost two years, the Taylors and Suttons maintained the shaky truce. But given the longevity of the feud, its scope, and the hatred it engendered, the two sides could keep the peace for only so long. The killing flared up again in 1876, culminating with the apparently pointless double murder of Dr. Philip Brassell and his son, George, on the night of September 19. By morning, word of the killing had spread throughout the area, and the people of DeWitt County had had enough. Dr. Brassell was a respected member of the community who had no particular quarrel with either Taylors or Suttons. Public indignation was so great that it was no longer safe for anyone to ally himself with or condone the murderers, and Judge Pleasants took advantage of the situation to once again demand the Rangers.[14]

In response, McNelly dispatched Lt. Lee Hall, who arrived in Clinton with a squad of Rangers on November 23 and camped in the pasture behind Judge Pleasants's house. Hall noted that local law enforcement, unaware that the judge had called for the Rangers, was unpleasantly surprised to see them on the streets of Clinton the following morning. The DeWitt County Sheriff's Office was holding about 150 murder indictments, not one of which had ever been served, and the presence of the Rangers only pointed up the inability—or unwillingness—of the county authorities to do anything about the feud.[15]

THE RANGER COMMANDER was born in North Carolina on October 9, 1849, as Jesse Leigh Hall. When he was nineteen years old, he went to Texas in search of excitement. Upon arrival, however, he found he had to support himself by teaching school in Grayson County, where the tendency of parents to mispronounce his middle name as "Lay" prompted him to change the spelling to "Lee." He was also called "Red" because of the color of his hair. During his first two years in Texas, he often volunteered to assist local peace officers, until, finally, he gave up teaching to become city marshal of Sherman, the county seat. He established a reputation as an honest, dependable officer and was appointed sergeant-at-arms to the state legislature for the spring and summer of 1876. In August, he was named a lieutenant of McNelly's company.[16]

Court was scheduled to convene in Clinton to try criminal cases on December 18. Two days before the docket was to be called, Hall wrote Adjutant General Steele:

> I am confident of arresting the murderers of Dr. Brazzell [*sic*] and his son. I hold now thirty-one murder indictments and know where I can find the men. All of these criminals have friends throughout the county, because more than half of the county is mixed up in this matter. They are so involved in deeds of blood that they cannot afford to have any member of the brotherhood sent to prison. The people are completely terrorized and cowed by the assassins and cutthroats who got their hands in, shedding blood during the Taylor-Sutton troubles, then joined so-called vigilant associations, and are now killing off witnesses and intimidating juries by threats of violence, so that we believe it is impossible to secure a conviction.[17]

Despite Hall's misgivings, the grand jury met as scheduled and indicted Deputy Sheriff Bill Meador, Deputy Sheriff Joe Sitterlie, William Cox, Jacob Ryan, David Augustine, Frank Heister, and Charles Heissig for the murders of Dr. Brassell and his son. All the suspects were members of the Sutton faction. Hall received the warrants on December 20 and, with Judge Pleasants's blessings, determined to execute them as soon as possible.

"I want you to do your part," the judge told the Ranger, "and I will see that the courts deal justice. Together, we can bring order out of chaos."[18]

HALL KNEW JOE Sitterlie planned to get married on December 22, and the Sutton faction would be out in force to help celebrate. He decided to round up the suspects during the festivities. The night was cold and drizzly, and the dance was held at a home a few miles outside of Cuero.[19]

While the Suttons partied, Hall rode into the Ranger camp and told his men to saddle up.

"We won't go far, so you needn't take any blankets," he said. "We'll be back tonight."

About two hundred yards from the house where the party was under way, Hall ordered the men to dismount. They slipped up to the house, which was a "dog trot" consisting of two separate rooms connected by an open gallery. It was brightly lit, and the Rangers could see dancers through the windows. Ranger George Durham remembered the fiddlers playing "Cowboys' Christmas Ball" as the caller chanted the words. Only Joe Sitterlie and Bill Meador, the two deputies, were armed. The others had checked their guns at the door in deference to frontier custom.

Hall positioned his men around the building. Four Rangers with double-barreled shotguns were put at the ends of the long porches. The music changed to "Oh, Suzanna!" After making certain each man was in place and ready, Hall walked into the house, armed with a carbine.

"Do you want anyone here, Ranger?" Joe Sitterlie demanded.

"We're Rangers. Joe Sitterlie, you're under arrest."

"You go to hell," Sitterlie replied.

"You're under arrest," Hall repeated. "Come with me."

"Go to hell, Ranger," Sitterlie said again. "This is my wedding night. I ain't coming. If you got enough men come and get me."

"I've got enough men," Hall told him. "I've got papers here for six others: Bill Meador, Bill Cox, Jake Ryan, Dave Augustine, Frank Heister, and Charley Heissig. If you don't want to come peaceably, then clear the women and children from the room. We'll take you."

After years of bloodshed, the Sutton women were used to gunfights and didn't flinch. One of them asked: "Mr. Big Texas Ranger, would it be all right if we women stood alongside this wall where we could see?"

"Lady, you can do as you feel like," Hall said. "I'm here to take out these seven men."

After more arguing and tough talk, the Sutton men began to realize they were outgunned by the Rangers surrounding the house. They began to back down. One of the women suggested allowing the dance to continue until morning, after which the men would accompany the Rangers. Sitterlie gave his word they would go quietly. After taking Bill Meador into immediate custody as a hostage, Hall agreed.

"But remember," Hall cautioned, "he dies if any attempt is made to break him loose. That's a Ranger law."

The dance continued, and several Rangers joined the festivities under the watchful eye of their lieutenant. Then, at sunup, the Rangers took the suspects into custody. Judge Pleasants ordered them held without bond.[20]

ATTORNEYS FOR THE accused spent a week filing motions for habeas corpus, apparently disputing the evidence against their clients. When court convened, the Rangers disarmed every spectator so that, for the first time, fear and intimidation within the courtroom were not factors in DeWitt County. Three Rangers, their carbines cocked, stood by Judge Pleasants as he prepared to rule on the motions.[21] The judge regarded the crowd for a moment, then said in a calm but firm voice:

> This county is and has been for years a reproach to the fair name of the State of Texas. Over it have roamed bands of lawless men, committing terrible outrages, murdering whomever met their disdain, shooting down men from ambush in the most cowardly manner possible. Here in this very room, listening to me now, are murderers who long ago should have been hanged. At this time, I do not speak of the prisoners at the bar, but of you who yet are free. You are murderers, bushwhackers, midnight assassins.
>
> Some of you have dared to threaten me with cowardly, unsigned letters, and I have needed to bring state soldiers into this court of justice. I learn that you have blamed the sheriff of this county for calling upon the Rangers to assist in restoring order. No, it was not the sheriff who had the Rangers sent here; it was I. I called for them and I am going to see that they remain here in this county until it is as peaceful and law-abiding as any in the State—as quiet and orderly as any in the Union. I tell you now, beware! The day of reckoning is surely coming. It is close at hand. When you deal with the Texas Rangers, you deal with men who are fearless in the discharge of their duty and who will surely conquer you.
>
> I shall send these men at the bar to jail to await trial for as wicked and cowardly a murder as ever disgraced this State. It is but the beginning. Others will soon follow them. The reign of the lawless in DeWitt County is at an end!
>
> Lieutenant Hall, clear the room, sir![22]

Because of legal maneuverings, the cases dragged on for years. Charges against Meador were finally dropped in 1894. Cox, Ryan, and Sitterlie were convicted, but the convictions were overturned on appeal. Cox, Sitterlie, and Jim Heister moved to New Mexico, where Sitterlie became a leading citizen and worked to live down his past. Dave Augustine ultimately was convicted, but on October 30, 1899, thirty years after the feud began and twenty-three years after the Brassell murders, he received a governor's pardon. The Taylor-Sutton Feud was finally over.

WHILE LEE HALL rounded up feudists in DeWitt County, McNelly had most of his company on the Mexican border, where, according to Wilburn King's Ranger history, they "proved so active, vigilant, daring, and successful, in dealing with lawless characters and with hostile Mexicans, as to secure a permanent good name for themselves and beneficial results to the border, by their gallant and zealous performance of duty."[23]

This, of course, is a matter of opinion. Trouble did indeed exist on the Mexican border. Nevertheless, McNelly's efforts, while effective, were sometimes criticized as high-handed even in his own time, and there is some evidence that he was not always particular about whether his bandit-hunting turned up the right people.

The lawless area was the Nueces Strip, in the southernmost part of Texas, a region of almost impenetrable brush between the Nueces River in the north and east and the Rio Grande in the south and west. Settled by the Spaniards in the 1700s, it originally was part of the province of Nuevo Santander, and later the Mexican state of Tamaulipas. Texas did not gain permanent and official possession until the Treaty of Guadalupe Hidalgo in 1848, and even then and for many years afterward, some Mexicans were ready to fight about it. Banditry and cattle rustling were major industries in the Strip, with the close proximity of the Mexican border aggravating the situation.

The Mexican government inadvertently contributed to the discord by creating the *zona libre,* or free zone, a narrow strip of land running along the Mexican side of the border where foreign goods—specifically from the United States—could be imported without paying the exorbitant duties levied throughout the rest of the nation. Although the zone was designed to alleviate the problems of the border people who routinely acquired goods in the United States that were prohibitively expensive or unavailable in Mexico, it also provided a cover for bandits transporting stolen American goods and livestock into Mexico.[24]

The generally unstable conditions became worse after 1870 when Juan N. Cortina—the same Cortina who had created so much mayhem on the border in the late 1850s—became governor of Tamaulipas and from his position of authority orchestrated cattle raids as far north as Corpus Christi. Adjutant General Steele believed Cortina controlled the entire cattle-stealing industry between Camargo and the mouth of the river and accused him of shipping stolen Texas cattle from the Rio Grande to Cuba. Brig. Gen. Edward O. C. Ord, commander of the army's Department of Texas, agreed, but was restricted by government policy from retaliating. In 1873, units of the Fourth United States Cavalry created an international incident by striking sixty miles into Coahuila in an unauthorized but tacitly approved raid. Since then, however, the federal government had tried to avoid affronts to Mexican sovereignty. Rangers, though, did not always observe such restrictions, and it was in response to border cattle thievery and banditry that McNelly was ordered to the border.[25]

ON MARCH 26, 1875, bandits raided practically to the Nueces itself, attacking settlements within a few miles of Corpus Christi. More raids were reported in early April, prompting Nueces County sheriff John McClure to telegraph Steele:

> Is Capt. McNally [*sic*] coming[?] we are in trouble[.] five ranches burned by disguised men near Laparra last week[.][26]

McNelly, however, was already on his way. He had reorganized his company on April 1 and left for the Nueces Strip on April 10. Arriving in Corpus Christi, he found that his first priority was to bring the local population under control. Many depredations had been committed not only by Mexican bandits, but by Americans, either desperadoes or self-appointed "posses" and vigilance committees.

"The acts committed by Americans in this section are horrible to relate," he reported to Steele, "many ranches have been plundered and burned, and the people murdered or driven away; one of these parties confessed to me in Corpus Christi as having killed eleven (11) men, on their last raid."[27]

Clamping down, he published a special order in the local newspaper stating:

> In consequence of the recent outrages committed in this portion of the country by armed bands of men acting without authority of law, I find it necessary to notify all such organizations that after the publication of this order I will arrest all such bands and turn them over to the civil authorities of the counties where they are arrested, and nothing but the actual presents [*sic*] of some duly accredited officer of the County or State will protect them from arrest.
>
> L. H. McNelly
Capt Co A Vol Mil[28]

The order created a furor, not only in Corpus Christi, but elsewhere in the state. It was called "the McNelly Pronunciamento," and the San Antonio *Daily Express* went so far as to call McNelly the "captain of a Corporal's guard" who presumed to issue orders "like an emperor." Unconcerned by the public reaction, McNelly rode on toward Santa Gertrudis, headquarters of the near-legendary King Ranch, where Capt. Richard King was building one of the greatest cattle empires in the world. The ranch had always been a target for attack, and Ranger George Durham noted that the main house

> was more like an army arsenal inside. In one big room there were eighty stands of Henry repeating rifles and maybe a hundred boxes of shells. Two men stood in the lookout tower day and night and there was always a man at the ready for each of those rifles. But that didn't stop the raiders.

The Rangers rested for a few days enjoying the hospitality of the ranch. Noticing the poor quality of horses the state provided, Captain King gave them fine blooded remounts, pointing out that if he didn't, the bandits would probably steal them. "Most of those rascals are mounted on my stock, and I at least want to do as good by you," he told McNelly.[29]

CONTINUING SOUTH TOWARD the Rio Grande, McNelly found that raids by "posses" and vigilantes had forced the Mexican and *tejano* populations to band together "for their own protection and under the orders of the Deputy Sheriff. . . . Mexican citizens have no security for life or property in this section whatever."[30]

The Rangers ran into one such posse, a rough-looking, undisciplined group whose leader informed McNelly they planned to ride with him.

"I've got all the men I need," McNelly replied. "I'm going to disband and disarm these men and return them to their homes."

"They won't do that," the posse leader said.

"Then I'm ordering you to. Disband and disarm them."

"They won't do that for me," the man told him.

"They will for me," McNelly snapped. He had been chewing the end of an unlit cigar, which his men recognized as a sign he was growing impatient.

When the posse leader said they would have to vote on it, McNelly gave him ten minutes, but added, "If you don't vote to lay down those arms and surrender to the regular law of Texas, my Rangers will move on you and lay them down for you."

"Meaning we're the same as outlaws?" the man asked.

"I can't prove you are right now," McNelly said. "I don't know what all you posses have been doing. But at the end of ten minutes you will be. You will be reckoned as armed outlaws. And we've been sent in to kill them."

With that, he took out his watch. As time passed and the posse members argued among themselves, he took his pistol from his holster, and the other Rangers followed suit. Finally, the posse leader rode up and handed his own pistol to McNelly.

"You may keep it," McNelly told him. "But use it only to defend your home."[31]

THE RANGERS WERE now deep into an area where they could expect a fight. In camp one night, McNelly lined them up and told them that soon they would go out on scouting details of two and three men each.

"There are only two kinds of people for us—outlaws and law-abiding," he said. "Treat these law-abiding folks with all respect, regardless of color or size. Don't enter a house unless the man invites you in. Don't take a roasting ear [of corn] or melon unless he tells you to. If his dog barks at you, get away from it. Don't shoot it. Let them know we're their friends sent down to help them.

"As for the others," he continued, "place under arrest and bring into camp everybody else. Horseback or afoot, singly or in groups. Arrest them, fetch them into camp.

"Until further orders, all prisoners will be put under the old Spanish law—*la ley de fuga*—which means the prisoner is to be killed on the spot if a rescue is attempted."

McNelly made it clear that the bandits did not fight by any accepted rules of civilized warfare and neither would he. He had no compunction about killing, and saw no need to keep prisoners alive if they made nuisances of themselves. Ranger Durham later admitted that he had misgivings about McNelly's methods, calling them "too harsh. But," he added, "those were orders."[32]

In Edinburg, McNelly's company relieved Capt. Neal Coldwell, who had established a solid reputation as an Indian fighter and bandit hunter on the northern frontier but had been unable to control depredations along the Rio Grande. Soon afterward, McNelly established a base camp at Las Rucias, about midway between Edinburg and Brownsville, before continuing downriver to Brownsville. There it was learned that a buyer for the Cuban market had arranged to purchase two thousand head of cattle from Cortina, most of which had American brands. A ship was lying offshore in Mexican waters to take them on board. Meanwhile, American cattle on the Mexican side were driven back away from the river, probably in fear of the Rangers, whose arrival had created a minor panic in Mexico. Ranchers upriver from Matamoros were organizing to repel what they believed was an impending invasion, sentinels were posted at the crossings, and women and children were being sent away from the houses at night.[33]

THE BREAK CAME on June 5, when McNelly learned sixteen Mexicans had crossed the river eight miles below Brownsville on a cattle-stealing expedition. He dispatched Pidge Robinson with eighteen men to the crossing of the Arroyo Colorado on the north side of the Rio Grande delta to scout the area and locate them. Three days later, Pidge reported he had captured one of the band, and McNelly joined him with the main company.

McNelly's method of interrogating prisoners—confirmed by recollections of Rangers Durham and William Callicott—was simple, brutal, and effective. A *tejano* member of his company, Ranger Jesús Sandoval, had an affinity for hanging and, in fact, had once hanged four Mexicans for stealing cattle on his ranch. Sandoval, whom the Rangers called "Casuse" in a vague attempt at the Spanish pronunciation of his first name, lashed the prisoner's hands behind his back, put a rope around his neck, and dragged him to the nearest tree. The rope was thrown over the branch and the prisoner was hoisted up until he almost strangled. If the prisoner proved stubborn, he would be jerked up and then allowed to fall, repeated several times until he talked.

Subjected to the Sandoval third degree, Pidge's prisoner told McNelly that the raiders consisted of sixteen men, sent by Cortina to the vicinity of the oft-raided La Parra Ranch to round up cattle for Cuba. He was standing rear guard when the Rangers caught him.

McNelly sent a scout to follow the trail of the main band and deployed his men to guard every crossing of the arroyo for twenty miles. A second prisoner was taken and, after a few minutes under a tree with Jesús Sandoval, said the bandits planned to drive three hundred head of cattle across the arroyo that night and push on to the river the next day. The prisoners were turned over to Sandoval, who rode away with them and shortly afterward returned alone. The members of the company later learned that he had completed the job of hanging them, something that undoubtedly McNelly already knew.

NOW THAT HE had his information, McNelly stationed his men on top of a knoll overlooking the stream and remained there until 2 A.M., when a scout rode in and reported that the bandits had crossed four miles to the east earlier that night. The Rangers mounted immediately, riding southeast toward the bay, hoping to either find the trail or get in front of them. About 7 A.M., they spotted the bandits with the herd about eight miles away. Seeing the Rangers, the thieves began running the herd. After a three-mile chase, they drove the cattle to a little island in a marsh, known locally as a resaca. Then they moved to the opposite side out onto the plain of Palo Alto, east of the field where General Taylor had defeated the Mexican army almost thirty years before, and prepared to fight.[34]

"We could see with the naked eye the mounted men and the stock," Durham remembered. "The country was open hardpan, except for a few clumps of dagger [yucca] and some salt cedar and marsh grass."

The Rangers spurred their horses until they reached the edge of the marsh about five hundred yards from where the cattle thieves had dug in. Then McNelly gathered them together.

"Boys," he said, "across this resaca are some outlaws that claim they're bigger than the law—bigger than Washington law, bigger than Texas law. Right now we'll find out if they're right or if they're wrong. This won't be a standoff or a dog fall. We'll either win completely, or we'll lose completely."[35]

The marsh was filled with about eighteen or twenty inches of mud and water. The bandits were behind a bank between four and five feet high. McNelly formed a skirmish line, placing his men five feet apart, and moved in. They were ordered to keep their carbines slung and pistols holstered, not to fire until ordered, and to fire directly ahead, not to the right or left. As soon as they moved into the morass, the bandits behind the bank opened fire, as did mounted members of the gang who had remained with the herd on the island to the left. The Rangers continued into the gunfire at a slow walk, their horses unable to move faster in the muck.

Firing grew heavier as the Rangers got halfway across, but the bandits' marksmanship was poor and they fired low. Still, McNelly pressed forward without firing a shot. "That must have spooked them," Durham commented. "It sure spooked me."

Cpl. William I. Rudd's horse was wounded, and he jumped clear as the animal fell. Other horses went down, either wounded or stumbling in the mud. Finally, when the Rangers came within seventy-five or a hundred yards of the bank, most of the bandits jumped on their horses and began riding off. As soon as McNelly's men got on hard ground, they spurred their horses and gave chase. When they were within pistol range, the bandits broke into a gallop. Most of the Rangers' horses were too tired to keep up, so McNelly sent three men on the best mounts to head them off and force a stand. The bandits stood their ground until McNelly himself arrived with four or five additional men.[36]

Several of the bandits broke through the Ranger line and started toward the Rio Grande. "After that," McNelly reported, "it was a succession of single hand fights for six miles before we got the last one." All twelve bandits guarding the cattle were killed, and it was later determined the final death toll was fifteen. Looking back on it, McNelly couldn't suppress a grudging admiration for the cattle thieves.

> I have never seen men fight with such desperation. Many of
> them after being shot from their horses, and severely wounded

three or four times would rise on their elbows and fire at my men as they passed.[37]

McNelly's only casualty was eighteen-year-old L. B. "Berry" Smith, who remains the youngest Texas Ranger to die in the line of duty. They captured twelve horses with rifles, pistols, and saddles and recovered 265 head of cattle.

About that time, Cameron County sheriff James J. Brown arrived with a posse of *tejanos*. Riding hard, they had seen much of the fight, but their horses were too tired to get there in time. The bodies of the dead bandits were turned over to Brown, and members of his posse positively identified all of them as Cortina's.[38]

Returning to Brownsville, the Rangers found the city in an uproar. The poorer residents, who were either Mexican or of Mexican descent, viewed Cortina as a hero and took the killing of his men as a personal affront. In Mexico itself, Cortina supporters were threatening to kill ten Americans for each of their people who died in the fight. The total garrison at Fort Brown was only 250 officers, soldiers, and servants, and McNelly doubted they would be able to prevent an incursion into Brownsville by the number of men Cortina could command.

Despite the weakness of the garrison, the soldiers turned out to bury Berry Smith with military honors. Among the mourners was his father, Ranger D. R. "Old Man" Smith, who was also a member of the company. Old Man Smith had been detailed as camp guard and had asked McNelly before the fight to leave his son, too, because he was an only child. McNelly agreed, but Berry had insisted on going along. Now an escort of soldiers and Rangers followed the coffin to the military cemetery at Fort Brown, where a rifle team fired a salute as the body was lowered into the ground.

The bodies of the dead bandits were stacked in the square in Brownsville. McNelly wanted them displayed as an example of what Rangers did with cattle thieves.[39]

WITH THE THREAT of a Cortinista incursion, most people believed McNelly planned to strike the first blow with a raid into Mexico. Several Rangers announced they would not fight across the river and took their discharges, and McNelly, who did not tolerate dissent, practically drove them out of camp.[40]

As time passed, however, there was little activity on either side. Despite the threats, the Palo Alto fight had severely shaken Cortina's people, and they tended to avoid the area. A major hindrance was removed when the Mexican government, bowing to U.S. diplomatic pressure and no doubt tired of unstable conditions on the border, summoned Cortina to Mexico City under arrest.

With Cortina under more or less permanent detention in the capital, his mantle of leadership passed on to lesser men. The cattle thieves shifted their operations upriver toward Camargo and operated on a smaller scale. After scouting the lower Rio Grande area through the summer, McNelly took his company up to Laredo in September, then, feeling ill, departed for his home in Brenham to recuperate. Pidge Robinson was left in charge during his absence. With little to do in Laredo, Pidge resumed his literary endeavors. He had stopped writing for the *Statesman* in December 1874, apparently after a falling-out with the editor. In October, however, the Pidge letters resumed, this time in the pages of the rival Austin *State Gazette.*[41]

The first letter described Casuse Sandoval's dexterity with a rope. "He is *so* kind and *so* considerate that it is almost a pleasure to be hanged by such a nice gentleman," Pidge wrote. "Cortina, before his arrest, would have given his right arm to have caught Sandoval on the Mexican side . . . and even now it is as much as his life is worth if he should be seen in Matamoras [*sic*]."[42]

MCNELLY RETURNED TO find bandit activities had resumed in the Brownsville area. Over two hundred head of cattle had been stolen, and driven across the river and on to Monterrey. At this point, he appears to have begun thinking seriously of an incursion into Mexico. He discussed the situation with Col. Joseph H. Potter, Twenty-fourth Infantry, at Fort Brown, who gave him the impression that General Ord might lend support. He also was encouraged by Capt. DeWitt Clinton Kells, commander of the U.S. gunboat *Rio Bravo,* which patrolled the Rio Grande. Kells, an adventurer who had been part of American filibuster William Walker's ill-fated invasion of Nicaragua in the 1850s, seemed eager for an incident, and ready to provoke one himself if the Mexicans would not oblige.[43]

The army was ready to do its part within the legal constraints of an international boundary. On November 8, 1875, two detachments of the

Eighth Cavalry were ordered out of Fort Brown, one under Lt. H. J. Farnsworth to Fort Ringgold, and the other commanded by Capt. James F. Randlett "with all the commissioned officers, and as many enlisted men of his company . . . as can be armed and mounted" to Edinburg. Randlett was specifically ordered to "scout the country after armed bands of *Mexican Cattle Thieves and Marauders*" and to make "the utmost endeavors" to recover stolen property and arrest the thieves.[44]

Randlett arrived in Edinburg on November 12, established his camp, and, the following day, began sending small details of troops to patrol the countryside, look for trails of cattle thieves, and become acquainted with the area and people. About dark on November 16, he learned that a party of about fifteen cattle thieves had crossed into Texas looking for cattle, and probably would return the following night. Presuming that they would return to Mexico at Las Cuevas crossing, about twenty miles up-river from Edinburg, he took thirty men to intercept them and sent a message to the adjutant at Fort Brown asking that a backup detail be sent from Ringgold.[45]

McNelly, meanwhile, arrived in Edinburg and on November 17 received word that the cattle thieves were definitely heading toward Las Cuevas. Assembling his company, he arrived at the crossing the following day, and learned that Randlett had found the thieves crossing the river with about 250 stolen cattle and opened fire. The Mexicans returned fire, holding off the troops long enough to eventually get all but about twenty-five head into Mexico. McNelly met with Maj. D. R. Clendennin, who had arrived with a backup detail from Ringgold and assumed command.[46] The two men went over the options, and McNelly telegraphed Adjutant General Steele:

> A party of raiders have crossed two hundred & fifty cattle at Los Cuevos [*sic*] they have been firing on Maj Clendennin[']s men[.] he refuses to cross without further orders[.] I shall cross tonight if I can get any support.
>
> LH McNelly[47]

Clendennin was opposed to the crossing, but apparently indicated (or so McNelly chose to believe) that he would support the Rangers if they got into trouble on the Mexican side. With that, McNelly again telegraphed to Steele:

> I commence crossing at one oclock tonight[.] have thirtyone men[.] will try & recover our cattle[.] the U.S. troops promise to cover my return[.] Lt Robinson has just arrived making a march of fifty five miles in six hours.[48]

At 1 A.M., November 19, while the soldiers fired into Mexico to draw attention, the Rangers marched down the bank single-file, leading their horses. The men climbed into boats; the animals were to swim. All went well until the horses, exhausted from Pidge Robinson's forced march, became mired in the mud and quicksands of the banks. "It was calculated that with the best of luck and no accident all of them could be safely landed on the Mexican bank by Christmas Eve," Pidge told his readers. After struggling to get five animals across the river, McNelly decided the effort was useless and ordered the others left on the Texas side. The horses were unsaddled and turned loose. The Rangers would fight on foot.[49]

TODAY, LAS CUEVAS is called Díaz Ordaz, and is a typical modern Mexican small town. It is reached either by highway from Camargo or by driving to Los Ebanos, Texas, and taking the hand-drawn ferry, preserved as the last of its kind on the boundary between the United States and a foreign country. In the 1870s, it was a large settlement, more of a village than a ranch, with a substantial population. McNelly believed the cattle were held there, defended by between 250 and 300 men. He hoped to surprise them by dashing in, taking the first house, and holding it until relieved by the U.S. troops he presumed would come to his aid. He was aware, as he later told Steele, that "[n]ot one of us could get back without the aid of their troops," and said he had made that position clear to the army officers before crossing the river.

The Rangers walked two and a half miles until, about daylight, they came to a large picket fence cutting across the trail with houses beyond. This must be Las Cuevas, they thought. Casuse Sandoval moved along the perimeter and found a gate. McNelly formed up his men and gave his orders. Kill everyone but the old men, women, and children. Then he pulled open the bars of the gate.

"Stand to one side, boys. Casuse has not had a chance to breathe Mexican air or give a yell in Mexico for over twenty years. We'll let Casuse wake them up."

Sandoval, one of the five men with horses, shoved his hat back and took the other riders through the gate. Then he dug in his spurs and gave a Comanche yell, and the five charged among the picket huts, their pistols blazing. The others ran in from behind.

"If the angels of heaven had come down on that ranch the Mexicans would not have been more surprised," Ranger Bill Callicott remembered. "We were the first Rangers they had seen since the Mexican War."

Some of the men were gunned down as they cut wood for the morning's cooking fires. "Every moving thing was a fair target," Durham remarked.

Soon all was quiet. A woman who was questioned gave some unsettling information. This was not Las Cuevas. This was the ranch of Las Cachutas. Las Cuevas was half a mile farther up the trail. The Rangers had attacked the wrong settlement and, according to McNelly's official report, killed four men. Pidge, however, estimated the toll as seven killed and nine wounded, probably a more accurate figure considering the indiscriminate gunplay.

McNelly was less concerned with the error (which he later tried to justify by claiming the men were pickets for the main force) than with the fact that all hope of surprise now was lost. Nevertheless, he moved on to Las Cuevas and, coming over a rise, saw it ahead. The village had two sides closed by a six-foot stockade. There were several groups of *jacales*—picket houses with thatched roofs—and a chapel in the middle of town.[50]

The Rangers moved in but were met by almost three hundred men, about a third of whom were mounted. To Pidge, it seemed like the column of horsemen stretched more than a hundred miles downriver, all the way to Matamoros. The others held the ground and corrals in front of the village. McNelly immediately saw that his hope of taking and holding one of the houses was futile. The nearest house was still a hundred yards away, and the Mexicans had the ground in between. Both sides began shooting. The Ranger fire took its toll, but the Mexicans quickly recovered, especially after a group of mounted men rode in from the direction of Camargo and their leader took control. "His trappings were all silver-garnished, and his horse was a blooded animal," Durham remembered. McNelly recognized him as Gen. Juan Flores Salinas, who owned the ranch and controlled the surrounding area, a man who could organize the Mexicans into a coherent unit. Flores divided the mounted men, sending them around the Rangers on either side, to come in from behind.

"Every man break for the river, or we'll be cut off," McNelly ordered. "Keep low and don't shoot unless overhauled. Break lines and make it your own way."

The river was more than two miles away in a direct line through heavy brush. Had the Mexicans known the true situation, Durham believed, they would have moved in and cut them to pieces. As it was, Sgt. George Hall with four mounted Rangers held them back and they advanced slowly, giving the others time to get ahead. They reached the river without opposition.

McNelly's next move defies comprehension. Instead of crossing the river back into Texas under the covering fire of U.S. troops, he ordered his men to dig in. He told them that the Mexicans would believe they had fled in panic across the river. Even so, there was no reason for him to remain, because he had totally failed in his objective. Perhaps he was still hoping to induce the soldiers into coming over. Whatever his motives, he established the mounted men as a picket line in the brush, then retreated about 150 yards across an open field.

Soon they heard gunfire, and the pickets came dashing across the field with Mexican horsemen chasing them. George Hall and John B. Armstrong lost their horses and came running on foot. McNelly's men opened fire, killing Juan Flores, and the Mexicans retreated. Soon Lieutenant Randlett crossed the river with thirty soldiers and a Gatling gun, and opened fire.

"If there is an inanimate object in this whole world for which I have a pure and unadulterated veneration, respect and love, that object is a Gatling gun," Pidge later told his readers. Right now, though, he had little time to reflect. Despite the heavy fire, the Mexicans held firm, and McNelly ordered him to charge and break them up.[51]

A QUIET DESCENDED over the river. About 5 P.M., a Mexican appeared with a flag of truce and a letter addressed to "Commander of the American forces on Mexican soil." McNelly refused to receive it, so it was handed to Randlett. The message was from the mayor of Camargo, under whose jurisdiction Las Cuevas fell. He assured the recipient that Mexican authorities were taking steps "to secure the capture of the cattle thieves and their punishment in conformity with the law," and demanded United States forces withdraw from the country.[52]

Randlett had no option but to comply. McNelly, however, refused to consider it until the Mexicans delivered the stolen cattle and the thieves. After some negotiation, both sides agreed to a cease-fire and settled down for the night.

As the fight dragged into its second day, the army dealt with the implications of a military incursion into a foreign nation that, officially at least, was friendly. In San Antonio, General Ord had received orders from army headquarters to stay on the U.S. side of the boundary. He telegraphed Colonel Potter at Fort Brown to advise the Mexican authorities that United States soldiers would not cross the river. Potter, in turn, notified Maj. A. J. Alexander, who had superseded Major Clendennin at Las Cuevas crossing, that McNelly was on his own as long as he remained in Mexico.

"Inform him that you are directed not to support him in anyway [*sic*] while he remains on Mexican territory," Potter directed. "If McNelly is attacked by Mexican forces on Mexican ground do not render him any assistance."[53]

As the day progressed, the Mexicans appeared amiable. Early in the morning, they had raised a flag of truce and returned the horses lost by George Hall and Armstrong. One of the saddles was missing, but they promised to look for it and return it later in the day. In turn, McNelly agreed to keep his flag of truce up and to give one hour's notice before resuming the fight. Privately, he realized his situation was becoming desperate. He was surrounded and he knew the Mexicans had been reinforced. He began to consider asking the Mexicans for terms. Thomas F. Wilson, the U.S. consul in Matamoros, believed he had no choice and sent a telegram advising him to surrender to Mexican federal authorities.

In one last effort to avoid humiliation, McNelly decided to try a bluff. At 4 P.M. on November 20, he notified the Mexicans that he expected the stolen stock and thieves to be delivered to him at Rio Grande City by 10 A.M. the following day. Otherwise he would advance immediately against their lines. Several notes were exchanged, and the Mexicans agreed to consider it.

That was enough for McNelly. He had saved face. He led his men back across the river and up to Fort Ringgold. The following day, sixty-five

head of cattle were delivered, and the mayor of Camargo and a delegation of citizens called with assurances that Mexico would take steps to
stop the raids.

McNelly did not believe it, but it did not matter.[54] He had made a terrific fool of himself by attacking the wrong settlement, and had caused
the deaths of innocent people. He had created an international incident.
And he had put his own men in serious danger of annihilation. In the end,
however, he had managed to save his command, and make enough impression on the Mexican officials to get at least a portion of the stolen
cattle returned.

Chapter 13

Bad Times for Badmen

One of the problems perennially facing the Texas Rangers was money. When Indians or badmen were active, or when the Mexican border was in turmoil, the legislature willingly voted money for a frontier force. When things were quiet—and sometimes even when they weren't—the need for law enforcement or defense somehow didn't seem as immediate, and lawmakers began cutting back until the next emergency.

As early as October 27, 1874, when the Frontier Battalion was only five months old, Major Jones was forced to issue a general order forbidding the sharing of rations with "camp-followers and loafers" who hung around the camps on the pretext of waiting for an opening for enlistment. "In view of the fact that it may be necessary to disband a portion of the command before a great while, no more recruits will be received until further orders."[1]

A year later, on October 25, 1875, he issued yet another order stating:

> On account of the meager appropriation for frontier defense, for the current year and the consequent necessity for economizing its expenditures as much as possible; on the 30th of November next commanders of companies will reduce the force of their re-

spective companies by discharging all except two Sergeants, one corporal, and seventeen privates, giving to the men discharged final statements of their accounts, as has been done heretofore in similar cases.[2]

The dilemma with these cutbacks was that although the Indian threat was drawing to a close and the iron-fisted rule of Porfirio Díaz ultimately would bring the Mexican border under control, the badman problem remained serious. In a lengthy report to Adjutant General Steele in December 1874, Jones wrote:

> Besides . . . scouting for Indians, the battalion has rendered much service to the frontier people by breaking up bands of outlaws and desperadoes who had established themselves in these thirty settled Counties [patrolled by the Rangers], where they could depredate upon the property of good citizens, secure from arrest by the ordinary process of law, and by arresting and turning over to the proper civil authorities many cattle and horse thieves, and other fugitives from justice. . . .
>
> Although the force is too small and the appropriation insufficient to give anything like adequate protection to so large a territory, the people seem to think we have rendered valuable service to them, and there is a degree of security felt in the frontier counties, that has not been exhibited [or] experienced for years before.[3]

Despite Jones's reasoning, the legislature continued to cut funds, and each year he had to juggle the books to find enough men and equipment to do the job. The situation was particularly serious because the decade of the 1870s was the era of a group of killers who might easily be styled the "Big Four" of Texas, and even of the entire Midwest. The worst was, of course, John Wesley Hardin. "It has been said by some wag that Texas, the largest state in the Union, has never produced a real world's champion at anything," Sgt. James B. Gillett remarked. "Surely this critic overlooked Hardin, the champion desperado of the world." Second only to Hardin was John King Fisher, followed in no particular order by the murderous Bill Longley and stylish, Yorkshire-born Ben Thompson.[4]

Of the four, the Rangers were most concerned with Hardin and Fisher, a frustrating situation because those two, together with Thompson, were almost folk heroes in Texas and often more popular than the lawmen who hunted them. Badmen defied authority, and this appealed to the independent nature of the average Texan as the state began assuming the trappings of a modern regulatory bureaucracy. And because the badmen took on unpopular institutions, such as banks, railroads, and the autocratic cattle kings, ordinary citizens and cowhands were often ready to cover for them and help them along.[5]

AS PREVIOUSLY NOTED, Wes Hardin had returned to his family home in Comanche County after the killing of Bill Sutton. Accompanied by Jim Taylor, he arrived in Comanche, the county seat, about April 28, 1874, and despite a $500 reward for Taylor stemming from the feud with the Suttons, they had a quiet month racing horses, while Wes joined his brother Joe's cattle business.

Joe Hardin's "business" generally involved phony bills of sale on stolen cattle, bills of sale on nonexistent herds, or herds that on delivery turned out to be short-counted. This was not lost on the honest cattlemen of the neighborhood; even before Wes's arrival they had called on the law to do something about the Hardins and their associates.[6]

The situation boiled over on May 26, John Wesley Hardin's twenty-first birthday. He had a standing feud with Deputy Sheriff Charles Webb of adjacent Brown County, and when Webb showed up in Comanche in the midst of Hardin's birthday revelries, Wes, his cousin Bud Dixon, and Jim Taylor gunned him down on the street in broad daylight. As he died, Webb managed to get off one shot, grazing Hardin in the left side. Wes and his associates escaped to his parents' home, where his mother dressed his wound, then hid out a few miles west of Comanche.[7]

On May 30, twenty-two citizens of Comanche County petitioned Governor Coke for a detachment of Rangers to end lawlessness in general, and specifically to capture John Wesley Hardin and Jim Taylor. The petition, however, had been anticipated, because Company A, consisting of fifty-five men under command of Capt. John R. Waller, had arrived in Comanche three days earlier. One Ranger remembered, "The country was overr Run [*sic*] with lawless caracters [*sic*] & among them was that notorious Killer John Wesley Hardin."[8]

As far as Hardin was concerned, the coming of the Rangers virtually guaranteed that he would be lynched if caught.

> The sheriff told [Waller] he could and would arrest me whenever he was sure he could protect me. He tried to get Waller to assist him in doing this, but Waller was really the captain of a "vigilant" band and would not do it. Even my father and brother told Waller that if he would himself guarantee me protection, I would come in and surrender. Waller could guarantee nothing, but persisted in hunting me with his mob, composed of the enemies of all law and order. He aroused the whole country and had about 500 men scouting for me, whose avowed purpose was to hang me.[9]

For once, Hardin's observations may have been more accurate than self-serving, for, as his biographer Leon Metz has pointed out, Waller was notoriously indifferent to the safety of prisoners. As events soon would show, he did not particularly care whether or not a jailed suspect fell victim to a lynch mob.[10]

THE RANGERS WENT to work immediately. Wes's parents, the Rev. and Mrs. James G. Hardin; Wes's wife, Jane; Joe Hardin and his wife; Tom and Bud Dixon; and several other Hardin relatives and adherents were detained. James Hardin and the women were placed under house arrest, while the others were lodged in a two-story stone building on the Comanche town square that served in lieu of a jail. Three days later, on May 30, the Rangers learned that Wes, Alec Barekman (another of his innumerable cousins), Jim Taylor, and Hamilton Anderson were camped about six miles west of Comanche, and several running gunfights ensued. During one of these fights, Hardin's horse was slightly wounded, and the Rangers seem to have mistakenly assumed they had wounded Hardin himself.

Wes Hardin realized old friendships and family connections no longer protected him from the outraged citizenry. Barekman and Anderson, however, did not understand the gravity of the situation. They had had enough. Separating from Hardin and Taylor, they hoped to slip home, but on June 1, the Rangers found them and gunned them down.

Barekman and Anderson were not the only ones to die that day. About midnight, some twenty prominent cattlemen gathered in Brown County and, heavily armed, rode toward Comanche. Arriving at the stone build-ing where Joe Hardin and the others were being held, they disarmed the guards and announced they had come for the men who had killed Charles Webb. In fact, they had come to clean up the Hardin gang, because they took not only the Dixon boys, who had been present when Webb was killed, but Joe Hardin, who had been elsewhere. The three were strung up from a live oak tree a short distance out of town with Joe protesting his innocence right up until the rope choked him off for good.[11]

Waller's company stayed in Comanche until June 12, and a report of the Frontier Battalion's activities during that period observes:

> **Company "A"**   Between May 28 and June 12, [18]74, Capt. Jno.
> R. Waller's command made over 22 arrests of Cattle Thieves and
> desperadoes. Turned over to Sheriff of DeWitt County, 7 prison-
> ers (members of John [Wesley] Hardin's gang) and to Sheriffs of
> other counties, the remainder of the parties arrested. John Hardin
> was wounded by Capt. Waller, but made good his escape.

There was no mention of the lynching of Joe Hardin and the Dixon boys, but more than six decades later, in 1937, one of Waller's Rangers, J. H. Taylor, admitted that "three was mobbed."[12]

JOE'S LYNCHING CONVINCED Wes that the time had come to leave Texas. He fled to Gainesville, Florida, where he assumed the name John Swain and purchased a saloon. His wife, Jane, and infant daughter, Mollie, joined him there, staying as long as he deemed it safe. Then, in early 1875, he sold the saloon and the family moved first to Micanopy, south of Gainesville, then northeast to Jacksonville, near the Georgia line.[13]

Meanwhile, in January 1875, the Texas legislature authorized Gover-nor Coke to pay a reward of $4,000, a phenomenal sum for that era, for Hardin's apprehension and "delivery of the body" to the Travis County Jail in Austin. The resolution did not specify whether "the body" need be dead or alive. Although his twenty-second birthday was still four months away, it was estimated Hardin had killed twenty-seven men, and he had the highest price on his head of any fugitive in the history of Texas.[14] By 1876, he was so infamous that the adjutant general's annual *List of Fugi-tives from Justice,* which normally carried detailed physical descriptions and personal information, simply stated:

> Hardin, John. . . . Murder; he is the notorious desperado, John
> Wesley Hardin.[15]

Apparently no other description was necessary.

IN THE SPRING of 1877, Lt. Lee Hall gave Sgt. John B. Armstrong the go-ahead to apprehend Hardin. The son of a Tennessee physician, Armstrong had arrived in Texas in 1872, at the age of twenty-two. Already he had been wandering four years, after being run out of his hometown in the wake of various scrapes with Reconstruction authorities. In Texas, he joined an Austin militia unit known as the Travis Rifles, and from there moved on to McNelly's company.[16] Describing him, Ranger Napoleon A. Jennings wrote:

> He had a singularly mild blue eye, and experience on the frontier
> has taught me that mild blue eyes usually indicate anything but
> mildness of disposition. His handsome face was full of charac-
> ter. His carriage was as erect as that of a grenadier and, despite
> his great size, he was extremely graceful in all his movements.
> He was a dashing fellow, and always ready to lead a squad of
> Rangers on any scout that promised to end in a fight.[17]

Although the official history of the Armstrong family states that the prospect of bringing in Hardin aroused the Ranger's "sporting blood," there can be little doubt the hefty reward was a factor as well, because, as Leon Metz notes, in the nineteenth century the opportunity for reward money persuaded many men to go into law enforcement in the frontier West; Rangers frequently chased fugitives across state lines and international boundaries in hopes of collecting the bounty.[18]

If Armstrong was motivated by financial gain, he nevertheless was the right man for the job. His tenacity in carrying out his assignments had earned him the nickname "McNelly's Bulldog." Earlier in the year, in DeWitt County, he had arrested several of the feudists without hesitation.[19]

HALL AND ARMSTRONG had no idea where Hardin was, and they decided that the best approach would be to hire a detective. The first man they hired turned up nothing. Then Hall learned that Hardin was supposedly living at an unspecified location in Florida under the alias John Swayne. With that information, the Rangers contacted John Riley (Jack) Duncan of Dallas, a former policeman who had a reputation as the best detective in Texas. Governor Richard Hubbard, who had succeeded Coke, gave Duncan official status by appointing him a special Ranger assigned to work with Armstrong on the Hardin case. They were to track down and capture or kill John Wesley Hardin—it really didn't matter which.

It was common knowledge that the Hardins were a close-knit clan, as were Wes Hardin's in-laws, the Bowens of Gonzales County. Wherever Wes was, Jane and the children were probably nearby. And Jane's brother, Joshua Robert Bowen, who for some unknown reason had the nickname Brown, was on the run with a $500 price on his head. Chances were that he was with Wes and Jane, and between the two families, someone would keep in touch with the folks back home. On that premise, Jack Duncan wandered down to Gonzales County posing as a man named Williams who, although supposedly a merchant, was himself in trouble with the law. There he became friendly with Neill Bowen, Hardin's father-in-law, and discussed buying Bowen's store.[20]

All the hunches paid off. Duncan's involvement with the store allowed him to intercept a letter from Brown Bowen to his father, Neill, sent from Pollard, Alabama. In that letter, Jane sent her love. The return address was to J. H. Swain, close enough to John Swayne, the alias they had been given.

Duncan's next problem was to arrange his own sudden disappearance from Gonzales County without arousing suspicion. He sent a wire to Armstrong stating, "Come and get your horse." About a day later, the Rangers arrived and arrested "Mr. Williams," the fugitive merchant, who was placed in irons, loaded into a wagon, and taken to Cuero in DeWitt County. Soon he and Armstrong were on the train to Austin to meet with Governor Hubbard over extradition. After arranging for warrants to be forwarded for both John Wesley Hardin and John Swain, Duncan and Armstrong took the train to Montgomery, Alabama, arriving on June 20, 1877. From there, Duncan wandered down to Pollard, this time posing as a transient, and learned that John Swain was in Pensacola, Florida, gambling. He also learned that William D. Chipley, superintendent of the Pensacola Railroad, had had an altercation with a drunken Brown Bowen in the Pensacola terminal in an earlier trip to that city, and that Bowen had threatened to kill him.

After exchanging telegrams with Armstrong and Duncan, Chipley took the train to meet them in Alabama. Because the Texas warrants had not arrived, the superintendent was accompanied by a Pensacola judge and Escambia County, Florida, sheriff William Henry Hutchinson. The Florida authorities obtained Armstrong's assurances that Bowen would be arrested as well, even though he was not with Hardin in Pensacola at the time. While Chipley had no particular love for Hardin, he vehemently hated Bowen and did not want him wandering around after Hardin was arrested.

With Hardin gambling in Pensacola, the group agreed to wait until he prepared to return to Alabama, and take him on the train in the Pensacola station. On August 23, Hardin and three friends, Shep Hardy, Neal Campbell, and Jim Mann, boarded the train. Sheriff Hutchinson already had placed about twenty deputized citizens in and around the station. Then he, Deputy A. J. Perdue, Armstrong, and Duncan got on the train and found Hardin and his friends relaxing in the smoking car. Hutchinson and Perdue apparently had no idea of the identity of the suspect, only that he was wanted in Texas.

There are many versions of what happened next. The best-known is that on seeing Armstrong's Colt's revolver with the classic Ranger seven-and-a-half-inch barrel, Hardin shouted, "Texas, by God!" and went for his own gun, but it caught in his suspenders. Hardin himself claimed that Hutchinson and Perdue came in and said, "Surrender! Hold up your hands," to which he shouted, "Robbers! Protect me!" and went for his gun, and a struggle ensued. Whatever the case, a melee erupted with Hardin, Hutchinson, and Perdue rolling around in the aisle, kicking, cursing, and shouting, until Armstrong came into the car and ended it by bringing his revolver crashing down on Hardin's head.

Meanwhile, young Jim Mann, who had done nothing illegal, panicked. Not understanding what was happening, he went for his gun and fired a couple of wild shots before he was killed by Deputy Martin Sullivan. The train pulled out of the station, and during the trip north, Armstrong informed Hutchinson and Perdue that J. H. Swain was, in fact, John Wesley Hardin. According to Hardin, the two Florida lawmen received $500 each for assisting the Rangers.[21]

Hardin arrived in Austin on August 28 and was lodged in Travis County Jail. A series of legal battles ensued, with Hardin contending that because the Texas warrants had never arrived, there were no warrants in

Florida and there had not been a proper extradition—he had been kidnapped. In modern times he would be upheld, but in 1877 he was not.

He also used the time to work on his image. Hardin could be docile when he wanted to be, and part of the reason he had managed to avoid the law so long was a certain personal charm. He also knew the power of newspapers, and began giving interviews. It paid dividends. Although he is known to have killed twenty-seven men, he was tried for only one—the killing of Deputy Sheriff Charles Webb. On September 29, 1877, a Comanche County jury convicted him of second-degree murder and sentenced him to twenty-five years in prison.[22]

The irony was that Brown Bowen, who was apprehended a short time after Hardin, was hanged in Gonzales for a killing that actually might have been Hardin's twenty-eighth. At least that's what Bowen said during and after his trial, and there is evidence that he probably was telling the truth. But people never really liked Bowen, who was mean-tempered and vindictive even under the best circumstances. Quite likely, Brown Bowen was hanged in part because he lacked Hardin's style and finely tuned sense of public relations.[23]

TEXAS'S NUMBER TWO badman, John King Fisher, was perhaps the most eccentric and colorful. Starting off as a small-time thief, he had a natural gift for leadership and lofty ambitions that rapidly made him wealthy. He was more settled than most gunmen, generally confining his operations to south Texas and the Mexican border, where he almost could have been called a prominent citizen. He had a sizable ranch near Carrizo Springs, northwest of Laredo, that became a headquarters for fugitives from the law. Eventually, King Fisher commanded more than a hundred loyal men.[24]

The ever observant Ranger Jennings, who first met Fisher when the latter was about twenty-five, was probably not exaggerating when he called the badman

> the most perfect specimen of a frontier dandy and desperado that I ever saw. He was all, beautifully proportioned, and exceedingly handsome. He wore the finest clothing procurable, but all of it was the picturesque, border, dime novel kind. His broad-brimmed white Mexican *sombrero* was profusely ornamented with gold and silver lace and had a golden snake for a band. His fine buck-

skin Mexican short jacket was heavily embroidered with gold. His
shirt was of the finest and thinnest linen and was worn open at the
throat, with a silk handkerchief knotted loosely about the collar.

Fisher's chaps, Jennings wrote, were made from the skin of a Bengal tiger.
He had seen the tiger in a circus and taken a fancy to the skin. His gang
had taken over the circus long enough to kill the tiger and take the hide.

Nevertheless, there was substance behind the show. Fisher was a cold-
blooded gunman who, by the time he was twenty-six, boasted probably
with some accuracy that he had killed a man for every year of his life.
According to Jennings, he "was an expert revolver shot, and could handle his six-shooters as well with his left hand as with his right. He was a
fine rider, and rode the best horses he could steal in Texas or Mexico."[25]

BECAUSE MOST OF King Fisher's crimes were against Mexicans, who were
not popular in south Texas at the time, and because he retained first-rate
legal council, he generally managed to stay one jump ahead of the law.[26]
In early 1876, however, he pushed too far, because he appeared on the
List of Fugitives from Justice with the notation "Theft of geldings; committed February, '76; indicted April, same year."[27] That attracted the attention of Leander McNelly, whose jurisdiction included Fisher's
domain.

On May 31, McNelly notified Adjutant General Steele from Laredo
that he was going after King Fisher. Fisher's ranch was in Dimmit
County, on the upper Nueces River, ninety or so miles to the northwest.
The Rangers were armed with new caliber .44-40 Winchester repeating
rifles, thirty of which had been sent to them as a token of appreciation by
Capt. Richard King. They were a welcome change from the heavy
Sharps, and the Rangers were pleased with the new weapon, but
McNelly himself may have had mixed emotions. He disliked wasting
ammunition, and the Sharps, which had to be reloaded after each shot,
encouraged the men to fire accurately and conserve ammunition. A repeating rifle with a full magazine might prompt them to "blaze away."[28]

Arriving in Carrizo Springs, McNelly sent a second letter to Steele, in
which he described a classic range war:

> The country is under a perfect reign of terror from the number
> and desperate character of the thieves who infest this region. The

country is rich in stock, but very sparsely settled, and the opportunities and inducements for anyone to steal are very great.

This county (Dimmit) is unorganized and is attached to Maverick County for judicial purposes. About one-half the white citizens of Eagle Pass [the Maverick County seat] are friends of King Fisher's gang. The remainder of the citizens there are too much afraid of the desperadoes to give any assistance in even keeping them secure after they have been placed in jail, and they would never think of helping to arrest any of them. On my arrival here, I found the people greatly terrified, and on the eve of deserting their homes and property to save their lives—the homes which for years they had defended against Indians and invading Mexicans alternately, and never once thought of leaving. Some of the oldest and best citizens told me that, in all of their frontier experience, they had never suffered so much as from these American robbers. For weeks past they have not dared to leave their homes for fear of being waylaid and murdered.

Every house in this part of the country has been repeatedly fired into by armed men, from fifteen to twenty in number at a time. The ranchmen's horses and cattle have been driven from their range, and even from pens at the houses, until the people are left almost destitute of means of support. If anyone had the temerity to protest against being robbed, he was told that he had just so many days to live if he did not leave the country. Some of those who had the courage to remain have been foully murdered.[29]

McNelly spent three or four days in Carrizo Springs, gathering information on Fisher and his headquarters. Much of it was obtained from a storekeeper who had trouble with the bandits. He also retained a boy named Drew Taylor, who knew the best route to Fisher's ranch on Pendencia Creek, ten miles out of town, just beyond the north point of Lake Espantosa.

ESPANTOSA IS A Spanish word, more or less meaning "haunted." Formed by an old channel of the Nueces River, Lake Espantosa is notorious in that part of south Texas as a sort of ghost lake. Strange beings are said to appear in the mists that sometimes cover its surface. In frontier days, unwary travelers who camped there supposedly vanished without a trace.

Even stagecoaches and wagons attempting to ford at night disappeared into its depths, according to local lore, and the spirits of the lost roam after dark. In modern times its banks are a lovers' lane because its demonic reputation assures privacy, and in the nineteenth century it was a hangout for badmen for the same reason.[30]

If McNelly was even aware of the lake's reputation, he was as indifferent to it as he was to Fisher's reputation. Learning that Fisher would be home with about thirty men on a particular day, the captain decided to bring him in. He left a small guard in camp and took twenty-five men out toward Pendencia Creek. They were divided into two squads about two miles apart. Scouts rode ahead with orders to arrest anyone they saw. Fisher did not know the Rangers were coming, and McNelly did not intend for him to find out.

When the Rangers reached a fork where the road to Fisher's ranch branched from the main trail, they found a sign that said: THIS IS KING FISHER'S ROAD—TAKE THE OTHER.

Nearing the ranch, McNelly assembled his men in heavy brush, cautioning them, "There may be women present, so don't shoot till they open fire. We'll give them a chance to surrender."

The Rangers formed into a skirmish line and slowly moved through the brush until they sighted the main house in a cottonwood grove. About half a dozen men were playing cards in a lean-to shed. The Rangers formed up in a half-circle, their Winchesters ready. McNelly raised his hand and they charged, jumping their horses over a small fence and coming into the yard.

Surprise was complete. The only show of resistance was when Ranger A. L. Parrott and Fisher gunman Frank Porter faced each other with leveled rifles, but Parrott followed a McNelly adage: no gunman could shoot if he was facing the officer and you had his eye. Parrott's nerve held and Porter's didn't. The badman threw his rifle to the ground.

McNelly had just stepped through the door of the main house when Fisher came into the front room.

"I'm Ranger Lee McNelly," he said. "Lock your hands behind your head and come out."

Fisher didn't argue.[31]

The Rangers took Fisher and nine of his men to Eagle Pass, on the Rio Grande about forty miles west of Carrizo Springs, and lodged them in the county jail. McNelly, whose health was failing, remained in camp sending scouting parties to comb the area and try to round up more of the gang. Two days later, he and several Rangers were taking a group of prisoners to Eagle Pass when they ran into Fisher and his men on their way home. Fisher boasted that they had made bail and could make bail anytime they were arrested.

Disgusted and undoubtedly in considerable pain, McNelly said, "If we ever come up here again, we'll come to kill, and if you keep up your system of robbery and murder, you'll be hearing from us."

Fisher laughed.[32]

LEANDER MCNELLY PERSONALLY was in no position to make good on his threat. His tuberculosis was entering its final stages, and he went to San Antonio for treatment. Some time later, several members of his company went to the city on business, making their headquarters at the Menger Hotel, where McNelly was bedridden. To avoid tiring him, Cpl. W. L. Rudd acted as go-between, but occasionally the others would go up to his room for a visit. During one of those visits, Durham noticed that McNelly "was just the same color as the bedsheets." After a few minutes of conversation, the captain went into a coughing fit. Rudd took Durham by the arm and said, "Let's get out."

"But I couldn't move," Durham remembered. "I just looked at Captain and maybe sort of puddled up."[33]

During their conversation, McNelly told Durham he expected the company to be disbanded after that year's election. He had become too controversial. His strong-arm methods were a campaign issue, and his raids into Mexico were creating such furor along the border that some members of the legislature were pushing for appointment of a discreet, level-headed officer to the company, one who would curb the captain's enthusiasm. This had been the reason behind Lee Hall's appointment as lieutenant—to keep an eye on him and perhaps even to be groomed as his replacement. The Rangers suspected the latter. Durham commented that Hall's arrival "meant Captain [McNelly] was on his way out. . . . So we didn't fall over ourselves welcoming Lieutenant Hall."[34]

KING FISHER STILL ran loose, and the area above Laredo remained his private fiefdom. From his bed, McNelly ordered members of his company to clean up the Fisher gang. John Armstrong was to proceed to Carrizo Springs with twenty-five men and set to work. He started his men off that night. Determined to surprise Fisher, he ordered the men to carry only ammunition without the usual trail packs of extra equipment. They were to arrest anyone they saw. The following day, they remained in "dry camp," which is to say no fires allowed for cooking or coffee, and that night came to the vicinity of Carrizo.

By sunup they had five prisoners, "and we persuaded them to talk," Durham observed dryly. One of the prisoners was Noley Key, a young horse thief who associated with Fisher's gang. According to Jennings, Armstrong "took Key aside and drew from him the information that a band of horse thieves were in camp on the banks of Lake Espantoso [*sic*], six or seven miles distant." Durham was more explicit, admitting that they hoisted Key "a couple of feet off the ground" with a rope around his neck until he agreed to guide the Rangers.[35]

Key said there were about six or eight horse thieves holding a herd of horses stolen from east Texas, which would be driven northwest toward the Devil's River in another day or so. King Fisher himself had departed for west Texas a couple of days earlier with 150 steers. That night, Armstrong set a guard over the prisoners and sent a detail to investigate bandit activities at another ranch. Then he took six Rangers and Noley Key toward the lake. They rode for about an hour until they were within a quarter of a mile of the camp, then dismounted. Rangers Thomas N. Devine and Thomas N. Evans were detailed to watch both the horses and Key. If Key tried to escape, they were to kill him. Although Armstrong said this within Key's earshot to make certain he understood his situation, the prisoner was slightly deaf and may not have heard him.

Leaving the others behind, Armstrong, Durham, Jennings, A. L. Parrott, and George Boyd started on foot toward the horse thieves' camp.

"Boys," Armstrong told them, "we are going to capture those thieves or kill them. The reason I did not bring more men along was because I was afraid that these fellows wouldn't resist if we were so many. Key tells me that they stood off the sheriff and his posse a few nights ago, and so they'll be looking for officers and be prepared to fight. That's just what we want. If they only fire at us, we can rush in on them and kill them all. Nothing but that will break up this gang of cold-blooded desperadoes. I only hope they'll show fight. Now, come along and don't make any noise."[36]

The Rangers slipped up, circling so that the desperadoes had their backs to the lake. By the light of the half-moon, they could see a sentry about fifty yards out from the camp. To the north were the shadows of the stolen horses with several riders as herd guard. Seven men sat around a large campfire. Before the Rangers could move in, however, the sentry saw them and fired.

"Damn you, you'll shoot at an officer, will you?" Armstrong shouted.

"The scrap was on," Durham commented. "We crouched and charged in with our repeater rifles blazing away, wasting ammunition. But we sprayed the camp good."

Jennings added, "We rushed in on them and there was a continual blaze from the firearms."

Caught between the Rangers and the lake, the thieves never got completely organized, and they fired haphazardly. Some jumped into the water, but three men, already wounded, held their ground and kept firing. One of them, a hard case named John Martin, emptied his pistol and threw it away, then drew a knife and started toward George Boyd. The Ranger raised his Winchester, but it jammed. He managed to jump backward as Martin slashed at him, then got out his own knife. Boyd was small, wiry, and light on his feet, while Martin was staggering from a bullet wound in his hip. Even so, he managed to cut Boyd before the Ranger jumped on him and the two tumbled into the lake. They rolled and splashed for a couple of minutes until Boyd emerged dizzy and bleeding heavily. Martin was dead.

Jennings, meanwhile, was facing a desperado named Jim McAlister. The badman was emptying his revolver and yelling loud obscenities when the Ranger fired. The bullet caught McAlister in his open mouth, and he went down with part of his jaw shot off.

The entire fight lasted only three or four minutes, but Jennings estimated two hundred shots were fired. Three of the badmen were dead, and McAlister was badly wounded. The rest managed to escape by jumping into the lake. About that time, they heard firing in the direction of their horses and hurried back. They found Evans and Devine standing close together.

"Where's Noley Key?" Armstrong demanded.

"Dead," Devine answered.

"Dead?"

"Yes. When he heard the firing, he jumped up and started to run, and we fired at him. One of us killed him, for there's a bullet hole in his back."

They went over and found Key's body, facedown.[37]

Returning to the main camp, they learned that the detachment sent to the other ranch had seven prisoners, and had killed one who they said resisted arrest.[38]

Despite the night's work, King Fisher continued to elude them. Durham sourly commented, "Maybe King Fisher was the head and brains of this stock-rustling bunch [at Lake Espantosa]. I don't know. All I know is that we never did make a case on him."[39]

Fisher continued to reign supreme over south Texas. Soon after the Lake Espantosa fight, he moved up to Uvalde County and managed to become chief deputy. In 1884, he even ran for sheriff and appeared to be a sure bet, because he had no opposition. He never made it, though, because in March of that year, he and his good friend Ben Thompson were gunned down in a drunken brawl in a San Antonio saloon. Ranger sergeant James B. Gillett noted the event by scribbling "Killed" next to Fisher's name in the index of his copy of the *List of Fugitives from Justice*.[40]

The deaths of Fisher and Thompson and John Wesley Hardin's imprisonment accounted for three of Texas's "Big Four" badmen. In spite of the dozens of killings on their combined records, only Bill Longley paid the extreme penalty, going to the gallows in Giddings, east of Austin, on October 11, 1878. Like Brown Bowen, Longley expressed some irritation at the unfairness of his sentence compared with Hardin's, but then people didn't care much for Longley either.[41]

LEANDER MCNELLY NEVER again assumed effective command of his company. He remained on disability until November 20, and aside from escorting five members of the feuding Suttons from DeWitt County to jail in Galveston, he performed no further duties for the state. On January 21, 1877, his physician notified Adjutant General Steele that he would be unfit for duty for the remainder of the winter. Soon after, when McNelly's company was reorganized, his name was deleted from the roster. The official reason was health. Steele pointed out that McNelly underwent medical treatment almost continuously from July 1876 through January 1877, and at state expense.

"The bills paid on his account were nearly one-third of the whole amount paid for his company," the adjutant general explained, adding, "I do not consider that the command of the few men that can be paid from the small remnant of the appropriation for this company as the proper place to put an incompetent man, no matter what his previous service may have been."

Durham, however, attributed the dismissal to McNelly's high-handed methods. In particular, the near-strangulation of and suspicious death of Noley Key at Lake Espantosa brought an adverse public reaction; although McNelly was not present, these were his men following his well-known procedures.

Whatever his faults, many felt McNelly had been treated shabbily. But it made no difference. He had angered too many people, and he had to go. McNelly returned to his farm and lived another ten months, dying on September 4, 1877. He was thirty-three years old.

When the company was reorganized, Lee Hall, promoted to captain, was placed in command. Wilburn King, the history-minded future adjutant general, described Hall as "well fitted to command a body of men intended for peculiarly arduous service against ruthless and cruel Mexican cut-throats, as well as against many desperate criminals of his own race. . . ."

Durham, however, was not so loose with his praise. Hall, he said, "knew his way around," but most of the Rangers believed that Armstrong or Pidge Robinson should have been promoted to command. "Lee Hall was a good man," he wrote. "But he wasn't a Captain McNelly."[42]

Chapter 14

The Salt War

The Trans-Pecos region, running westward from the Pecos River to El Paso, has always been almost a separate world from the rest of Texas, and as previously noted, the concept of Rangers did not arrive until after the Civil War, when Capt. Gregorio García formed his short-lived company during Reconstruction. With the creation of the Frontier Battalion, García's son-in-law, Telesforo Montes of San Elizario, was authorized to muster a company on May 27, 1874. Like García's company, most of the members were local, and Montes's Rangers were designated the Minute Company of the Frontier Battalion.

The Minute Company spent the next two years fighting various Apache bands who raided even into the suburbs of San Elizario and nearby Socorro. Montes's failure to subdue the Indians was through no lack of effort on his own part or the part of his men; they had several fights, killed a number of marauders, and recovered stolen stock. But the vast region of the Trans-Pecos was simply too much for a small band of men against the many bands of Indians, and there are no reported activities of this company after August 31, 1876. Thus when the El Paso Salt War erupted a year later, an ad hoc Ranger company had to be organized from what was available, and what was available was not adequate for the violence that ensued.[1]

Of all the blood-soaked difficulties in the Terrible Seventies, the El Paso Salt War went far beyond an ordinary feud. It was, in effect, a clash of races and cultures similar to the Cortinista conflicts on the Lower Rio Grande. The source of the bloodshed in El Paso, however, was common table salt. In the desert areas of the Southwest, salt was more sought-after than gold. Not only did it make food palatable, it was vital in a hot environment where perspiration rapidly drained the body of the salt necessary for survival, and was essential for curing meat and dairy products in the days before refrigeration. Men fought and died over rights to salt deposits just as bitterly as they fought over gold or cattle.

The racial issue came into play in part because of politics and in part because of different legal and cultural views. To the Hispanic population, salt deposits were public domain. This stemmed from ancient Spanish custom maintaining that all waters and mineral deposits belonged to the crown. A Spanish land grant might or might not include water and mineral rights, according to the will and pleasure of the sovereign. In the salt-starved provinces of the north, in what is now west Texas and New Mexico, as early as 1611 the crown decreed free access to local deposits, in effect placing them in the public domain, a principle Mexico continued upon gaining independence. Consequently, by the time that part of the continent came under U.S. rule, there was a long-established tradition of public use of salt deposits in the region.

The Americans, on the other hand, had a strong sense of private ownership and use, of both land and resources. Even the public domain was subject to lease for private commercial development, and upon discovering how completely the local population depended on salt, newly arrived entrepreneurs filed for leases on public deposits or in some cases claimed outright ownership. The determination of the Mexicans to continue taking salt as they needed it and the determination of the Americans to charge a fee or control the market set the stage for trouble. In 1854, a minor squabble erupted between Mexican salt transporters and pioneer El Paso County resident James Wiley Magoffin over use of deposits in New Mexico where Magoffin claimed exclusive rights. This dispute, however, paled in comparison to the bloody Salt War of 1877.[2]

The bloodshed centered around a string of salt beds at the base of Guadalupe Peak, the tallest mountain in Texas, located about 110 miles due east of the new community of El Paso and ninety miles from San Elizario, then the county seat. *Tejanos* and Mexicans had been exploiting the beds for many years before 1862, when the area's Anglo-Saxons learned of their existence. Development was slow, however, because of the established roads to New Mexico deposits, and because the politicians were loathe to offend the largely *tejano* voting population that used the Guadalupe beds. Nevertheless, the deposits were especially valuable because of "the abundance and purity of the salt yielded from them," and local businessmen moved to gain control. By the summer of 1877, Charles Howard of El Paso had title to virtually all the Guadalupe salt beds and posted notice that no more salt would be drawn without approval from himself or his agents.

Howard, who arrived in El Paso in 1872 and briefly served as district judge, was cold, calculating, and ruthless. Contemporaries described him as a man to be feared. Two who did not fear him were Louis Cardis, a member of the state legislature whose word was "little less than law" in the Hispanic community, and Antonio Borajo, an autocratic priest who ruled his San Elizario parish with the iron-fisted determination of an inquisitor-general.[3] They advised the *tejanos* and Mexicans to take the salt and disregard Howard's fees. Howard responded by announcing his determination to kill Cardis.

The breaking point came in September 1877, when Howard had two Mexicans arrested and fined for taking salt from the Guadalupe beds without paying his fees. A mob waylaid him in Ysleta and held him for three days, debating whether or not to kill him. By now, however, Cardis was beginning to realize that things were getting out of control, and he pleaded with the mob to release Howard. In a hopeful turn of events, Borajo recently had been transferred to a parish across the river in Mexico, and the new priest helped Cardis calm the crowd. Howard was freed on a $12,000 bond signed by four friends, John G. Atkinson, Charles E. Ellis, Jesus Cobos, and Tomás García, an act that would later cost Atkinson and Ellis their lives. Yet these and other killings could have been averted had Howard chosen at this juncture to be reasonable. Cardis was earnestly trying to avert a feud, but the near-lynching left Howard even more implacable.[4]

THE EL PASO Salt War began on October 10, when Howard picked up a double-barreled shotgun loaded with buckshot and walked down to S. Schutz & Bro. store in El Paso, where Cardis, who often conducted business there, was lounging in a rocker. Cardis tried to duck behind a desk, but Howard blasted him in the stomach with one barrel and in the heart with the other.[5] Fearing for his own life, Howard fled across the state line to Mesilla, New Mexico. El Paso County sheriff Charles Kerber went to see him, but agreed that it would not be safe for him to return to El Paso. Kerber made arrangements with the Mesilla sheriff to protect Howard from the vengeance of Cardis's supporters, while he telegraphed Adjutant General Steele for Rangers. "The Mexicans intend to revenge the death of Cardis, but a company of your State police would quiet them very much," he said. Steele responded by ordering Major Jones to El Paso to investigate and to have a company of the Frontier Battalion "in position to march at once in case of necessity for the use of troops."[6]

To reach remote El Paso, Jones had to take the train from Austin to Santa Fe, New Mexico, by way of Topeka, Kansas. At Santa Fe, he boarded a stagecoach, finally arriving in El Paso after ten days. The trip convinced him that it was futile to try to bring in one of the regular companies of the Frontier Battalion as Steele had instructed. Instead, he decided to raise a company locally. The new twenty-man unit was mustered into service on November 12, 1877, as a detachment of Company C, Frontier Battalion, under command of Lt. John B. Tays. The Rangers were stationed in San Elizario, where trouble, if any, could be expected to break out.[7]

The men who formed the detachment were less than desirable. As C. L. Sonnichsen noted in his history of El Paso, not one of them would have been a Ranger under normal conditions. Lieutenant Tays, likewise, was not a good choice to command Rangers in a trouble spot. He was not highly educated, and supported himself with odd jobs. The best that could be said of him was that he was relatively honest for the times, brave, and hardworking. Nevertheless, this motley collection was the best Jones could do.[8]

ON NOVEMBER 16, Howard returned to El Paso and surrendered to Jones. He was taken before the local justice of the peace for arraignment, and was released after posting a $4,000 bond. After a meeting with several Cardis associates, Howard returned to Mesilla, and Jones went back to Austin.[9]

All was quiet until December 1, when a train of about sixteen carts and wagons started from San Elizario to draw salt from the Guadalupe beds. Fearing bloodshed, Governor Hubbard sent a telegram to several leaders of the *tejano* community, warning them to obey the laws, presumably meaning to pay Howard's fees or stay away from the salt beds.

"You can control your people, if you will, I'm informed," the governor said. "Do so."

Twelve days later, Howard returned to San Elizario with a Ranger escort. Experience had taught him nothing, and he filed a suit to seize the salt from the train, which was expected to arrive that day.[10]

Howard's latest action, and the governor's support of his position, was more than the community could bear. The year 1877 had been bad for the small *tejano* farmers along the river. The Rio Grande was almost dry, and crops were failing. A few pesos or dollars gathered by selling salt would have helped immensely. Indians had been active, stealing horses and mules and setting everyone's nerves on edge. Many were in debt to John G. Atkinson, who had posted part of the bond for Howard. Citizens of Mexico were no better off, not only being hurt by drought and Indians, but also caught up in the civil strife that ultimately brought Porfirio Díaz to power. The people were ready for anything. Howard and his friends, they agreed, were the source of their ills. Even if the Mexicans and *tejanos* did not have the legal right to the salt, they felt they had the moral right. Mexico's tradition of defiance and resistance to whatever civil authority was currently in power—invariably justified on moral grounds— looked appealing and perhaps could be applied in Texas as well. They reasoned that the time had come for action.[11]

As December 12 wore on, Howard went to Ysleta to take care of some business. Fearing for his life, Lieutenant Tays took a detachment of Rangers to meet him and escort him back to San Elizario. At the edge of town, they were confronted by *tejano* leader Chico Barela and a picket of about eighteen men. The Rangers and Howard rode through the line and into town, but Tays realized this was only the edge of a much larger mob. He consolidated his forces and prepared for trouble, doubling the guard around the adobe building that served as Ranger quarters and putting several men on the roofs of adjacent houses. Then Tays sent a Ranger to El Paso to request backup from a detachment of troops that had recently arrived from Fort Bayard, New Mexico, in response to pleas from local citizens for military protection. A squad of soldiers rode out to San Elizario, but were confronted by the mob and told to mind their own business, and the officer in charge apparently lost his nerve and ordered the troops back to El Paso. The Rangers were on their own. The fate of Howard and his friends was now sealed.[12]

THE RIOT BROKE out about 10 P.M., when members of the mob roped Howard associate Charles Ellis, dragged him through the streets, slashed him to death with knives, and mutilated his corpse. Then they moved against the Ranger quarters. Tays deployed his men but ordered them not to fire until fired upon. The mob came within a hundred yards of the building, then halted, apparently to take positions for a siege. The rest of the night passed quietly.

Dawn revealed the Ranger quarters surrounded by three lines of pickets, beyond which were several squads of about twenty mounted men each, placed about two hundred yards apart. Rawhide entanglements had been set up to block a charge by the Rangers, although individuals could move about. John Atkinson managed to reach Ranger quarters with a trunk containing a substantial amount of money. As Atkinson passed through the mob's lines, he was told the Rangers had three hours to deliver Howard or they would come in and get him.

About mid-morning, the mob opened up on the building with a fusillade, mortally wounding a Ranger sergeant. The shooting continued all day and into the next. The rioters charged several times but were beaten back.[13]

THE SIEGE, WHICH began on Wednesday, lasted until Sunday night, when a cease-fire was negotiated. After a quiet night, Tays woke up Monday morning to find that the mob had erected fortifications and dug rifle pits. When he met with the leaders, they told him that unless the Rangers surrendered Howard, they would blow up the quarters. As for Howard, all he had to do was surrender and relinquish all claim to the Guadalupe salt beds. After that, he was free to do as he pleased.

Howard wasn't fooled. "I will go," he told Tays, "as it is the only chance to save your lives, but they will kill me."

Tays was against it. He said the Rangers were prepared to hold the building and protect him to the end.

"It is useless for us to attempt to stand them off any longer," Howard replied. "This is our only chance to escape." He told everyone goodbye and gave his valuables to one of his agents, John McBride. Then he and Tays walked over to meet the leaders of the mob. Howard's Spanish was rudimentary, and Tays spoke none at all, so he sent back to the Ranger quarters for Atkinson to translate. When Atkinson arrived, the leaders took him into another room, where he offered to turn his money over to the leaders of the mob in exchange for the lives of Howard, McBride, himself, and the Rangers. Chico Barela agreed and swore by the Holy Cross to uphold his end of the agreement. A flag of truce was sent to the Ranger headquarters, and to persuade them to surrender, Atkinson told them Tays had arranged an armistice and ordered them to come out. They agreed, becoming the only Rangers in history to surrender.

Tays, of course, had not been consulted, and when he saw the Rangers filing out to be disarmed, he was furious. The leaders came back and told him to go with his men. He replied that he had brought out Howard in good faith and didn't plan to leave until the agreements between Howard and the mob were finalized. At that point, twelve armed men appeared and hustled him into another room, while they decided what to do with Howard, Atkinson, and McBride. It didn't take long.

Chico Barela was the holdout. Regardless of what he personally thought of Howard, Atkinson, and McBride, he had given his solemn oath to preserve their lives. To reinforce it, he sent a runner across the river to inform the priest Borajo. The reply was not what he expected. "Shoot all the gringos," Borajo advised, "and I will absolve you." That ended it as far as the other leaders of the mob were concerned. Barela continued to protest, but by now the mob was out of control.

Howard was brought out first. One witness recalled, "He walked erectly, with his hands behind him." At the command to halt, Howard stopped and turned to face the mob. A firing squad was formed, and moved up about ten feet from Howard, who calmly watched. Finally, in broken Spanish, he said, "You are now about to execute three hundred men," apparently referring to the reprisals that were sure to follow. Then he pulled open his shirt and shouted, "Fire!"

Howard fell, badly wounded but not dead. The mob moved in and hacked him to death. The body was thrown into a nearby well.

Atkinson and McBride were next. McBride was described as "melancholy," but Atkinson was defiant. This was too much for Chico Barela. He had shed no tears over Howard (his daughter had been engaged to Louis Cardis before Howard murdered him), but Atkinson and McBride were another matter. He had given his solemn oath that they would live, and he intended to uphold it. Picking up on that, Atkinson, who spoke fluent Spanish, asked the members of the mob if they intended to violate the oaths their leaders had made on their behalf. Someone shouted, "Finish them!"

"Then, there is no remedy?" Atkinson asked.

"No! No!" the crowd shouted.

"Then let me die with honor. I will give the word." With that, he removed his coat and vest and opened his shirt. "When I give the word, fire at my heart. Fire!"

McBride died instantly, but Atkinson was hit five times in the stomach. He staggered, then recovered and shouted, "Higher, you sons of bitches!"[14]

Two more shots rang out, and he fell, but was still alive. He motioned to his head, and the commander of the firing party finished him.

Many members of the mob wanted to kill the Rangers as well, but Chico Barela was finally regaining control over a portion of the men, and said they would fight if there were any more killings. The Rangers were given their horses and escorted as far as Ysleta. Then the mob began plundering San Elizario.[15]

AT THIS POINT, Col. Edward Hatch, commander of Fort Bayard, arrived with a large contingent of troops. Faced with regular soldiers under a determined commander, the mob quickly dispersed, and with peace restored, the reprisals began. Rangers began searching houses and gunning down anyone they believed even remotely connected with the mob, without bothering to determine whether they were, in fact, guilty.

A woman named Mariana Núñez testified she and her husband were in the kitchen of their home in Socorro when Sheriff Kerber arrived with "about a dozen Rangers who gunned down her husband and ransacked the house." Two Mexicans were arrested in Ysleta and readied for transfer to San Elizario. A party was headed in that direction, consisting of thirty or forty men, including Sheriff Kerber, Lieutenant Tays and Rangers, and soldiers. There were also two wagons containing coffins for Howard, Atkinson, and McBride. A cavalry officer who saw the two Mexicans brought out noted their hands were bound and they had to be helped into one of the wagons. On the road, the two prisoners were shot while "trying to get away."[16]

Even more ominous were reports that men identified as "rangers" ransacked houses for money, raped at least one woman, and in several cases broke into houses and searched them, demanding to know where the women were. Most of these outrages appear to have been the work not of the Rangers themselves, but of a gang of toughs brought in from New Mexico by Sheriff Kerber to form a posse and supposedly help the

Rangers restore order. In fact, the majority report of the military commission that investigated the Salt War—and that was by no means friendly to the Rangers—stated that the New Mexico men "seem especially to be responsible for the rapes, homicides, and other crimes of which the people justly complained."[17]

Even so, the Rangers were not altogether blameless. Tays himself admitted being present when Mariana Núñez's husband was gunned down at the kitchen door. He contended it was self-defense, although there is little evidence to support that claim. Tays also witnessed the killing of the two bound prisoners on the road, and identified two Rangers as the men responsible. A local saddler, Antonio Cadena, positively identified Tays as one of a group of Rangers who, together with Sheriff Kerber, ransacked his house, confiscated his pistol and bullets, and made off with a bridle, saddle, spurs, and two horses.[18]

The bodies of the two prisoners killed by the Rangers were still lying by the road when Colonel Hatch rode past to inspect the towns in the vicinity. Approaching Socorro, he heard gunshots in the town. Hatch hunted up Sheriff Kerber and let him know in no uncertain terms that he expected the local authorities to do something about the reprisals. This was followed by a general order stating, "Outrages in the name and under color of the law, and by those who ought to be its representatives and guardians, will not be tolerated." He also indicated he would use troops if necessary. The reprisals began to wind down, although, contrary to Hatch's orders, Kerber made no attempt to arrest any of the Rangers or New Mexico men that the colonel held responsible.[19]

IN JANUARY 1878, Major Jones grudgingly obeyed an order from Adjutant General Steele to serve on a U.S. military commission to investigate the violence, including the conduct of the Rangers. Anxious to avoid straining the already fragile diplomatic situation with Mexico, the army commissioners downplayed the involvement of Mexican citizens, indicating that the Salt War was a largely local matter. They also glossed over the military's failure to act in time to avert the crisis. Losses through plunder and destruction of property were estimated at about $12,000. Finally, the army commissioners hinted that the Rangers were culpable for some of the violence.[20]

Jones would have none of it, and he prepared a minority report contradicting most of the findings. Mexican citizens, he maintained, were very heavily involved in the violence and plunder and came to Texas for that purpose, and the authorities in their country took no steps to prevent it. He criticized the military for its failure to act and indicated that many of the reprisals, "atrocities," and "outrages" were the result of the federal government's failure to maintain peace. Jones also estimated damage at $31,000. About the only thing everyone agreed on was that Fort Bliss should be reactivated and a permanent military presence established, as it subsequently was.[21]

No one was ever tried for the violence. Howard, of course, was dead, negating any action on the Cardis murder. As for the siege in San Elizario, a grand jury indicted six leaders of the mob, but all fled into Mexico and were never brought to justice.

The El Paso Salt War was over. Ironically, in the wake of all the bloodshed and misery, the locals henceforth quietly paid the fees to draw salt from the Guadalupe beds.[22]

PART 5
FROM FRONTIER DEFENDERS TO STATE POLICE

Chapter 15

The Last of the Old Guard

In Texas, at least, Sam Bass was probably one of the last of the traditional badmen, and one of the most durable. In his own time, he was the subject of paperback "penny dreadfuls" hawked in railroad stations and on trains, as well as local poetry and a contemporary ballad that was a favorite among cowboys on the trail. In the 120 years since his death, there has probably been as much written about him as about any desperado who ever roamed the West. The late Ramon Adams, a leading authority on Western badmen, had some two hundred books concerning Bass in his personal library. Some of the penny dreadfuls—so flimsy that they fell apart after one or two readings and now are among the rarest of all Western books—have been reprinted as minor classics.

When measured against John Wesley Hardin, King Fisher, Ben Thompson, and Bill Longley, Bass seems almost a prankster. Although virtually illiterate and generally slovenly, he had a charming personality, loved to joke and show off, and was not given to killing unless absolutely cornered. To much of the public, he was a sympathetic figure, a sort of frontier Robin Hood with a reputation for generosity. With one or two notable exceptions, none of his robberies was very profitable, and in some cases he only took part of the available money, so as not to leave his victims completely destitute. And the fact that he was taking on railroads, express companies, and the U.S. Mail (all unpopular in Texas at the time) won him widespread public support.[1]

Sam's legendary criminal career spanned only two years, beginning in 1876, when he joined a band of Dakota highwaymen. After a year of incredibly unsuccessful attempts to rob stagecoaches, the gang ended up in Nebraska, where, on September 18, 1876, they took $60,000 in $20 gold pieces from a train. With his share of the loot, Sam Bass went to Denton, Texas.[2]

Bass remained in Denton, freely spending his share of the train holdup and gathering about him a gang of drifters and layabouts. He lay low for several months and then, on January 26, 1878, robbed the Fort Worth–Weatherford stage, taking about $400 in cash and several gold watches. Sam disliked stagecoaches, however. The Nebraska train robbery had been good to him, and he wanted to take on the railroads. On February 22, the gang robbed the Texas Central, inaugurating the biggest series of train robberies in the history of the state—four within a seven-week period and all within twenty miles of Dallas. In every case, the robbers were seen riding in the direction of Denton, leaving no doubt in anyone's mind that the same gang was involved in all of them.

The fourth robbery was at Mesquite on April 10. By now the railroads were ready. Bass's gang met with a hail of gunfire, and several of his men rode off carrying buckshot. Two days later, Adjutant General Steele ordered Major Jones to take personal charge of the hunt for the robbers. Because there were no Ranger companies in the Dallas area, he would organize a squad that nominally would be part of Company B.[3]

JONES ARRIVED IN Dallas on April 14 and offered command of the new detachment to Junius "June" Peak, a former lawman then serving as city recorder. Initially Peak obtained a leave of absence from his duties with the city, and was commissioned as a lieutenant. He never returned to his desk in city hall, however, for on June 1 he became captain of Company B.

The Rangers were not alone. Although none of the robberies brought Bass an appreciable amount of money, they involved the express companies and the mails. Consequently, Dallas was swarming with Pinkerton detectives and federal lawmen, all trying to get a crack at the train robbers.[4]

So many strange lawmen were showing up in the Denton area that they ran the risk of being mistaken for bandits and picked up or shot by other lawmen. In one instance, June Peak's Rangers collided with a posse under Deputy Sheriff Tom Gerren. Mistaking the Rangers for members of the gang, one of the posse opened fire, and the Rangers were preparing to shoot back when the error was discovered.[5]

On May 12, the Rangers, together with a sheriff's posse, caught Bass and his men in camp in Wise County. The desperadoes had been running for several days, trying to avoid the growing crowd of lawmen. Now they stood their ground and returned fire. The lawmen, however, were stronger and more heavily armed and pushed into camp. Gang member Arkansas Johnson was killed, and the rest fled, abandoning their horses in a clump of timber. The Rangers assumed they would find the robbers with their horses and stopped to hunt them down, giving Bass and his remaining comrades time to flee on foot. Then, mounted on stolen horses, they returned to their familiar haunts around Denton.

Five days after the fight, Peak's detachment was reduced from thirty-one to fifteen men, and they were ordered essentially to sit quietly in Dallas and abandon the chase. No one could understand why the Rangers had suddenly lost interest, but it was all part of a master plan worked out by Major Jones to put an end to Sam Bass, once and for all.[6]

THE PLAN WAS suggested by James W. Murphy, who was scheduled to go on trial in federal court in Tyler for harboring Bass. On May 21, Murphy proposed to June Peak and Deputy U.S. Marshal Walter Johnson that he join the gang and betray Bass to the lawmen. Johnson and Peak took him to see Jones, and he repeated his proposal. Jones ordered Murphy to wait while he discussed it with U.S. Attorney A. J. Evans. Half an hour later, he returned with the arrangements. Murphy would leave town early the next morning, and it would be announced in court that he had skipped bail. Evans would quietly protect the men who had posted Murphy's bond. If he could deliver any of the five members of the Bass gang, all charges against him would be dismissed. If, through no fault of Murphy's, none of the gang were captured, his cooperation would be entered on his behalf at his trial. Evans drew up the memorandum the same day.[7]

Murphy skipped bail as arranged and returned to his home in Denton County. The supposed "escape" of a federal prisoner while in Ranger custody brought sneers from newspaper editors throughout the state, some of whom ridiculed Peak by name. One of Murphy's bondsmen, who was not let in on the deal and believed his money forfeit, accused the Rangers of incompetence. Peak silently endured it. In mid-June, Bass stopped by for a visit at Murphy's farm, and arrangements were made to capture the gang that night. Unfortunately, the sheriff's posse failed to appear. Over the next four days, Murphy made several other attempts to contact lawmen, all of which failed for one reason or another. He did manage, however, to attract unwanted attention to himself.

On June 17, the Bass gang, with James W. Murphy as its newest member, rode south. Bass hoped to pull one last job and then lie low in Mexico for a while. Murphy's life was in serious danger, and he knew it. Already, Bass had learned he was a spy and had made up his mind to kill him. Believing it better not to try too much bluff, Murphy told him about the deal with Jones, but claimed he had agreed to give himself a chance to escape. Bass appeared jovial enough, and in Waco bought a round of drinks, paying for it with the last $20 gold piece from his Union Pacific haul in Nebraska. Nevertheless, Murphy was closely watched, and he made no further efforts to contact lawmen until the gang arrived in Belton, about sixty miles north of Austin, on July 13. There Murphy sent a letter to Sheriff William C. Everhart in Denton advising him that the gang was on its way to Round Rock to rob either the bank or the railroad office. By now he was desperate; he did not know how long he could maintain his cover. Farther south, in Georgetown, he wrote again, this time to Major Jones, saying they would rest their horses for a few days before heading on to Round Rock. He was convinced that if the lawmen didn't act soon, he would be killed.[8]

When Jones received Murphy's letter from Belton, the nearest Ranger unit was Capt. N. O. Reynolds's Company E, which he believed was at Lampasas, some sixty miles to the northwest. There being no telegraph, he ordered Cpl. Vernon Wilson to ride to Lampasas and tell Reynolds to hurry to Round Rock. Wilson rode all night, killing his horse with the effort, only to find Company E had moved fifty-five miles farther to San Saba. Wilson made the daylong trip by stagecoach, finally reaching Reynolds after more than twenty-four hours on the road. Jones, meanwhile, had ordered three Rangers at the Capitol to ride the fifteen miles to Round Rock and conceal themselves.

The next day Jones arrived in Round Rock on the morning train, accompanied by Travis County deputy sheriff Morris Moore. They met with Williamson County deputy sheriff A. W. Grimes, informed him of the situation, and advised him to watch for strangers. Both deputies were former Rangers.

At San Saba, an eight-man detachment of Company E left camp at sunset on July 18 and rode all night. A storekeeper heard them pass in the night, and told his customers the next morning "that hell was to pay somewhere as the rangers had passed his store during the night on a dead run." At sunrise, Friday, July 19, Reynolds halted at the crossing of the North San Gabriel River, forty-five miles from Round Rock, and gave them half an hour to eat, have coffee, and rest the horses. He held his watch on them the entire time. They reached Round Rock between 1 and 2 P.M. that afternoon and went into camp outside of town, while Reynolds rode in to report to Major Jones.[9]

Soon after, Lee Hall arrived. Adjutant General Steele, worried that Reynolds wouldn't make it in time, had ordered him to form a posse to back up Jones, his few Rangers, and the two deputies. Hall took John B. Armstrong, a couple of his Rangers, and a scout, along with his brother, Dick Hall, and a friend from San Antonio. About three miles outside of Round Rock, Hall directed them to go into camp, while he went into town to consult with Jones.[10]

AFTER SUPPER ON FRIDAY, Bass's gang rode into Round Rock. He planned to rob the bank the following morning, and he wanted to look over the building and determine the best escape route. Besides Bass and Murphy, the gang included Frank Jackson, whose friendship was the only thing keeping Murphy alive, and Seaborn Barnes, who wanted Murphy dead. As they approached town, Murphy realized this might be the day he had been waiting for, and he stopped at a feed store on the pretext of getting feed for the horses. Their guard momentarily down, Bass, Jackson, and Barnes continued on, tying their horses in the alley behind the bank. Walking past the building, they came to a store, where they stopped to buy some tobacco.

All was quiet. The Rangers were scattered about the area. Dick Ware, whom Jones had sent up from Austin, was in the barbershop getting a shave. The two deputies, Moore and Grimes, were lounging on the sidewalk keeping an eye on the strangers. Jones had ordered them to report any suspicious activities to him, but when Moore said he thought one of the men was armed, Grimes decided to investigate. He went into the store and approached Bass.

"I believe you have a pistol," he said.

"Yes, of course I have a pistol," Bass answered. With that, the three drew their guns and fired point-blank into Grimes. Moore, who had followed Grimes to the store, emptied his revolver without hitting anything, then went down with a bullet in the lung.

Hearing the gunfire, Hall grabbed his rifle and came out onto the street in time to see Grimes fall facedown in front of the store and Moore supporting himself against the wall. Dick Ware had rushed out of the barbershop and was already in a single-handed fight with the three robbers. A slug hit a hitching post, sending splinters into Ware's face, but he kept firing. Jones charged in, armed only with a small-caliber Colt's double-action revolver (probably a Lightning or Thunderer model). Other Rangers were joining the fray.

The three desperadoes reached their horses, where Barnes went down with one of Ware's bullets in his brain. Bass was mortally wounded, but Jackson untied his horse and assisted him into the saddle. Standing in the door of the feed store, Murphy saw them ride past. Bass was pale and bleeding.[11]

The next day, the Rangers found the dying Sam Bass concealed in a live oak thicket three miles out of town. By his own choice, he was alone. Loyal to the end, Jackson had wanted to stay and make a stand, but Bass ordered him on his way. Before he left, Jackson bound his wounds as best he could and tried to make him comfortable. The Rangers carried him back to town, where two physicians confirmed that death was imminent.

Bass lived until Sunday afternoon. As long as he had strength, he chatted genially with Major Jones, but he refused to give any information about friends who were still at large or that might convict those who had been arrested. "If a man knows anything, he ought to die with it in him," he remarked. The information died with him at 3:58 P.M. on July 21, 1878, his twenty-seventh birthday. Frank Jackson vanished from history, but there is good evidence that he got on the right side of the law and became a prosperous New Mexico rancher.[12]

JUST AS SAM Bass's death marks the passing of the traditional Texas badman, the Apache disturbances of the late 1870s mark the passing of the Texas Ranger as an Indian fighter. By then, the Trans-Pecos region was virtually the only place left in Texas where the Rangers could still find Indians to fight. Even the deadly northwest frontier was reasonably safe.

The army had subdued the Kiowas, Comanches, and other Plains tribes, and the few young warriors who did slip into Texas to steal horses or cattle were promptly chased back to their reservations in Oklahoma. One man who served in the northwest in 1880 remarked, "There was not much that happened that was very exciting while I was with the Rangers. We caught several cattle thieves, and some criminals wanted in other parts of Texas and some wanted in other states."[13]

The Trans-Pecos, however, was still the domain of the Western Apaches, and even Lieutenant Tays's ill-starred El Paso Rangers had an Indian fight. It happened during a scouting expedition shortly after the Salt War siege in San Elizario. Approaching some springs, he divided the men into two groups of six each, to get water by detachments. As the first group rounded some rocks, they ran into a band of ten or twelve Indians riding away from the water holes. Both sides were startled, the Indians heading for the rocks, and five of the Rangers diving into a nearby gully. The sixth, identified as a Russian nobleman, chose to stand upright and fight like a "gentleman," and was quickly cut down.

The four-day siege at San Elizario had steeled the nerves of the Rangers, who now gave a better account of themselves. One, George Lloyd, accidentally slammed a .45-caliber Colt shell into the receiver of his .44 Winchester. The rifle jammed as he closed the breech, and he had to use his knife to unscrew the side plates, remove the shell from the chamber, and screw the side plates back on, with Indians firing at him the whole time. He got his rifle back together and withdrew with the other Rangers.[14]

Tays resigned on March 25, 1878, and the company was disbanded for more than a year before newly commissioned Lt. George Wythe Baylor was ordered to reorganize it. The prospect of fighting Indians had prompted Baylor to apply for a position in the Rangers. Indian fighting was in his blood. His brother was the notorious John R. Baylor, who had created such turmoil on the northwest frontier in the 1850s, and George Baylor had had his share of scrapes with the Indians. According to his own recollection, he joined the Rangers by writing Jones and asking him "if he had any Indians out west that he wanted killed and scalped."[15]

Jones, who had succeeded Steele as adjutant general, was less concerned with Indians than with peace and harmony in El Paso County. Although the Salt War had ended, ill feeling still remained. Some of Tays's former Rangers still held a grudge, believing Tays "had a streak of yellow in him" and had himself ordered their surrender. The two factions still glared at each other across the barrier of language and culture, and Jones wanted someone who could reconcile them. "I would have to use a great deal of discretion in order to avoid further trouble," Baylor later wrote. He was allowed to build his company around a nucleus of experienced Rangers from the central part of the state.

Baylor was well suited for the job. He spoke Spanish reasonably well. Both he and his brother, John, had spent time in the area as Confederate officers during the Civil War and had many friends and acquaintances. The detachment, accompanied by Baylor's wife and three daughters, left San Antonio on August 2, 1879, and arrived at their headquarters in Ysleta on September 12. During one stage of the journey, the Rangers and a band of Mescalero Apaches shadowed each other, but neither party did anything to provoke a fight.[16]

BAYLOR'S FIRST ENCOUNTER with Indians came in October, when Capt. Gregorio García informed him Apaches had attacked hay cutters downriver. The Rangers followed the trail to the Rio Grande, then asked permission to cross from authorities in the nearby Mexican town of Guadalupe. It was a touchy situation. Guadalupe was home to many of the Mexicans who had participated in the Salt War, and it was the parish of the fiery priest Antonio Borajo. No Ranger had been in that part of Mexico since the Salt War. But the hereditary hatred between Mexican and Apache outweighed any other grievance. The Rangers received permission and entered the town to an enthusiastic greeting from the citizens, many of whom had suffered losses to the Apaches. A detail of volunteers from Guadalupe and the nearby town of San Ignacio organized to help the Texans hunt down the Indians.

On learning that the Apaches had killed a herder near a stage stop some twenty miles south of Guadalupe, the Rangers and Mexicans took off in pursuit. The trail led into a mountain canyon, where the Rangers and Mexicans left their horses and moved in on foot. The Mexicans dashed ahead, found the Indians concealed among the rocks, and opened the fight. The Rangers joined in, and shooting continued until dark. Finally, realizing that the Apaches covered the available water holes and were in a position to charge and take their horses, the Rangers and Mexicans withdrew. "The next night," Baylor wrote, "we spent with the hospitable *ciudadanos* [citizens] of Guadalupe, who treated us royally." The hatreds of the Salt War were rapidly vanishing in the face of a common enemy.[17]

A MONTH LATER, the Warm Springs Apache chief Victorio bolted his reservation in New Mexico, inaugurating a brief but bloody conflict known as the Victorio War. Ranger James B. Gillett remembered Victorio as "probably the best general ever produced by the Apache tribe. He was a far better captain than old Geronimo ever was, and capable of commanding a much larger force of men."

Victorio understood the significance of the Rio Grande, knowing that neither country could send its troops into the other. He would raid in the United States, then cross into Mexico. When the immediate furor died down, he would raid in Mexico, then take refuge in the United States. "This," according to Baylor, "was a most unfortunate state of affairs, for many of the best and bravest men of each country lost their lives before an agreement was reached allowing the troops of each country to cross the boundary at will."

The dead included twenty-nine leading citizens of the Mexican town of Carbajal, members of two volunteer expeditions sent out from the town and ambushed and massacred by the Apaches. The other towns in the area began forming a militia company, and they sent to Ysleta asking for Baylor's help. Among the leaders of the Mexican contingent was Chico Barela, one of the leaders of the mob at San Elizario in the Salt War. Meeting him, the Rangers "gave the old fellow to understand that we were now fighting a common enemy and should act in harmony together."[18]

Together the Rangers and Mexicans made several expeditions deep into Chihuahua. Victorio, however, knew the desert and its resources and led them in fruitless pursuits for almost a year. Finally, on October 14, 1880, Mexican regular troops caught up with him. Victorio, sixty warriors, and eighteen women were killed, and the Mexicans took sixty-eight prisoners.

Shortly before the fight with the Mexicans, a small group of warriors and their families deserted and returned to Texas, where they attacked a cavalry camp, killing several soldiers and an Indian scout. For the next two months, they raided the road to El Paso, attacking immigrant trains and military camps. In January 1881, they attacked a stagecoach and killed several people, including a prominent judge. Baylor was notified,

244 © From Frontier Defenders to State Police

and on January 29, 1881, he caught up with the Apaches in their camp in the Diablo Mountains west of Guadalupe Peak. The Indians were wrapped in blankets against the cold, making it hard to distinguish men from women. In the ensuing fight, four warriors, two women, and two children were killed and several were taken prisoner. The Rangers found clothing and military equipment, as well as articles taken from the stage.

This was the last Indian fight in Texas. Baylor had mixed emotions. On the one hand, he was satisfied with the outcome, because he knew this would end the state's Indian wars forever. But he was not happy that some of the women and children had been killed or wounded. Recalling one two-year-old boy with a toe shot off, Baylor admitted, "I was the bold warrior that shot his toe off as we charged through the camp."[19]

THE DAYS OF the traditional Texas Ranger were over. The death of Major Jones in 1881 coincided with the resignation of many of the leading captains of the Frontier Battalion. Although the battalion itself lingered on until 1900, there really was no further reason for it. The frontier line no longer existed. Texas had no more Indians to fight, and the few great gunfighters and badmen who remained were starting to feel their age. More and more of the state's law enforcement requirements were being handled by local deputies and police, who often did not want the Rangers in their bailiwicks. Much of the Ranger's own efforts began to resemble routine police work. The single advantage that the Ranger still had over the locals was his statewide authority.[20]

The Texas Ranger continued to ride a horse, because automobiles had yet to be introduced, but overall there was a more modern air. One of those who had trouble adjusting was George Wythe Baylor. His heart was not in the new role. He was an Indian fighter and not a hunter of fugitives from justice. The problem was aggravated by the high turnover in his company. Few men stayed more than six months, and they rarely got to know each other well. This situation attracted undesirables and hard cases, some of whom were themselves fugitives. In one letter to Austin, Baylor noted that at least nine former Rangers of Lieutenant Tays's old detachment had been "killed as highwaymen" since their discharge, and one of his own Rangers was killed for horse stealing.[21]

Some were little more than bounty hunters, ignoring ordinary lawbreakers in favor of those with large rewards. The public, however, was less concerned about reward money than law and order, and said so in letters to the capital. As early as November 1880, Jones had pointedly told Baylor that citizens of El Paso were complaining that he was not making enough effort to hunt for fugitives. "Unless you can make a good showing to the legislature of the work done by the frontier and special forces," Jones said, "you will not likely get another appointment."[22]

There was an ongoing feud with El Paso city marshal Dallas Stoudenmire, who complained to Jones's successor, Adjutant General Wilburn H. King, about unruliness among the Rangers who came into town. "They . . . take great delight in throwing obstructions in my way whilst in the discharge of my duties," Stoudenmire wrote. "They come to town fully armed and remain as long as they please, get full [of liquor] and go back to camp shooting up the streets."

King passed the complaint on to Baylor, who was affronted and claimed that Stoudenmire was part of the problem, being a heavy drinker, and also involved with some feuds of his own. In fact, he contended, only the presence of the Rangers prevented the marshal from settling a grudge with his enemies by gunplay.[23]

Nevertheless, even Gillett, who liked and admired Baylor, admitted that he was a poor judge of character and indifferent to discipline.

> All men looked alike to him, and he would enlist anyone when there was a vacancy in the company. The result was that some of the worst San Simon Valley [New Mexico] rustlers got into the command and gave us no end of trouble, nearly causing one or two killings in our camp.[24]

Despite the differences, Baylor outlasted Stoudenmire, who resigned as city marshal on May 29, 1882, and was succeeded by Gillett. Ultimately Baylor adjusted to the new conditions and remained with the Rangers until April 15, 1885, when his unit, Company A, was disbanded.[25]

IN SOUTH TEXAS, Lee Hall's succession of Leander McNelly likewise represented a shift away from the traditional Ranger. Hall had no intention of emulating McNelly, concentrating instead on obtaining arrests and indictments and generally keeping things quiet. Still, he faced a problem that was all too familiar to Jones, McNelly, and other Ranger commanders of the nineteenth century—money. By the summer of 1877, the legislature was considering disbanding his company as an economy measure. Addressing the issue as members of the West Texas Stock Association prepared to meet in Goliad, the *Goliad Guard* urged the stockmen to act on their own to keep Hall's men in the field.

> Hall's Company has restored peace to the country, and we are just beginning to enjoy the fruits of the victory they have achieved, but no well informed man will deny the fact that security will cease as soon as the Police is [*sic*] disbanded. The people cannot afford to lose the vantage ground gained by these brave men. If they allow this advantage to be lost by indifference or illiberality on their part, the relapse into crime and outlawry will rebound with greater disasters upon them than before, and the valuable services of our police force in the past will have been thrown away. . . . Legislative appropriations have been exhausted, but the people of Western Texas are too much interested to fail to contribute from their own private means a sufficient amount to retain Hall's company in service, and we believe the Legislature of Texas too loyal to the great State they represent to refuse to appropriate at their next session money to refund the contributions of private citizens.[26]

Nevertheless, the company was disbanded, an act that proved premature, because the Southwest was still too unsettled. To rectify the mistake, the legislature in 1879 authorized a special company with Hall as captain. For the next several years, Hall and his successors policed the Nueces Strip, rounding up fence-cutters and cattle thieves and bringing them to the conventional justice of the courtroom. Occasionally they also ventured over into DeWitt County, to make sure the Taylors and Suttons remained quiet.[27]

THE NEW EMPHASIS on courtroom justice was yet another shift from tradition. The classic Ranger settled things with a rope or a firearm, but the new generation was beginning to rely on due process, improvising some semblance of due process where none was readily available. The definitive case of improvisation was in the rough-and-tumble railroad construction camps on the Pecos River west of Del Rio. The Rangers had been dispatched at the request of the railroad contractor, who complained to the adjutant general about the hard cases that hung around the camps. A detachment arrived under Capt. T. L. Oglesby and began cleaning up.

The problem was that the nearest court with jurisdiction was over two hundred miles away in Fort Stockton, and in 1882 the round-trip was twelve days on horseback, in a parched desert. A solution presented itself in July of that year, when the Rangers arrested a man named Joe Bell for aggravated assault. Rather than ride all the way to Fort Stockton, the Rangers hauled him before Roy Bean, an aging, gray-bearded saloon keeper who, like a biblical patriarch, dispensed homespun justice built on sagacity, common sense, and a feel for the locale. Although he had no legal authority whatsoever, Bean found Bell guilty. The Rangers were satisfied, and Captain Oglesby recommended that the saloon keeper be formally appointed justice of the peace. Bowing to frontier realities, the Pecos County Commissioners' Court formalized Roy's position by naming him justice of the peace on August 2, 1882, thereby creating the legendary Judge Roy Bean.[28]

A classic product of the frontier, Roy Bean never admitted to being completely honest either as a judge or as a businessman. He amused himself by fleecing the customers in his saloon and daring them to do anything about it. None did. Generally speaking, the "law" as interpreted by Judge Roy Bean was his will, enforced by his overbearing personality, a natural talent for bluff, and the Rangers who stopped by from time to time. In reality, Roy owed his position to the fact that he was the only person who could demand—and get—respect from the brawling railroad men and frontier toughs. And in the Pecos country, the respect of the railroad men and frontier toughs counted for a lot more than the conventional law of the civilized world.

IT IS IRONIC that one of the most famous of all Ranger sayings, "One riot—one Ranger," comes not from the frontier but from urban disturbances. The statement is attributed to Capt. William J. McDonald, whose protégés included President Theodore Roosevelt, and who represented the new generation of Ranger. The remark itself is apocryphal, but like many such sayings, it developed from a series of real incidents where McDonald dealt with potentially dangerous problems of the modern, industrial era.

Like many other Rangers of the new generation, McDonald got his start in one of the old frontier companies, but was young enough to make the shift when the frontier began to die. By the mid-1890s, when Texas was plagued with a series of labor disputes, he and his men often were used to put down disturbances. Among them was a strike of workers at the Fort Worth and Denver Railroad that had brought operations in Wichita Falls to a standstill.

McDonald went alone to Wichita Falls, to the hall where the workers were holding a closed meeting. When the doorkeeper refused him entry, he said, "I am Captain McDonald of the Rangers, and I'm here to talk to you men and see what the trouble is. You're all here now, and I think I'll talk to you together."

"Where are your Rangers?" the doorkeeper demanded.

"I didn't bring any. I don't need any. I'm a pretty good single-handed talker, myself."

With that, he pushed past the doorkeeper and confronted the angry strikers, eventually persuading them to take their grievances to the president of the railroad.

McDonald used the same ploy with striking coal miners in Thurber in east Texas, telling the president of the mines, "I'm using my men in other places. I'll look around a little and do what I can."

Like many labor disturbances of the era, this one had anarchist elements, and when McDonald arrived at the miners' meeting, a speaker was advocating blowing up the mines. He interrupted and told the group, "I'm here alone, but I'll have my men here, if I need them, and I'll hang just such fellows as this man," indicating the speaker.

One of the crowd shouted he would be killed if he continued to interfere.

"That's been tried on me more than once without much success," McDonald replied. "You see I'm here yet."

The classic McDonald emerged when Dallas community leaders asked for a company of Rangers to break up an impending prizefight. McDonald stepped off the train alone, and the mayor asked, "Where are the others?"

"Hell!" McDonald snapped. "Ain't I enough? There's only one prizefight!"[29]

Chapter 16

Gunmen, Pugilists, and a "Fistic Carnival"

By 1895, the Texas frontier had been reduced to an isolated strip along the Rio Grande. Starting just beyond Brownsville, near the mouth, the wild country ran north and west, following the river until it reached El Paso. El Paso itself was the biggest thing in the Trans-Pecos. No longer a cluster of settlements centering around Fort Bliss or a suburb of San Elizario, it was the county seat. The arrival of the railroads in 1881 boosted the city until, by 1895, it had thirteen thousand people. As the hub of the railroads, it had become completely Americanized and even showed signs of respectability, although the usual frontier mixture of good and bad (with a large helping of the latter) could make a Saturday night pretty lively.[1]

El Paso's better nature, such as it was, could be credited in part to the Texas Rangers. Owen White, an El Paso boy who grew up to become an important contributor to *The American Mercury, The New York Times,* and other leading Eastern publications, recalled a Saturday night when various gamblers, gunmen, and imported hoodlums from the East decided to take over El Paso for their own amusement. They were shooting up the place when a handful of Rangers rode into town.

"The result was instantaneous; it was miraculous," White remembered. "The good citizens in El Paso breathed easily; the bad ones put their guns out of sight and kept quiet; and all that the Rangers did was to sit around their camp, roll cigarettes, and, once in a while, go over to the saloon and get a drink."[2]

The Rangers were supported by the local Law and Order League, who were determined to clean up the town. Reformers pressured the city council into appointing gunfighter Jeff Milton chief of police. Upon taking office, Milton ran the gamblers out of town and generally made life easier for decent citizens. With the next election, however, Milton was fired and the gamblers were back in business. The Law and Order League petitioned Austin for more Rangers to bolster the company in Ysleta. Then they went to court and got injunctions against the gambling houses. The injunctions had little impact, but they demonstrated that the league meant business.[3]

DOWNRIVER, PEACE WAS being established in the railroad camps under the watchful eyes of the Rangers and Judge Roy Bean. Seldom did anyone challenge their combined authority, and when someone tried, the reaction was swift and decisive. In one rare incident, a naive attorney had the temerity to question one of the judge's rulings. Turning to the senior Ranger present, Roy inquired, "Sergeant?"

"Yes, sir."

"What are your orders here?"

"To stand behind you in everything you say," the sergeant replied.

"What would you do if I told you to take this fellow out and hang him?"

"I'd take him out and hang him."

The lawyer now saw reason behind Roy's ruling and let the matter drop for the time being, although he later complained (futilely, of course) to higher authorities.[4]

Roy had bluffed the attorney, and it worked. Despite a later Hollywood reputation for ruthlessness, he never hanged anyone. He never had that kind of authority, and he was smart enough to know how far he could bend the law. But for all his flaws and eccentricities, Judge Roy Bean was the only law in the Pecos region, and the Rangers were ready to back him in whatever he chose to do.

FOR ALL THE efforts of the Rangers, Judge Roy Bean, and the El Paso Law and Order League, the strip along the Rio Grande was still a rough area, particularly in the Trans-Pecos. El Paso was a frontier town, and as such had the dubious distinction of being home to some of the West's last practicing gunfighters. On the side of law and order was shootist Jeff Milton. George Scarborough, who played both sides of the law, was currently serving as deputy U.S. marshal and assisted the Rangers from time to time.

Also playing both ends against the middle were the two John Selmans, father and son. John Sr. was well known to the Rangers as a man who had spent much of his life outside the law. He had been a key figure in a bloody feud in Shackelford County in the mid-1870s, and later headed a west Texas gang of cutthroats known as Selman's Scouts. By the mid-1880s he had pushed his luck about as far as he dared. The time had come to settle down, to look toward a more respectable career and give more attention to his family. With the move to El Paso, he began the transformation to a venerable, if somewhat dishonest, figure known to the local community as "Uncle John." He now served as constable, and was said to shake down the local prostitutes for payoffs. John Jr. was a police officer of equally dubious reputation.

In the spring of 1895, El Paso's diverse collection of gunslingers was joined by the most notorious killer of all, John Wesley Hardin. Hardin had walked out of prison on February 17, 1894, after serving slightly less than sixteen years of his twenty-five-year sentence. The years behind bars had taught him to tone down his viciousness, and he used the time to study law. Six weeks after his release, he received a full pardon, and he was admitted to the bar on July 21. A change of venue on one of his legal cases had brought him to El Paso, and he decided to establish his practice there. Still prone to gambling and drunken brawls, he was not exactly a model citizen, but he generally managed to stay within the law.[5]

Hardin's arrival in El Paso was simply one gunfighter too many as far as John Selman, Sr., was concerned. He had lived in El Paso for about ten years and was fifty-five, getting on in years for a gunfighter. Unlike Hardin, he didn't go around looking for trouble, but neither did he back away from it. He was particularly touchy about any threat involving his family, and with John Jr. serving as a police officer in the rough-and-tumble border town, he had ample opportunity to get touchy. Age may have outwardly mellowed him, but John Selman remained a ruthless, cold-blooded killer. Thus, in the summer of 1895, El Paso had two gunfighters on a collision course—Hardin with his tendency to look for trouble, and Selman with his tendency to accommodate.[6]

Of all the gunmen in El Paso, Hardin naturally attracted the most attention. It seemed everyone was interested in him. In August, Ranger captain John Hughes and gunfighting deputy marshal George Scarborough were helping Davis County officials track down bandits who had robbed a store and killed a local peace officer in Valentine, 145 miles southeast of El Paso. As they combed the mountains of the Big Bend country, Hardin's name came up.

"They say Wes Hardin is cutting capers in El Paso," the Davis County sheriff told Hughes. "What's going to happen, Captain?"

"Why, someone will kill him," Hughes observed.

"Who?"

"See that man in the blue britches?" Hughes asked, indicating Scarborough. "He might do it."[7]

HUGHES WAS RIGHT about someone killing Hardin, but wrong about who would do it. While the posse sought the bandits, Hardin was exchanging threats with gunfighter-turned-constable John Selman. All summer, trouble had been brewing between the two, much of it centering around John Jr., who had arrested the widowed Hardin's latest paramour for being drunk and disorderly. About 7 P.M. on August 19, Uncle John encountered Hardin on the street. Words and insults flew, and the two men separated.[8] Hardin went to the Wigwam Saloon and got gloriously drunk. About 10 P.M., he staggered into the Acme Saloon. He was rolling dice for drinks at the bar with Henry S. Brown when Selman slipped up to the door of the saloon. Hardin threw the dice on the counter and said, "Brown, you've got four sixes to beat."

Selman's gun exploded. The .45-caliber slug struck Hardin in the back of the head and came out through his left eyelid. He was dead before he hit the floor. Selman pumped two more bullets into the prone body for good measure. Two .41-caliber Colt's revolvers were found on the body, but he had not used either. He never knew what hit him.[9]

The next morning, Hughes and Scarborough boarded the train for El Paso, after their fruitless hunt for the Valentine killers. As he checked their passes, the conductor asked, "Have you heard the news in El Paso?"

"What news?" Scarborough asked.

"Why, Wes Hardin was killed."

"Who did it?"

"John Selman," the conductor replied.

"I'll bet he shot him in the back," was Scarborough's only comment.[10]

Eight months later, on April 5, 1896, Scarborough and Selman got into an argument in an alley behind the Wigwam. Guns flashed, and Selman went down. He died the next morning, following surgery.[11]

THE DEATHS OF John Wesley Hardin and John Selman marked the end of the era of the gunfighters. Texas was becoming civilized in spite of itself. By the time Hardin died, even prizefighting was coming under fire. But the sport wasn't going down without a full count. One of the most absurd matches in the history of boxing brought virtually every Ranger in Texas to El Paso and, for one brief moment of glory, made a forgotten little whistle-stop in the middle of the desert the center of attention for the sporting crowd on both sides of the Atlantic.

Pugilism was still very popular with the male population of Texas during the final decade of the nineteenth century, but the United States as a whole was in the throes of conscience. Temperance societies abounded, animal rights activists were vocal, and boxing was seen as a bastion of sin because of the violence within the ring, its male orientation, the large purses, and the fortunes that changed hands in wagers. By 1895, when Dallas promoter Dan Stuart secured a match between undefeated heavyweight champion James J. (Gentleman Jim) Corbett and Australian contender Robert (Ruby Bob) Fitzsimmons, Texas was one of the few states in the Union where fighters could face off for prize money. A prohibitionary statute did exist, but it was ambiguous enough to be ineffective.[12]

The fight initially was set for Dallas. The purse was $15,000, with a $10,000 side bet between Corbett and Fitzsimmons. Stuart began constructing an arena, and the attention of the sporting world turned toward Dallas. Preparations were well under way when Governor Charles Culberson, himself a Dallas man, speaking for what he considered "the better class of citizens" of Texas, announced there would be no prizefighting in the state. When Stuart countered that the existing Texas law was invalid, Culberson convened a special session of the legislature to get an improved version.[13]

With prizefighting so severely restricted in the United States, the showdown between Stuart and Culberson was followed throughout the country. "If it should turn out that Stuart has the law on his side," the *Chicago Tribune* predicted, "Dallas is certain to hold one of the biggest crowds on the day that the carnival begins that have ever gathered at a ringside in this or any other country, and should the Governor be right, then it looks as though the battle would certainly take place on Mexican soil and within easy reach of San Antonio."

Regardless of where the fight was held, "Chicago will have a big representation . . . already two special trains have been arranged for and the chances are that still another will be found necessary to accommodate the crowd who propose to take the journey." Odds were two to one in favor of Corbett, and were rising to three to one.[14]

THE THIRTY-TWO-year-old Culberson was no prig. One of his friends and supporters told a *Chicago Tribune* sportswriter that the governor

> stands ready without the slightest hesitation to sample most any kind of invigorator . . . in a bottle. When he is irritated he can swear like a teamster, and he doesn't hesitate to garnish the ordinary conversation with a reasonable degree of profanity.[15]

But Culberson had come up through various local and state offices to the governorship with powerful support from the Dallas pulpits, and now he had to stand by them in the prizefighting controversy.[16]

One Dallas County elected official (who asked not to be identified because he couldn't afford to alienate the church vote) told *Chicago Tribune* sportswriter George Siler that if the governor ran out of other options,

> he could play the rangers on us. These rangers are sort of a little standing army; they are entirely under the command of the Governor, and they make a speciality of going it blind and shooting up everybody and everything the Governor tells them to.

The man doubted Culberson would go to that extreme, but said if he did, "there's likely to be a heap of trouble," because a large percentage of the anticipated sixty thousand fight fans would be cowboys. "Now a cow puncher doesn't like a Texas ranger, no how, and if he ever meets him in Dallas at this fight, and there is enough of him to make it worth while, there's liable to be trouble in a minute." In fact, the Dallas man said, Ranger vs. Cowboy would be a bigger event than Fitzsimmons vs. Corbett.[17]

While Culberson lobbied a not-so-compliant state legislature, a Dallas judge ruling in another case overturned Texas's existing law prohibiting prizefighting. Attorney General Martin M. Crane prepared to battle it out in appeals. It seemed everybody was getting into the act. Looking ahead, in case Texas did ban the fight, federal officials announced they would not permit the fight north of the Red River in the Indian Territory. Culberson's wife was quoted as saying, "[I]f Texans want a prizefight, let them have it, I say. . . . What's use of poor Charles working himself to death to prevent something the whole State wants?" Meanwhile, on September 28, Ruby Bob Fitzsimmons arrived in Houston to wide public acclaim, and he gave an exhibition fight that night.[18]

WITH SOME EFFORT, Culberson managed to get the necessary vote in the legislature, and a clear-cut law against prizefighting went on the books in Texas. Not a man to be discouraged, Dan Stuart then announced that the fight would be held in Hot Springs, Arkansas. After more than a century, what happened next is not clear, but Arkansas governor James P. Clarke appears to have quashed it by having Corbett and Fitzsimmons arrested for conspiracy to assault each other.[19]

Corbett, who was not particularly interested in boxing in the first place, had grown weary of delays. On November 11, he attended a fight in Nevada—the only Western state where professional boxing was still legal—and watched Irish heavyweight Peter Maher trounce Steve O'Donnell. This was Corbett's way out. Although he had no right to do so, he announced he was retiring the championship in favor of Maher. Fitzsimmons, however, made no objections; he had already beaten Maher in 1892, and was confident he could do it again.

Dan Stuart was also happy, because as 1895 drew to a close with no fight, sunshine appeared on the western horizon. The El Paso business community, more interested in promoting their city than in the fine points of Texas law, had offered him $6,000 to stage a fight between Fitzsimmons and Maher. The community leaders envisioned the bout as the main event of a "Great Fistic Carnival," with lesser prizefights, baseball, football, shooting matches, a rodeo, and bullfights across the river in Ciudad Juárez.[20]

El Paso was the ideal spot for a grand event. The Southern Pacific ran through the city on its way to the West Coast, giving the sporting crowd easy access to the city from both directions. It was conveniently located to New Mexico and Arizona, federal territories outside the realm of conventional state law. Júarez was in the Mexican state of Chihuahua, beyond the reach of U.S. law.

Culberson was not interested in El Paso's grand scheme, and he ordered Adjutant General W. H. Mabry to send a detachment of Rangers to make sure the fight did not occur. This brought an immediate denunciation of the governor, Mabry, and the Rangers by the indignant members of the El Paso city council, who firmly believed that it was no one's business in Austin how they ran their community.[21]

The *El Paso Herald* lobbied hard for "that scrapping match," bluntly stating that local citizens were less interested in "the scientific display of the manly art itself" than in the money it would bring. In fact, the *Herald* commented that if Stuart brought the fight to El Paso, he would find local morals exceedingly flexible. Stuart was happy to oblige, and the fight was set for February 14, 1896, either in El Paso or in the immediate vicinity.[22]

As far as Mabry was concerned, state law was not subject to local option. He ordered Captain Hughes to move his Rangers into town from their camp at Ysleta and prevent the match.[23] The entry of the Rangers provided new grist for the cartoon mills of the New York newspapers. The *World* portrayed a Ranger as a disheveled frontiersman with drooping mustache, stringy, unkempt, chest-length hair, outsized sombrero with a Bowie knife stuck through the brim, rifle slung over his shoulder, heavy cartridge belt, and fringed trousers. Each hand held a six-shooter bearing a more than passing resemblance to Colt's giant, intimidating Walker Model. The muzzles were stuck in Fitzsimmons's and Maher's faces, and the Ranger was daring either of them to throw a punch.[24]

After all was said and done, community standards in El Paso were not as flexible as the city's newspaper presumed. The Law and Order League swung into action, as did the El Paso Ministers' Union. Both were determined to stop the fight, not only in their city, but anywhere within a convenient radius, regardless of jurisdiction. The Ministers' Union correctly guessed that if El Paso couldn't host the match, Stuart would hold it just across the line in New Mexico, where neither federal nor territorial law prohibited it. When New Mexico authorities explained they were powerless to stop the fight in their territory, the ministers began lobbying the U.S. Congress. Responding to the growing furor, Congress outlawed both prizefighting and bullfighting "for money or for other things of value, or for any championship" in federal territories. Violation was a felony, with a penalty of one to five years in prison.[25]

Soon after, Adjutant General Mabry arrived in El Paso with his other three captains. Forty Rangers were on hand to prevent the fight. President Grover Cleveland dispatched U.S. Marshal Edward Hall and thirteen deputies to make certain the match did not slip over into federal territory. These efforts spurred Mexico to action. Gen. Miguel Ahumada, governor of Chihuahua, was a grim, stern man with a reputation for using the military to suppress lawlessness in his state. True to form, he sent a cavalry detachment to the border to make certain the fistic carnival did not occur in Mexico. They were followed by the governor himself, who crossed the Rio Grande into El Paso on February 11 to confer with local officials. As a courtesy, he also met with leaders of the local business community, but he remained inflexible. He would not allow the fight in Chihuahua.[26]

"If men come into Mexico and intend to break the law they will be arrested and if they resist arrest they will be shot. That's all there is to the matter," Ahumada said. He warned that spectators and newspaper correspondents would be considered participants in the fight, and would be subject to prosecution or worse under the laws of Mexico.[27]

A day later, the great John L. Sullivan arrived in El Paso and rode to his hotel in an open carriage to the acclaim of the crowds. Sullivan's head was bandaged because of what one news correspondent politely called a "railroad accident." He had fallen off the observation platform of a train going forty miles an hour between Rock Island and Peoria, and had been found unconscious by the roadbed. Those in the know said he had been drinking again, but regardless of circumstances, he was badly hurt. Asked his opinion of the coming fight, Sullivan, who didn't care for Fitzsimmons, predicted Maher would win. So did two of the nation's leading astrologers, who combined their efforts under the name Astor-Hazelrigg and said the stars were definitely in the Irishman's favor.[28]

SPECTATORS WERE POURING into town. Already there were some fifteen hundred with more on the way, paying as much as five dollars a night for a cot in a hallway. Then, only two days before the bout, Maher was out of it, at least for the time being. Earlier in the week, alkali dust had blown into his face during a *remolino,* a vicious Southwestern whirlwind that blows up for only a few seconds but throws dust and sand with incredible force. The Irishman was diagnosed as suffering from ophthalmia and could barely see his hand in front of his face.

Maher's sudden vision problems raised suspicions. Some said he was losing his nerve. Others believed Stuart himself had concocted the ailment to buy time (and build excitement) while he considered all his options. Mabry suspected a ruse, and Fitzsimmons's manager, Martin Julian, was disgusted with delays and ready to claim a forfeit. But for some fight fans who had followed the match from Dallas to Hot Springs to El Paso, this was the final straw, and they began leaving.[29]

John L. Sullivan, however, was convinced that it was no act. "I feel sorry for Maher," John L. wrote to the New York *World*. "His eyes are in bad shape."[30] Maher's backer, John J. Quinn, assured the public through the pages of the *World* that although Maher was in great pain and his vision was poor, he was beginning to recover and would "give a good account of himself" in the coming fight.[31]

WHILE THE SPORTING world waited, Mabry kept everyone involved under tight scrutiny. Rangers watched the railroad depot, with orders to note and follow any fight paraphernalia that might be unloaded. They duly reported cars containing the platform, carnival paraphernalia, and Kinetoscope equipment (Stuart's real profit—if any—would come from showing films of the fight throughout the country). The Rangers also followed Fitzsimmons and Maher, and Capt. Bill McDonald became a constant companion of the unwilling Stuart.[32]

Stuart found the situation irritating, but otherwise was not impressed. "Nothing short of lightning or the destruction of the earth by fire and flood can stop the contest we have arranged to pull off," he remarked. Surveillance was so close that some people only vaguely connected with the fight complained that Mabry and Culberson were running a police state.[33]

Mabry was also ready with accusations. Stuart, he alleged, was exercising "a kind of censorship" over news correspondents, telling them if their dispatches were not favorable to the fight, they would not be allowed to attend. Consequently, Mabry said the city council's resolution condemning Culberson's efforts received wide distribution. On the other hand, a resolution of support from the Ministers' Union, which Mabry contended "represented a large class among the best citizens approving the Governor's action and upholding my methods," was hardly mentioned in the press. There were also rumors that Stuart had sent for ex-gunslinger Bat Masterson, himself a sporting man, to head up a hundred toughs and make certain nothing interfered with the fight. The New York *World,* which reported the events as they unfolded, called Masterson "Dan Stuart's sergeant-at-arms."[34]

Masterson arrived in El Paso, but was tight-lipped about his role in Dan Stuart's scheme of things. "As to my connection with the enterprise I can say nothing," he remarked, although he did not hesitate to call Stuart "an honorable sportsman." He commented, "To be sure, he has been in hard luck since he started pugilistic enterprises, but he is here to stay this time; and if it comes down to cases will pull the fights off just to show that a Texan is not to be bluffed." That said, Bat turned his eloquent wrath against the moralists and politicians.

> That all the commotion has been stirred up because two men are going to box with five-ounce gloves seems to me to be utterly ridiculous. When the Senate and House of Representatives of this great country can find nothing better to do than to make a law prohibiting boxing contests in the Territories it is high time something was done.[35]

UNFORTUNATELY FOR STUART and Masterson, Mabry had a better grasp of public opinion. Citizens were getting tired of the large influx of people, not all of whom were of the best character. The out-of-towners naturally provided a boost to gambling and prostitution, and the entire situation was becoming a nuisance. Even the pro-fight *Herald* was starting to complain about the "tin horns" streaming into the city.

Downriver near the confluence with the Pecos, the Rio Grande flowed around a sandbar situated midstream, straddling the international boundary. This sandbar was a no-man's-land, unclaimed by either the United States or Mexico and therefore under no one's jurisdiction—a fact not lost on Judge Roy Bean, who sat in his Jersey Lilly Saloon in the nearby town of Langtry. For now he minded his own business, peddling cold beer and watered-down whiskey to thirsty passengers during the Southern Pacific's twenty-minute watering stop and shortchanging them until the whistle of the departing train told them they could argue no longer.

All the while, he was following Stuart's frustrated efforts in El Paso, waiting for the right moment to intervene.[36]

Just when the promoter's situation seemed hopeless, Roy acted. Stuart received a telegram advising him that he and his fighters would be welcome in Langtry. Ranger Ed Aten boarded the train carrying all the lumber and equipment, not knowing for certain where it was bound. When everything was finally off-loaded at the little whistle-stop town of a few dozen people, 389 miles downriver from El Paso, Aten immediately telegraphed Mabry, who sourly observed:

> The prize fighters were merely dough in the hands of Mr. Stuart and the hundreds of others who were present for the money they hoped to win, and would have fought in the ring, wherever located, if unmolested by officers at that time.[37]

Dan Stuart, the fighters, the spectators, and supporting cast boarded the train for Langtry shortly before midnight on February 20. So did Mabry and twenty-six Rangers. When the conductor asked the adjutant general for tickets, he produced authorization from Culberson and said the state would pay the bill. The conductor did not argue.[38]

Some fight fans may have felt more comfortable with the Rangers along for the ride. The New York *World* correspondent reported:

> There were "bad men" aboard the train. They were of the variety who declared they would see the fight without the necessary tickets, and confided to everybody that there would be music if Dan Stuart or any Denver man-killer interfered with their sport. By Denver man-killer they meant "Bat" Masterson. . . . These bad men had an uncomfortable manner of fingering their firearms when speaking of the most commonplace things, and some of the more timid Eastern gentlemen agreed among themselves that sporting life was not quite up to what it was cracked to be.[39]

John L. Sullivan was among those who found the Texans' fascination with six-shooters unsettling. "I don't like this gun business," he wrote. "A true man should be able to take care of himself with the weapons provided by nature." He felt lawmakers would better serve the public by regulating firearms instead of "such innocent and manly sport as boxing."[40]

The Texans, of course, felt the public best served by not regulating either boxing or firearms. They were accustomed to handling their own disputes and did not necessarily feel that every law that came out of Austin was a good law. The law against boxing, for example, was viewed as an effort to satisfy a small but politically vocal segment of the community at the expense of the majority of the state's citizens. And as a law unsupported by the majority, it was not subject to respect or obedience, and neither were its enforcers.

Among the noncitizens ready to challenge the lawmen was Bat Masterson. The train stopped for lunch at Sanderson, and Bat sat next to Bill McDonald in a Chinese restaurant. According to Albert Bigelow Paine, McDonald's friend and biographer, a dispute arose between the Ranger and the gunfighter. Paine wrote a few years after the incident, "Bat has since given up all his reckless ways and become a good citizen, but at that time he was training with the unreformed and not feeling very well, anyhow."

Masterson decided the Chinese waiter wasn't tending to him fast enough, and demanded attention. When the Chinese replied he was working as fast as he could, Bat lost his temper and jerked up a table caster to hit him.

"Don't you hit that man!" McDonald ordered.

"Maybe *you'd* like to take it up!" Bat retorted.

"I done took it up!" McDonald replied.

Bat thought better of it, sat back down, and finished his meal quietly.[41]

Or so wrote Paine. Masterson vehemently denied it, claiming that he and McDonald were longtime friends who never quarreled about anything, and branding Paine's story "a brazen, cowardly lie." Nevertheless, the Masterson-McDonald standoff has joined the lore, not only of the fight, but of the Rangers and Bat Masterson.[42]

THE TRAIN PULLED into Langtry at 3 P.M. on February 21 in a cold, drizzling rain. Judge Roy Bean was ready for the sporting crowd, waiting at the platform and extending his personal welcome with an invitation to stop by the Jersey Lilly for beer at a dollar a bottle before stumbling down the rugged path to the river. Mabry was skeptical. Familiar with Roy's reputation for deviousness, he lined his Rangers up for inspection to demonstrate that—just this once—Judge Roy Bean was not the only law west of the Pecos.

But Roy was one jump ahead. The ring, he assured them, was outside state or federal jurisdiction. Nobody need worry about any laws being broken. Mabry was still suspicious, but Hughes accepted the situation with good grace. He knew Roy, although they had never dealt with each other in an official capacity, and if the conniving old jurist could make some money swindling the sporting crowd, that was fine with Hughes—provided the fight itself was held outside Texas jurisdiction.[43]

A newspaper correspondent described the scene as the crowd made its way toward the ring.

> Over a rocky road, winding about the precipitous cliffs along the Rio Grande, the crowd wended its way to the sandy beach of the river. Forty-two Mexicans had carried the ring material down to the river bank last night after working hard all day upon a roadway down from the bluff. A narrow wooden footbridge had been put up across the swiftly flowing stream. The crowd stumbled over the stony path and waded ankle deep in the sand, guided by little Jimmy White, a boy who came from Toronto to be at the fight.
>
> The battle-ground was a sandy flat upon a big bend in the Rio Grande River, on the Mexican side. It was just two miles from the village of Langtry. The ring was protected from outsiders' view by a canvas wall. The board floor was covered with canvas, over which rosin was sprinkled. At one side was the frame compartment for the taking by the kinetoscope of the pictures of the fight as it proceeded. On the opposite side of the ring were two little tents for the principals.[44]

This was overly optimistic. The sky was too overcast for the Kinetoscope and there would be no films of the fight. And the canvas walls of the amphitheater were not high enough to block a clear view from the bluffs on either side. Now that they were sure no state or federal laws were being broken, the Rangers joined a nonpaying crowd of some two hundred Mexicans from across the river to watch the show from beyond the amphitheater.[45]

As it turned out, the months of political and legal sparring were more interesting than the main event. For one brief moment (literally) Maher put up a good fight. Then Fitzsimmons knocked him silly. Referee

George Siler, the *Chicago Tribune* sportswriter and boxing expert who had covered the initial disputes in Dallas, said it lasted one minute forty-three seconds. The *El Paso Herald* figured 1:25, and the New York *World* said 1:35. Whatever the time, the fight ended before the Rangers and spectators on the banks even got comfortable.[46]

Dan Stuart's Great Fistic Carnival was over. After all the wrangling, threats, charges and countercharges, and tens of thousands of dollars of expenses, it would be fair to say that probably the only person who came out ahead on the deal was Judge Roy Bean.[47]

Chapter 17

Tarnished Star

The Texas Rangers entered the twentieth century with another of their periodic reorganizations, this one prompted by a reinterpretation of the 1874 law creating the Frontier Battalion. The law stated that "officers" of the battalion had the power to execute criminal processes and make arrests in accordance with the criminal procedures of the state. Traditionally, the term "officer" had been taken to mean any Ranger. In 1900, however, attorneys challenged the arrest power of rank-and-file Rangers, on the grounds that such powers were extended only to *commissioned* officers of the battalion. On May 26 of that year, the state's attorney general agreed, nullifying the authority of every Ranger below the rank of second lieutenant.[1]

The ruling effectively ended the existence of the Frontier Battalion, because most of its men now had no legal power. But Governor Joseph D. Sayers was loath to entirely dismantle the Ranger Service and requested an opinion on the extent to which it could continue to function. On June 1, using the second opinion, Sayers reduced the battalion to four companies, each consisting of three commissioned officers and three privates. Only commissioned officers could make arrests, but they could summon the privates to assist if necessary. Meanwhile, the legislature set to work to correct the defects in the law and, on July 8, 1901, passed a bill creating a "ranger force" whose responsibility would be "protecting the frontier against marauding and thieving parties, and suppressing lawlessness and crime throughout the state." The new force consisted of four companies of twenty men each, including one captain and one sergeant. Commanding officers were John A. Brooks, Company A; W. J. "Bill" McDonald, Company B; J. H. Rogers, Company C; and John R. Hughes, Company D. All were veteran captains of the Frontier Battalion.[2]

Given the limited resources and statewide jurisdiction, the new companies were frequently shifted from one part of Texas to the other, generally in the west and along the Mexican border. Despite efforts by law enforcement and the military from the United States and Mexico, the border area was still a violent no-man's-land where criminals from both countries congregated and took refuge. In many ways, little had changed in the sixty years since the Mexican War, and it was perhaps the last place in Texas where the Rangers used traditional frontier methods. A shootout near Del Rio, in December 1906, was reminiscent of the classic American West.

Five Rangers had cornered murderer Ed Putnam in a house near town. The family who lived there managed to get out, but one of the daughters told Capt. J. H. Rogers that Putnam had "a funny look in his eyes." About that time, a shot came from the house, and the Rangers scattered under cover around the building. The ensuing fight lasted an hour, with Putnam dashing from window to window, firing whenever he had a chance. The Rangers poured lead into the house until, finally, a shot from Ranger Frank Hamer went into Putnam's heart.

The house was in ruins. The Rangers counted more than three hundred bullet holes in the walls. Examining Putnam's body, they found his pockets full of shells, enough to hold the Rangers off at least until dark and escape, had not Hamer shot him.[3]

THE YEAR 1906 was also busy for Capt. Bill McDonald. About midnight on August 13, a group of men had run through downtown Brownsville firing their weapons into the buildings. One man was killed and two wounded. The townspeople blamed soldiers of the First Battalion, Twenty-fifth Infantry, a black unit stationed at Fort Brown. The citizens resented the posting of black troops to Fort Brown, and almost from their arrival in Brownsville, a little more than two weeks earlier, citizens and soldiers had clashed verbally and physically. Whether the soldiers actually were guilty of the August 13 shooting has never clearly been established. McDonald, however, went to Brownsville with the notion that they were. He had with him two Rangers and District Judge Stanley Welch.[4]

Although McDonald also believed that the military would try to cover up the incident and block a civilian investigation, he found the officers at Fort Brown remarkably cooperative. They allowed him onto the post to question officers and enlisted men, an act that brought criticism from one national civil rights group. Based on his investigation, McDonald secured warrants for the arrest of twelve soldiers. In September, after a three-week session, which included a charge from Judge Welch that was heavy with racist overtones, the Cameron County Grand Jury was unable to reach a conclusion, and the soldiers were released. At the behest of Brownsville citizens, Fort Brown was deactivated. The enlisted men of all three companies subsequently were dishonorably discharged without trial on orders of President Theodore Roosevelt.[5]

Only three months after the Brownsville incident, Judge Welch was dead, shot in his sleep in Rio Grande City, where he was holding court. The shooting occurred on the eve of a hotly contested election, which, combined with the killing, brought together the conditions for a riot. On orders from Governor Samuel W. T. Lanham, McDonald went to Rio Grande City at the head of several men. They reached the railhead at Sam Fordyce, twenty miles downriver from Rio Grande City, late in the day and hired a hack for the remainder of the trip. It was a rough area, and travelers frequently were waylaid.

After dark, the Rangers were met by a second hack, approaching from the opposite direction. Their driver pulled over to allow the other to pass, but when it came within about thirty paces, they saw a rifle flash and a bullet sped by.

"Hold up there!" McDonald shouted. "We are Texas Rangers! Stop that shooting!"

One of the Rangers repeated the warning in Spanish.

Three men with rifles leaped out of the other vehicle, shouting in Spanish and firing. Four of their companions also opened fire, and the Rangers shot back. The fight lasted about thirty seconds, the men as close as twelve feet apart. When it was over, four of the assailants were dead, one was wounded, and two captured. There appeared to have been no particular reason for the fight, other than the mutual animosity that often existed between Rangers and border people.[6]

The fight on the road was McDonald's last. He arrived in Rio Grande City to find the situation had substantially calmed, and soon after, the transfer of Captain Hughes's Company D to the city did much to restore peace to the area. Two months later, on January 16, McDonald left the Rangers to accept an appointment as state revenue agent. The murder of Judge Welch was never solved.[7]

DESPITE THE TROUBLES in Rio Grande City, even the frontier along the border was drawing to a close. The railroad reached Brownsville in 1904, and the area was opened up for settlement. Where previously the only communities along the first two hundred miles beyond the mouth of the Rio Grande were Brownsville, Edinburg, Rio Grande City, and Roma, dozens of new towns sprang up as the rails extended upriver. Edinburg itself no longer occupied the original site. After floods threatened the county buildings, the city was relocated fifteen miles inland in 1908, and old Edinburg became known as Hidalgo. Investors, home seekers, farmers, and speculators arrived by the trainload to take advantage of the lush, fertile river delta. Although Rangers still were periodically involved in border affairs, settling an occasional blood feud, hunting down cattle thieves, and investigating disputed elections, much of the area was peaceful, and the bulk of law enforcement fell on local sheriff's deputies, town marshals, and newly established police forces.

In 1910, however, the thirty-year regime of Porfirio Díaz was overthrown, plunging Mexico into seven years of revolution that ultimately killed more than a million people. By 1913, there was a complete breakdown of law and order. The chaos in Mexico, which was no longer able to police itself, combined with the close proximity of the border, gave a boost to bandit activity in the ranching area around the newly established cities of the Lower Rio Grande. William W. "Bill" Sterling, who later became the last adjutant general to command Rangers, recalled that Rangers and customs inspectors chained twenty prisoners to mesquite trees after one raid on a bandit hideout. The old Anglo-Saxon population, which had gotten along reasonably well and even intermarried with local Mexicans and *tejanos,* was supplanted by new arrivals from the Midwest who were suspicious of anyone who had a dark face and spoke Spanish.[8]

As the chaotic conditions on the border progressed, they began taking on political overtones. There was a resurgent nationalism among some of the Hispanic people of the Southwest because of several factors. Part of it was in response to discrimination by newly arrived Midwesterners. Part came from resentments that had smoldered since the end of the Mexican War. And part was due to the various international workers' revolutionary movements then current in most industrialized nations. All found expression in the Plan of San Diego, a manifesto that originated in early 1915 among Mexican citizens and disgruntled *tejanos* influenced by the revolutionary movement in general and the revolution in Mexico in particular.

The plan, named for the little south Texas town of San Diego, which the conspirators used as a base, called for a race war pitting Hispanics, blacks, and the growing Japanese population against the Anglo-Saxons throughout the American Southwest. A new Hispanic republic would be forged from Texas, California, Arizona, New Mexico, and Colorado, and the blacks would be given six additional states. Ancestral Indian lands would be restored, and every Anglo-Saxon male over the age of sixteen would be put to death. Efforts were made to secure support in Mexico by promising participation for any Mexican citizen, regardless of political faction.

There is some evidence of German influence in the Plan of San Diego. Europe was then embroiled in the First World War, and German agents were active among the various revolutionary factions in Mexico. There was also a concerted (albeit unsanctioned) effort in the German Foreign Office to keep the Americans involved with Mexico so that they would stay out of Europe.[9]

THE PLAN OF San Diego was exposed on January 19, 1915, when one of the plotters was arrested in McAllen with a copy of the plan. It created a minor panic among area residents, and a county law officer later recalled:

> Resentment toward strange Mexicans reached a new high, and several were found shot to death. Some of them may or may not have been bandits. People were shooting first and not talking afterward.[10]

Nevertheless, the plot brought a new round of heavy raiding along the Lower Rio Grande, and the Texas Rangers were woefully inadequate for the situation. In June 1915, the service had only thirty-four men in three companies. Two of these companies, A, commanded by Capt. J. J. Sanders, and B, under Capt. J. Monroe Fox, were ordered to the Lower

Rio Grande, and a fourth company, D, under Capt. R. L. Ransom, was organized and sent to the border. Fort Brown and Fort Ringgold were regarrisoned with regular troops.

Ranger Company B began its border service under a shadow that would haunt it until it was disbanded in disgrace three years later. One of its members resigned, claiming the sergeant was chronically drunk, and that a Ranger killed in a fight with Mexican smugglers had been deserted by his comrades. No action was taken on the allegations.[11]

In the summer of 1915, people had little inclination to worry about internal Ranger disputes. On July 4, a band of Mexican irregulars crossed the border and raided about sixty miles into Cameron County, killing three people. This began a series of raids and reprisals, culminating with the activities of Luis de la Rosa, a *tejano* revolutionary from Rio Hondo, a small farming community on the Arroyo Colorado, about thirty miles north of Brownsville. He initiated his campaign by tearing up railroad trestles and cutting telegraph wires, prompting military authorities to assign soldiers to guard trains between Harlingen and Raymondville. On August 6, he flaunted his opinion of Anglo-Saxon law and order by raiding Sebastian, a small town about ten miles north of Harlingen, and murdering Alfred L. Austin, president of the quasi-vigilante Sebastian Law and Order League, and his son, Charles. From there he turned his attention to the greatest and most venerable symbol of Anglo-Saxon authority in south Texas—the King Ranch.[12]

THE 825,000-ACRE King Ranch is divided into four divisions, covering parts of six counties. Stretched out in a single line, its fence rows would be two thousand miles long. Today it is a family corporation owned by the descendants of Richard and Henrietta M. King through their youngest daughter, Alice Gertrudis King, and her husband, Robert Justus Kleberg. The ranch's prestige and influence are evident throughout south Texas— in the cities of Kingsville and Alice, Kleberg County, and several H. M. King High Schools. The southernmost division is Norias, which begins about ten miles north of Raymondville. The headquarters of the Norias Division, which attracted Luis de la Rosa's attention, is about twenty miles farther north.

On August 7, de la Rosa's men joined forces with twenty-five Mexicans led by officers of one of the factional armies of Mexico and rode north, planning to attack the house and railroad shed at Norias. They were spotted crossing one of the big ranches between the railroad and the coast, and their presence was reported to Caesar Kleberg, manager of the Norias Division, who telephoned Brownsville for Rangers and troops. Captains Ransom and Fox, several of their Rangers, and a squad of soldiers from Fort Brown left on a special train on the afternoon of August 8. Meanwhile, King Ranch cowboys, themselves descendants of Mexican *vaqueros* imported by Richard King in the 1850s, prepared to defend the division. These men, called *kineños,* or King's people, held their jobs by hereditary right; their only loyalty was to the ranch and the King-Kleberg family.

When the Rangers and soldiers arrived at Norias, the *kineños* were ready with horses. The soldiers remained at the headquarters, while the Rangers and cowboys rode south to intercept de la Rosa's men. Soon after their departure, the regularly scheduled train arrived from Brownsville, bringing three customs inspectors and a deputy sheriff. The group waited for the others, and after supper, customs inspector Marcus Hines walked out on the porch and remarked, "I see the Rangers coming back. They didn't meet those bandits."

"Rangers, hell!" another man remarked. "That's bandits a-comin'!"

The customs inspectors and soldiers took a prone position on the railroad grade as de la Rosa's men approached from the east across the tracks. The confident Mexicans had not bothered to reconnoiter and were unaware of a bull-proof fence of heavy wire parallel to the track in the brush ahead of them. Those in the lead slammed into the fence, and their companions piled in behind them. The defenders opened fire.

The startled Mexicans fell back, leaving behind eight dead, with several dead or wounded horses. Some of the horses were screaming in pain, and one of the defenders later remarked he had never before heard that kind of sound from a horse. A soldier was shot in the heel, and two of his companions started to pull him back into the ranch building. As they dragged him he was hit again, below the knee.

The Mexicans charged several more times, each time becoming entangled in the fence. When they finally broke off the fight, about 8:30 P.M., they left behind five more dead. Two U.S. soldiers were killed. About an hour later, the Rangers and cowboys came back. Fox and two others tied ropes around the dead Mexicans and dragged them behind their horses through the brush. Somebody took a photograph, and thousands of copies were distributed as a warning to future raiders.[13]

Far from frightening the Mexicans, the treatment of the Norias dead only intensified ill feeling. Among other things, it established to the devoutly Roman Catholic Mexicans and *tejanos* that Ranger vengeance extended not only to this life but to the hereafter as well. By dragging the bodies into the brush and leaving them for coyotes and vultures, the Rangers denied the dead the final sacraments of their religion, including burial in consecreated ground. This only emphasized that the Hispanic people could expect little if any mercy if they crossed a Ranger. Even some members of the Anglo-Saxon community were offended, but these were by far the minority.[14]

Mexicans, likewise, were ready to shoot first and ask questions later. One tactic was for a small group of bandits to allow itself to be cornered, then wave a white cloth and offer to surrender. Then, as the Rangers approached, the main band would open fire from the brush. Once they had fallen into this trap a few times, the Rangers habitually killed anyone waving a white cloth. Both sides were accused of maintaining "black lists" of people from the opposite ethnic group that someone might want killed.[15]

LUIS DE LA ROSA, meanwhile, was far from finished. Returning to the Rio Grande, he and his men skirmished with army patrols over the next two days, resulting in the death of one of his own men and a U.S. soldier. Then, in September, a second group of partisans led by Aniceto Pizana cut a swath of murder through Cameron County.

It was de la Rosa, however, who pulled the most daring raid of all, the destruction of the night train to Brownsville on October 17, 1915. The train had pulled out of San Benito as usual for the twenty-mile run to Brownsville, but at 11 P.M., Cameron County sheriff W. F. Vann was notified it was overdue. He telephoned Harlingen and found it had left on time. Then he tried San Benito and the line went dead. It had been cut. At 1 A.M., a porter from the train called and told him it had been wrecked near Olmito, about seven miles up the line. The porter had run three miles to a ranch to find the phone.

Vann and his deputies rushed up to Olmito. The first thing they found was a burning trestle. From the light of the fire, they saw the wrecked train beyond. To de la Rosa, the railroad represented everything detestable about American rule. He believed trains were segregated into Mexican and Anglo sections, an erroneous assumption, because Mexicans and *tejanos* were permitted in first class. Nevertheless, the belief exemplified all the irrationality that had taken over the border conflict, and de la Rosa was just as determined as Captain Fox to make an example.[16]

Arriving at Olmito ahead of the train, de la Rosa's men had removed the fishplates connecting two rails, then pulled out the spikes that held one of the rails in place. They attached a heavy wire to one of the rails and waited. As the train approached, they pulled the rail out. The locomotive went over onto its side. Live steam poured into the cab, scalding the engineer to death and badly burning the fireman. The cars tumbled off and piled up behind the locomotive. The baggage and mail cars rolled over, but the two passenger cars remained upright, although one of the coaches was leaning to one side, throwing the occupants off balance.

From the brush, de la Rosa's men opened fire on the coaches. Passengers inside could hear them shouting, "Viva Carranza! [Mexican revolutionary leader and provisional president Venustiano Carranza] Viva Luis de la Rosa! Viva Aniceto Pizana!" Then, apparently realizing the train was not segregated and that he risked killing his own people, de la Rosa ordered a cease-fire and sent some of his men into the coach. Among the passengers, two soldiers were killed, and the county health officer was mortally wounded. Another soldier and former Ranger Henry Wallis were badly wounded. After robbing some of the passengers and setting fire to the trestle, de la Rosa's men departed.[17]

THE SHERIFF'S POSSE was accompanied by Captain Ransom and several Rangers, and by soldiers. As the sun came up, Deputy John Peavey and his brother, Clarence, searched the brush and found the tools de la Rosa's men had used to pull out the rail. Then Peavey and some deputies followed the trail of horse tracks and scattered plunder from the train to the river, where the bandits had crossed.

Returning to the wreck, they found that the Rangers had killed four *tejanos* for no other reason than that they lived in the immediate vicinity and therefore were presumed guilty. The sight disgusted Peavey, who was convinced he had tracked the real killers to the river and the Rangers had murdered innocent men. "I had seen things like this before," he later wrote, "but to me it still seemed cold and cruel."

Sheriff Vann agreed. He despised Ransom, whose primary qualification was his connection with Governor James "Pa" Ferguson, and had opposed Ransom's appointment as company captain. Sharp words had been exchanged after Ransom announced he intended to kill the men. When Vann said he would have no part of it, Ransom accused him of cowardice.[18]

RESPONDING TO THE growing violence on the lower border, the possible conspiracy raised by the Plan of San Diego, and the raids of revolutionary leader Francisco "Pancho" Villa in New Mexico and the Big Bend of Texas, the Wilson administration called the National Guard into federal service on the Mexican border. The Lower Rio Grande area became one vast military camp. Governor Ferguson created units of Special Rangers to handle the crisis on behalf of the state. Faced with the growing might and power of the United States in the Lower Rio Grande, the raiding gradually tapered off. Upriver in the Del Rio area, Ranger Frank Hamer entered into an agreement with the *rurales,* the ruthless Mexican rural gendarmerie, whereby Hamer actually crossed the border and rode with the Mexicans, heading off trouble before it could reach Texas.[19]

The Big Bend country, however, was a virtual war zone. Even today the most isolated, rugged, and mountainous area of the state, it is virtually impossible to completely seal off and patrol. For more than two decades, this area was almost the private preserve of Capt. John R. Hughes, who had weathered the various reorganizations of the Ranger Service to become senior captain. Although Hughes's company was shifted elsewhere from time to time as the situation required, he invariably returned to west Texas, where he became known as the "Border Boss."

Hughes's great advantage was his knowledge of the people on both sides of the river, which enabled him to communicate with the leaders of the various revolutionary factions in Mexico. He was particularly friendly with Pancho Villa, and the two men had great respect for each other. His regular contact with the Revolutionaries brought accusations in both Mexico City and Washington of Ranger partisanship, although in fact he was obtaining advance information of impending battles that might reach the border and warning the leaders not to let stray shots fall into Texas. He also sent detachments of Rangers to march along the river parallel to Mexican troops to make certain they kept to their side.[20]

Hughes, however, was not able to entirely control so vast an area. Gunrunning through the Big Bend country was generally easy and always profitable, particularly since the Revolutionaries tended to pay in silver or in cattle. Even U.S. soldiers and Texas Rangers were known to engage in the trade, the soldiers stealing and selling machine guns from government armories. The arms trade was accompanied by the same violence that characterizes today's drug trade in that region. It was aggravated by cattle and horse stealing and attacks on remote ranches. Unlike the violence of the Lower Rio Grande, which had political overtones through the Plan of San Diego, these raids were little more than ordinary banditry. No one was safe; in 1913, two U.S. Customs inspectors and an inspector for the Texas Cattle Raisers Association were gunned down as they escorted a prisoner. One of the customs inspectors was mortally wounded.[21]

The situation received a new twist through two unrelated events. On January 31, 1915, Hughes retired from the Rangers. A lifelong bachelor and always thrifty, he had acquired substantial business interests in El Paso and New Mexico, and his departure removed a stabilizing influence over the Revolutionary leaders in their relations with Texas. The same year, the Wilson administration recognized Pancho Villa's rival, Venustiano Carranza, as de facto president of Mexico, providing arms and assistance to Carranza while placing an embargo against Villa. This cost Villa prestige and denied him the means to continue his war. He retaliated with a series of raids, first against Carranza strongholds in Chihuahua, culminating in 1916 with attacks on Columbus, New Mexico, and various border settlements in Texas.[22]

ASIDE FROM HIS age (he was sixty and had been a Ranger for a record twenty-eight years), Hughes's retirement was prompted by politics. As governor, Pa Ferguson was a firm practitioner of patronage and cronyism, and he made his appointments accordingly. The quality of state service, including the Rangers, declined, and this was reflected by Capt. Monroe Fox's Company B, which was transferred to the Big Bend country as federal troops took over defense of the Lower Rio Grande. Even at best, Fox faced an impossible assignment—patrolling more than four thousand square miles of wild, unfamiliar country from his headquarters in Marfa with only eleven Rangers. It was made worse by the fact that only a few of his men were duly appointed peace officers, and even these were largely Ferguson's Special Rangers. The rest were informal appointments—men who simply showed up and offered to help.[23]

The Rangers faced an atmosphere of hate and fear. The shooting of the three inspectors in 1913 had frightened many local ranchers. Three years later, in 1916, one of the survivors of the initial shooting, customs inspector Joe Sitters, who had since joined the Rangers, and Ranger Eugene Hulen, son of the adjutant general of Texas, were gunned down and killed near the little town of Porvenir. The attacks on lawmen, the flood of refugees fleeing the chaos in Mexico, and bandit raids against the ranches and settlements created a situation that could explode into mindless violence at any moment.[24] One local citizen summed up the feelings of the Anglo-Saxon community in the Big Bend:

> We used to contend with the Comanches every light moon. We knew what we were going up against when we seen a bunch of Comanches. . . . You meet a bunch of Mexicans and you don't know what you are going up against; whether they are civilized or not.[25]

The breaking point came on Christmas Day 1917, when bandits attacked Lucas C. Brite's ranch about midway between the town of Valentine and the Rio Grande. Like many of the large, isolated spreads in the region, Brite's was less a ranch than a small community, with its own post office and a general store that served not only the ranch hands but citizens and other ranchers in the surrounding area. Shouting, *"Mueran a los gringos!"*[26] the bandits shot up the ranch and looted the store, although they failed to break open the large safe. The raid was more noise and plunder than anything else, until the mail hack from Candelaria, on the Rio Grande, arrived. They opened fire, killing two passengers and taking the mail driver prisoner. Initially they were inclined to turn the driver loose, but when he began to argue with them about his mules, they cut his throat. After about five hours of terrorizing the ranch people, the bandits rode away. The next day, U.S. troops caught fifteen of them four miles above the river, killed ten, and recovered some of the plunder from the ranch. The rest managed to cross into Mexico after a running fight.[27]

THE ANGLO COMMUNITY demanded retaliation for the Brite raid, and suspicion fell on Porvenir, a little community of 140 people, a large number of whom were refugees from Mexico, with the balance being native *tejanos*. It was located on the Texas side of the river, a few miles up from

Pilares, Chihuahua. The people scratched out a living raising cattle and goats and did their trading at Brite's store, a hard day's ride on horseback. The only semblance of modernity was a school. Local ranchers, who viewed the Porvenirians as squatters on ranch land, claimed it was a bandit hideout, and Captain Fox and his Rangers were ready to believe it. On January 23, 1918, Fox ordered a detachment of his Rangers to investigate the town. En route, they were joined by local ranchers, bringing the total number to about forty.

The Rangers and ranchers rode into Porvenir about 1 A.M., shook the local population out of bed and into the cold, and marched the men about a quarter of a mile along the road to the river. Then they began ransacking the huts looking for arms. They found one pistol belonging to John J. Bailey, the lone Anglo living in the village, and a Winchester rifle, a Mauser rifle with forty cartridges, a shotgun, and a .22-caliber rifle. The weapons were confiscated. Three of the men were placed under arrest because they wore a brand of shoe carried by Brite's store. The rest were told they could return to their homes. The three prisoners were taken to the Ranger camp in an abandoned railroad tunnel and questioned about the raid. The following day they were also released. One man departed for Mexico. The others returned to Porvenir, thinking the matter was over.[28]

The Rangers, however, had other plans. On January 27, they went to the Eighth Cavalry post at Camp Evetts, about four miles from Porvenir, where they presented Capt. Henry A. Anderson with a letter from Col. George Langhorne, commanding officer of the Eighth, directing him to assist the Rangers in pacifying Porvenir. Anderson balked. There was bad blood between the army and the Rangers, who frequently extorted money from the soldiers on trumped-up arrests. He also was familiar with Porvenir and its people, knew them to be peaceful and hardworking, and wondered just who or what he was expected to assist in pacifying. A phone call to Colonel Langhorne at Camp Marfa confirmed the orders, however, and Anderson ordered his men to get ready to ride. They were to cordon off the village, see that no one left, and confiscate all weapons.

The Rangers, soldiers, and four ranchers who had been on the previous raid to Porvenir arrived at the village just after midnight on January 28. The Rangers stood apart while the soldiers went through the village, turning everyone out. Someone built a fire, and the townspeople huddled around it, trying to get warm. The soldiers assured them they were searching for weapons, after which everyone could return to bed. One old gun and a few knives were recovered, but nothing suitable for bandit activity, and no plunder from Brite's.

When the soldiers finished, the Rangers moved in and herded fifteen men and boys along the road to the river, just as they had done a few nights earlier. They told Anderson he could withdraw his troops, that they would question the prisoners in Spanish. Anderson agreed, but considered it a waste of time. No weapons had been found, he said. He knew all of them and there were no bandits in Porvenir. Then he started his men back to Camp Evetts. A few minutes later, the soldiers heard a fusillade of gunshots. Anderson sent one trooper back to see what was happening. Arriving on the scene, the trooper found the Rangers standing over the corpses of the fifteen men and boys. Turning to the Rangers, the soldier "cursed them and told them 'what a nice piece of work you have done tonight!' "[29]

THE YOUNGEST OF the fifteen Porvenir victims was about sixteen. The oldest was about forty-seven. Harry Warren, teacher at the Porvenir school, saw the bodies laid out side by side where they had been killed. "Some were partly lying upon others, about a hundred or so yards from the road, by a little rock bluff," he wrote. The women, children, and old men fled across the river and found shelter in a little Mexican town, also named Porvenir. Later they obtained permission to transport the bodies to Mexico for burial.[30]

The incident might have been covered up and forgotten, except that schoolteacher Harry Warren would not allow it to be. "The quiet little village of Porvenir with its peaceful farms and happy homes was no more!" he wrote. "The Rangers and the four cow-men made 42 orphans that night.

"Now what was the cause of this wholesale destruction of these Mexicans, these peaceful farmers and small stock-raisers?" Warren asked.

He specifically named one of the ranchers who participated in both raids, saying the rancher had stolen mares and colts belonging to the Porvenir people and had taken them to Valentine for sale. Fearing prosecution, Warren said, the rancher decided to eliminate any witnesses by telling the Rangers that the Porvenirians were involved in the Brite raid. The Rangers were only too eager to believe him.[31]

278 ❂ From Frontier Defenders to State Police

Despite pressure from the military, which considered him a trouble-maker, Warren continued to speak out about the atrocity. He was aided by Justice of the Peace J. J. Kilpatrick of Candelaria, who accused the army of a cover-up. Soon the Porvenir survivors were giving statements in Mexican courts, and it took very little time for word to reach Washington, where the Mexican ambassador lodged a formal protest. The federal government began its own investigation into the affair.

In Austin, meanwhile, Captain Fox had lost his patron in the Governor's Mansion. Sometime earlier, Pa Ferguson had made the politically fatal mistake of trying to extend his patronage into the University of Texas. He was impeached, convicted, removed from office, and prohibited from ever again holding state office in Texas. Lieutenant Governor William P. Hobby was sworn in to succeed him. On June 6, 1918, Hobby disbanded Company B and fired five of its Rangers. Adjutant General James A. Harley demanded Fox's resignation. Fox complied, but claimed it was a political vendetta because of his Ferguson ties. This brought a scathing public reply from Harley.[32]

In an open letter to Fox, published in the *Brownsville Herald* on July 12, the adjutant general wrote:

> The Governor had personally nothing to do with your resignation nor any politics being in it.—The evidence disclosed, after a thorough investigation, as you know, *that fifteen mexicans [sic] were killed while in the custody of your men after they had been arrested and disarmed. This is verified by all proof* even to the admission from the parties and information gathered by this office and by *agents of the United States Government.* We are not interested in your politics when a question of the honor and decency of the state is involved. . . . You know as all peace officers should know that every man whether he be white or black, yellow or brown, *has the constitutional rights to a trial by jury,* and that no organized band operating under the laws of this state has the right to constitute itself judge and executioner and shooting men upon no provocation when they are helpless and disarmed. We are fighting a world war now to overthrow ruthless autocracy and do not propose to tolerate it here at home. You were not forced to resign by the Governor for political reasons, but your forced resignation came in the interest of humanity, decency, law and order.[33]

THIS WAS NOT the end of the affair. In Austin, State Representative J. T. Canales of Brownsville, a collateral descendant of old Juan Cortina, leveled eighteen charges of abuse and corruption against the Rangers. Addressing a joint committee investigating the conduct of the Rangers, Canales said:

> There are now and have been for some time, in the state Ranger force men of desperate character, notoriously known as gunmen, their only qualification being they can kill a man first and then investigate afterward. The character of these men is notorious and well known and the Adjutant General is either negligent in the selection of his men or else it is his policy to have such characters in the Ranger force to terrorize and intimidate the citizens of the state.[34]

This was more than Adjutant General Harley was willing to tolerate, and he responded with a five-page letter putting much of the blame squarely on the legislature itself. " 'Every laborer is worthy of his hire,' " Harley wrote, "and no man is going to render higher service than the standard you fix for him by his remuneration, save in a few exceptional cases." For years, he said, the Rangers had labored under low pay, shortages of equipment, and other handicaps that could easily be remedied by legislative action. Nevertheless, he said, as an organization, the Rangers had rendered faithful and valiant service.[35]

It was an admirable effort on the adjutant general's part, and it contained a certain amount of truth. Even so, testimony revealed incidents such as the killings after the Olmito train wreck, pistol whippings, extortion, torture, floggings, and other abuses of power. Porvenir was the centerpiece, and although testimony was not taken, many pages of depositions were placed on the record. When it was over, the legislature abolished the Special Rangers, reducing the service back to four companies, each with a captain, a sergeant, and no more than twelve privates. Citizens were allowed to bring charges against Rangers, and the adjutant general was required to investigate and, if the evidence warranted, take legal action.[36]

Canales had detractors who accused him of political ambitions, but even historian and Ranger partisan Walter Prescott Webb admitted that his true aim seemed to have been to improve the quality of the service.

Canales himself expressed support for the Ranger Service as a whole, going so far as to introduce legislation to increase the pay and upgrade the caliber of applicant for the service. Longtime ranger Bill Sterling remarked, "Many members of the House and Senate knew the charges brought by Mr. Canales to be true, but they believed that the Rangers could be saved by a good housecleaning. . . . I always supported the position taken by Judge Canales."[37]

The Dallas *News* went one step farther, editorializing:

> The service which Mr. Canales has rendered in this matter merited a more generous recognition than it received from the committee. Merely to admit that Mr. Canales was "prompted by no improper motives" is to ignore that he rendered a large public service in disclosing a state of affairs which neither the people nor the Legislature knew anything about, which would probably have suffered to continue indefinitely if he had not the courage and sense of responsibility necessary to force a consideration of it. . . .
>
> Apparently one of the chief recommendations which a man seeking employment as a Ranger has been able to give himself in the past has been that he is dexterous in the manipulation of a sixshooter and not averse to the use of it. So long as that talent and that proclivity are made the chief qualifications for service, it will be inevitable that the force will be made up in a large part of men who are not morally fitted to exercise the freedom and discretion which, it seems, must be given them, to make them effective.[38]

Conclusion:
The End and the Myth

The 1920s and 1930s were a traumatic period for the Texas
Rangers. One question in the minds of many was exactly what a Ranger
was supposed to do in a modern society. Texas-born New Yorker Owen
White saw the Ranger as an honored relic of an earlier, simpler era, but
out of place in a world of superfluous and artificial values.

"The Texas Ranger is no more!" White lamented. "And he has
passed away, not gloriously, with his boots on and wrapped in a wind-
ing sheet of his own six-shooter smoke but, ignominiously and
supinely he has succumbed to the hysteria of a nation and, along with
a number of other time-honored and excellent institutions, he has become a collateral victim of the operations of the deadly Volstead
Act."[1]

Rangers had not been reduced to mere Prohibition agents under the
federal Volstead Act. They still were statewide peace officers. Nevertheless they, like the many other "time-honored and excellent institutions," were having to adjust to modern times. With the end of the
border disturbances, the Rangers turned their attentions to general law
enforcement and investigation, typical of that going on throughout the
country. The two great issues of the period were Prohibition and the
Ku Klux Klan. In enforcing the Prohibition laws, both state and federal agents were hindered by Texas's long seacoast, the close proxim-

ity of Galveston to Cuba, the eight-hundred-mile border with Mexico, and the general problems of enforcing a law that nobody wanted or respected.

If Prohibition was viewed as a national joke, the Klan posed a far more serious situation in Texas, at least in the immediate postwar period. One citizen remembered, "It was all Democrats, but within the Democratic Party, you were either pro–Ku Klux or you were anti–Ku Klux. The Republicans . . . well, they were just quiet Republicans." White-hooded horsemen were bold enough to ride openly down the main streets of Texas towns in daylight parades.[2]

Pa Ferguson hated the Klan. Prohibited by the legislature from holding office, he ran his wife, Miriam, on an anti-Klan platform. Ma Ferguson's election signaled the end of the Klan's real influence in Texas. With public opinion largely behind her, she secured legislation severely curtailing its activities. Despite this virtue and a generally progressive program, there was never any question that Pa was actually calling the shots, and Ma's two nonconsecutive administrations marked the return of patronage and cronyism, particularly with the Rangers. One of her first acts was to discharge the entire Ranger Service. She then commissioned 2,300 "special" Rangers, some of whom were convicted felons.

Even when a Ranger was conscientious about his job, it brought trouble. Efforts to clean up crime and corruption in the "oil patch" of the Texas Panhandle brought cries of state interference in local affairs. This culminated in a suit to enjoin the Rangers from involving themselves in local government.[3]

Nevertheless, good Rangers like Frank Hamer, Clint Peoples, and Manuel T. Gonzaullus managed to uphold the integrity of the service. Known as the "Lone Wolf," Gonzaullus was a Catalan, born in Barcelona. Nevertheless, as he walked down the streets of the rough oil towns, he seemed almost the embodiment of the classic Ranger. A newspaper editor who knew him in his prime wrote:

> He was distinguished in appearance; rather heavily built, he moved with a silent tread, and his keen gray eyes seemed to be acutely aware of every person within their range. [He] had dark hair, olive complexion, and long, graceful fingers. He wore a neat, dark suit, boots, a large, white hat, and a broad belt with a big buckle. There was one other detail—a holster on each hip.[4]

Of all the old Rangers, Frank Hamer made the transition from horse to automobile with the most ease. He had joined the Rangers in 1906, dropped out for several years while he worked in local law enforcement, then rejoined in 1915. He had seen service throughout central and west Texas and along the Mexican border. Even so, he is probably best remembered as a modern law officer who used old Ranger scouting methods to track Bonnie Parker and Clyde Barrow to their bloody end in the famous shootout in Louisiana in 1934.[5]

The Bonnie and Clyde affair represented the end of one era and the beginning of another. The days of the horse-mounted Ranger who had to be as much a tracker and a gunfighter as a lawman were over. The age of the criminologist, with his automobile and crime scene kit, had begun. The transition for the Rangers became complete in 1935 when a reform administration swept the Fergusons from office and completely overhauled the state law enforcement system. On August 10, 1935, the Rangers were amalgamated with the Highway Patrol to form the Department of Public Safety.

As of 1996, the Ranger Service was composed of 105 men and women organized into six field companies headquartered in Houston, Garland (near Dallas), Lubbock, San Antonio, Midland, and Waco, and a headquarters company in Austin. Each field company includes a captain, a lieutenant, and about seventeen Rangers. All Rangers below lieutenant hold the rank of sergeant in the Department of Public Safety. Unlike DPS patrol officers, however, Rangers do not wear uniforms.[6]

In Austin, the Ranger Division is commanded by the senior Ranger captain, supported by an assistant commander and approximately sixteen noncommissioned staff members. Nevertheless, in keeping with the frontier tradition, individual Rangers are scattered and decentralized in order to cover all 254 counties in Texas with maximum freedom of action.[7]

WHILE THE REAL Texas Ranger adapted to new methods and social values, the Texas Ranger of myth took on a new dimension, brought on by mass communications and mass marketing. Rangers had entered the realm of literature as early as the mid-nineteenth century, when Texas pioneers became aware of their role in history and began compiling memoirs and interviewing old comrades. Most of these were historical and nostalgia pieces, and it was several more decades before the

Ranger became a key component of fiction. Many authors wrote Western stories in the nineteenth century. Among them was William Sidney Porter, who, as O. Henry, wrote stories about a character based on Capt. Lee Hall. But Western fiction did not truly come of age until 1902, with the publication of Owen Wister's *The Virginian*. Describing cowboy life in Wyoming, *The Virginian* was the prototype, and has been so widely imitated that the original now seems trite. Nevertheless, Wister opened the door for Western novelists, most notably Zane Grey, who ultimately churned out fifty-four high-quality Westerns, most of which are still in print. Grey's novels were set over the entire region, covering many different Western types in a wide variety of locales. Among his titles was *Lone Star Ranger,* dedicated to John R. Hughes, the Border Boss.

Hughes himself did much to promote the legend. Following his retirement, he grew a large, bushy beard and adopted Hollywood-style Western clothes, portraying the type of Texas lawman that people expected to see in the era of Tom Mix. He became a regular fixture as grand marshal of parades throughout the state. Yet somehow people knew that beneath the showmanship, he was the tough old Border Boss of the closing years of the frontier. Hughes, however, had outlived his era and his contemporaries. He became despondent and, at eighty-six, shot himself.[8]

The 1920s and 1930s were the golden age of pulp magazines, heirs to the nineteenth-century dime novels that had made celebrities out of people like Buffalo Bill Cody. One of the earliest pulps was *Frontier Times,* which made its debut in the fall of 1923. Published in Bandera, Texas, by J. Marvin Hunter, the magazine billed itself as preserving the record of "Frontier History, Border Tragedy, Pioneer Achievement." Hunter himself was a member of a pioneer Texas family, and when *Frontier Times* began publication, many of the early settlers were still alive. The magazine contained firsthand accounts and interviews, and scarcely an issue appeared without one or more items by or about early Rangers, or announcements of Ranger reunions.

Although *Frontier Times* was essentially a regional publication, it attracted a wide national following and continued for half a century until it was ultimately absorbed into *True West*. Now the senior Western magazine, *True West* also publishes Ranger material, although these days it is from a purely historical point of view. Meanwhile, Western Publications of Stillwater, Oklahoma, parent company of *True West,* reprints the early issues of Hunter's *Frontier Times* on a subscription basis.

Hunter's aim was just as he stated—to preserve the history of the vanishing frontier—and much of the proceeds from the magazine, as well as its spin-off books and pamphlets, went toward his Frontier Times Museum, which still operates in Bandera.[9] Under his ownership, *Frontier Times* was a prosaic magazine, printed on cheap paper; it was virtually devoid of photography and its graphics consisted of only a few designs monotonously repeated. The articles themselves were not judged by excitement and readability as much as by whether they reflected life as it really was on the frontier. Not so the pulp magazines published in the East. They had beautifully rendered, action-packed cover art to match the short stories and novellas inside. The American West was a favorite theme, and among the many Western pulps was *Texas Rangers,* published during the 1930s by Better Publications of New York.[10]

THE MOST FAMOUS Texas Ranger of all made his debut on radio station WXYZ in Detroit on the evening of January 30, 1933. Listeners heard Rossini's *William Tell* Overture, followed by hoofbeats and the shout of "Hi-yo, Silver!"

According to the story line, young Ranger John Reid was part of a company headed by his older brother in pursuit of the dastardly Cavandish gang. The gang ambushed the Rangers, killing them all—or so they thought. When the noble Indian Tonto discovered the massacre scene, the desperately wounded John Reid was the sole survivor. As Tonto said when he nursed Reid back to health, "You Lone Ranger."

The Lone Ranger was an immediate hit. A black mask made from his brother's shirt concealed his identity. He rode a beautiful white stallion named Silver. He carried silver bullets. And always at his side was his faithful companion, Tonto. Several motion pictures were made from the radio show, but the definitive Lone Ranger came to television in 1949 in the person of Saturday-afternoon-serial king Clayton Moore. Aside from looking the part, Moore was an excellent actor, as was Jay Silverheels, who played Tonto. Together they carried the series until 1961, as well making two color feature films. Since then, the Lone Ranger has been presented as a cartoon character, and there was an effort at another motion picture in 1981, but these seem like cardboard imitations compared to Moore and Silverheels.[11]

A more realistic approach was *Tales of the Texas Rangers,* which first aired on NBC Radio on July 8, 1950. Produced by Stacy Keach, Sr., the show was to the Texas Rangers what *Dragnet* was to the Los Angeles Police Department. Each of the ninety-seven radio episodes was based on an actual case, and all scripts were approved by Col. Homer Garrison, then director of the Texas Department of Public Safety. Just as *Dragnet* centered around the character of Sgt. Joe Friday, *Tales of the Texas Rangers* centered around Ranger Jace Pearson, portrayed by veteran Western movie star Joel McCrea. Many of the episodes were based on the experiences of Capt. Manuel "Lone Wolf" Gonzaullas, a thirty-year veteran who served as Keach's technical adviser.

Tales of the Texas Rangers attracted a nationwide following and made a successful transition to television. After McCrea left the series, the Jace Pearson role was played at various times by Craig Stevens (who later portrayed television detective Peter Gunn), Willard Parker, and Harry Lauter. It also served as the basis of a Dell comic book series, although the comic book plots were imaginary. Interestingly enough, Gonzaullas owned half the rights to the radio and television programs.[12]

Walker, Texas Ranger, television's Ranger offering of the 1990s, presents a totally different image. Ranger Cordell Walker (played by martial arts superstar Chuck Norris) is a thoroughly modern law enforcement officer—at least as modern as Hollywood will allow for Texas. He drives a four-by-four on public highways, leans toward an automatic pistol, has a computer and a fax machine, and deals with current problems like drugs and alien smuggling. The Rangers themselves don't particularly care for the black hat Norris wears on the show (they prefer white or pearl gray), and they hate the long hair and beard. They do, however, sense and appreciate the values the Walker character represents.[13]

These values are evident in the performance of their duties as lawmen, duties that still carry the dangers facing any peace officer. On Thursday, January 22, 1987, Ranger Stan Guffey of Brady died in the rescue of a two-year-old girl held hostage by Brent Albert Beeler, a habitual criminal who had already kidnapped and tortured to death a twenty-two-year-old woman. Beeler himself was killed by Guffey's partner, Ranger Johnnie Aycock, and the little girl was returned unharmed to her parents. Guffey was the third Texas Ranger to die in the line of duty since the Ranger Division was placed under the Department of Public Safety in

1935. He had been with the department for eighteen years, and left a widow and four children.[14]

RANGERS CONTINUE TO fascinate the people of Texas. A handwritten letter by a famous Ranger like Leander McNelly or James B. Gillett will fetch hundreds of dollars from collectors. Just as the East has its Civil War reenactment groups, so does Texas have Ranger reenactments, many of whose participants are themselves lawmen and/or are descended from old-time Rangers. There are Ranger trading cards, each carrying the portrait of a famous past or present Ranger with his service record on the back. The Texas Ranger Hall of Fame in Waco, the main center for Ranger preservation and research, records an average of ninety thousand visitors a year. Ranger memorabilia can be found in many of the state's major museums, and even in smaller towns like Falfurrias on U.S. 281 in deep south Texas, where the local museum has a highly developed and well-presented Texas Ranger Room. Out in Langtry, Judge Roy Bean's Jersey Lilly Saloon still stands, although the Texas Department of Transportation has completely destroyed the effect by landscaping and other "improvements." The visitor's center (which overwhelms and obscures the Jersey Lilly itself) has dioramas and displays of Roy's life, and Dan Stuart's Fistic Carnival figures prominently.

The fascination with the Rangers—old and new—shows that Owen White was unduly pessimistic (if not flat-out *wrong*) when he wrote:

> The old-time Texas Rangers had almost abolished themselves
> . . . by being efficient and worthy, and it only remained for the
> newer representatives of the formerly great organization to complete its demolition by deserting its traditions.[15]

The Texas Rangers have not abolished themselves. They have survived not by deserting their traditions but by reinventing themselves, by adjusting—even if grudgingly—to new eras, new values, and new circumstances. Every time it seems the Rangers have become an anachronism, they prove beyond any doubt that they are still relevant and necessary. As they approached a new century and a new millennium, Texas governor George Bush assessed their role for the future:

> The Texas Rangers will continue to be the elite unit of the Department of Public Safety, whose job is to be good investigators.

The days of "one-man/one-riot" are over, but "one complicated situation/one Ranger" will still hold true. The Texas Rangers are revered as a wholly unique and efficient law enforcement agency. They are a symbol of what we have been and what we are. One Ranger still covers hundreds of miles of territory. The frontier is shrinking and we are entering a new era, but Texas will always have the Rangers.[16]

Notes

Abbreviations

AG	(U.S.) Adjutant General
AAG	(U.S.) Assistant Adjutant General
AAAG	(U.S.) Acting Assistant Adjutant General
AGO	(U.S.) Adjutant General's Office
DPS	Department of Public Safety
RG	Record Group
TAGF	Texas Adjutant General's Files (original files)
TAGR	Texas Adjutant General's Records (transcripts)

Introduction: Are They Still There?

1. Jaime Aron, Associated Press report, McAllen *Monitor,* May 11, 1997.
2. Sterling, *Trails and Trials,* 524.
3. Texas Legislature, *General Laws, 11th Legislature,* 10; Department of Public Safety, *Annual Report, 1994,* 9; Weiss, "The Texas Rangers Revisited," 622; Cox, *Silver Stars,* 2. Most sources state the "Texas Rangers" designation did not appear until the creation of the Frontier Battalion in 1874. However, the name appears in the Act to Provide for the Protection of the Frontier of the State of Texas, Section 1, approved September 21, 1866.
4. DeShields, "Indian Raid, Pursuit and Fight," 1.
5. Donaly Brice, conversation with the author, August 22, 1996.

1: Life and Death in a Harsh Land

1. Wooten, *Comprehensive History of Texas,* 2:329
2. Gillett, *Six Years,* 21. Some Rangers joined the army during the Mexican War and Civil War and continued to call themselves Rangers. This was simply a figure of speech or a frame of mind, because, as soldiers, they were no longer Texas Rangers.
3. *Texas Almanac,* 303.
4. Sonnichsen, *I'll Die Before I'll Run,* 14–15; Nackman, "Making of the Texan Citizen Soldier," 234, 240.
5. Weddle, *San Juan Bautista,* 66–67, 90–91; Bancroft, *North Mexican States and Texas,* 1:609–14.
6. Wallace and Hoebel, *The Comanches,* 26–27; Mooney, "Calendar History," 163.

7. Wallace and Hoebel, *The Comanches,* 45.

8. Newcomb, *Indians of Texas,* 108, 138.

9. Bancroft, *North Mexican States and Texas,* 1:626–27. The complete story of this ill-fated mission is told by Robert S. Weddle, *The San Saba Mission.*

10. Weddle, *San Saba Mission,* 188.

11. Bancroft, *North Mexican States and Texas,* 2:54–55.

12. Ibid., 2:55.

13. Most of this material on Moses Austin comes from the first two chapters of Eugene C. Barker, *The Life of Stephen F. Austin;* Bancroft, *North Mexican States and Texas,* 2:56–57; and Mary Austin Holley, *Texas,* 282–83.

14. Fehrenbach, *Lone Star,* 134–35; Barker, *Stephen F. Austin,* 23–25.

15. Moore, "Bastrop," 1:410.

16. Ibid., 1:410; Kuykendall, "Reminiscences," 6:3:248; Fehrenbach, *Lone Star,* 135; Bancroft, *North Mexican States and Texas,* 2:57n–58n.

17. Fehrenbach, *Lone Star,* 135; Barker, *Stephen F. Austin,* 25.

18. Barker, *Stephen F. Austin,* 25–28; Holley, *Texas,* 281–82, 284.

19. Smithwick, *Evolution of a State,* 42.

20. Ibid., 42; Kuykendall, "Reminiscences," 7:1:49–50.

21. Barker, *Stephen F. Austin,* 12, 31–32; Martinez to Austin, August 24, 1821, quoted in Barker, "The Government of Austin's Colony," 225.

22. Holley, *Texas,* 285.

23. Newcomb, *Indians of Texas,* 59; Jenkins, *Recollections,* 158–59; Kuykendall, "Carankawa Indians," 178–79; Smithwick, *Evolution of a State,* 3.

24. Newcomb, *Indians of Texas,* 78; Smithwick, *Evolution of a State,* 3; Jenkins, *Recollections,* 159.

25. Barker, *Stephen F. Austin,* 91; Wilbarger, *Indian Depredations,* 198.

26. Barton, "The Anglo-American Colonists Under Mexican Militia Laws," 61–62.

27. Kuykendall, "Reminiscences," 6:3:248; Barker, *Stephen F. Austin,* 88. Barker and Kuykendall spell the name "Morrison," but his signature is "Morrisson."

28. Kuykendall, "Reminiscences," 7:1:31. Barker, *Stephen F. Austin,* 88–89, says the ranger/militia commander was Andrew Robinson. This version is from J. H. Kuykendall, who was there at the time. Barker and Kuykendall agree that Bell was named *alcalde.*

29. Barker, *Stephen F. Austin,* 91; Austin to Guerra, secretary to the commanding general, undated (about November 1823), in Barker, *Austin Papers,* 1:672; Kilgore, *A Ranger Legacy,* 21–22.

30. "A List of American Settlers in the Colorado (District), March 4th, 1823," facsimile in Winkler, *Manuscript Letters,* 18–22; Kilgore, *A Ranger Legacy,* 21–22; Morrisson to Col. José Felix Trespalacios, June 5, 1823, facsimile in Winkler, *Manuscript Letters,* 23. "Dollar" no doubt refers to the Spanish-Mexican eight real, or "piece of eight," a large silver coin that circulated on par with the U.S. dollar and was legal tender in the United States until 1857. Oddly enough, although only ten men were enlisted, Austin's subsequent correspondence with the government continued to list the number of men at the fourteen authorized by Trespalacios.

31. Early correspondence variously refers to San Antonio by that name, or as "St. Antonio" or "Bexar."

32. Morrisson to Trespalacios, July 5, 1823, facsimile in Winkler, *Manuscript Letters,* 26–27.

33. Kilgore, *A Ranger Legacy,* 26.
34. Garcia to Bastrop, July 16, 1823, in Barker, *Austin Papers,* 1:672–73 (my translation).
35. Jenkins, *Recollections,* 160; Wilbarger, *Indian Depredations,* 200–1; Kuykendall, "Reminiscences," 6:3:247–48, 7:1:30. Most accounts give the name "Brotherton," although he probably was Robert Brotherington, a member of Austin's Old Three Hundred. See Burnam, "Reminiscences," 16n.
36. Kuykendall, "Reminiscences," 7:1:30–31, says nine or ten were killed, while Moore (Burnam, "Reminiscences," 15n) recalled twenty-three. Wilbarger (*Indian Depredations,* 201), who was not present for the fight, claimed the settlers killed nineteen of the twenty-one warriors in the camp. All agree that there were no white losses.
37. Burnam, "Reminiscences," 16n; Jenkins, *Recollections,* 160.
38. Moore in Burnam, "Reminiscences," 16n.
39. Morrisson to Kuykendall, August 3, 1823, in Barker, *Austin Papers,* 1:676.
40. Barker, *Stephen F. Austin,* 40–41; Yoakum, *History of Texas,* 1:227.
41. Decree of the Commanding General, May 28, 1823, in Barker, *Austin Papers,* 1:597 (my translation); Barker, "Government of Austin's Colony," 226.
42. Barker, *Stephen F. Austin,* 89; Austin, Address to the Colonists, August 5, 1823, in Barker, *Austin Papers,* 1:678–79.
43. Wilkins, *The Legend Begins,* 7.
44. Austin to Guerra, November 1823, in Barker, *Austin Papers,* 1:711 (my translation; in Spanish, the double negative is the emphatic form). The powder most likely came from government stores and would have been intended for the .75-caliber smoothbore muskets that were then standard issue in the Mexican army. These weapons required a coarse-grained, slow-burning powder, while the light .45- or .50-caliber rifles of the Texans needed a fine-grained, fast-burning powder. The annual catalogs published by Dixie Gun Works, Union City, Tennessee, contain many pages of technical information on black powder.
45. Austin to Guerra, November 1823, in Barker, *Austin Papers,* 1:711 (my translation).

2: Indian Raids and Revolution

1. Barker, *Stephen F. Austin,* 94; Webb, *Texas Rangers,* 20. The Tonkawa attitude toward the Karankawas is described in Kuykendall, "Reminiscences," 6:3:252.
2. Barker, *Stephen F. Austin,* 94; Kuykendall, "Reminiscences," 7:1:35.
3. Kuykendall, "Reminiscences," 7:1:35.
4. Ibid., 7:1:35–36; Barker, *Stephen F. Austin,* 94–95; Holley, *Texas,* 159–60.
5. Austin to Militiamen, about May 1, 1826, in Barker, *Austin Papers,* 2:2:1317–18.
6. Barker, *Stephen F. Austin,* 144–45.
7. Kuykendall, "Reminiscences," 7:1:32–33.
8. Austin, "To the Settlers in what is called 'Austin's Colony,' in Texas," November 1, 1829, reprinted in Gammel, *Laws of Texas,* 1:21.
9. De Leon, *They Called Them Greasers,* 1–5.
10. In the spring of 1998, I translated between a Puerto Rican who did not speak English and a McAllen, Texas, postal clerk who did not speak Spanish. When I was finished, the Puerto Rican told me, *"Usted habla bien cristiano,"* which is to say, "You speak the Christian language [i.e., Spanish] very well."

11. Bancroft, *North Mexican States and Texas,* 2:84–87.

12. Henson, *Juan Davis Bradburn,* 126.

13. De Leon, *They Called Them Greasers,* 5–7.

14. Bancroft, *North Mexican States and Texas,* 2:87–90; Wilkins, *The Legend Begins,* 8–9; Morton, "Mier y Teran," 47:1:30; Ramsey, *The Other Side,* 9–11.

15. The Fredonia Rebellion appears in many histories of Texas and is thoroughly examined in Bancroft, *North Mexican States and Texas,* 2:98ff., and Barker, *Stephen F. Austin,* 148ff. See also "Document Relating to Mexican Land Grant to Cherokee Indians [Undated]," Winfrey and Day, *Texas Indian Papers,* 1:9.

16. Kuykendall, "Reminiscences," 7:1:38–39.

17. Barker, *Stephen F. Austin,* 163; Morton, "Mier y Teran," 47:1:33–34.

18. This period is discussed in Howren, "Causes and Origin," 415–17; Bancroft, *North Mexican States and Texas,* 2:114–15.

19. Yoakum, *History of Texas,* 1:260–61.

20. Kuykendall ("Reminiscences," 6:3:250) spells the name "Cavanagh." "Cavina" is probably a corrupted spelling.

21. Wilbarger, *Indian Depredations,* 209–10; Jenkins, *Recollections,* 160–61. Wilbarger dated the Cavina massacre in 1830, while John Holmes Jenkins, who edited his great-great-grandfather's memoirs, placed it in 1831. The Jenkins date is used because it is based on research while Wilbarger was relying on memory.

22. Barker, *Stephen F. Austin,* 342, 345.

23. Austin's view of his life and work and his financial problems are discussed in Barker, *Stephen F. Austin,* Chapter 9. His work with the convention is in ibid., 348–49.

24. In Mexico one still occasionally hears the expression *como vendió Santa Anna,* which roughly translates as "sold out like Santa Anna."

25. Santoni, *Mexicans at Arms,* 50.

26. Santa Anna is the subject of many works. Bancroft (*History of Mexico,* 5:138–41) gives a good capsuled description. Also notable are his own autobiography, *The Eagle,* edited and extensively annotated by Ann Fears Crawford, and Wilfrid Hardy Callcott's *Santa Anna: The Story of an Enigma Who Once Was Mexico.*

27. Richardson, *Texas,* 79–80; Bancroft, *History of Mexico,* 5:139–42.

28. Bancroft, *History of Mexico,* 5:140; Linn, *Reminiscences,* 40.

29. Richardson, *Texas,* 79–85; Wilkins, *The Legend Begins,* 11–12; "The Govr. of the State . . . ," Lamar Papers No. 2438, *Papers of Mirabeau Buonaparte Lamar,* 4:1:242.

30. Barker, "Journal of the Permanent Council," 260–62; Gammel, *Laws of Texas,* 1:527; Wilkins, *The Legend Begins,* 12.

31. Wilkins, *The Legend Begins,* 14.

32. "Journals of the Consultation Held at San Felipe de Austin," Gammel, *Laws of Texas,* 1:543.

33. Ibid., 1:600; Wilkins, *The Legend Begins,* 18.

34. Smithwick, *Evolution of a State,* 82; Wallace and Hoebel, *Comanches,* 63.

35. Brown, *Indian Wars and Pioneers,* 25–26.

36. Ibid., 26.

37. Kilgore, *A Ranger Legacy,* 34.

38. Smithwick, *Evolution of a State,* 1.

39. Wilkins, *The Legend Begins,* 16. Smithwick's life is told in his memoir, *Evolution of a State,* from which most of this sketch is drawn.

40. The Alamo was formerly the Mission of San Antonio de Valero, and was commonly called "Valero." The term "Alamo" probably came into use in the late eighteenth century, when a company of Spanish frontier troops from Alamo de Parras, Chihuahua, was posted there.
41. Travis to "Andrew Ponton, Judge, and the Citizens of Gonzales," February 23, 1836, quoted in Brown, *History of Texas,* 1:550.
42. Williamson "To the Governor and Council of Texas," February 25, 1836, quoted in ibid., 1:537.
43. Ibid., 1:438–39; Lord, *A Time to Stand,* 97, 125.
44. Travis's letter, which was carried in relays to all the settlements, is in such demand that the Texas State Archives keeps facsimile copies stacked on the front desk. This version is taken from the facsimile of Travis's own hand. The letter has also been reprinted in virtually every book about the Alamo.
45. Lord, *A Time to Stand,* 126–28; Bancroft, *North Mexican States and Texas,* 2:209. It is generally believed the mysterious rider was a British officer in Mexican service. The only other potential candidate, Juan Davis Bradburn, a Virginia-born Mexican officer, was in Copano on the Gulf Coast at the time. See Margaret Swett Henson, *Juan Davis Bradburn,* 120–21. John W. Smith, who guided the Gonzales Rangers into the Alamo, left the fort for the last time on March 3, three days before the final assault, carrying Travis's final plea for help.
46. Filisola, *Representación,* 175; Crawford, *The Eagle,* 50–51. Ironically, Filisola himself was from the Italian peninsula.
47. Smithwick, *Evolution of a State,* 82.
48. Ibid., 82–86.
49. Ibid., 87; Wilkins, *The Legend Begins,* 18.
50. Yoakum, *History of Texas,* 2:179–81.

3: Serving the Republic

1. Hacker, *Cynthia Ann Parker,* 6–7.
2. Hogan, *Texas Republic,* 198; James W. Parker in Lofton et al., *Rachel Plummer Narrative,* 5. The history of the Parker family may be found in Hacker, *Cynthia Ann Parker.*
3. The main source of information on this raid is found in Lofton et al., *Rachel Plummer Narrative,* which contains accounts by survivors and rescued captives.
4. Erath, "Memoirs," 26:4:271–72; Sawyer to Coleman, August 12, 1836, quoted in Wilkins, *The Legend Begins,* 27; Smithwick, *Evolution of a State,* 108.
5. Smithwick, *Evolution of a State,* 112.
6. Ibid., 151; Erath, "Memoirs," 26:4:273.
7. Erath, "Memoirs," 26:4:273.
8. Duval, *Early Times in Texas,* 30–31.
9. Smithwick, *Evolution of a State,* 108; Jenkins, *Recollections,* 50n.
10. Erath, "Memoirs," 26:4:275.
11. Ibid., 26:4:274–75.
12. Smithwick, *Evolution of a State,* 113.
13. Ibid., 113–15; Jenkins, *Recollections,* 50–51.
14. Smithwick, *Evolution of a State,* 116–17, 154; Jenkins, *Recollections,* 50n.
15. Wallace and Hoebel, *The Comanches,* 259.
16. Lee, *Three Years Among the Comanches,* 143–44.
17. Greene, *The Last Captive,* 57.

18. Richardson, *Texas,* 107.

19. Ibid., 50–51; Barker, *Stephen F. Austin,* 442–43.

20. An act defining the pay of Mounted Riflemen, now and hereafter in the ranging service on the frontier, December 10, 1836, in Gammel, *Laws of Texas,* 1:74.

21. Treaty Between Texas and the Tonkawa Indians, November 22, 1837, Winfrey and Day, *Texas Indian Papers,* 1:28–30; Treaty Between Texas and the Lipan Indians, January 8, 1838, ibid., 1:30–32.

22. "Brazos," *Life of Robert Hall,* 45.

23. Robinson, "Cannibal Heroes," 33.

24. "Brazos," *Life of Robert Hall,* 46.

25. Smithwick, *Evolution of a State,* 179.

26. Richardson, *Texas,* 111; Siegel, *Poet President of Texas,* 51.

27. Lamar's life and career are discussed in Siegel, *Poet President,* and Lamar's own monumental six-volume *Papers of Mirabeau Buonaparte Lamar,* which remains one of the most important sources for this period of Texas history.

28. Siegel, *Poet President,* 54–58; Webb, *Texas Rangers,* 48–53. The Indian and Mexican policies are also extensively discussed in Vols. 2 and 3 of *Papers of Mirabeau Buonaparte Lamar,* particularly nos. 1613 (3:230) and 1805a (3:393). Lamar's interest in Mexican relations is mentioned in nos. 959 (2:373–74) and 973 (2:389–90).

29. Myers Papers, Folder 10.

30. An act to authorize the raising of a company of fifty-six men for the ranging service, January 15, 1839, Gammel, *Laws of Texas,* 2:44; An act to provide for the raising of three Companies of Mounted Volunteers for frontier service against the hostile Indians, January 23, 1839, ibid., 2:78; "a corps of rangers . . . ," An act for the raising of certain Troops therein named, January 26, 1839, ibid., 2:93.

31. Webb, *Texas Rangers,* 46; Jenkins, *Recollections,* 179; "My heart rose to my throat . . . ," Brown, *Indian Wars and Pioneers,* 70–71.

32. Brown, *Indian Wars and Pioneers,* 71–72; Jenkins, *Recollections,* 179n; "raised a hideous yell . . . ," Houston *Telegraph* (later known as *Telegraph and Texas Register*), June 5, 1839.

33. Houston *Telegraph,* June 5, 1839.

34. Webb, *Texas Rangers,* 47.

35. Siegel, *Poet President,* 102–3; Lamar Papers 1049, *Papers of Mirabeau Buonaparte Lamar,* 2:437–40; White, *News of the Plains and Rockies,* 2:150; Austin *Daily Bulletin,* December 15, 1841. The Texans had surrendered to Mexican authorities in New Mexico in scattered groups in September and October 1841, but apparently by December word had not reached the Austin paper, which received its information in a roundabout way via the head of the Santa Fe Trail in Missouri and then through New Orleans. See Bancroft, *Arizona and New Mexico,* 322–23.

36. Webb, *Texas Rangers,* 71; proclamation, Lamar Papers 1972, *Papers of Mirabeau Buonaparte Lamar,* 488–95; Connor, "Austin, 1839–1842," 79.

37. White, *News of the Plains and Rockies,* 2:150; Webb, *Texas Rangers,* 71–72; Bancroft, *Arizona and New Mexico,* 323.

38. The term "cow-boy" originated with these bandits, who initially had rounded up abandoned Mexican cattle in the area between the Nueces and the Rio Grande and driven them into Texas for sale. From there, they expanded into general banditry, although "cowboy" ultimately came to mean anyone who worked cattle for a living. See DeShields, *Border Wars of Texas,* 190; Dobie, "Mustang Gray," 110.

39. Lamar Papers 1742, *Papers of Mirabeau Buonaparte Lamar,* 3:350–51.
40. Lamar Papers 2081, ibid., 3:563–65. Kinney's questionable allegiance is discussed in Wilkins, *The Legend Begins,* 93–94.
41. Lamar Papers 2081, *Papers of Mirabeau Buonaparte Lamar,* 3:563–65.
42. Linn, *Reminiscences,* 322.
43. Ibid., 322–24. Linn translated for the survivor when he gave a deposition on the massacre to the authorities in Victoria. Gray's story is told in Dobie, "Mustang Gray: Fact, Tradition, and Song."

4: A Great Captain and a New Weapon

1. Houston to J. Pinckney Henderson, February 20, 1844, in Williams and Barker, *Writings,* 4:268.
2. Lockhart, "Jack Hays' Visit to Washington, Texas," 3.
3. Hays is the subject of many scattered pieces, but only one serious biography, *Colonel Jack Hays: Frontier Leader and California Builder,* by James Kimmins Greer. An abridged version that deletes most of the material on Hays's life after he left Texas was published as *Texas Ranger: Jack Hays in the Frontier Southwest.* Aside from Greer's work, the most complete biography is "Jack Hays, the Intrepid Texas Ranger," a compilation edited by J. Marvin Hunter and published as a series in *Frontier Times* magazine in 1927. The series was reprinted in pamphlet form the following year. Much of Hunter's material was taken from an unpublished manuscript, "Sketch of Colonel John C. Hays, the Texas Rangers, Incidents in Texas and Mexico, Etc.," compiled by Hays's friend and associate Maj. John Caperton, who got most of his material from Hays himself. The biographical sketch in the text is derived primarily from Hunter's initial installment in *Frontier Times,* Vol. 4, no. 5 (February 1927), and from Greer, *Colonel Jack Hays,* 15–21. Houston mentioned his friendship with Harmon Hays in a letter to John C. Hays, September 14, 1842, in Williams and Barker, *Writings,* 4:144–45.
4. Brice, *Great Comanche Raid,* 3.
5. Henry W. Karnes to Albert Sidney Johnston, secretary of war, January 10, 1840, Winfrey and Day, *Texas Indian Papers,* 1:101–2; Johnston to Fisher, January 30, 1840, ibid., 1:105–6.
6. Matilda Lockhart never completely recovered from the abuse and died within three years of her liberation. See Wilbarger, *Indian Depredations,* 3–4.
7. Brice, *Great Comanche Raid,* 22–25; Wilbarger, *Indian Depredations,* 23–24; DeShields, *Border Wars,* 289–90.
8. Brice, *Great Comanche Raid,* 26–27; DeShields, *Border Wars,* 294–95.
9. Brice, *Great Comanche Raid,* 28–33; Linn, *Reminiscences,* 338–41; Houston *Telegraph,* August 19, 1840.
10. Brice, *Great Comanche Raid,* 29.
11. "Brazos," *Life of Robert Hall,* 53–54.
12. Ibid., 54–55; Lee, *Three Years Among the Comanches,* 17; DeShields, *Border Wars,* 299–301; Wilbarger, *Indian Depredations,* 31–33; Felix Huston to Archer, August 12, 1840, Houston *Telegraph,* August 26, 1840; Wilkins, *The Legend Begins,* 84–85.
13. Wilkins, *The Legend Begins,* 86–89.
14. Brice, *Great Comanche Raid,* 69; Greer, *Colonel Jack Hays,* 34–39.
15. An Act to Complete the Organization of the Militia, January 18, 1841, Gammel, *Laws of Texas,* 2:115–16; Wilkins, *The Legend Begins,* 91–92.

16. Lee, *Three Years Among the Comanches,* 21.
17. Greer, *Texas Ranger,* 10.
18. Sowell, *Early Settlers and Indian Fighters,* 20.
19. Robinson, "The Forgotten Fight at Bandera Pass," 23.
20. Roemer, *Texas,* 132.
21. DeShields, "Jack Hays['] Fight on the Gaudaloupe [*sic*]," 1.
22. Lamar Papers 2432, *Papers of Mirabeau Buonaparte Lamar,* 4:1:234; Hunter, "Jack Hays," 4:5:28; Robinson, "Forgotten Fight at Bandera Pass," 23. "Jaeger" or "Yager" generally refers to the U.S. Model 1841 rifle, although it might also mean the so-called Kentucky rifle, also common on the frontier.
23. Wilson, *Colt, an American Legend,* 10.
24. Ibid., 16.
25. Wilbarger, *Indian Depredations,* 72.
26. Koury, *Arms for Texas,* 9–10.
27. Ibid., 29.
28. Hockley to Albert Sidney Johnston, March 28, 1839, reprinted in ibid., 78–81.
29. Memucan Hunt, Secretary of the Navy, to Captain E. W. Moore, April 29, 1839, in ibid., 29; Moore quoted in ibid., 42.
30. Greer, *Colonel Jack Hays,* 94–95.
31. Hays to Archer, July 1, 1841, Lamar Papers 2431, *Papers of Mirabeau Buonaparte Lamar,* 4:1:234. There are several conflicts between these accounts. In such cases, Hays's report to Archer is used.
32. Lamar Papers 2432, ibid., 4:1:234–35.
33. Lockhart, "Jack Hays' Visit to Washington, Texas," 1–2.
34. Lee, *Three Years Among the Comanches,* 27.
35. Reid, *Scouting Expeditions,* 111–12.
36. Ibid., 112. Near the end of the nineteenth century, Creed Taylor, who had served with Hays's Rangers in the 1840s, mentioned the Enchanted Rock Fight, which he said occurred in 1841, although he admitted he "was not with him" in that fight. James T. DeShields recorded Taylor's reminiscences as "Jack Hays['] Fight on the Gaudaloupe [*sic*]," 2.
37. Reid, *Scouting Expeditions,* 111.
38. Opinion of the Secretary of State on the Financial and War Policy of the Country, December 22, 1841, in Jones, *Memoranda and Official Correspondence,* 124–25.
39. James, *The Raven,* 320–21.
40. Houston to Margaret Lea Houston, December 29, 1841, Roberts, *Personal Correspondence,* 155; Houston to Hays, September 14, 1842, in Williams and Barker, *Writings of Sam Houston,* 4:144–45; James, *The Raven,* 321.
41. Wilkins, *The Legend Begins,* 18–19, 117.
42. Sowell, *Life of "Big Foot" Wallace,* 55.
43. Ibid., 55–58.
44. Ibid., 58–59; Hogan, *Texas Republic,* 258.
45. Sowell, *Life of "Big Foot" Wallace,* 90–91; Richardson, *Texas,* 120; Brown, *Indian Wars and Pioneers,* 140–41; Lee, *Three Years Among the Comanches,* 63–68.
46. Sowell, *Life of "Big Foot" Wallace,* 94.
47. Houston to Hays, September 14, 1842, in Williams and Barker, *Writings of Sam Houston,* 4:144–45.

48. Hunter, "Jack Hays," 28–29; Caperton, "Sketch of Colonel John C. Hays," 11–13.
49. Greer, *Colonel Jack Hays,* 94–95.
50. Wilkins, *The Legend Begins,* 175.
51. Thomas G. Western to Sam Houston, June 16, 1844, in Winfrey and Day, *Texas Indian Papers,* 2:72–73; "some sixty-five or seventy warriors . . . ," Maverick, *Memoirs,* 76–77; "two cylinders and both loaded," Rufus Perry to John H. Jenkins, in Jenkins, *Recollections,* 145. The fight is reconstructed from several sources that do not entirely agree on minor points, but generally tell the same story. Mrs. Maverick heard it from Hays twelve days after the fight, upon his return to San Antonio.
52. Thomas G. Western to Sam Houston, June 16, 1844, in Winfrey and Day, *Texas Indian Papers,* 2:73.
53. Bridges, *Black Powder Gun Digest,* 51–53; Rose, *Gen. Ben McCulloch,* 68.

5: Bound for the Rio Grande

1. Richardson, *Texas,* 121–23; Fehrenbach, *Lone Star,* 262–66. Jones's life and career are discussed in Gambrell, *Anson Jones: The Last President of Texas.*
2. Eisenhower, *So Far from God,* 30.
3. Ibid., 30; Weems, *To Conquer a Peace,* 55–58.
4. Jones to Taylor, August 6, 1845, U.S. Congress, House of Representatives, Executive Document No. 60, 30th Congress, First Session (hereinafter cited as HED 60): 83–84.
5. "reputation as a partisan," Taylor to AG USA, September 14, 1845, ibid., 107; Bliss to Hays, September 12, 1845, TAGF.
6. Grant, *Personal Memoirs,* 53.
7. Sowell, *"Big Foot" Wallace,* 122. Sowell was born in 1848, five years after his cousin J. L. Shepard was shot for drawing a fatal bean. The memory remained in the family, however, and Sowell knew many equally bitter survivors of the lottery.
8. Taylor to AG USA, November 19, 1845, HED 60:114; Wilkins, *Highly Irregular Irregulars,* 24.
9. "Brazos," *Life of Robert Hall,* 77.
10. Local residents don't usually consider the Arroyo Colorado to be a branch of the Rio Grande, the river proper (and international boundary) being the main or southern channel. The area between the arroyo and the main channel is, in fact, a large delta island.
11. Henry, *Campaign Sketches,* 59–65; Wilkins, *Highly Irregular Irregulars,* 24–25. Unless otherwise stated, all distances along the Rio Grande, where the author was born, reared, and presently lives, are overland, and do not account for the various bends and twists of the river that can double or triple the figure.
12. Henry, *Campaign Sketches,* 77–79; Wilkins, *Highly Irregular Irregulars,* 25; Eisenhower, *So Far from God,* 63.
13. Henry, *Campaign Sketches,* 83.
14. Taylor to AG USA, April 26, 1846, HED 60:288; Brooks, *Mexican War,* 108. Wilkins (*Highly Irregular Irregulars,* 25) lists Walker's company as having ninety-one privates. Brooks's figure is used here because of timeliness of his account.
15. Kuykendall, "Col. Samuel H. Walker," 1–3; Webb, *Texas Rangers,* 84; Wilkins, *Highly Irregular Irregulars,* 24; Lee, *Three Years Among the Comanches,* 70.
16. Kuykendall, "Col. Samuel H. Walker," 7.

17. Weems, *To Conquer a Peace,* 126.

18. Eisenhower, *So Far from God,* 74; Henry, *Campaign Sketches,* 85; Taylor to AG USA, May 3, 1846, HED 60:289–90; Brooks, *Mexican War,* 108.

19. Taylor to AG USA, May 3, 1846, HED 60:288–89; Brooks, *Mexican War,* 108–9; Lee, *Three Years Among the Comanches,* 71–72.

20. Taylor to AG USA, May 5, 1846; Brown to Taylor, May 4, 1846, both HED 60:292–94.

21. Taylor to AG USA, May 20, 1846, ibid., 299.

22. Holland, "Diary of a Texan Volunteer," 1–2.

23. Wilkins, *Highly Irregular Irregulars,* 36–41; Caperton, "Sketch of Colonel John C. Hays," 42–43.

24. Wilkins, *Highly Irregular Irregulars,* 26.

25. "Arms turned in by Cap[tain] Walker, July 22, 1846," Walker Papers. These arms were turned in by Walker when his company's initial enlistment expired, and before being incorporated into the First Texas. Interestingly enough, none of the revolvers were turned in, although some accessories were.

26. McCulloch's life is covered by Victor M. Rose in *The Life and Services of Gen. Ben McCulloch.*

27. Reid, *Scouting Expeditions,* 26.

28. Ibid., 26.

29. Grant to Julia Dent, July 25, 1846, Grant, *Personal Memoirs,* 918. Not until the twentieth century were United States regular officers empowered to exercise full military control and discipline over state troops in federal service. During the nineteenth century, they were primarily the responsibility of their own officers, who often were elected by the men they commanded and likewise could be removed.

30. Oates, "Texas Rangers in the Mexican War," 66.

31. Lane, *Adventures and Recollections,* 56.

32. Clayton and Chance, *March to Monterrey,* 31; Bauer, *Mexican War,* 87; Brooks, *Mexican War,* 163.

33. Reid, *Scouting Expeditions,* 53.

34. Clayton and Chance, *March to Monterrey,* 37.

35. Ibid., 37; Reid, *Scouting Expeditions,* 59.

36. Reid, *Scouting Expeditions,* 60–61. Reid suggests this celebration was held in Matamoros, but Lieutenant Dilworth's diary (Clayton and Chance, *March to Monterrey,* 37) indicates the first units of Rangers had arrived in Reynosa on June 21. Reid may have compiled anecdotes from several different companies, presenting them as personal experiences.

37. Holland, "Diary of a Texan Volunteer," 11.

38. Ibid., 12. Much of Holland's diary for July 1846 is a litany of illness and death. Aside from climate and terrain—totally different from the pine forests of east Texas—tropical fevers and the deplorable sanitary conditions of military camps claimed the lives of many troops, especially volunteers, during the months they spent along the Rio Grande in the Mexican War. Construction crews occasionally discover large numbers of graves at the sites of the American camps on the Mexican side of the river.

39. Ibid., 19.

40. Ibid., 12.

41. Reid, *Scouting Expeditions,* 56–57.

42. Ibid., 57–58.
43. Well into August, Taylor did not believe the Mexicans would attempt to defend the city. By the end of the month, however, he had information on Monterrey's fortifications and Mexican defense preparations and realized he would have to fight. See Bauer, *The Mexican War,* 89.
44. Reid, *Scouting Expeditions,* 46–47; Clayton and Chance, *March to Monterrey,* 36.
45. Clayton and Chance, *March to Monterrey,* 35.
46. Reid, *Scouting Expeditions,* 66. In *Buffalo Hump and the Penateka Comanches,* Jodye and Thomas Schilz do not mention any depredations by Buffalo Hump along the Rio Grande in 1846, although they say (32–33) that the following year he led a major raid deep into Coahuila and Chihuahua. General Taylor, however, reported "extensive depredations upon the Mexican inhabitants of Mier." Taylor to AG USA, August 3, 1846, HED 60:402.
47. Wilkins, *Highly Irregular Irregulars,* 65; "to have a parley . . . ," Reid, *Scouting Expeditions,* 66.
48. Reid, *Scouting Expeditions,* 67–68.
49. Ibid., 68–74.

6: Glory and Infamy

1. Wilkins, *Highly Irregular Irregulars,* 75–78; Reid, *Scouting Expeditions,* 125.
2. Wilkins, *Highly Irregular Irregulars,* 75–80; Bauer, *The Mexican War,* 90; Clayton and Chance, *March to Monterrey,* 63.
3. Reid, *Scouting Expeditions,* 127–29; Bauer, *The Mexican War,* 90; Clayton and Chance, *March to Monterrey,* 63.
4. Holland, "Diary of a Texan Volunteer," 25; Bauer, *The Mexican War,* 90.
5. Bauer, *The Mexican War,* 90–92; Holland, "Diary of a Texan Volunteer," 25.
6. Wilkins, *Highly Irregular Irregulars,* 83.
7. Holland, "Diary of a Texan Volunteer," 25.
8. Eisenhower, *So Far from God,* 120–21; Caperton, "Sketch of Colonel John C. Hays," 43; Chamberlain, *My Confession,* 80.
9. Quoted in Smith, *Chile con Carne,* 82.
10. Caperton, "Sketch of Colonel John C. Hays," 44; Eisenhower, *So Far from God,* 130; Reid, *Scouting Expeditions,* 152–53.
11. Sowell, *Life of "Big Foot" Wallace,* 122–23.
12. Reid, *Scouting Expeditions,* 159.
13. Quoted in Caperton, "Sketch of Colonel John C. Hays," 45.
14. Sowell, *Life of "Big Foot" Wallace,* 123; "Steel clashed against steel . . . ," Chamberlain, *My Confession,* 90. Chamberlain was not present at the battle of Monterrey, being in San Antonio with Gen. John E. Wool's troops at the time. He did, however, fight at Buena Vista and had firsthand knowledge of combat in northern Mexico. He probably drew his account of Monterrey from conversations with Rangers, from official records, and from other published accounts, and it is considered, within the limitations of secondhand information, to be an accurate description (see William H. Goetzman's introduction to *My Confession,* 8–9).
15. Chamberlain, *My Confession,* 92.
16. Sowell, *Life of "Big Foot" Wallace,* 123.
17. Holland, "Diary of a Texan Volunteer," 26; Eisenhower, *So Far from God,* 141; Oates, "Texas Rangers in the Mexican War," 68.

18. Barry, *Buck Barry,* 38–39.
19. Oates, "Texas Rangers in the Mexican War," 68.
20. Ibid., 68; Wilkins, *Highly Irregular Irregulars,* 106–7; Henry, *Campaign Sketches,* 222; Eisenhower, *So Far from God,* 144–47; Taylor to AAG USA, HED 60:430.
21. Melchior Hoffer to Walker, August 14, 1846, and Mary Bordley to Walker, November 6, 1846, both in Walker Papers; Wilkins, *Highly Irregular Irregulars,* 114.
22. Wilkins, *Highly Irregular Irregulars,* 114.
23. Ibid., 114; Wilson, *Colt: An American Legend,* 18–20.
24. Colt to John Mason, December 1, 1846, Walker Papers.
25. Wilson, *Colt: An American Legend,* 23–26; Colt to J. T. Walker, December 16, 1846, Walker Papers. Jonathan T. Walker was Samuel Walker's brother.
26. Colt to Samuel Walker, January 18, 1847, Walker Papers; Wilson, *Colt: An American Legend,* 26–28; Webb, *Great Plains,* 177–79.
27. Quoted in Ford, *Rip Ford's Texas,* 87n.
28. Wilkins, *Highly Irregular Irregulars,* 123–25; Chance, *Mexico Under Fire,* 113.
29. Dobie, "Mustang Gray," 109–12.
30. Chance, *Mexico Under Fire,* 113; Chamberlain, *My Confession,* 6, 10.
31. Smith, *Chile con Carne,* 294–95.
32. Dobie, "Mustang Gray," 112.
33. Lamar Papers No. 2326, *Papers of Mirabeau Buonaparte Lamar,* 4:1:167–68.
34. Lane, *Adventures and Recollections,* 53–59; Chamberlain, *My Confession,* 350, n113.
35. Taylor to AG USA, June 16, 1847, HED 60:1178.
36. Smith, *Chili con Carne,* 293–94.
37. Webb, *Texas Rangers,* 113–15; Samuel H. Walker to Jonathan T. Walker, August 4, 1847, Walker Papers.
38. Webb, *Texas Rangers,* 114–16; Oates, "Texas Rangers in the Mexican War," 70.
39. Samuel H. Walker to Jonathan T. Walker, October 15, 1847, Walker Papers.
40. Eisenhower, *So Far from God,* 349.
41. Webb, *Texas Rangers,* 114–16; Greer, *Colonel Jack Hays,* 170–71; Ford, *Rip Ford's Texas,* 81–85.

7: A New Era

1. Technically, Santa Fe was claimed by Texas, being east of the Rio Grande. The federal government, however, had never really acknowledged the claim and finally settled the matter by purchasing the disputed territory from Texas as part of the Compromise of 1850.
2. Caperton, "Sketch of Colonel John C. Hays," 67–73; Maverick, *Memoirs,* 95–96; Greer, *Colonel Jack Hays,* 216–21. During the Hays era, the term "El Paso" referred to "el Paso del Norte" (the Pass of the North), a ford of the Rio Grande between mountain chains at the bend where the river turns north into New Mexico. A small American settlement called Hart's Mill was established at the pass itself, and several other settlements grew up along the river above and below Hart's Mill. These ultimately consolidated into the modern city of El Paso. On the opposite side, the Mexican city of El Paso del Norte is now known as Ciudad Juárez. Citizens of El Paso, Texas, sometimes call their city "Pass of the North" in deference to its geographical location.

3. These companies are discussed in Henry W. Barton, "Five Texas Frontier Companies During the Mexican War." Horton sent several letters to Secretary of War William Marcy and other federal officials, which are reprinted in Winfrey and Day, *Texas Indian Papers,* 5:8–13 and 17–19.
4. Webb, *Texas Rangers,* 127–28; "With the exception . . . ," Olmsted, *Journey Through Texas,* 298.
5. HR 352, Payment of Texas Volunteers, 1.
6. Ibid., 1–2; Wood to Fitzhugh, January 15, 1848, and Wood to S. P. Ross, March 14, 1848, both in *Texas Indian Papers,* 3:100.
7. Harris, *Gila Trail,* 30. The Tarrant County Courthouse in Fort Worth is located on the site of the old military post.
8. Myers Papers, Folder 10; Webb, *Texas Rangers,* 128–29.
9. HR 352, 2. When the state applied to the federal government for reimbursement for the three companies requisitioned by the army, the House Committee on Military Affairs determined that the United States should reimburse Texas the cost of the initial two companies as well, stating that "this call for volunteers was absolutely necessary for the safety of the citizens" and the governor would have been derelict in his duty not to order it.
10. Ford, *Rip Ford's Texas,* 141.
11. Ibid., 142–43; Webb, *Texas Rangers,* 142–43.
12. Ford, *Rip Ford's Texas,* 149; Petition from the Citizens of Rio Grande to Bell, undated [1850], Winfrey and Day, *Texas Indian Papers,* 3:138–39.
13. Ford's life is covered in W. J. Hughes's biography, *Rebellious Ranger: Rip Ford and the Old Southwest,* and in his own memoirs, *Rip Ford's Texas.*
14. Ford, *Rip Ford's Texas,* 145.
15. Ibid., 147.
16. Ibid., 150–54.
17. Olmsted, *Journey Through Texas,* 300.
18. Nat Benton, claims against the state, January 8, 1856, and March 31, 1857, TAGF; Executive Department to Col. H. K. Craig, U.S. Ordnance Department, undated, 1858, TAGF.
19. Wilson, *Colt,* 30.
20. Barton, "The United States Cavalry and the Texas Rangers," 508–9.
21. Hughes, *Rebellious Ranger,* 106.
22. H. Clay Davis to Bell, July 9, 1852, TAGR.
23. Harmon, "United States Indian Policy in Texas," 382. Harmon's basic information is sound, although the article should be used with caution because of specific problems in spelling and dates. For example, he says "Fort Marvin Scott" for Fort Martin Scott (Fredericksburg), places Fort Phantom Hill in James County when it actually is in Jones County, and dates the establishment of Fort Stockton during the period 1849–53, when in fact it was founded in 1859.
24. Olmsted, *Journey Through Texas,* 301–2.
25. Untitled documents, RG 401, TAGF.
26. Governor Elisha M. Pease to "Gentlemen of the Senate and House of Representatives," August (day illegible) 1856, ibid.
27. Robinson, "Life and Death of an Indian Lover," 18.
28. Davis to Bell, September 19, 1853, Winfrey and Day, *Texas Indian Papers,* 5:155–57.

29. Harmon, "United States Indian Policy in Texas," 394.
30. Neighbors to Bvt. Maj. Gen. D. E. Twiggs, commander DT, extract in Twiggs to Lt. Col. L. Thomas, AAG USA, January 20, 1858, HR 535, *Claims for Spoliations,* 5.
31. Neighbors to Twiggs, extract, ibid., 5.
32. Ford, *Rip Ford's Texas,* 223–24; Runnels to Ford, January 28, 1858, TAGF; Brown, *History of Texas,* 2:375.
33. Ford, *Rip Ford's Texas,* 227–32; Ford to Runnels, undated (May 12, 1858), TAGR. The first two pages of the report are missing; the extant copy, a transcript in the University of Texas Center for American History, begins with the discovery of the main camp.
34. Ford to Runnels, undated (May 12, 1858), TAGR. A more dramatic account of the fight appears in Wilbarger, *Indian Depredations,* 320–26. Wilbarger (320) states that Iron Jacket got his name because "he wore a coat of scale mail, a curious piece of armor, which doubtless had been stripped from the body of some unfortunate Spanish knight slain, perhaps, a century [*sic*] before—some chevalier who followed Coronado, De Leon, La Salle [*sic*]. . . ."
35. Runnels to John B. Floyd, secretary of war, August 9, 1858, HR 535, *Claims for Spoliations,* 6; Ford, *Rip Ford's Texas,* 239n.
36. Ford, *Rip Ford's Texas,* 239n.
37. "with power and authority . . . ," Appointment of a Peace Commission, June 6, 1859, TAGF; Klos, " 'Our People Could Not Distinguish One Tribe from Another,' " 611, 615; Webb, *Texas Rangers,* 167–72; Neighbours, *Robert Simpson Neighbors,* 198ff.; Hacker, *Cynthia Ann Parker,* 23; Robinson, "Life and Death of an Indian Lover," 18–19. An opposing view of the situation is offered by Ranger James Buckner Barry in his memoirs, appropriately titled *Buck Barry.* Barry (112–17) contends the threat from the Comanche reservation was very real, and that the reservation Comanches routinely joined in the depredations of their hostile kin against surrounding settlements. He maintains that an ad hoc company of Rangers with Baylor as their commander was the logical—indeed the only possible—response to the situation, because they could get no relief from either the agency personnel or troops at Fort Belknap. In fact, Barry says (113–14) that at one point, having chased marauders from the Comanche reservation to the Lower Brazos Reserve at Belknap, they were fired on by U.S. soldiers and Indian auxiliaries, initiating a fight that "was bloody for a while." Eventually Baylor, who Barry said was loath to continue fighting federal troops, ordered his company to fall back and break off the action. John Henry Brown, who commanded a Ranger company involved in the reservation dispute, claims the persecution of the reserve Indians was "more or less distorted for political effect." While Brown admitted that the hysteria led to "the killing of probably two small parties of unoffending Indians, still it was unquestionably true that more or less of the depredations . . . were perpetrated by the Indians belonging to one or the other of the two reservations." Brown, *Indian Wars and Pioneers,* 121.
38. Sul Ross's life is discussed in Judith Ann Benner's biography, *Sul Ross, Soldier, Statesman, Educator.* Ross himself mentioned the adoption in a letter (July 12, 1884) to James T. DeShields, reprinted in Wilbarger, *Indian Depredations,* 333. One of the most remarkable and intellectually gifted of all Ranger leaders, Ross not only became governor but also served as a Confederate general, framer of the present state constitution, and president of Texas A&M College. Sul Ross State University in Alpine, Texas, is named in his honor.

39. Benner, *Sul Ross,* 47–48.
40. DeShields, *Border Wars of Texas,* 162–63.
41. Benner, *Sul Ross,* 49–50; Hacker, *Cynthia Ann Parker,* 24.
42. Gholson, "The Death of Nacona," 1; Hacker, *Cynthia Ann Parker,* 27. Gholson dictated his story on August 26, 1931. It should be remembered that Rangers of the period often were very young men, and he would have been in his late teens or early twenties at the time of the fight.
43. Gholson, "The Death of Nacona," 1–4; Hacker, *Cynthia Ann Parker,* 26–27. The famous Nacona™ brand of Western boot is named for Peta Nacona.
44. Gholson, "The Death of Nacona," 4.
45. Hacker, *Cynthia Ann Parker,* 28.
46. Ibid., 33–35. One of her sons was Quanah Parker, the last great Comanche war chief.

8: The Cortina War

1. The name is often erroneously spelled "Cortinas." The character Pedro Flores in Larry McMurtry's novel *Lonesome Dove* is based on Cortina, as is Benito Garza in James A. Michener's *Texas.* See Thompson, *Juan Cortina,* 7–8.
2. Thompson, *Juan Cortina,* 11.
3. Canales, *Juan N. Cortina Presents His Motion,* 5; Ford, *Rip Ford's Texas,* 261.
4. Ford, *Rip Ford's Texas,* 261. During the Cortina War, Ford relentlessly hunted Cortina. In the Civil War, however, Ford's wife refugeed to Matamoros, where Cortina protected her, establishing a love-hate relationship between the two men. Ford intervened on Cortina's behalf when the latter fell afoul of the Díaz regime in Mexico in 1876. See Thompson, *Juan Cortina,* 3.
5. Ford, *Rip Ford's Texas,* 261–64; Webb, *Texas Rangers,* 176.
6. Webb, *Texas Rangers,* 175–76; Coker, *News from Brownsville,* 295–96; Canales, *Juan Cortina Presents His Motion,* 9–10; Rayburn and Rayburn, *Century of Conflict,* 64.
7. Affidavit of Robert Shears, January 14, 1860, U.S. Congress, *Difficulties on Southwestern Border,* 129–30; Thompson, *Juan Cortina,* 13–12; Rayburn and Rayburn, *Century of Conflict,* 64–65.
8. "Long live Cheno Cortina! Death to the gringos! Long live the Republic of Mexico!"
9. In his official report, U.S. Appraiser General W. P. Reyburn said Neale had killed two Mexicans in fits of jealousy, and Morris "had perpetrated many Mexican murders." Reyburn to F. A. Hatch, November 21, 1859, U.S. Congress, *Difficulties on Southwestern Frontier,* 65.
10. Reyburn to Hatch, November 21, 1859, ibid., 65–66; Heintzelman to Lee, March 1, 1860, U.S. Congress, *Troubles on Texas Frontier,* 3–4; Thompson, *Juan Cortina,* 12; Rayburn and Rayburn, *Century of Conflict,* 66–67; Glaevecke, "A Story of Old Times," 23.
11. Webb, *Texas Rangers,* 179–81; "lay the town in ashes . . . ," Heintzelman to Lee, March 1, 1860, U.S. Congress, *Troubles on Texas Frontier,* 4–5; "For God's sake, urge the government . . . ," anonymous citizen to New Orleans *Picayune,* October 10, 1859, U.S. Congress, *Difficulties on Southwestern Frontier,* 40.
12. Runnels to Tobin, October 13, 1859, TAGF.
13. Heintzelman to Lee, March 1, 1860, U.S. Congress, *Troubles on Texas Frontier,* 5–6; Webb, *Texas Rangers,* 181–82. Heintzelman implied they lynched Cabrera,

and Webb cites Rip Ford in actually accusing them of it. The broken-neck story was told by Judge Harbert Davenport and published in Webb, 181.

14. Heintzelman to Lee, March 1, 1860, U.S. Congress, *Troubles on Texas Frontier,* 6–8; P. Jordan to "Dr. W.," November 14, 1859, RG 401-100, TAGF; Hughes, *Rebellious Ranger,* 162.

15. Heintzelman to Lee, March 1, 1860, U.S. Congress, *Troubles on Texas Frontier,* 7; Twiggs to Secretary of War John B. Floyd, November 28, 1859, U.S. Congress, *Difficulties on Southwestern Frontier,* 73.

16. Heintzelman to Lee, March 1, 1860, U.S. Congress, *Troubles on Texas Frontier,* 6–8; Thompson, *Fifty Miles and a Fight,* 138.

17. Ford, *Rip Ford's Texas,* 266; Runnels to Ford, November 17, 1859, TAGF.

18. Ford, *Rip Ford's Texas,* 266–67; Hughes, *Rebellious Ranger,* 162–63.

19. Heintzelman to Lee, March 1, 1860, U.S. Congress, *Troubles on Texas Frontier,* 7–8; Heintzelman to Twiggs, December 16, 1859, U.S. Congress, *Difficulties on Southwest Frontier,* 87–88. Ford (*Rip Ford's Texas,* 267) says the fight was December 6. Heintzelman's date is used, as his report to Twiggs was dated only two days after the fight.

20. Ford, *Rip Ford's Texas,* 267–68; Heintzelman to Lee, March 1, 1860, U.S. Congress, *Troubles on Texas Frontier,* 8; Thompson, *Fifty Miles and a Fight,* 143.

21. Headquarters, Department of Texas, Special Orders No. 113, December 16, 1859, U.S. Congress, *Difficulties on Southwestern Frontier,* 88–89; Heintzelman to Lee, March 1, 1860, U.S. Congress, *Troubles on Texas Frontier,* 8; Ford, *Rip Ford's Texas,* 269–70; Hughes, *Rebellious Ranger,* 163; Thompson, *Fifty Miles and a Fight,* 142, 146–48.

22. Heintzelman to Lee, March 1, 1860, U.S. Congress, *Troubles on Texas Frontier,* 8–9; Ford, *Rip Ford's Texas,* 270. The nineteenth-century Edinburg on the Rio Grande is designated on modern maps as Hidalgo. The present city of Edinburg, founded in the first decade of the twentieth century, is some fifteen miles inland.

23. Heintzelman to Lee, March 1, 1860, U.S. Congress, *Troubles on Texas Frontier,* 9; Ford, *Rip Ford's Texas,* 270–71. *"Quién vive?"* literally translates as "Who lives?", which is to say, "Which side do you support?" In Mexico, it is used in lieu of "Who goes there?" The reply is *"Viva [cualquier político, general, cacique o causa],"* meaning "Long live [whatever politician, general, chieftain or cause]," thus identifying the other party.

24. Heintzelman to Lee, March 1, 1860, U.S. Congress, *Troubles on Texas Frontier,* 9; Ford, *Rip Ford's Texas,* 271. A modern visitor to Rio Grande City will be able to identify the hill, which is now surmounted by the Starr County Courthouse, although the river has shifted about a mile to the southwest and is no longer adjacent to the town. Cortina's line probably ran along the modern esplanade from the courthouse to the drop-off at the former riverbank.

25. Heintzelman to Cooper, December 27, 1859, U.S. Congress, *Difficulties on Southwestern Frontier,* 97; Heintzelman to Lee, March 1, 1860, U.S. Congress, *Troubles on Texas Frontier,* 9–10; Ford, *Rip Ford's Texas,* 271–75; List of wounded in the battle of Rio Grande City, Dec. 27, 1859, TAGF; Thompson, *Fifty Miles and a Fight,* 155.

26. Tobin to Houston, December 28, 1859, TAGF; Tobin to Houston, January 2, 1860, TAGR; Ford, *Rip Ford's Texas,* 276–77; Heintzelman to Lee, March 1, 1860, U.S. Congress, *Troubles on Texas Frontier,* 10; Thompson, *Fifty Miles and a Fight,* 161–62.

27. Tobin to Runnels, December 16, 1859, TAGR.
28. Ford to Houston, December 29, 1959, ibid.
29. Tobin to Heintzelman, January 2, 1860, TAGF; Heintzelman to Lee, March 1, 1860, U.S. Congress, *Troubles on Texas Frontier,* 10.
30. Navarro to Houston, February 15, 1860, U.S. Congress, *Difficulties on Southwestern Frontier,* 120–22; Campbell to Capt. J. B. Ricketts, Commander at Ringgold Barracks, January 28, 1860, U.S. Congress, *Troubles on Texas Frontier,* 19.
31. Heintzelman to Navarro and Taylor, February 2, 1860; Special Order, Office of State Commissioners, February 2, 1860, both in U.S. Congress, *Difficulties on Southwestern Frontier,* 118–19. Despite Littleton's support of Tobin during the election, Ford considered him a good officer. See Hughes, *Rebellious Ranger,* 169.
32. Heintzelman to Lee, March 1, 1860, U.S. Congress, *Troubles on Texas Frontier,* 10–11; Ford, *Rip Ford's Texas,* 281–83; Webb, *Texas Rangers,* 187–88.
33. Ford, *Rip Ford's Texas,* 283.
34. Ford to Heintzelman with addendum, February 4, 1860, U.S. Congress, *Troubles on Texas Frontier,* 63.
35. Ford, *Rip Ford's Texas,* 283–86.
36. Heintzelman to García, February 5, 1860, U.S. Congress, *Troubles on Texas Frontier,* 65.
37. Long, *Memoirs of Robert E. Lee,* 76–80; Samuel Cooper, AG USA, to Lee, February 24, 1860, U.S. Congress, *Difficulties on Southwestern Frontier,* 133; Lee to Cooper, March 15, 1860, U.S. Congress, *Troubles on Texas Frontier,* 78.
38. Lee to Cooper, April 11, 1860, and Lee to Trevino, April 2, 1860, both in U.S. Congress, *Troubles on Texas Frontier,* 83–84; diary entry, April 10, 1860, quoted in Long, *Memoirs of Robert E. Lee,* 80. The original (1848) post commander's house at Fort Ringgold is still shown to visitors as "the Robert E. Lee house," although there is no evidence that he ever stayed there. Departmental commanders generally carried their own well-appointed camping equipment, rather than trust the often rudimentary housing at frontier posts. Upon its disposal by the War Assets Administration in 1948, the entire century-old post of Fort Ringgold was deeded to the Rio Grande City School District. Many of the buildings of the original antebellum post still exist, although in an advanced state of deterioration; preservation is hampered by state laws concerning the use of school funds. State education and school building maintenance laws, unfortunately, were not designed around the possibility that they would apply to one of the oldest and best-preserved military posts in the trans-Mississippi West. Classes and support services are housed in buildings erected when the post was reconstructed beginning in 1867. Visitors to the post are subject to the standard state regulations concerning public schools.

9: Confederate Frontier

1. Long, *Memoirs of Robert E. Lee,* 85–87; Smith, *Frontier Defense,* 19; Barry, *Buck Barry,* 132; Twiggs to Col. Samuel Cooper, AG USA, November 28, 1859, U.S. Congress, *Difficulties on Southwestern Frontier,* 73–74.
2. Holden, *Lambshead,* 86; "some white men . . . ," Barry, *Buck Barry,* 120–23; Davis, *The Texas Rangers,* 43.
3. Smith, *Frontier Defense,* 21–22.
4. Darrow, "Recollections of the Twiggs Surrender," 33; Smith, *Frontier Defense,* 22–23; Barry, *Buck Barry,* 126–27; An Act to provide for the protection of the

Frontier of the State of Texas, February 7, 1861, *Laws of the Eighth Legislature,* 10; An Act Making an appropriation to pay for supplies furnished the troops now on the frontier, February 8, 1861, *Laws of the Eighth Legislature,* 1. Henry McCulloch commanded six different companies of Rangers between 1846 and 1851, gaining a reputation as an Indian fighter along the Nueces Strip and in the Hill Country of west-central Texas. See Brown, *History of Texas,* 2:356–59.

5. Report of Bvt. Maj. Gen. D. E. Twiggs, February 19, 1861, *Official Records of the Union and Confederate Armies in the War of the Rebellion* (hereinafter cited as *OR*), 1:1:503ff.; Darrow, "Recollections of the Twiggs Surrender," 34.

6. Long, *Memoirs of Robert E. Lee,* 87–88; Darrow, "Recollections of the Twiggs Surrender," 36.

7. Barry, *Buck Barry,* 126–27. By a "majority" vote, Barry apparently believed that the convention was expressing a popular mandate. It is academic, however, because when the referendum was held, most Texas counties voted overwhelmingly to secede, the opposition being mainly in the pro-Union German settlements.

8. Headquarters, Camp Cooper, Texas, Orders No. 12, February 16, 1861, *OR* 1:1:541–42.

9. Carpenter to Commanding Officer of the State Troops of Texas, February 18, 1861; Dalrymple to Carpenter, February 18, 1861; Carpenter to Dalrymple, February 19, 1861, all ibid., 542–43.

10. Barry, *Buck Barry,* 127–28; "seized by an armed force . . . ," Col. C. A. Waite, commander DT, to Lt. Col. E. D. Townsend, AAG US, May 25, 1861, *OR,* 1:1:552–53.

11. Davis, *The Texas Rangers,* 43–44. Terry's Texas Rangers are mentioned in many works on the Civil War. One of the most notable is *Terry Texas Ranger Trilogy,* a compilation of reminiscences by three veterans of the unit, published by State House Press in Austin.

12. Smith, *Frontier Defense,* xii–xiii, 169.

13. Walker to Benjamin McCulloch, March 4, 1861, *OR,* 1:1:609–10; Henry McCulloch to Barry, March 27, 1861, Barry, *Buck Barry,* 128–29.

14. Clark to Davis, April 4, 1861, *OR,* 1:1:621; Walker to John Hemphill, April 11, 1861, ibid., 621–22; Smith, *Frontier Defense,* 28–30.

15. Headquarters, Troops in Texas, General Orders No. 8, May 24, 1861, *OR,* 1:1:574–75; Williams, *Texas' Last Frontier,* 50–51; Noah Cox to Clark, May 7, 1861, TAGR.

16. Barry, *Buck Barry,* 130–31.

17. Ibid., 131–38.

18. Mooney, *Calendar History,* 176, 311.

19. Ibid., 176–77; "Our people . . . carried war . . . ," quoted in Robinson, *The Indian Trial,* 34; Lubbock to Ford, September 18, 1863, Winfrey and Day, *Texas Indian Papers,* 4:77.

20. Loving to Lubbock, undated (1862), Winfrey and Day, *Texas Indian Papers,* 4:67–68.

21. Smith, *Frontier Defense,* 41–43.

22. Ibid., 44–45.

23. Quoted in Haley, *Charles Goodnight,* 69.

24. Ibid., 69–82.

25. Brig. Gen. R. M. Gano and Brig. Gen. Nathaniel Terry to Magruder, August 12, 1863, *OR*, 1:26:2:159–60; Lubbock to J. S. Ford, commandant of conscripts, September 18, 1863, Winfrey and Day, *Texas Indian Papers*, 4:77.
26. Holden, *Lambshead*, 93; Proclamation by the Governor (March 26, 1864), Winfrey and Day, *Texas Indian Papers*, 4:80–81.
27. Ledbetter, *Fort Belknap*, 109–10.
28. Hamby, "An Indian Raid in Young County," Elm Creek Raid Statements; Carson to Col. James Bourland, October 16, 1864, *OR*, 1:41:1:885–86. This onslaught, generally called the Elm Creek Raid or Young County Raid, was the basis of Matt Braun's 1972 novel *Black Fox*, which was made into a television miniseries with Christopher Reeve in 1995. It was Reeve's last acting performance before his near-fatal riding accident.
29. Henry Williams to Laura V. Hamner, March 11, 1921, Elm Creek Raid Statements; Ledbetter, *Fort Belknap*, 111–18; Carson to Col. James Bourland, October 16, 1864, *OR*, 1:41:1:886; Barry, *Buck Barry*, 179.
30. Barry, *Buck Barry*, 178–79; Haley, *Charles Goodnight*, 116–19.
31. Smith, *Frontier Defense*, 168–69. Interestingly enough, the Dove Creek fight involved not the Plains tribes but the Midwestern Kickapoos, en route from their ancient homeland to Mexico in the face of unyielding white pressure. When overtaken by the Texans, the Kickapoos sent a delegation under a flag of truce to demonstrate their peaceful intentions, but the whites attacked anyway and were badly mauled by the well-armed, disciplined Indians.

10: Reconstruction

1. Rister, "Documents," 9:18–19.
2. Metz, *John Wesley Hardin*, 93–94; Ramsdell, *Reconstruction in Texas*, 67.
3. Sheridan, *Personal Memoirs*, 2:229–32; Fehrenbach, *Lone Star*, 402.
4. Petition from Lampasas County to J. W. Throckmorton, July 15, 1866, in Winfrey and Day, *Texas Indian Papers*, 4:95–96; various letters, ibid., 97–107.
5. An Act to provide for the protection of the Frontier of the State of Texas, September 21, 1866, Texas Legislature, *General Laws of the State of Texas—1866*, 10–12.
6. Fehrenbach, *Lone Star*, 402–3, 408; Webb, *Texas Rangers*, 219; Nelson, "Rebirth, Growth, and Expansion of the Texas Militia," 1–2; Davis, *Texas Rangers*, 46; Gard, *Sam Bass*, 31. No doubt ad hoc Ranger companies continued to function without formal state sanction; a section of the Texas Adjutant General's Files designated "Ranger Reminiscences" contains an account by William B. Roberts, who said he served in a company commanded by his brother, Capt. Alexander Roberts, that scouted in the Hill Country west of Austin in 1868 and 1869. Unfortunately, William Roberts wrote his recollections in April 1937, almost seventy years after the events he described. Consequently, many of the details are confused, and the reader is hard put to ascertain the veracity of the account.
7. Richardson, *Texas*, 211–12; Fehrenbach, *Lone Star*, 416. The Laredo citizens' meeting is discussed in a letter from Davis to Governor Elisha M. Pease, March 13, 1854, in Winfrey and Day, *Texas Indian Papers*, 5:159–63. Davis's problems as governor were aggravated because his own integrity did not always extend to his appointees. In 1872, Adjutant General James Davidson absconded with $37,454.67 of state money (see Nelson, "Rebirth, Growth, and Expansion of the Texas Militia," 4–5). It also should be noted that although Reconstruction for-

mally ended in Texas on April 16, 1870, when civil government officially was restored, Radical Reconstructionist rule continued until the end of the Davis administration in January 1874.

8. Webb, *Texas Rangers,* 221; Richardson, *Texas,* 213; Gard, *Frontier Justice,* 224. The overall concept and performance of the Texas State Police is reevaluated in Baenziger, "The Texas State Police During Reconstruction."

9. Salmon to Newcomb, June 25, 1870, with subsequent postscript, Winfrey and Day, *Texas Indian Papers,* 4:316–17. In stating no persons were killed, Salmon was referring to that particular raid because, in a report to Newcomb dated June 23, 1870, he noted that since spring 1865, twelve persons had been killed by Indians, and five captured in Wise County. The Indians were invariably identified as Kiowas and Comanches. Ibid., 4:314–17.

10. W. E. Jones to Davis, July 20, 1870, ibid., 4:324–25.

11. An Act to Provide for the Protection of the Frontier, June 13, 1870, *General Laws of the Twelfth Legislature,* 5–8; Robinson, *The Indian Trial,* 48–49; Davis, *Texas Rangers,* 46.

12. Sowell, *Rangers and Pioneers,* 235.

13. Eckhart, "Texas Ranger's Badge," 48–49. Some vintage photographs show aging Rangers wearing "reunion" badges issued to commemorate reunions of early Rangers.

14. Timmons, *El Paso,* 107–9; Day, "El Paso's Texas Rangers," 156.

15. Day, "El Paso's Texas Rangers," 156; Certification of Indian Wrongs by Gregorio García, Winfrey and Day, *Texas Indian Papers,* 4:90; List of Animals Stolen by Apaches in San Eluario [*sic*], ibid., 91–92; List of Animals Stolen by Apache in El Paso County, ibid., 92–93.

16. Sansom to Davidson, November 26, 1870, TAGF. Sansom commanded one of the ad hoc companies called up by Governor Pease during the raids on the western settlements in 1856.

17. Heineman to Falcon, December 30, 1870, TAGF.

18. Sowell, *Rangers and Pioneers,* 233ff.

19. Ibid., 270.

20. The Henry rifle was a highly efficient heavy-caliber, lever-action magazine rifle that preceded the familiar Winchester. "Needle gun" probably indicated the .50-caliber breech-loading Springfield military rifle, generally called "needle gun" because the long barrel and slender forestock gave it the general shape of a sewing needle. The term was also applied to its successor, the Model 1873 Springfield, caliber .45-70.

21. Lt. A. C. Hill to Davidson, February 9, 1871, TAGF.

22. Hill to Davidson, February 9, 1871, ibid.; Carter, *On the Border with Mackenzie,* 51.

23. Hill to Davidson, February 9, 1871, TAGF; Robinson, *The Indian Trial,* 52; Sowell, *Rangers and Pioneers,* 271–75.

24. Sowell, *Rangers and Pioneers,* 270–71.

25. Ibid., 270; Sowell, *Texas Indian Fighters,* 701.

26. Cox to Davidson, October 4, 1870, TAGF.

27. Cox to Davidson, November 3, 1870, ibid.

28. Cox to Davidson, November 22, 1870, ibid.

29. Hill to Davis, May 17, 1871, and J. Cicero Jenkins to Davis, June 4, 1871, both ibid.

30. Sherman departed Fort Griffin before the return of two scouting expeditions from the post, one Ranger and one military. Had he waited, he might have learned the seriousness of the problem sooner without having to be convinced by a subsequent massacre. See Robinson, *The Indian Trial,* 59.
31. The complete story of the raid, the trial and conviction of the chiefs, and their effect on the frontier is found in Robinson, *The Indian Trial.*
32. The 1873 election and its aftermath are discussed in Moneyhon, "Edmund J. Davis in the Coke-Davis Election Dispute of 1874."

11: The Frontier Battalion

1. Prassel, *Western Peace Officer,* 155; Davis, *Texas Rangers,* 49–50; Webb, *Texas Rangers,* 307–9; King, "Texas Ranger Service," 345; An Act to provide for the protection of the Frontier of the State of Texas against the invasion of hostile Indians, Mexicans, or other marauding or thieving parties, April 10, 1874, Texas Legislature, *General Laws of the State of Texas, 1874,* 88.
2. King, "Texas Ranger Service," 345.
3. Ibid.; Davis, *Texas Rangers,* 49–50.
4. Gillett, *Six Years,* 19–20.
5. Roberts, *Rangers and Sovereignty,* 34; Gillett, *Six Years,* 25.
6. An Act to provide for the protection of the Frontier of the State of Texas against the invasion of hostile Indians, Mexicans, or other marauding or thieving parties, April 10, 1874, Texas Legislature, *General Laws of the State of Texas, 1874,* 84–89; Adjutant General's Office, General Order No. 2, May 6, 1874, TAGF; Gillett, *Six Years,* 17–18.
7. Roberts, *Rangers and Sovereignty,* 16.
8. Webb, *Texas Rangers,* 309, 312.
9. Ibid., 310–11.
10. Jones to Steele, August 9, 1874, TAGF.
11. Jones to Steele, September 14, 1874, ibid.
12. Jones to Steele, December 1, 1874, TAGR.
13. Roberts, *A Woman's Reminiscences,* 11.
14. McConnell, *Five Years a Cavalryman,* 296.
15. Roberts, *A Woman's Reminiscences,* 13–15; Prassel, *Western Peace Officer,* 157.
16. Frontier Battalion, Exhibit "D," undated, TAGF.
17. Roberts, *Rangers and Sovereignty,* 77.
18. Ellington, "When Cattle Trails Were Highways," 13–14.
19. An Act to provide for the protection of the Frontier of the State of Texas against the invasion of hostile Indians, Mexicans, or other marauding or thieving parties, April 10, 1874, Texas Legislature, *General Laws of the State of Texas, 1874,* 86; Headquarters Company E, Frontier Battalion, Petition, July 31, 1874, TAGF.
20. The definitive history of the Red River War is James L. Haley's *The Buffalo War.* It is also discussed in Nye, *Carbine and Lance,* and Robinson, *The Indian Trial.*
21. "Loss [*sic*] Valley Fight," 100–1; Jones to Steele, July 14, 1874, TAGF; McIntire, *Early Days in Texas,* 126–27n1; Robinson, *The Indian Trial,* 165–66. The Kiowa version of the fight and the events leading to it are in Nye, *Carbine and Lance,* 102ff. W. S. Nye, who was stationed at Fort Sill in the 1920s and 1930s, interviewed many Kiowa warriors who had participated in raids into Texas, preserving their accounts for posterity.

22. The white (or often pearl-gray) hat was not simply a cliché. The light color reflects heat, lessening the possibility of sunstroke during the long Texas summers. Even now, many working cowboys prefer light shirts and hats.

23. "Loss Valley Fight," 100–2; Jones to Steele, July 14, 1874, TAGF; Nye, *Carbine and Lance*, 195–96; Z. T. Wattles to editor, *Observer*, August 22, 1874, undated newspaper clipping, TAGF. In his report to Adjutant General Steele, Jones said the Indians were joined by a second band of warriors, bringing their total to at least a hundred. The Kiowa accounts to Nye do not mention a second band.

24. Nye, *Carbine and Lance*, 197; "Loss Valley Fight," 102.

25. Nye, *Carbine and Lance*, 197–200; "Loss Valley Fight," 102–3; Jones to Steele, July 14, 1874, TAGF.

26. Jones to Steele, July 23, 1874, TAGF.

27. Gillett, *Six Years*, 18.

28. Jones to Steele, December 1, 1874, TAGR.

29. Sonnichsen, *I'll Die Before I'll Run*, 9; Hendricks, *The Bad Man of the West*, 19–20.

30. Webb, *Texas Rangers*, 326; Roberts, *Rangers and Sovereignty*, 87ff.; Douglas, *Famous Texas Feuds*, 147–50.

31. Douglas, *Famous Texas Feuds*, 152–53; Gillett, *Six Years*, 48–49.

32. Webb, *Texas Rangers*, 325; Gillett, *Six Years*, 49; Jones to Steele, September 28, 1875, TAGF.

33. Gillett, *Six Years*, 49–50.

34. Webb, *Texas Rangers*, 327–28; Douglas, *Famous Texas Feuds*, 159–60.

12: The Rise of McNelly's Rangers

1. Austin *Daily Democratic Statesman*, July 14, 1874, reprinted in Parsons, *"Pidge,"* 26.

2. The company was organized in 1873 and incorporated into the regular Ranger Service two years later.

3. Durham, *Taming the Nueces Strip*, 3; McNelly to Steele, various letters and telegrams, 1875, TAGR.

4. Douglas, *Gentlemen in the White Hats*, 120; King, "Texas Ranger Service," 2:350.

5. McNelly is discussed in Webb, *Texas Rangers;* Douglas, *Gentlemen in the White Hats;* Durham, *Taming the Nueces Strip;* Jennings, *A Texas Ranger;* Parsons, *"Pidge,"* and many other Ranger works. Chuck Parsons is presently writing his biography for State House Press. McNelly's own papers in the Center for American History deal primarily with his Civil War career. Ben Proctor's introduction to the Lakeside Press 1992 reprint of the Jennings book contains an excellent summary of McNelly's life and career.

6. *"Pidge"* (T. C. Robinson), Austin *Daily Democratic Statesman*, September 24, 1874, reprinted in Parsons, *"Pidge,"* 44.

7. Douglas, *Famous Texas Feuds*, 70–71; Parsons, *"Pidge,"* 26–27.

8. Sonnichsen, *I'll Die Before I'll Run*, 83. Robinson's life is detailed in Parsons, *"Pidge."* Although he enlisted in McNelly's company under the assumed name T. Chanders, the Rangers knew his true identity and refer to him as Robinson. The *"Pidge"* letters, which are reprinted in full by Parsons, are first discussed in detail in C. L. Sonnichsen's *I'll Die Before I'll Run*, 84. To the best of my knowledge, we are not related.

9. Austin *Daily Democratic Statesman,* August 8, 1874, reprinted in Parsons, *"Pidge,"* 37–38.

10. Austin *Daily Democratic Statesman,* September 2, 1874, reprinted in ibid., 40. Like Creed Taylor, Tumlinson was a veteran Ranger of the Jack Hays era and a member of the "Fighting Tumlinson" clan.

11. Sonnichsen, *I'll Die Before I'll Run,* 84–86; McNelly to Steele, August 7 and 8, 1874, TAGR; Parsons, *"Pidge,"* 38; Austin *Daily Democratic Statesman,* September 2, 1874, reprinted in Parsons, *"Pidge,"* 39–41.

12. Austin *Daily Democratic Statesman,* October 14, 1874, reprinted in Parsons, *"Pidge,"* 45.

13. Austin *Daily Democratic Statesman,* October 14 and November 12, 1874, both reprinted in ibid., 45–48; Sonnichsen, *I'll Die Before I'll Run,* 88–89; Webb, *Texas Rangers,* 237–38.

14. Sonnichsen, *I'll Die Before I'll Run,* 98ff.; Raymond, *Captain Lee Hall,* 65.

15. Sonnichsen, *I'll Die Before I'll Run,* 103; Jennings, *A Texas Ranger,* 286.

16. Hall's life is discussed in Dora Neill Raymond, *Captain Lee Hall of Texas.*

17. Hall to Steele, December 18, 1875, quoted in Jennings, *A Texas Ranger,* 289.

18. Raymond, *Captain Lee Hall,* 70; "I want you to do your part . . . ," quoted in Jennings, *A Texas Ranger,* 290.

19. Sonnichsen, *I'll Die Before I'll Run,* 105–6. Durham (*Taming the Nueces Strip,* 166) remembers the wedding as Christmas Eve.

20. Although the generally accepted account is Jennings, *A Texas Ranger,* 290ff., most of this description of the showdown at the wedding comes from Durham, *Taming the Nueces Strip,* 166–69. Durham is considered more reliable, and his account is more in keeping with the customs of the time. See also Sutton, *Sutton-Taylor Feud,* 74–77.

21. Sonnichsen, *I'll Die Before I'll Run,* 109.

22. Jennings, *A Texas Ranger,* 298–99.

23. King, "The Texas Ranger Service," 2:350.

24. The free zone is discussed by Samuel E. Bell and James M. Smallwood in *The Zona Libre 1858–1905.*

25. Ibid., 25; Thompson, *Juan Cortina,* 72. The main sources of information on McNelly's activities on the border are the records in the Texas Adjutant General's Files, T. C. Robinson's *"Pidge"* letters, and Ranger George Durham's memoir, *Taming the Nueces Strip.* Napoleon A. Jennings's *A Texas Ranger* devotes considerable space to the border conflict, but that part of his book should be used with caution. Despite the general accuracy of his account and its autobiographical format, Jennings did not join McNelly's company until the following year, and drew his material on the border conflict from interviews and eyewitness accounts of actual participants. For recent and unbiased evaluations of Jennings, see Jenkins, *Basic Texas Books,* 280–84, and Ben Proctor's introduction to the 1992 Lakeside Press edition of the Jennings book.

26. Parsons, *"Pidge,"* 72; McClure to Steele, April 18, 1875, TAGR.

27. Parsons, *"Pidge,"* 72; McNelly to Steele, April 29, 1875, TAGR. McNelly left San Antonio on April 10, and apparently took two weeks to ride the 150 miles to Corpus Christi. Why it took so long was not explained.

28. Headquarters Company A, Volunteer Militia, Special Order, April 27, 1875, TAGR.

29. San Antonio *Daily Express,* quoted in Parsons, *"Pidge,"* 72; Durham, *Taming the Nueces Strip,* 29–33. Durham's description of the arsenal probably referred to the old King Ranch commissary building, which was fortified, rather than the house proper.
30. McNelly to Steele, April 29, 1875, TAGR.
31. Durham, *Taming the Nueces Strip,* 35–37.
32. Ibid., 38, 40.
33. Ibid., 40–42; Parsons, *"Pidge,"* 74; Webb, *Texas Rangers,* 239.
34. McNelly to Steele, June [?], 1875, TAGR. Sandoval's interrogations are described in Durham, *Taming the Nueces Strip,* 54, and in Webb, *Texas Rangers,* 242–43. Webb interviewed Callicott and reprinted the interview verbatim.
35. Durham, *Taming the Nueces Strip,* 58–59.
36. Ibid., 59–60; McNelly to Steele, June [?], 1875, TAGR.
37. McNelly to Steele, June [?], 1875, TAGR; Parsons, *"Pidge,"* 77–78.
38. McNelly to Steele, June [?], 1875, TAGR; Parsons, *"Pidge,"* 74.
39. Webb, *Texas Rangers,* 242, 250–51; Durham, *Taming the Nueces Strip,* 66, 69; McNelly to Steele, June [?], 1875, TAGR. The post cemetery at Fort Brown was closed in 1912, and the bodies were removed to Alexandria, Louisiana. Today the old cemetery site is occupied by the Fort Brown Motor Hotel, the Chancery of the Diocese of Brownsville, and apartment and office complexes.
40. Durham, *Taming the Nueces Strip,* 67–68.
41. Thompson, *Juan N. Cortina,* 72; Parsons, *"Pidge,"* 78–81; Webb, *Texas Rangers,* 256.
42. Austin *State Gazette,* September 20, 1875, reprinted in Parsons, *"Pidge,"* 82–83.
43. Webb, *Texas Rangers,* 256; Austin *State Gazette,* March 4, 1876, reprinted in Parsons, *"Pidge,"* 92–93.
44. Headquarters, Fort Brown, Texas, Special Orders No. 156, November 8, 1875, copy in TAGR.
45. Randlett to AAAG, District of the Rio Grande, December 1, 1875; Randlett to AAAG, District of the Rio Grande, November 16, 1875, both in ibid.
46. McNelly to Steele, November 22, 1875, ibid.
47. McNelly to Steele, November 18, 1875, ibid.
48. McNelly to Steele, November 19, 1875, ibid.
49. Austin *State Gazette,* January 19, 1876, reprinted in Parsons, *"Pidge,"* 88; McNelly to Steele, November 22, 1875, TAGR; Durham, *Taming the Nueces Strip,* 104.
50. McNelly to Steele, November 22, 1875, TAGR; Durham, *Taming the Nueces Strip,* 107–9; Callicott to Webb in Webb, *Texas Rangers,* 264–65; Austin *State Gazette,* January 19, 1876, reprinted in Parsons, *"Pidge,"* 88.
51. McNelly to Steele, November 22, 1875, TAGR; Durham, *Taming the Nueces Strip,* 110–14; Webb, *Texas Rangers,* 265–67; Austin *State Gazette,* January 19, 1876, reprinted in Parsons, *"Pidge,"* 88–89.
52. McNelly to Steele, November 22, 1875; García "To the Commander of the American forces on Mexican Soil," November 19, 1875, both TAGR. In Mexico a municipality combines the function of city and county, and so the mayor's jurisdiction covers a much larger area than the immediate boundaries of his city.
53. Ord to Steele, November 19, 1875, and Potter to Alexander, November 20, 1875, copies in TAGR.

54. McNelly to Steele, November 22, 1875, and Wilson, copy of telegram to unnamed official, November 20, 1875, both in ibid.

13: Bad Times for Badmen

1. Headquarters, Frontier Battalion, General Order No. 5, October 27, 1874, TAGF.
2. Headquarters, Frontier Battalion, General Order No. 6, October 25, 1875, TAGF.
3. Jones to Steele, December 1, 1874, TAGR.
4. Gillett, *Six Years,* 85; Hendricks, *Bad Man of the West,* 48.
5. Cook, *Fifty Years on the Old Frontier,* 59–60.
6. Hardin, *Life,* 88; Marohn, *Last Gunfighter,* 65–66; Metz, *John Wesley Hardin,* 130ff.
7. Metz, *John Wesley Hardin,* 136–38; Hardin, *Life,* 90ff.
8. Metz, *John Wesley Hardin,* 141–42; J. H. Taylor, "Ranger Reminiscences," TAGF.
9. Hardin, *Life,* 93.
10. Metz, *John Wesley Hardin,* 142.
11. Hardin, *Life,* 95ff.; Metz, *John Wesley Hardin,* 142ff.
12. Frontier Battalion, Exhibit "D," undated; J. H. Taylor, "Ranger Reminiscences," both in TAGF.
13. Hardin, *Life,* 107; Metz, *John Wesley Hardin,* 158, 160–62.
14. Metz, *John Wesley Hardin,* 158ff.; Hardin, *Life,* 112; Parsons and Parsons, *Bowen and Hardin,* 59.
15. Texas Adjutant General's Office, *A List of Fugitives from Justice,* 27.
16. Smith, *Armstrong Chronicle,* 84–85. Most works spell Armstrong's middle name "Barclay," but Smith, who wrote her book with the cooperation of the Armstrong family, uses "Barkley." The confusion appears to arise because some descendants spell their own names "Barclay."
17. Jennings, *A Texas Ranger,* 131.
18. Smith, *Armstrong Chronicle,* 101; Metz, *John Wesley Hardin,* 165. Webb (*Texas Rangers,* 298) also attributes Armstrong's interest to "sporting blood."
19. Metz, *John Wesley Hardin,* 165.
20. Metz, *John Wesley Hardin,* 165; Hardin, *Life,* 114; Parsons and Parsons, *Bowen and Hardin,* 59–60; Raymond, *Captain Lee Hall,* 130.
21. Metz, *John Wesley Hardin,* 167–70; Hardin, *Life,* 114–17; Parsons and Parsons, *Bowen and Hardin,* 60; Marohn, *Last Gunfighter,* 111; Webb, *Texas Rangers,* 299. Hardin, who wrote his memoirs years later and whose memory was faulty on small details, said he was captured on July 23. Armstrong's report to Adjutant General Steele, reprinted in Webb (300), gives the date as August 23. All other sources agree.
22. Marohn, *Last Gunfighter,* 111–12; Metz, *John Wesley Hardin,* 178ff.; Hardin, *Life,* 136.
23. The Bowen case is discussed in Parsons and Parsons, *Bowen and Hardin.*
24. Fisher, "Life and Times," 233–36.
25. Jennings, *A Texas Ranger,* 238–39; Raymond, *Captain Lee Hall,* 55. The story of Fisher's killing the Bengal is from Jennings. Durham (*Taming the Nueces Strip,* 150) says he understood that Ben Thompson shot the tiger and had the chaps made as a gift for Fisher. The two man-killers were close friends.
26. Fisher, "Life and Times," 237–38.
27. Adjutant General's Office, *A List of Fugitives from Justice,* 153. George Durham

(*Taming the Nueces Strip,* 143) said Fisher's name was not in "The Book," as the *List of Fugitives from Justice* was called, but Durham was writing in 1934 and his memory appears to have been faulty on that point.

28. Durham, *Taming the Nueces Strip,* 134; Parsons, "Gunfire at Espantosa Lake," 23. Although this conflicts with McNelly's request for Winchesters in the Taylor-Sutton Feud, it is generally agreed that he did prefer the Sharps. He may have requested the Winchesters because the numerous gunfights dictated a repeating rifle, and because DeWitt County, which is heavily wooded, is not suitable terrain for the long-range Sharps.

29. McNelly to Steele, reprinted in Jennings, *A Texas Ranger,* 231–32.

30. Parsons, "Gunfire at Espantosa Lake," 21; Durham, *Taming the Nueces Strip,* 138–39.

31. Jennings, *A Texas Ranger,* 234; Durham, *Taming the Nueces Strip,* 139ff.; Fisher, "Life and Times," 239.

32. Jennings, *A Texas Ranger,* 239–41. McNelly's health is discussed in Durham, *Taming the Nueces Strip,* 148.

33. Durham, *Taming the Nueces Strip,* 155–56.

34. Durham, *Taming the Nueces Strip,* 156–58; Raymond, *Captain Lee Hall,* 38–39. Hall was sworn in as an officer of the company on August 10, 1876.

35. Durham, *Taming the Nueces Strip,* 158; Jennings, *A Texas Ranger,* 257–58; Parsons, "Gunfire at Espantosa Lake," 22.

36. Durham, *Taming the Nueces Strip,* 158–59; Armstrong quoted in Jennings, *A Texas Ranger,* 258–59.

37. Durham, *Taming the Nueces Strip,* 159–60; Jennings, *A Texas Ranger,* 259–61; Parsons, "Gunfire at Espantosa Lake," 22–24. According to Jennings, McAlister was still alive in 1892. Parsons cites Armstrong's report to McNelly in saying there were only four horse thieves in camp. The report is reprinted in Webb, *Texas Rangers,* 296.

38. Durham, *Taming the Nueces Strip,* 161; Parsons, "Gunfight at Espantosa Lake," 24.

39. Durham, *Taming the Nueces Strip,* 161.

40. Adjutant General's Office, *A List of Fugitives from Justice,* reprinted by State House Press as *Fugitives from Justice: The Notebook of Texas Ranger Sergeant James B. Gillett,* 193.

41. Metz, *John Wesley Hardin,* 191–92; Rosa, *Taming of the West,* 68.

42. Steele quoted in "The Reason Why Capt. McNelly Was Not Retained," undated, unattributed newspaper clipping, TAGF; Webb, *Texas Rangers,* 288; Durham, *Taming the Nueces Strip,* 158, 161–62; King, "Texas Ranger Service," 352.

14: The Salt War

1. Day, "El Paso's Texas Rangers," 157–58.

2. Bowden, "Magoffin Salt War," 95–96; Smith, "El Paso Salt War," 58–59.

3. Quotes from Majority Report, with Accompaniments, of Board to Investigate Recent Troubles in El Paso County, Texas, 45th Congress, Second Session, *El Paso Troubles in Texas,* 15 (hereinafter cited as "Majority Report"); "little less than law," W. M. Dunn, judge advocate-general, to Secretary of War, April 12, 1878, ibid.; Sonnichsen, *Pass of the North,* 182–83; Smith, "El Paso Salt War," 59.

4. Sonnichsen, *Pass of the North,* 193, 195–98, 200; Smith, "El Paso Salt War,"

60–61; J. A. Zabriskie to Edward H. Hatch, January 11, 1878, and deposition of B. S. Dowell, January 11, 1878, *El Paso Troubles in Texas,* 53–54.

5. Statement of A. Krakauer, February 1, 1878, *El Paso Troubles in Texas,* 60.
6. Kerber to Steele, October 18, 1877, and Steele to Jones, October 24, 1877, both ibid., 153.
7. Smith, "El Paso Salt War," 61; Sonnichsen, *Pass of the North,* 201.
8. Sonnichsen, *Pass of the North,* 202.
9. Minority Report, Board of Commissioners Appointed to Investigate the Troubles in El Paso County, Texas, *El Paso Troubles in Texas,* 26 (hereinafter cited as "Minority Report").
10. Ibid., 26–27; Hubbard to Cisto Solelnie, Leon Granillo, and Chico Barela, December 10, 1877, *El Paso Troubles in Texas,* 114.
11. Deposition of Solomon Schutz, March 18, 1878, ibid., 32–33; Sonnichsen, *Pass of the North,* 203–6.
12. Statement of J. B. Tays, December 20, 1877, *El Paso Troubles in Texas,* 80; statement of Capt. Thomas Blair, 15th Infantry, December 19, 1877, ibid., 56; Sonnichsen, *Pass of the North,* 206. Fort Bliss at El Paso recently had been deactivated by the War Department, making Fort Bayard the nearest U.S. military post.
13. Statement of J. B. Tays, December 20, 1877, *El Paso Troubles in Texas,* 80–81; "The San Elizario Massacre, As Related by an Eye-Witness," Mesilla, New Mexico, *Independent,* January 17, 1878, reprinted in ibid., 97; Smith, "El Paso Salt War," 62; Sonnichsen, *Pass of the North,* 206–7. Tays said Atkinson had $700, while the "Eye-Witness" (Juan Nepumoceno García) stated it was $11,000. Sonnichsen quoted the latter figure, which is probably nearer correct, given the extent of the transactions Atkinson was trying to protect.
14. *"Mas arriba, cabrones!"* Literally translated, the word *cabrón* refers to a goat, but in common usage, which Atkinson no doubt intended in view of the circumstances, it means "son of a bitch." *Cabrones* is the plural form.
15. Statement of J. B. Tays, December 20, 1877, *El Paso Troubles in Texas,* 81; "Eye-Witness," Mesilla *Independent,* reprinted in ibid., 97–98; Sonnichsen, *Pass of the North,* 209; Smith, "El Paso Salt War," 86.
16. Statement of Mariana Núñez, February 3, 1878, *El Paso Troubles in Texas,* 83; statement of J. W. Campbell, February 5, 1878, ibid., 84; statement of H. O. Matthews, February 3, 1878, ibid., 85; statement of Capt. Charles D. Beyer, Ninth Cavalry, February 3, 1878, ibid., 85; statement of John B. Tays, February 12, 1878, ibid., 87.
17. Dunn to Secretary of War, April 12, 1878, ibid., 4; various statements, ibid., 85ff. One local citizen, J. P. Miller, stated that two men broke into his home and threatened to kill him unless he told them where the women were; he positively identified the intruders as part of the New Mexico gang. Statement of J. P. Miller, March 7, 1878, ibid.
18. Statement of John B. Tays, February 12, 1878, ibid., 86–87; statement of Antonio Cadena, March 4, 1878, ibid., 93. A statement of Dr. J. K. Ball, a surgeon who arrived at the Núñez house shortly after the killing, casts doubt on Ranger claims of self-defense; statement of J. K. Ball, February 14, 1878, ibid., 88. Colonel Hatch frankly stated he did not believe the Rangers. Edward Hatch to Col. John H. King, President, Military Commission, February 14, 1878, ibid., 94.
19. Hatch to King, February 8, 1878, ibid., 87; Headquarters, District of New Mexico, General Field-Orders No. 1, December 24, 1878, ibid., 88.

20. Dunn to Secretary of War, April 12, 1878, ibid., 4–5, Majority Report, ibid., 13ff.
21. Minority Report, ibid., 19ff.
22. Day, "El Paso's Texas Rangers," 159; Sonnichsen, *Pass of the North,* 210.

15: The Last of the Old Guard

1. Sam Bass is the subject of a phenomenal amount of literature, the classics being Wayne Gard's *Sam Bass* and two reprinted "penny dreadfuls," *A Sketch of Sam Bass the Bandit,* by Charles L. Martin, and *"Hands Up!" The History of a Crime,* by Al Sorenson. Among the general surveys of badmen, George D. Hendricks's *The Bad Man of the West* probably is the best for detailed material on Bass. Ramon Adams's introduction to the University of Oklahoma Press edition of Martin's book has much good information, as do Adams's own extensive works. A capsuled but useful description of the real Bass also appears in Robert Elman's *Badmen of the West.* On pages 371–72 of *The Texas Rangers,* Webb reprints excerpts from a poem about Bass that was popular when he was a boy in west Texas in the 1890s. Excerpts of the cowboy ballad are quoted in Raymond, *Captain Lee Hall,* throughout Chapter 12.
2. Gard, *Sam Bass,* 68–70; Elman, *Badmen of the West,* 214–15. The Big Springs train robbery is the subject of Sorenson's book *"Hands Up!"*
3. Gard, *Sam Bass,* 106–7; Webb, *Texas Rangers,* 374.
4. Webb, *Texas Rangers,* 374–75.
5. Martin, *Sketch of Sam Bass,* 105.
6. Ibid., 120–23; Webb, *Texas Rangers,* 377.
7. Statement of J. W. Murphy, July 24, 1878; Evans, Memorandum in Regard to Jas. Murphy, May 21, 1878, both TAGF.
8. Statement of J. W. Murphy, July 24, 1878, ibid.; Gard, *Sam Bass,* 169–72; Webb, *Texas Rangers,* 280–83; Gillett, *Six Years,* 116–18.
9. Gillett, *Six Years,* 120–23; Raymond, *Captain Lee Hall,* 160.
10. Raymond, *Captain Lee Hall,* 160. Raymond cites an 1895 newspaper article by Hall stating that Murphy had been communicating with him as well as Everhart, but other sources do not mention it. Murphy had very little opportunity to communicate, and would have kept his letters to the minimum because he feared for his life, with good reason. Gard (*Sam Bass,* 206) says Hall was ordered to Round Rock by Major Jones, who also summoned Armstrong and the others when he began to worry about whether Reynolds's Rangers would arrive in time.
11. Gillett, *Six Years,* 123–25; Gard, *Sam Bass,* 210; Raymond, *Captain Lee Hall,* 161–62.
12. Gard, *Sam Bass,* 214ff., 231; Gillett, *Six Years,* 126–27.
13. Peterson, *"Facts As I Remember Them,"* 54.
14. Day, "El Paso's Texas Rangers," 159.
15. Ibid.; Baylor, *Into the Far, Wild Country,* 273. The latter work is a compilation of a series of articles Baylor wrote for the *El Paso Herald* from 1899 to 1906, edited and annotated by Jerry Don Thompson.
16. Baylor, *Into the Far, Wild Country,* 273–75; Day, "El Paso's Texas Rangers," 160; Gillett, *Six Years,* 140–41.
17. Baylor, *Into the Far, Wild Country,* 276–81; Gillett, *Six Years,* 153–59.
18. Baylor, *Into the Far, Wild Country,* 284; Gillett, *Six Years,* 161–66.
19. Baylor, *Into the Far, Wild Country,* 313–15; Gillett, *Six Years,* 200–3; Webb, *Texas Rangers,* 402–3.

20. Webb, *Texas Rangers,* 425; Prassel, *Western Peace Officer,* 158. In Texas the authority of a law enforcement officer is restricted to his or her own jurisdiction, i.e., city police within the city limits and county sheriffs within the county.
21. Day, "El Paso's Texas Rangers," 161; Baylor to W. H. King, adjutant general, September 30, 1881, TAGR; Metz, *Dallas Stoudenmire,* 71–72.
22. Metz, *Dallas Stoudenmire,* 71–72; Jones to Baylor, November 27, 1880, TAGR.
23. Stoudenmire to King, March 29, 1882; Baylor to King, April 26, 1882, both TAGR; Metz, *Dallas Stoudenmire,* 78–79. Besides their professional association, Gillett was Baylor's son-in-law (see Day, "El Paso's Texas Rangers," 164).
24. Gillett, *Six Years,* 143.
25. Baylor, *Into the Far, Wild Country,* 29; Day, "El Paso's Texas Rangers," 162.
26. *Goliad Guard,* May 26, 1877.
27. King, "Texas Ranger Service," 2:352.
28. Williams, *Texas' Last Frontier,* 279; Sonnichsen, *Roy Bean,* 80, 88.
29. McDonald's life is covered in Paine, *Captain Bill McDonald, Texas Ranger.* Most of this material comes from Chapter 28.

16: Gunmen, Pugilists, and a "Fistic Carnival"

1. Metz, *John Wesley Hardin,* 222.
2. White, *Them Was the Days,* 118.
3. Sonnichsen, *Pass of the North,* 356–57.
4. Sonnichsen, *Roy Bean,* 85–87.
5. Sonnichsen, *Pass of the North,* 356; Metz, *John Wesley Hardin,* 208, 211, 219–21.
6. Selman's life is covered in Metz, *John Selman, Gunfighter.* The Shackelford County Feud, which extensively involved the Rangers, is detailed in Sonnichsen, *I'll Die Before I'll Run,* and Robinson, *The Frontier World of Fort Griffin.*
7. DeArment, *George Scarborough,* 126–27; Martin, *Border Boss,* 155.
8. Statement of John Selman, *El Paso Daily Herald,* August 20, 1895, reprinted in Hardin, *Life,* 142.
9. White, *Them Was the Days,* 106; DeArment, *George Scarborough,* 127–29; Metz, *John Wesley Hardin,* 264–65, 272.
10. Martin, *Border Boss,* 155; DeArment, *George Scarborough,* 127.
11. Metz, *John Selman,* 198; Robinson, *Frontier World of Fort Griffin,* 144.
12. Sonnichsen, *Roy Bean,* 175; Time-Life, *The Gamblers,* 220. The Texas statutes governing both human and animal combat are discussed in Miletich, *Dan Stuart's Fistic Carnival,* 26, and *Chicago Tribune,* September 18, 1895.
13. The preliminaries are covered in Miletich, *Dan Stuart's Fistic Carnival,* and in Time-Life, *The Gamblers,* 220.
14. *Chicago Tribune,* September 2, 1895.
15. Ibid., September 30, 1895.
16. Ibid.
17. Ibid.
18. Ibid., September 19, 28 (Mrs. Culberson's remark), and 29, 1895.
19. Time-Life, *The Gamblers,* 220; Paine, *Captain Bill McDonald,* 194–95.
20. DeArment, *George Scarborough,* 137; Riley, "Prizefight," 40.
21. Paine, *Captain Bill McDonald,* 195.
22. DeArment, *George Scarborough,* 138.
23. Sonnichsen, *Roy Bean,* 179.
24. New York *World,* February 12, 1896.

25. Sonnichsen, *Roy Bean,* 180; DeArment, *George Scarborough,* 138–39.

26. DeArment, *George Scarborough,* 139; Mabry to Lieutenant Governor George T. Jester, February 27, 1896, in Paine, *Captain Bill McDonald,* 400; Riley, "Prizefight," 41; Miletich, *Dan Stuart's Fistic Carnival,* 151–54.

27. New York *World,* February 13, 1896.

28. Ibid.; Miletich, *Dan Stuart's Fistic Carnival,* 129–30.

29. Sonnichsen, *Roy Bean,* 183; Miletich, *Dan Stuart's Fistic Carnival,* 161, 164–65; New York *World,* February 16, 1896.

30. New York *World,* February 16, 1896.

31. Ibid.

32. Mabry to Jester, February 27, 1896, in Paine, *Captain Bill McDonald,* 400; Martin, *Border Boss,* 164; New York *World,* February 13, 1896.

33. Stuart quoted in Riley, "Prizefight," 41; Miletich, *Dan Stuart's Fistic Carnival,* 161–62.

34. Mabry to Jester, February 27, 1896, in Paine, *Captain Bill McDonald,* 399; New York *World,* February 22, 1896.

35. New York *World,* February 12, 1896.

36. Sonnichsen, *Roy Bean,* 152, 178; Sonnichsen, *Pass of the North,* 361.

37. Mabry to Jester, February 27, 1896, in Paine, *Captain Bill McDonald,* 401; Sonnichsen, *Roy Bean,* 174; Miletich, *Dan Stuart's Fistic Carnival,* 173.

38. Miletich, *Dan Stuart's Fistic Carnival,* 175.

39. New York *World,* February 22, 1896.

40. Ibid., February 16, 1896.

41. Paine, *Captain Bill McDonald,* 197–98.

42. Masterson's biographer Robert K. DeArment discusses the episode in "That Masterson-McDonald Standoff."

43. Sonnichsen, *Roy Bean,* 187; Miletich, *Dan Stuart's Fistic Carnival,* 181; Martin, *Border Boss,* 165.

44. New York *World,* February 22, 1896.

45. Miletich, *Dan Stuart's Fistic Carnival,* 182.

46. Ibid., 183, 229n13; New York *World,* February 22, 1896.

47. Sonnichsen, *Roy Bean,* 189.

17: Tarnished Star

1. Webb, *Texas Rangers,* 453.

2. Ibid., 457; Martin, *Border Boss,* 175.

3. Jenkins and Frost, *"I'm Frank Hamer,"* 22–30.

4. The Brownsville Affray, as it is called, is covered in detail by Ann J. Lane in *The Brownsville Affair* and by John D. Weaver in *The Brownsville Raid.* Lane concentrates more on the national civil rights implications, while Weaver looks at the incident itself and concludes that the soldiers were framed. Members of many old Brownsville families dispute Weaver's findings. Most of the material on McDonald's involvement comes from Chapters 38, 39, and 40 of Paine, *Captain Bill McDonald.*

5. Lane, *Brownsville Affair,* 19–20, 29–30. Judge Welch's charge, reprinted on pages 357–59 of Paine, *Captain Bill McDonald,* accuses the soldiers of "fiendish malice and hate, showing blacker than their skins." Paine's book, written three years after the incident, casts McDonald in a heroic mold, defending the integrity of Texas cit-

izenry and law against the federal government and its odious black soldiers. This, of course, reflected national attitudes of the era. Ninety years later, however, the same text makes McDonald appear at best amateurish in this particular incident.

6. This incident is told in Paine, *Captain Bill McDonald,* Chapter 41.
7. Ibid., 271–73.
8. Sterling, *Trails and Trials,* 21. The so-called Bandit War on the Lower Rio Grande is described fully by Sterling and in John R. Peavey, *Echoes from the Rio Grande.*
9. The Plan of San Diego and its impact on the border disturbances are detailed by James A. Sandos in *Rebellion in the Borderlands.* German influence is discussed in Sandos, 96–97; Jenkins and Frost, *"I'm Frank Hamer,"* 50–56; and Sterling, *Trails and Trials,* 25. Sterling also considers possible Japanese influence.
10. Sterling, *Trails and Trials,* 25; quote from Peavey, *Echoes from the Rio Grande,* 101.
11. Sandos, *Rebellion in the Borderlands,* 86–87; Justice, *Revolution on the Rio Grande,* 45.
12. Sandos, *Rebellion in the Borderlands,* 87–88; Peavey, *Echoes from the Rio Grande,* 100–1; Sterling, *Trials and Trails,* 32–33.
13. Jenkins and Frost, *"I'm Frank Hamer,"* 57–59; Sandos, *Rebellion in the Borderlands,* 89–90.
14. Sandos, *Rebellion in the Borderlands,* 92.
15. Ibid., 98; Jenkins and Frost, *"I'm Frank Hamer,"* 60.
16. Robinson, "When Bandits Wrecked the Night Train," 41–42; Sandos, *Rebellion in the Borderlands,* 104.
17. Robinson, "When Bandits Wrecked the Night Train," 42; Sandos, *Rebellion in the Borderlands,* 101–4; Peavey, *Echoes from the Rio Grande,* 120.
18. Peavey, *Echoes from the Rio Grande,* 121–22; Sandos, *Rebellion in the Borderlands,* 103–4.
19. Justice, *Revolution on the Rio Grande,* 10–14; Jenkins and Frost, *"I'm Frank Hamer,"* 62–65. The *rurales,* or Guardia Rural (Rural Guard), officially were dissolved with the collapse of the Díaz regime, although some units continued to function as the only semblance of law and order. Their closest counterparts were perhaps the Guardia Civil during the Franco regime in Spain.
20. Martin, *Border Boss,* 186ff.
21. Justice, *Revolution on the Rio Grande,* 6–9.
22. Ibid., 9–11, 17; Martin, *Border Boss,* 205–9.
23. Justice, *Revolution on the Rio Grande,* 36; Martin, *Border Boss,* 205.
24. Justice, *Revolution on the Rio Grande,* 9, 36.
25. Sam H. Neill, quoted in ibid., 21.
26. "Death to the gringos!"
27. Justice, *Revolution on the Rio Grande,* 21ff.; Warren, "The Raid on Luke Brite's Ranch," Warren Papers.
28. Justice, *Revolution on the Rio Grande,* 36–37; Warren, "The Porvenir Massacre," Warren Papers; In re of the Investigation of the El Porvenir Fight [*sic*], of January 28, 1918, in Presidio County, Texas Legislature, Proceedings of the Joint Committee of the Senate and the House in the Investigation of the Texas State Ranger Force (hereinafter cited as "Proceedings"), 1586ff. The Proceedings contain eyewitness statements on the Porvenir massacre, which were given in a Mexican court and appear in the Texas legislative record in translation. Many of the

statements are virtually identical except for a few details, giving the impression of rehearsed testimony. Before reaching that conclusion, however, one must consider the fact that a large number of these people were illiterate, and the Mexican notaries, upon realizing that most people were testifying essentially to the same thing, may have prepared a standardized statement, changing it only when details of the testimony varied.

29. Justice, *Revolution on the Rio Grande,* 37–39; Proceedings, 1586ff.; "cursed them . . . ," Warren, "The Porvenir Massacre," Warren Papers.
30. Warren, "The Porvenir Massacre," Warren Papers.
31. Ibid.
32. Justice, *Revolution on the Rio Grande,* 40–45; Fehrenbach, *Lone Star,* 639.
33. Harley to Fox, June 11, 1918, copy of letter attached to Memorial of the Mexican General Commission of Claims, Warren Papers.
34. Proceedings, 148.
35. Harley to W. H. Bledsoe, Chairman of the Joint Committee, copy in ibid.
36. Various entries, ibid.; Justice, *Revolution on the Rio Grande,* 46.
37. Webb, *Texas Rangers,* 513–14; Sterling, *Trails and Trials,* 51.
38. Dallas *News,* February 21, 1919.

Conclusion: The End and the Myth

1. White, *Them Was the Days,* 112.
2. John F. Barron to the author, undated interview (1975).
3. Prassell, *Western Peace Officer,* 158–59. The impact of the Ferguson era on the Rangers is described in full in Sterling, *Trails and Trials.*
4. House, "Rip-roaring Days," 19.
5. Hamer's story, with much material on the Bonnie and Clyde case, is told in Jenkins and Frost, *"I'm Frank Hamer."*
6. Mike Cox to the author, telephone conversation, September 3, 1996.
7. DPS, *Annual Report, 1994,* 10.
8. Askins, *Texans, Guns and History,* 184.
9. Hunter, "How the Greatest Museum in the South Was Built," 220–21.
10. Heide and Gilman, *Cowboy Collectibles,* 24–25.
11. Ibid., 62ff.
12. Malsch, *"Lone Wolf" Gonzaullas,* 195–96. A tape of a 1952 radio episode with Joel McCrea is available in "The Smithsonian Collection. Old Time Radio Detectives and Crime Fighters."
13. Cartwright, "Chuck Norris," 103.
14. *San Antonio Express-News,* January 24, 1987; Mike Cox to the author, telephone conversation, September 3, 1996.
15. White, *Them Was the Days,* 126.
16. George W. Bush to the author, October 21, 1996.

Bibliography
Government Documents and Publications

Cox, Mike. *Silver Stars and Sixguns: The Texas Rangers*. Austin: Texas Department of Public Safety, 1995.

Ellington, G. W. "When Cattle Trails Were Highways." Ranger Reminiscences. Typescript. Record Group 401. Office of the Adjutant General. Texas State Library and Archive, Austin.

Gammel, Hans Peter Nielson, comp. *The Laws of Texas, 1822–1897*. 10 vols. Austin: Gammel Book Company, 1898.

Mooney, James. "Calendar History of the Kiowa Indians." *Seventeenth Annual Report of the Bureau of American Ethnology, 1895–96*. Part I: 129–445. Washington, D.C.: Government Printing Office, 1898. Reprinted. Washington, D. C.: Smithsonian Institution Press, 1979.

State of Texas. Department of Public Safety Public Information Office. *Annual Report, 1994, Texas Department of Public Safety*. Austin: Department of Public Safety Reproduction Office, n.d. (1995).

———. Office of the Adjutant General. *A List of Fugitives from Justice*. Austin: Adjutant General's Office, 1878. Reprint, as *Fugitives from Justice: The Notebook of Texas Ranger Sergeant James B. Gillett*. Austin: State House Press, 1997.

———. Record Group 401. Texas State Library and Archive, Austin.

———. Ranger Reminiscences. Record Group 401. Texas State Library and Archive, Austin.

———. Texas Adjutant General's Records. Center for American History, University of Texas, Austin.

———. Texas Legislature. *General Laws of the State of Texas Passed by the Eleventh Legislature*. Austin: State Gazette, 1866.

———. *General Laws of the State of Texas: Passed at the Session of the Fourteenth Legislature Begun and Held at the City of Austin, January 13, 1874*. Houston: A. C. Gray, State Printer, 1874.

———. *General Laws of the Twelfth Legislature of the State of Texas. Called Session*. Austin: Tracy, Siemering & Co., 1870.

———. *Laws of the Eighth Legislature of the State of Texas. Extra Session*. Austin: John Marshall & Co., State Printers, 1861.

———. Proceedings of the Joint Committee of the Senate and the House in the Investigation of the Texas State Ranger Force. January 13, 1919.

United States Congress. House of Representatives. 30th Congress, First Session, HR Executive Document No. 60. *Hostilities by Mexico. Message of the President of the United States Relative to an invasion and commencement of hostilities by Mexico*. May 11, 1846.

————. 31st Congress, First Session, HR No. 352. *Payment of Texas Volunteers.* [To accompany bill H.R. No. 314.] June 12, 1850.

————. 36th Congress, First Session, Executive Document No. 52. *Difficulties on Southwestern Frontier.*

————. Executive Document No. 81. *Troubles on Texas Frontier.*

————. 36th Congress, First Session, Report No. 535. *Claims for Spoliations Committed by Indians and Mexicans.* [To accompany bill H.R. No. 728.] May 18, 1860.

————. 45th Congress, Second Session, Executive Document No. 93. *El Paso Troubles in Texas.*

United States Department of War. *War of the Rebellion: A Compilation of the Official Records of the Union and Confederate Armies.* 130 vols. Washington, D.C.: U.S. Government Printing Office, 1891–1898.

Winfrey, Dorman H., and James M. Day, eds. *The Indian Papers of Texas and the Southwest 1825–1916.* 5 vols. Austin: Pemberton Press, 1966. Reprint. Austin: Texas State Historical Association, 1995.

Manuscripts

Caperton, John. "Sketch of Colonel John C. Hays, The Texas Rangers, Incidents in Texas and Mexico, Etc." Center for American History, University of Texas, Austin.

Davenport, Harbert. Papers. Texas State Library and Archive, Austin.

DeShields, James T. "Indian Raid, Pursuit and Fight." John Coffee Hays Items. Center for American History, University of Texas, Austin.

————. "Jack Hays Fight on the Gaudaloupe [*sic*]." John Coffee Hays Items. Center for American History, University of Texas, Austin.

Elm Creek Raid Statements. Earl Vandale Collection. Center for American History, University of Texas, Austin.

Gholson, Benjamin Franklin. "The Death of Nacona." Earl Vandale Collection. Center for American History, University of Texas, Austin.

Hamby, Thornton K. "An Indian Raid in Young County, Texas, Oct. 13th 1864." Elm Creek Raid Statements. Earl Vandale Collection. Center for American History, University of Texas, Austin.

Hays, John Coffee. Items. Center for American History, University of Texas, Austin.

————. Vertical File. Center for American History, University of Texas, Austin.

Kuykendall, J. H. "Col. Samuel H. Walker." Typescript. Samuel Hamilton Walker Vertical File. Center for American History, University of Texas, Austin.

Lockhart, John W. "Jack Hays' Visit to Washington, Texas." John Coffee Hays Items. Center for American History, University of Texas, Austin.

McNelly, Leander H. Papers. Center for American History, University of Texas, Austin.

Myers, James Will. Papers. Panhandle-Plains Historical Society, Canyon, Texas.

Vandale, Earl. Collection. Center for American History, University of Texas, Austin.

Walker, Samuel Hamilton. Papers. Texas State Library and Archive, Austin.

————. Vertical File. Center for American History, University of Texas, Austin.

Warren, Harry. Papers, 1835–1932. Archives of the Big Bend, Sul Ross State University, Alpine, Texas.

————. "The Porvenir Massacre in Presidio County, Texas, on January 28, 1918." Harry Warren Papers, 1835–1932. Archives of the Big Bend, Sul Ross State University, Alpine, Texas.

———. "The Raid on Luke Brite's Presidio County, Texas, on Xmas Day, 1917." Harry Warren Papers, 1835–1932. Archives of the Big Bend, Sul Ross State University, Alpine, Texas.

Books

Askins, Charles. *Texans, Guns and History.* New York: Bonanza Books, 1970.

Bancroft, Hubert Howe. *History of Arizona and New Mexico, 1530–1888.* Vol. 17 of *The Works of Hubert Howe Bancroft.* San Francisco: The History Company, 1889.

———. *History of Mexico.* 6 vols. Vols. 9–14 of *The Works of Hubert Howe Bancroft.* San Francisco: The History Company, 1883–88.

———. *History of the North Mexican States and Texas.* 2 vols. Vols. 15–16 of *The Works of Hubert Howe Bancroft.* San Francisco: The History Company, 1889.

Barker, Eugene C., ed. *The Austin Papers.* Annual Report of the American Historical Association for the Year 1919. 2 vols. Washington, D.C.: Government Printing Office, 1924.

———. *The Life of Stephen F. Austin, Founder of Texas, 1793–1836: A Chapter in the Westward Movement of the Anglo-American People.* Nashville and Dallas: Cokesbury Press, 1925. Reprint. Austin: University of Texas Press, 1980.

Barry, James Buckner. *Buck Barry, Texas Ranger and Frontiersman.* New ed. Waco: Friends of the Moody Texas Ranger Library, 1978. Reprint. Lincoln: University of Nebraska Press, 1984.

Bauer, K. Jack. *The Mexican War, 1846–1848.* New York: Macmillan, 1974. Reprint. Lincoln: University of Nebraska Press, 1992.

Baylor, George Wythe, and Jerry Don Thompson, eds. *Into the Far, Wild Country: True Tales of the Old Southwest.* El Paso: Texas Western Press, 1996.

Bell, Samuel E., and James M. Smallwood. *The Zona Libre 1858–1905: A Problem in American Diplomacy.* El Paso: Texas Western Press, 1982.

Benner, Judith Ann. *Sul Ross, Soldier, Statesman, Educator.* College Station: Texas A&M University Press, 1983.

"Brazos" (pseud.). *The Life of Robert Hall, Indian Fighter and Veteran of Three Great Wars. Also Sketch of Big Foot Wallace.* Austin: Ben C. Jones, Printer, 1898. Reprint. Austin: State House Press, 1992.

Brice, Donaly E. *The Great Comanche Raid: Boldest Indian Attack of the Texas Republic.* Austin: Eakin Press, 1987.

Bridges, Toby, ed. *Black Powder Gun Digest.* Chicago: Follett, 1972.

Brooks, N. C. *A Complete History of the Mexican War: Its Causes, Conduct, and Consequences: Comprising an Account of the Various Military and Naval Operations, from Its Commencement to the Treaty of Peace.* Philadelphia: Grigg, Elliot & Co., 1849.

Brown, John Henry. *History of Texas from 1685 to 1892.* 2 vols. St. Louis: L. E. Daniell, 1892. Reprint. Austin: Jenkins Publishing Company/The Pemberson Press, 1970.

———. *The Indian Wars and Pioneers of Texas.* Austin: L. E. Daniell, n.d. (1896). Reprint. Austin: State House Press, 1988.

Callcott, Wilfrid Hardy. *Santa Anna: The Story of an Enigma Who Once Was Mexico.* Norman: University of Oklahoma Press, 1936.

Canales, José T. *Juan N. Cortina Presents His Motion for a New Trial, 1951.* San Antonio: Artes Graficas, 1951.

Carter, Robert G. *On the Border with Mackenzie or Winning West Texas from the Co-manches.* Washington: Eynon Printing Company, Inc., 1935. Reprint. New York: Antiquarian Press, 1961.

Chamberlain, Samuel. *My Confession: Recollections of a Rogue.* Unexpurgated and Annotated Edition. Austin: Texas State Historical Association, 1996.

Chance, Joseph E., ed. *Mexico Under Fire, Being the Diary of Samuel Ryan Curtis, 3rd Ohio Volunteer Regiment During the American Military Occupation of Northern Mexico, 1846–1847.* Fort Worth: Texas Christian University Press, 1994.

Clayton, Lawrence R., and Joseph E. Chance, eds. *The March to Monterrey: The Diary of Lieutenant Rankin Dilworth, U.S. Army.* El Paso: Texas Western Press, 1996.

Coker, Caleb, ed. *The News from Brownsville: Helen Chapman's Letters from the Texas Military Frontier, 1848–1852.* Austin: Texas State Historical Association, 1992.

Cook, James H. *Fifty Years on the Old Frontier as Cowboy, Hunter, Guide, Scout, and Ranchman.* New Haven: Yale University Press, 1923.

Crawford, Ann Fears, ed. *The Eagle: The Autobiography of Santa Anna.* Austin: Jenkins Publishing Company/The Pemberton Press, 1967. Reprint. Austin: State House Press, 1988.

Dalton, Kit. *Under the Black Flag.* Memphis, Tenn.: privately printed, 1914. Reprint. Memphis: Larry J. Tolbert, 1995.

Davis, John L. *The Texas Rangers: Images and Incidents.* Rev. ed. San Antonio: University of Texas Institute of Texan Cultures at San Antonio, 1991.

DeArment, Robert K. *George Scarborough: The Life and Death of a Lawman on the Closing Frontier.* Norman: University of Oklahoma Press, 1992.

De Leon, Arnoldo. *They Called Them Greasers: Anglo Attitudes Toward Mexicans in Texas, 1821–1900.* Austin: University of Texas Press, 1983.

DeShields, James T. *Border Wars of Texas, Being an Authentic and Popular Account, in Chronological Order, of the Long and Bitter Conflict Waged Between Savage Indian Tribes and the Pioneer Settlers of Texas.* Tioga, Tex.: Herald Company, 1912. Reprint. Austin: State House Press, 1993.

Dixie Gun Works. Annual catalogs. Union City, Tenn.

Dobie, J. Frank. *Guide to the Life and Literature of the Southwest.* Rev. ed. Dallas: Southern Methodist University Press, 1952.

Douglas, C. L. *Famous Texas Feuds.* Dallas: Turner Co., 1936. Reprint. Austin: State House Press, 1988.

———. *The Gentlemen in the White Hats: Dramatic Episodes in the History of the Texas Rangers.* Dallas: South-West Press, 1934. Reprint. Austin: State House Press, 1992.

Durham, George, as told to Clyde Wantland. *Taming the Nueces Strip: The Story of McNelly's Rangers.* Austin: University of Texas Press, 1962; reprint, 1990.

Duval, John C. *Early Times in Texas or, the Adventures of Jack Dobell.* Austin: H.P.N. Gammel & Co., 1892. Reprint. Lincoln: University of Nebraska Press, 1986.

Eisenhower, John S. D. *So Far from God: The U.S. War with Mexico, 1846–1848.* New York: Random House, 1989.

Elman, Robert. *Badmen of the West.* Secaucus, N.J.: Castle Books, 1974.

Fehrenbach, T. R. *Lone Star: A History of Texas and the Texans.* New York: Macmillan, 1968. Reprint. New York: American Legacy Press, 1983.

Filisola, Vicente. *Representación Dirigida al Supremo Gobierno por el General Vicente Filisola, en defensa de Su Honor y Aclaración de Sus Operaciones como*

General en Jefe del Ejército Sobre Tejas. Mexico, D.F.: Ignacio Cumplido, 1836. Translated and reprinted in Carlos Castaneda, ed. *The Mexican Side of the Texas Revolution [1836] by the Chief Mexican Participants.* 2nd ed. Austin: Graphic Ideas Incorporated, 1970.

Ford, John Salmon, and Stephen B. Oates, ed. *Rip Ford's Texas.* Austin: University of Texas Press, 1963; reprint, 1994.

Gambrell, Herbert Pickens. *Anson Jones, the Last President of Texas.* Garden City, N.Y.: Doubleday, 1948.

Gard, Wayne. *Frontier Justice.* Norman: University of Oklahoma Press, 1949.

————. *Sam Bass.* Boston: Houghton Mifflin, 1936.

Gillett, James B. *Six Years with the Texas Rangers, 1875 to 1881.* New Haven: Yale University Press, 1925. Reprint. Lincoln: University of Nebraska Press, 1976.

Grant, Ulysses S. *Memoirs and Selected Letters: Personal Memoirs of U.S. Grant; Selected Letters, 1839–1865.* New York: Literary Classics of the United States, 1990.

Greeley, Horace. *An Overland Journey, from New York to San Francisco, in the Summer of 1859.* New York: C. M. Saxton, Barker & Co., 1860.

Greene, A. C. *The Last Captive.* Austin: Encino Press, 1972.

Greer, James Kimmins. *Colonel Jack Hays, Texas Frontier Leader and California Builder.* Rev. ed. Waco: W. M. Morrison, 1973.

————. *Texas Ranger: Jack Hays in the Frontier Southwest.* College Station: Texas A&M University Press, 1993.

Hacker, Margaret Schmidt. *Cynthia Ann Parker: The Life and the Legend.* El Paso: Texas Western Press, 1990.

Haley, J. Evetts. *Charles Goodnight, Cowman and Plainsman.* New ed. Norman: University of Oklahoma Press, 1949.

Haley, James L. *The Buffalo War: The History of the Red River Indian Uprising of 1874.* Garden City, N.Y.: Doubleday, 1976. Reprint. Norman: University of Oklahoma Press, 1985.

Hardin, John Wesley. *The Life of John Wesley Hardin as Written by Himself.* Seguin, Tex.: Smith and Moore, 1896. Reprint. Norman: University of Oklahoma Press, 1961.

Harris, Benjamin Butler. *The Gila Trail: The Texas Argonauts and the California Gold Rush.* Norman: University of Oklahoma Press, 1960.

Heide, Robert, and John Gilman. *Cowboy Collectibles.* New York: Harper and Row, 1982.

Hendricks, George D. *The Bad Man of the West.* San Antonio: Naylor, 1950.

Henry, W. S. *Campaign Sketches of the War with Mexico.* New York: Harper and Brothers, 1847.

Henson, Margaret Swett. *Juan Davis Bradburn: A Reappraisal of the Mexican Commander of Anahuac.* College Station: Texas A&M University Press, 1982.

Hogan, William Ransom. *The Texas Republic: A Social and Economic History.* Norman: University of Oklahoma Press, 1946. Reprint. Austin: University of Texas Press, 1980.

Holden, Frances Mayhugh. *Lambshead Before Interwoven: A Texas Range Chronicle, 1848–1878.* College Station: Texas A&M University Press, 1982.

Holley, Mary Austin. *Texas.* Lexington, Ky.: J. Clarke & Co., 1836. Reprint. Austin: Texas State Historical Association, 1990.

Hughes, W. J. *Rebellious Ranger: Rip Ford and the Old Southwest.* Norman: University of Oklahoma Press, 1964; reprint, 1990.

James, Marquis. *The Raven: A Biography of Sam Houston.* Indianapolis: Bobbs-Merrill, 1929; reprint, 1975.

Jenkins, John Holmes, III. *Basic Texas Books: An Annotated Bibliography of Selected Works for a Research Library.* Rev. ed. Austin: Texas State Historical Association, 1988.

———, ed. *Recollections of Early Texas: The Memoirs of John Holland Jenkins.* Austin: University of Texas Press, 1958; reprint, 1995.

———, and H. Gordon Frost. *"I'm Frank Hamer": The Life of a Texas Peace Officer.* Austin: Jenkins Publishing Company/The Pemberton Press, 1968. Reprint. Austin: State House Press, 1993.

Jennings, Napoleon A. *A Texas Ranger.* New York: Charles Scribner's Sons, 1899. Reprint. Chicago: R. R. Donnelley & Sons, 1992.

Jones, Anson. *Memoranda and Official Correspondence Relating to the Republic of Texas, Its History and Annexation. Including a Brief Autobiography of the Author.* New York: D. Appleton and Company, 1859. Reprint. Chicago: Rio Grande Press, 1966.

Justice, Glenn. *Revolution on the Rio Grande: Mexican Raids and Army Pursuits, 1916–1919.* El Paso: Texas Western Press, 1992.

Kilgore, D. E. *A Ranger Legacy: 150 Years of Service to Texas.* Austin: Madrona Press, 1973.

Koury, Michael J. *Arms for Texas: A Study of the Weapons of the Republic of Texas.* Fort Collins, Colo.: Old Army Press, 1973.

Lamar, Mirabeau Buonaparte. *The Papers of Mirabeau Buonaparte Lamar.* 6 vols. Austin: A. C. Baldwin & Sons (vols. 1–2); Von Boeckmann-Jones, Inc. (vols. 3–6), 1921–27.

Lane, Ann J. *The Brownsville Affair: National Crisis and Black Reaction.* Port Washington, N.Y.: National University Publications/Kennikat Press, 1971.

Lane, Walter Paye. *The Adventures and Recollections of General Walter P. Lane, a San Jacinto Veteran, Containing Sketches of the Texian, Mexican, and Late Wars, with Several Indian Fights Thrown In.* Marshall, Tex.: Tri-Weekly Herald Job Print, 1887. Reprint. Austin: Jenkins Publishing Company/The Pemberton Press, 1970.

Ledbetter, Barbara A. Neal. *Fort Belknap, Frontier Saga: Indians, Negroes and Anglo-Americans on the Texas Frontier.* Burnet, Tex.: Eakin Press, 1982.

Lee, Nelson. *Three Years Among the Comanches: The Narrative of Nelson Lee, the Texas Ranger.* Albany, N.Y.: Baker Taylor, 1859. Reprint. Norman: University of Oklahoma Press, 1991.

Linn, John J. *Reminiscences of Fifty Years in Texas.* New York: D. & J. Sadlier & Co., 1883.

Lofton, Rachel, Susie Hendrix, and Jane Kennedy. *The Rachel Plummer Narrative.* N.p., 1926.

Long, A. L. *Memoirs of Robert E. Lee, His Military and Personal History Embracing a Large Amount of Information Hitherto Unpublished.* J. M. Stoddart and Company, 1886. Reprint. Secaucus, N.J.: Blue and Gray Press, 1983.

Lord, Walter. *A Time to Stand.* New York: Harper and Brothers, 1961. Reprint. Lincoln: University of Nebraska Press, 1978.

McConnell, H. H. *Five Years a Cavalryman; or, Sketches of Regular Army Life on the Texas Frontier, Twenty Odd Years Ago.* Jacksboro, Tex.: J. N. Rogers & Co., 1889.

McIntire, Jim. *Early Days in Texas: A Trip to Hell and Heaven.* Kansas City, Mo.: McIntire Publishing Co., 1902. Reprint. Norman: University of Oklahoma Press, 1992.

Malsch, Brownson. *"Lone Wolf" Gonzaullas, Texas Ranger.* Rev. ed. Norman: University of Oklahoma Press, 1998.

Marohn, Richard C. *The Last Gunfighter: John Wesley Hardin.* College Station, Tex.: Early West/Creative Publishing Company, 1995.

Martin, Charles L. *A Sketch of Sam Bass, The Bandit; A Graphic Narrative; His Various Train Robberies, His Death, and Accounts of the Deaths of His Gang and Their History.* Dallas: Herald Steam Printing House, 1880. Reprint. Norman: University of Oklahoma Press, 1956.

Martin, Jack. *Border Boss: Captain John R. Hughes—Texas Ranger.* San Antonio: Naylor, 1942. Reprint. Austin: State House Press, 1990.

Maverick, Mary Ann. *Memoirs of Mary A. Maverick, Arranged by Mary A. Maverick and Her Son, Geo. Madison Maverick.* San Antonio: Alamo Printing Co., 1921. Reprint. Lincoln: University of Nebraska Press, 1984.

Metz, Leon Claire. *Dallas Stoudenmire, El Paso Marshal.* Austin: Jenkins Publishing Company/The Pemberton Press, 1969. Reprint. Norman: University of Oklahoma Press, 1979.

———. *John Selman, Gunfighter.* 2nd ed. Norman: University of Oklahoma Press, 1980.

———. *John Wesley Hardin, Dark Angel of Texas.* El Paso: Mangan Books, 1996.

Miletich, Leo N. *Dan Stuart's Fistic Carnival.* College Station: Texas A&M Press, 1994.

Neighbours, Kenneth Franklin. *Robert Simpson Neighbors and the Texas Frontier, 1836–1859.* Waco, Tex.: Texian Press, 1975.

Newcomb, W. W., Jr. *The Indians of Texas from Prehistoric to Modern Times.* Austin: University of Texas Press, 1961; reprint, 1980.

Nye, Wilbur Sturtevant. *Carbine and Lance: The Story of Old Fort Sill.* Third ed. Revised. Norman: University of Oklahoma Press, 1969.

Olmsted, Frederick Law. *A Journey Through Texas Or, a Saddle-Trip on the Southwestern Frontier: With a Statistical Appendix.* New York: Dix, Edwards & Co., 1857. Reprint. Austin: University of Texas Press, 1978.

Paine, Albert Bigelow. *Captain Bill McDonald, Texas Ranger: A Story of Frontier Reform.* New York: J. J. Little & Ives Co., 1909. Reprint. Austin: State House Press, 1986.

Parsons, Chuck. *"Pidge," a Texas Ranger from Virginia: The Life and Letters of Lieutenant T. C. Robinson, Washington County Volunteer Militia Company "A."* Wolfe City, Tex.: Henington Publishing Co., 1985.

Parsons, Chuck, and Marjorie Parsons. *Bowen and Hardin.* College Station, Tex.: Early West/Creative Publishing Company, 1991.

Peavey, John R. *Echoes from the Rio Grande.* Brownsville, Tex.: privately printed, 1963.

Peterson, John Allen, ed. *"Facts As I Remember Them": The Autobiography of Rufe LeFors.* Austin: University of Texas Press, 1986.

Prassel, Frank Richard. *The Western Peace Officer: A Legacy of Law and Order.* Norman: University of Oklahoma Press, 1972.

Ramsdell, Charles William. *Reconstruction in Texas.* New York: Columbia University Press, 1910. Reprint. Austin: University of Texas Press, 1970.

Ramsey, Albert C., ed. *The Other Side: Or Notes for the History of the War Between Mexico and the United States. Written in Mexico.* New York: John Wiley, 1850.

Rayburn, John C., and Virginia Kemp Rayburn, eds. *Century of Conflict, 1821–1913: Incidents in the Lives of William Neale and William A. Neale, Early Settlers in South Texas.* Waco, Tex.: Texian Press, 1966.

Raymond, Dora Neill. *Captain Lee Hall of Texas.* Norman: University of Oklahoma Press, 1940; reprint, 1982.

Reid, Samuel C., Jr. *The Scouting Expeditions of McCulloch's Texas Rangers; Or, The Summer and Fall Campaign of the Army of the United States in Mexico—1846.* Philadelphia: G. B. Zieber and Co., 1847. Reprint. Austin: Steck Company, 1935.

Richardson, Rupert Norval. *Texas, The Lone Star State.* 2nd ed. Englewood Cliffs, N.J.: Prentice-Hall, 1958.

Roberts, Daniel Webster. *Rangers and Sovereignty.* San Antonio: Wood Printing & Engraving Co., 1914. Reprint. Austin: State House Press, 1987.

Roberts, Lou Conway (Mrs. Daniel Webster Roberts). *A Woman's Reminiscences of Six Years in Camp with the Texas Rangers.* Austin: Press of Von Boeckmann-Jones Co., n.d. (1928). Reprinted in one volume with *Rangers and Sovereignty.* Austin: State House Press, 1987.

Roberts, Madge Thornall, ed. *The Personal Correspondence of Sam Houston.* Denton: University of North Texas Press, 1996.

Robinson, Charles M., III. *The Frontier World of Fort Griffin: The Life and Death of a Western Town.* Spokane: Arthur H. Clark Co., 1992.

———. *The Indian Trial: The Complete Story of the Warren Wagon Train Massacre and the Fall of the Kiowa Nation.* Spokane: Arthur H. Clark Co., 1997.

Roemer, Ferdinand. *Texas, with Particular Reference to German Immigration and the Physical Appearance of the Country.* Trans. by Oswald Mueller. San Antonio: Standard Printing Company, 1935. Reprint. Austin: Eakin Press, 1995.

Rosa, Joseph G. *The Taming of the West: Age of the Gunfighter, Men and Weapons on the Frontier, 1840–1900.* New York: Smithmark Publishers, 1993.

Rose, Victor M. *The Life and Services of Gen. Ben McCulloch.* Philadelphia: Pictorial Bureau of the Press, 1888. Reprint. Austin: Steck Company, 1958.

Sandos, James A. *Rebellion in the Borderlands: Anarchism and the Plan of San Diego, 1904–1923.* Norman: University of Oklahoma Press, 1992.

Santoni, Pedro. *Mexicans at Arms: Puro Federalists and the Politics of War, 1845–1848.* Fort Worth: Texas Christian University Press, 1996.

Schilz, Jodye Lynn Dickson, and Thomas F. Schilz. *Buffalo Hump and the Penateka Comanches.* El Paso: Texas Western Press, 1989.

Sheridan, Philip Henry. *Personal Memoirs of P. H. Sheridan.* 2 vols. New York: Charles L. Webster & Company, 1888.

Siegel, Stanley. *The Poet President of Texas: The Life of Mirabeau B. Lamar, President of the Republic of Texas.* Austin: Jenkins Publishing Company/The Pemberton Press, 1977.

Smith, David Paul. *Frontier Defense in the Civil War: Texas' Rangers and Rebels.* College Station: Texas A&M University Press, 1992.

Smith, Diane Solether. *The Armstrong Chronicle: A Ranching History.* San Antonio: Corona Publishing Co., 1986.

Smith, S. Compton, *Chile con Carne; Or, The Camp and Field.* New York: Miller and Curtis, 1857.

Smithwick, Noah. *The Evolution of a State or Recollections of Old Texas Days.* Austin: Gammel Book Company, 1900. Reprint. Austin: University of Texas Press, 1983.

Sonnichsen, C. L. *I'll Die Before I'll Run: The Story of the Great Feuds of Texas.* New York: Devin-Adair, 1962.

———. *Pass of the North: Four Centuries on the Rio Grande.* El Paso: Texas Western Press, 1968.

———. *Roy Bean, Law West of the Pecos.* New York: Macmillan, 1943. Reprint. Albuquerque: University of New Mexico Press, 1986.

Sorensen, Al. *"Hands Up!" or The History of a Crime. The Great Union Pacific Express Robbery.* Omaha: Barkalow Brothers, 1877. Reprint. College Station, Tex.: Early West/Creative Publishing Company, 1982.

Sowell, Andrew Jackson. *Early Settlers and Indian Fighters of Southwest Texas.* Austin: Ben C. Jones & Co., 1900. Reprint. Austin: State House Press, 1986.

———. *Life of "Big Foot" Wallace, the Great Ranger Captain.* Devine, Tex.: Devine News, 1899. New edition. Austin: State House Press, 1989.

———. *Rangers and Pioneers of Texas, Embracing a Concise Account of the Settlement of the Greater Part of the State.* San Antonio: Shepard Bros. & Co., 1884. Reprint. Austin: State House Press, 1991.

Sterling, William Warren. *Trails and Trials of a Texas Ranger.* Norman: University of Oklahoma Press, 1960.

Sutton, Robert C., Jr. *The Sutton-Taylor Feud.* Quanah, Tex.: Nortex Press, 1974.

Texas Almanac and State Industrial Guide, 1994–95. Dallas: Dallas Morning News, 1993.

Time-Life Books, Editors of. *The Gamblers.* The Old West (series). Alexandria, Va.: Time-Life Books, 1978.

Timmons, W. H. *El Paso: A Borderlands History.* El Paso: Texas Western Press, 1990.

Thompson, Jerry Don, ed. *Fifty Miles and a Fight: Major Samuel Peter Heintzelman's Journal of Texas and the Cortina War.* Austin: Texas State Historical Commission, 1998.

———, ed. *Juan Cortina and the Texas-Mexico Frontier, 1859–1877.* El Paso: Texas Western Press, 1994.

Wallace, Ernest, and E. Adamson Hoebel. *The Comanches, Lords of the South Plains.* Norman: University of Oklahoma Press, 1952.

Weaver, John D. *The Brownsville Raid.* New York: W. W. Norton, 1970. Reprint. College Station: Texas A&M University Press, 1992.

Webb, Walter Prescott. *The Great Plains.* New York: Ginn and Company, 1931. Reprint. New York: Grosset & Dunlap, 1971.

———. *The Texas Rangers: A Century of Frontier Defense.* 2nd ed. Austin: University of Texas Press, 1965.

Weddle, Robert S. *San Juan Bautista, Gateway to Spanish Texas.* Austin: University of Texas Press, 1968; reprint, 1991.

———. *The San Saba Mission, Spanish Pivot in Texas.* Austin: University of Texas Press, 1964; reprint, 1988.

Weems, John Edward. *To Conquer a Peace: The War Between the United States and Mexico.* Garden City, N.Y.: Doubleday, 1974. Reprint. College Station: Texas A&M University Press, 1988.

White, David A., comp. *News of the Plains and Rockies, 1803–1865*. Vol. 2. Spokane, Wash.: Arthur H. Clark Company, 1996.

White, Owen P. *Them Was the Days: From El Paso to Prohibition*. New York: Minton, Balch & Company, 1925.

Wilbarger, J. W. *Indian Depredations In Texas: Reliable Accounts of Battles, Wars, Adventures, Forays, Murders, Massacres, etc., etc., Together with Biographical Sketches of Many of the Most Noted Indian Fighters and Frontiersmen of Texas*. Austin: Hutchings Printing House, 1889. Reprint. Austin: Eakin Press and Statehouse Books, 1985.

Wilkins, Frederick. *The Highly Irregular Irregulars: Texas Rangers in the Mexican War*. Austin: Eakin Press, 1990.

———. *The Legend Begins: The Texas Rangers, 1823–1845*. Austin: State House Press, 1996.

Williams, Amelia W., and Eugene C. Barker, eds. *The Writings of Sam Houston*. 8 vols. Austin: University of Texas Press, 1938–43.

Williams, Clayton W. *Texas' Last Frontier: Fort Stockton and the Trans-Pecos, 1861–1895*. College Station: Texas A&M University Press, 1982.

Wilson, R. L. *Colt, An American Legend: The Official History of Colt Firearms from 1836 to the Present*. Sesquicentennial ed. New York: Abbeville Press, 1985.

Winkler, E. W., comp. *Manuscript Letters and Documents of Early Texians, 1821–1845, in Facsimile Folio Collection of Original Documents*. Austin: Steck Company, 1937.

Wooten, Dudley G., ed. *A Comprehensive History of Texas 1685 to 1897*. 2 vols. Dallas: William G. Scarff, 1898. Reprint. Austin: Texas State Historical Association, 1986.

Yoakum, Henderson. *History of Texas from Its First Settlement in 1685 to Its Annexation to the United States in 1846*. 2 vols. New York: Redfield Publishers, 1855. Reprint. Austin: Steck Company, 1935.

Articles

Baenziger, Ann Patton. "The Texas State Police During Reconstruction: A Reexamination." *Southwestern Historical Quarterly*, Vol. 72, no. 4 (April 1969): 470–91.

Barker, Eugene C. "The Government of Austin's Colony, 1821–1831." *Southwestern Historical Quarterly*, Vol. 21, no. 3 (January 1918): 223–52.

———. "Journal of the Permanent Council (October 11–27, 1835)." *Quarterly of the Texas State Historical Association*, Vol. 7, no. 4 (April 1904): 249–78.

Barton, Henry W. "The Anglo-American Colonists Under Mexican Militia Laws." *Southwestern Historical Quarterly*, Vol. 65, no. 1 (July 1961): 61–71.

———. "Five Texas Frontier Companies During the Mexican War." *Southwestern Historical Quarterly*, Vol. 66, no. 1 (July 1962): 17–30.

———. "The United States Cavalry and the Texas Rangers." *Southwestern Historical Quarterly*, Vol. 63, no. 4 (April 1960): 495–510.

Bowden, J. J. "The Magoffin Salt War." *Password*, Vol. 7 (Summer 1962): 95–121.

Burnam, Jesse. "Reminiscences of Capt. Jesse Burnam." *Quarterly of the Texas State Historical Association*, Vol. 5, no. 1 (July 1901): 12–18.

Cartwright, Gary. "Chuck Norris." *Texas Monthly*, Vol. 24, no. 9 (September 1996): 103, 147.

Connor, Seymour V. "Austin, 1839–1842." In *Capitols of Texas*, 79–100. Waco, Tex.: Texian Press, 1970.

Darrow, Caroline Baldwin. "Recollections of the Twiggs Surrender." In Robert Underwood Johnson and Clarence Clough Buel, eds., *Battles and Leaders of the Civil War,* 1:33–39. New York: Century Company, 1887. Reprint. New York: Thomas Yoseloff, 1956.

Day, James M. "El Paso's Texas Rangers." *Password,* Vol. 24 (Winter 1979): 153–73.

DeArment, Robert K. "That Masterson-McDonald Standoff." *True West,* Vol. 45, no. 1 (January 1998): 12–15.

Dobie, J. Frank. "Mustang Gray: Fact, Tradition, and Song." In *Tone the Bell Easy.* Publications of the Texas Folk-Lore Society, No. 10 (1932).

Eckhart, Larry. "Texas Ranger's Badge." *True West,* Vol. 40, no. 9 (September 1993): 46–49.

Erath, Lucy A. "Memoirs of Major George Bernard Erath." *Southwestern Historical Quarterly,* Vol. 26, no. 3 (January 1923): 207–33; no. 4 (April 1923): 255–80; Vol. 27, no. 1 (July 1923): 27–51; no. 2 (October 1923): 140–63.

Fisher, O. Clark. "The Life and Times of King Fisher." *Southwestern Historical Quarterly,* Vol. 64, no. 2 (October 1960): 232–47.

Glaevecke, Adolphus. "A Story of Old Times." In W. H. Chatfield, *The Twin Cities of the Border and the Country of the Lower Rio Grande,* 23. New Orleans: E. P. Brandao, 1893. Reprint. Brownsville Historical Association and Lower Rio Grande Valley Historical Society, 1959.

Harmon, George D. "The United States Indian Policy in Texas, 1845–1860." *Mississippi Valley Historical Review,* Vol. 17, no. 3 (December 1930): 377–403.

Holland, James K. "Diary of a Texan Volunteer in the Mexican War." *Southwestern Historical Quarterly,* Vol. 30, no. 1 (July 1926): 1–33.

House, Boyce. "Rip-roaring Days in the Oil Fields." *Southwest Review.* Reprint. *Frontier Times,* Vol. 23, no. 2 (November 1945): 15–20.

Howren, Alleine. "Causes and Origin of the Decree of April 6, 1830." *Southwestern Historical Quarterly,* Vol. 16, no. 4 (April 1913): 378–422.

Hunter, J. Marvin. "How the Greatest Museum in the South Was Built." *Frontier Times,* Vol. 22, no. 8 (May 1945): 217–32.

———, ed. "Jack Hays, the Intrepid Texas Ranger." *Frontier Times,* Vol. 4, no. 5 (Feb. 1927): 25–40; no. 6 (March 1927): 17–31; no. 7 (April 1927): 17–31; no. 8 (May 1927): 17–31.

Jones, Billy Mac. "Houston, 1837–1839." In *Capitols of Texas,* 57–74. Waco, Tex.: Texian Press, 1970.

Kelley, Dayton. "Columbia, 1836." In *Capitols of Texas,* 33–52. Waco, Tex.: Texian Press, 1970.

King, W. H. "The Texas Ranger Service and History of the Rangers, with Observations on Their Value as a Police Protection." In Dudley G. Wooten, ed., *A Comprehensive History of Texas 1685 to 1897,* 2:329–67. Dallas: William G. Scarff, 1898. Reprint. Austin: Texas State Historical Association, 1986.

Klos, George. " 'Our People Could Not Distinguish One Tribe from Another': The 1859 Expulsion of the Reserve Indians From Texas." *Southwestern Historical Quarterly,* Vol. 97, no. 4 (April 1994): 599–619.

Knopp, Kenn. "True to the Union." *Enchanted Rock Magazine,* Vol. 2, no. 12 (February 1996): 26–29, 31, 35.

Kuykendall, J. H. "Reminiscences of Early Texans: A Collection from the Austin Papers." *Quarterly of the Texas State Historical Association,* Vol. 6, no. 3. (January 1903): 236–53; Vol. 7, no. 1 (July 1903): 29–64.

Kuykendall, J. W. [J. H.]. "The Carankawa Indians." *Texas Almanac* 1872. Reprint. *Frontier Times,* Vol. 22, no. 6 (March 1945): 178–79.

"The Loss [*sic*] Valley Fight." *Frontier Times,* Vol. 7, no. 3 (December 1929): 100–4.

Moneyhon, Carl H. "Edmund J. Davis in the Coke-Davis Election Dispute of 1874: A Reassessment of Character." *Southwestern Historical Quarterly,* Vol. 100, no. 2 (October 1996): 131–51.

Moore, Richard W. "Bastrop, Baron de." In *The New Handbook of Texas,* ed. Ron Tyler et al., 1:410. Austin: Texas State Historical Association, 1996.

Morton, Ohland. "Life of General don Manuel de Mier y Teran as It Affected Texas-Mexican Relations." *Southwestern Historical Quarterly,* Vol. 46, no. 1 (July 1942): 22–47; no. 3 (January 1943): 239–54; Vol. 47, no. 1 (July 1943): 29–47; no. 2 (October 1943): 120–42; Vol. 48, no. 1 (July 1944): 51–66; no. 2 (October 1944): 193–218; no. 4 (April 1945): 499–546.

Nackman, Mark E. "The Making of the Texan Citizen Soldier, 1835–1860." *Southwestern Historical Quarterly,* Vol. 78, no. 3 (January 1975): 231–53.

Nelson, Christian G. "Rebirth, Growth, and Expansion of the Texas Militia, 1868–1898." *Texas Military History,* Vol. 2, no. 1 (February 1962): 1–16.

Oates, Stephen B. "The Texas Rangers in the Mexican War." *Texas Military History,* Vol. 3, no. 2 (Summer 1963): 65–85.

Parsons, Chuck. "Gunfire at Espantosa Lake." *True West,* Vol. 44, no. 10 (October 1997): 21–24.

Riley, Matthew K. "Prizefight on the Border: Fitzsimmons vs. Maher, 1896." *True West,* Vol. 41, no. 10 (October 1994): 38–43.

Rister, Carl Coke, ed. "Documents Relating to General W. T. Sherman['s] Southern Plains Indian Policy 1871–1875." *Panhandle-Plains Historical Review,* Vol. 9 (1936).

Robinson, Charles M., III. "Cannibal Heroes: Tough Little Tonkawas of Texas." *True West,* Vol. 40, no. 3 (March 1993): 32–42.

———. "The Forgotten Fight at Bandera Pass." *True West,* Vol. 39, no. 6 (June 1992): 22–24.

———. "The Life and Death of an Indian Lover." *True West,* Vol. 38, no. 10 (October 1991): 14–19.

———. "When Bandits Wrecked the Night Train to Brownsville." *True West,* Vol. 38, no. 9 (September 1991): 40–43.

Smith, Robert Barr. "The El Paso Salt War." *Wild West,* Vol. 10, no. 5 (February 1998): 58–62, 86.

Smith, Thomas T. "U.S. Army Combat Operations in the Indian Wars of Texas, 1849–1881." *Southwestern Historical Quarterly,* Vol. 99, no. 4 (April 1996): 500–41.

Weiss, Harold J., Jr. "The Texas Rangers Revisited: Old Themes and New Viewpoints." *Southwestern Historical Quarterly,* Vol. 97, no. 4 (April 1994): 620–40.

Miscellaneous

"The Smithsonian Collection. Old Time Radio Detectives and Crime Fighters." Schiller Park, Ill.: Radio Spirits Inc., in association with Smithsonian Institution Press, 1995.

Newspapers

Austin *Daily Bulletin*
Chicago Tribune
Dallas *News*
Galveston News
Goliad [Texas] *Guard*
Houston *Telegraph and Texas Register*
McAllen, Texas, *Monitor*
New York *World*
San Antonio Express-News

Index

Grateful acknowledgment is made to the following for permission to reprint and use the material listed below:

THE CENTER FOR AMERICAN HISTORY, THE UNIVERSITY OF TEXAS AT AUSTIN: Excerpts from the following items in the John Coffee Hays Collection: "Sketch of Colonel John C. Hays, The Texas Rangers, Incidents in Texas and Mexico, Etc," CN 2R35; excerpts from "Indian Raid, Pursuit and Fight" and "Jack Hays Fight on Gaudaloupe [sic]," both items by James T. DeShields, CN 3F176; "Jack Hays' Visit to Washington, Texas" by John W. Lockhart, CN 3F176. Excerpts from the following items in the Earl Vandale Collection: Elm Creek Raid Statements (various), CN 2H481; "The Death of Nocona" by Benjamin Franklin Gholson, CN 2H464; "An Indian Raid in Young County, Texas, October 13, 1864" by Thornton K. Hamby (from Elm Creek Raid Statements), CN 2H481. Excerpt from the following item from the Samuel Hamilton Walker Vertical File, housed in the Texas Collection Library: "Col. Samuel H. Walker" by J. H. Kuykendall. All items used by permission of The Center for American History, The University of Texas at Austin.

EAKIN PRESS: Excerpt from *Roemer's Texas 1845–1847* by Ferdinand Roemer, translated by Oswald Mueller. Reprinted by permission of Eakin Press.

GERALD B. HURST: Excerpts from *Buck Barry, Texas Ranger and Frontiersman* by James K. Greer. Reprinted by permission of Gerald B. Hurst.

TEXAS STATE HISTORICAL ASSOCIATION: Excerpts from *My Confession: Recollections of a Rogue,* unexpurgated and annotated edition by Samuel Chamberlain (Austin: Texas State Historical Association, 1996); excerpts from "Memoirs of Major George Bernard Erath" by Lucy A. Erath (*Southwestern Historical Quarterly,* Vol. 26, no. 4, April 1923, pp. 255–280); excerpts from "Diary of a Texan Volunteer in the Mexican War" by James K. Holland (*Southwestern Historical Quarterly,* Vol. 30, no. 1, July 1926, pp. 1–33); excerpts from *Fifty Miles and a Fight: Major Samuel Peter Heintzelman's Journal of Texas and the Cortina War* edited by Jerry Don Thompson (Austin: Texas State Historical Commission, 1998). All material reprinted by permission of Texas State Historical Association.

TEXAS WESTERN PRESS: Excerpts from *The March to Monterrey: The Diary of Lieutenant Rankin Dilworth, U. S. Army* edited by Lawrence R. Clayton and

About the Author

CHARLES M. ROBINSON III was born in Harlingen, Texas, and grew up on the Texas-Mexico border, where much of the action in this book occurred. He received a bachelor's degree from St. Edward's University in Austin, Texas, and a master's degree from the University of Texas-Pan American. His book *Bad Hand: A Biography of General Ranald S. Mackenzie* received the Texas Historical Commission's T. R. Fehrenbach Book Award, and *Satanta: The Life and Death of a War Chief* led to his being made an honorary member of the Chief Satanta (White Bear) Descendants. He lives in San Benito, Texas, and teaches U.S. history at South Texas Community College in McAllen, Texas. He is a member of the Western Writers of America, the Texas State Historical Association, Montana Historical Society, and various other organizations. He is presently writing a biography of Maj. Gen. George Crook.

About the Type

This book was set in Times New Roman, designed by Stanley Morison specifically for *The Times* of London. The typeface was introduced in the newspaper in 1932. Times New Roman has had its greatest success in the United States as a book and commercial typeface rather than one used in newspapers.